Practical DV Filmmaking

Acquisitions Editor: Elinor Actipis
Associate Editor: Becky Golden-Harrell
Assistant Editor: Robin Weston
Marketing Manager: Lucy Lomas-Walker
Cover Design: Fred Rose

Practical DV Filmmaking

Second edition

Russell Evans

AMSTERDAM • BOSTON • HEIDELBERG • LONDON • NEW YORK • OXFORD
PARIS • SAN DIEGO • SAN FRANCISCO • SINGAPORE • SYDNEY • TOKYO
Focal Press is an imprint of Elsevier

ELSEVIER

Focal Press is an imprint of Elsevier
30 Corporate Drive, Suite 400, Burlington MA 01803, USA
Linacre House, Jordan Hill, Oxford OX2 8DP, UK

First edition 2002
Reprinted 2003, 2004
Second edition 2006

Library of Congress Cataloguing in Publication Data
A catalog record for this book is available from the Library of Congress

British Library Cataloguing in Publication Data
A catalogue record for this book is available from the British Library

ISBN 13: 978-0-240-80738-6
ISBN 10: 0-240-80738-3

06 07 08 09 10 10 9 8 7 6 5 4 3 2 1

For information on all Focal Press publications visit our website at:
www.focalpress.com

Typeset by Charon Tec Pvt. Ltd, Chennai, India
www.charontec.com
Printed in the United States of America

Working together to grow
libraries in developing countries

www.elsevier.com | www.bookaid.org | www.sabre.org

ELSEVIER   BOOK AID
            International   Sabre Foundation

Contents

Acknowledgements

This book has been less stressful in preparation than it might otherwise have been, thanks to the support of a number of filmmakers who provided opinions and help and lent stills. Thank you to Amaru Amasi, Andy Glynne of London Documentary Group, Chris Allen of The Light Surgeons, everyone at Antenna, the staff of Addictive TV, Colin Spector, Raya, Neo (Jake Knight), Richard Graham, Phil Grabsky, Sean Martin, Jonnie Oddball, Matt Sheldon, James Sharpe, Liz Crow, Jon Rennie, Nick Ball, Max Sobol, Annie Watson, David Casals, Carl Tibbets, Gurchetan Singh, Debra Watson, Kevin Lapper, Mark Innocenti, Paul Cowling, Carlo Ortu, Emily Corcoran, Jon Price and Ed Spencer. Thanks also to Colonel Blimp, RSA Films and Anonymous Content.

The brilliant people at Focal Press have been supportive and friendly – many thanks are due to Elinor Actipis, Becky Golden-Harrell, Christine Tridente and Cara Anderson in Boston. In Focal Press at Oxford, thanks to Jenny Rideout and Christina Donaldson, who helped develop the first edition.

John Edmonds and Nick Wright provided much valuable feedback prior to publication; Lisa Hill offered advice on careers in the United States; and Michael Rabiger took time out from his own book (*Developing Story Ideas*) to help with my questions.

Nearer to home, thanks go to Esme, Zoe and Alfie for doing without Jane stories for a while. Much praise must go to my wife Wendy Klein, who offered calm solutions and additions to the ideas contained in the book, and helped develop the overall structure.

Introduction to the second edition

Since this book was first published in its first edition in 2002, it appeared to be prepared for the brave new world of the DV revolution. But in the accelerated development of current filmmaking, it later needed much revising to reflect what could be termed the post-revolutionary DV world. Arrivals such as streaming, web film and DVD have quickly become standard features of the filmmaking landscape, and have been joined by high definition, the rise of the VJ and the multiplicity of viewing formats. The new landscape left behind by these advances offers chances but also quandaries for the emerging film-maker. Faced with a world where there are no pre-set paths to follow, no continuous route of development in a career and more and more shifting technical benchmarks, the filmmaker of today needs a guidebook as never before.

Hopefully, users of this book will find the mix of technical and artistic guidance some help in enabling them to make the right steps in this changed landscape.

A large portion of the text has been altered and no chapter has been left unchanged, reflecting the sharp changes that have governed the last few years in DV. Significant changes have been made to the chapters dealing with how to find an audience for films. A new chapter on careers has been added, developed in part through my years as a lecturer in film and also from many interviews with filmmakers in Britain and the United States. The advice is designed to be real, practical and ready to be put into effect.

Perhaps the biggest sea change in video has been the emergence of new platforms to create video for – cell phones and email movies, for instance – and filmmakers have responded as they always have, by creating new art forms out of technical advances. But the necessity remains – as it always has – for a thread of meaning to run through all films, whether designed to create sensations, to raise political points or to make us laugh. Hopefully, the projects and text in this book will draw the filmmaker towards a closer appreciation of what is important to them and how to express it to an audience.

How to use this book

This book is going to work as a more flexible tool than standard reference books. You don't have to start at the front and work your way through; you can access it anywhere and make the most of what it offers. There are two reasons why it has been arranged like this: first, you may be coming with certain skills already in place and can skip certain sections; second, your idea of what you want to make is different for everyone.

In this sense, it is non-linear, like a ready-access CD or DVD. And just like DVDs, you can make your 'scene selection' by looking at the first page of each section to find out how to skip parts and go straight to the chapter you need now. At the start of relevant chapters, a 'quick start' section has been included to help you determine what is applicable to you right now so that you can get started quickly. You can then go back and examine areas in more detail later, when you need to.

A film course

You can also use this book in a linear fashion, so that you encounter the stages that you would if you were at film school. A film course would often take you through understanding how films 'work' – the way all the elements of filmmaking interact – and then onto planning and writing, learning how to shoot, and finally onto editing. This book goes a couple of steps further by then proposing a clear way of making your way into filmmaking as a career. Later, at the end of the book, there is also a section on what the industry you are going to enter looks like, to help you find your way through it. Inevitably, that last section is no more than a snapshot of a shifting industry, but it does attempt to point towards the major direction it is heading, including threats and opportunities that are on the horizon.

Projects

One of the features of this book is the practical projects which run throughout it. The aim is to suggest ways of developing your skills and putting what is discussed into practice. The projects are designed to push certain skills and ideas, and allow you to make big steps forward quickly. For instance, in the section on scriptwriting there are projects that are going to help you get to grips with putting meanings into your stories. After the music promo chapter there is a project designed to get you making your own promo and avoid the pitfalls of other filmmakers.

The non-linear approach to the book described above carries on in the projects too, as each one can be expanded for those who want more of a challenge. If you find that a certain project was useful you may then want to go to the more difficult version and push yourself further.

Boxes

To break up the text and include extra information, there are boxes throughout the chapters which give more information. These are in five types:

- *Film Views*. These boxes describe films that would help you to investigate further what that chapter is about.
- *Tips*. These boxes offer advice about certain points, such as technical tips and shortcuts.
- *Interviews*. Many filmmakers were interviewed for this book and their comments help relate the ideas in it to the real world. Quotes from their interviews feature in the text to illustrate points and ideas.
- *Did you know?* These boxes contain facts and snippets of information on the various subjects discussed in the book.
- *Weblinks*. These are links to sites that will expand on points in the text or just offer up-to-date advice. They also help make the text address international differences – for instance, on finance or distribution.

Finally, all the projects have been road-tested on students and filmmakers. They have been developed as people have responded to them and made use of them.

1 Overview

1. Think big

'Four years ago, if you had a video and you wanted people to see it, you had to invite them all over to your house for a beer. With the web, it's possible to produce a movie with almost no budget and get a million people to watch it.'

David Trescot, group product manager at Adobe, giving his view
about the ease with which you can now go out and make movies

There is no doubt that with a camcorder and an Internet connection you have one of the most powerful tools for communicating. If you have the energy and the will you can shoot a short movie on any subject, in your own unique style, show it to a global audience, and promote and advertise it yourself. You are more in control of the filmmaking process than any previous generation, and furthermore have less need for the established industry than ever before. Changes to the film industry as entertainment and as an art form are here to stay, and simply by possessing an Internet connection, a camcorder and basic editing software you are a part of it.

This is a great opportunity, but you may now be getting a sense of the problem that goes with it. Although inspiring, for many this is daunting. As the spotlight moves your way the need to have developed yourself as a filmmaker is profound; you need to find out what kind of films you make, how to come up with ideas good enough to film and how to get the knowledge that makes other people take you seriously. Your only obligation is to stand out from the crowd, do your own thing, don't emulate what everyone else is doing when the whole world starts making movies. Take advantage of this moment and start getting to know what it is that a movie by you looks like.

This isn't a new phenomenon even if the technology is in its infancy. Some of the finest directors have started their careers making films on no budgets, with no help from big studios. David Lynch made the classic film *Eraserhead* (1976) at weekends over a number of years while holding down a day job; within five years of its release he was being offered the chance to direct *Return of the Jedi*. George Romero made his seminal zombie film *Night of the Living Dead* (1969) with almost no funds, relying on the commitment of friends willing to be part-time zombies, but without being paid. Robert Rodriguez went from making a film with a borrowed camera – *El Mariachi* (1992) – to making hit films such as *From Dusk Till Dawn* (1995) and *Spy Kids* (2001).

The difference for today's filmmakers is that you can go further. Not only can you get hold of good cameras capable of broadcast quality images, but you can edit these films at home without having to endure the budget-crippling prices of the rent-by-the-hour edit unit. When it's finished you can show it on one of the many web cinemas, short film festivals or TV access slots. The potential is there to place your short movies in millions of homes around the world.

Digital video has affected the independent, low-budget filmmaker more than any other part of the film industry. These self-financing, ultra-resourceful people would make movies whatever it cost them and however long it takes. But it is now a realistic aim to say that you want to make movies and do so without mortgaging your soul. All you need is a camcorder, a computer, a limitless imagination and the desire to tell it your way.

2. The filmmaking process

To begin with, it would be useful to get to grips with the process of making a film as a whole. What do these people actually do? Why does it take so long between thinking of the film and getting down to shooting it?

The whole project starts life as an idea, in your imagination or as a response. You may have a story you wish to tell or a theme you want to work with. Whatever it is, it starts in darkness, probably a collection of images you see appearing in the film, played out in no real order in your mind's eye. Most directors favour getting as much material on paper as you can at this stage to establish the detail of an idea. Others suggest more idiosyncratic approaches. Robert Rodriguez recommends you 'stare at a blank projection screen. See your film, watch it from start to finish.' Whatever your initial idea, it is crucial to get to know it at this early stage as clearly as possible. Even though you have only a broad outline of the project you do have the initial spark: the images, atmosphere or look of the film. It is this that you should try to pin down and keep, as it will become the main creative thrust of the project, seeing you through the obstacles and possible wrong turns to come.

Stage 1: Planning

The first stage of making a movie is centred on getting the film developed as much as possible before you start shooting. Substantial changes during shooting are expensive and disrupt continuity, or worse can result in a discordant and messy film. Good planning means that when you start shooting you go through a smoother process. You will encounter surprises and have to make changes here and there, but planning means you encounter more of the right sort of surprises and know how to solve the less welcome ones. The aim is to let your ideas grow and develop to a point at which you know every aspect of the project better than anyone else. You know the relative significance of each part of the story, the kinds of motifs and ideas that are running through it, and the kind of atmosphere that is to dominate. In a sense, when you commit your ideas to paper you are taking them out of the comforting darkness of the imagination, where you don't notice the loose ends and rough structure of a film, and exposing them to light. Some aspects of your ideas survive, some don't, but it is better that the project changes now than later. Work on paper is cheap but work on film is expensive. An hour of scriptwriting can save you a day of shooting and a week of editing later in the process.

Visual blueprints

In planning your film you will make detailed written and visual blueprints of how the film will look and sound from the first to the last moment. Step 1 involves a written outline in the form of a short story. Even if your film does not rely on plot at all, you need basically and simply to write down all the scenes that you envisage in the order that you think they may occur. Getting to that stage may involve noting down all the elements of the film and producing several different versions of an outline. This rough draft we can call a treatment. Following that, you will produce a range of material which will trace the steps you take as you develop and grow the film.

Early visualizations

If you have ever found yourself doodling with a pen and paper then you will have some idea of what this stage of work involves. To some people what you draw when doodling is a true reflection of the natural inclinations of your mind; some people draw closed-in little boxes, tightly stuck together, others draw blossoming spirals or crystal-like structures. It doesn't take a certificate in psychology to work out the meanings of the things we find ourselves drawing; what you are doing is reflecting the current inner architecture of your thoughts, not the thoughts themselves as such but the shape they take. Whatever your doodles look like – dark and angular, bold and bright – these can be viewed as potential design notes for a film. Of course, this is only relevant if you are determined to find and display your own personal world view, as opposed to following the needs of a client or audience focus group.

In a practical sense, what you are doing when drawing visualizations is a long set of small sketches, per-haps each the size of a cigarette packet. Each one is a quick outline of a possible scene from the film. These are drawn in no particular order, but the order you draw them does say something about the relative importance of each to you. Each sketch should be quick and uncomplicated, showing the main elements in the shot and hinting at the kind of light in the frame. The aim is not to correct them or judge them in any way until you've gone through the whole exercise, with as many frames as possible on paper. Following this, you can then start to group your sketches together and compare the overall style of each frame.

Storyboard

The storyboard is used to explain the detail of the visual side of the film to a crew and allow those people working on a film to plan essential equipment and work schedules effectively. Working on a low budget with just yourself and a few friends does not excuse you from this process; it offers a chance to refine both the look and structure of your film and pare it down, stripping it of elements that divert from the idea, making it a project that fulfils the specific aims you had in mind right at the start.

In preparing a storyboard, you will draw frames on one vertical column of the paper with correspond-ing dialogue, notes or sound written next to it. This document is the most detailed visual and written description of the whole film, the single blueprint that you try to stick to throughout the shooting process.

Although storyboarding was rigidly adhered to by directors such as Alfred Hitchcock, for the most part it is simply the most accurate plan you have at this point, ready to be challenged and altered during filming.

Script

In films where you have a story, a script is going to be the only way to prepare it and iron out the inconsistencies. Even in films where there are no speaking roles you may find it useful to prepare a script showing only director's notes, as it gives yet another opportunity to hone your idea, add to it or subtract.

The importance of each stage of planning is relative to the sort of film you are making. Abstract, theme-based movies will demand more consideration of visual aspects, while character studies with intense dialogue will need more attention paid to the script. All films, however, need to go through an intense period of planning in order to emerge fully formed before a camera starts showing up the faults. Know your film.

Stage 2: Shooting

Shooting is to some a time where the film takes on a whole life of its own, to others a simple regurgitation of a paper storyboard. In practical terms, it seems simple enough: plan out a series of shots, go and shoot them just as you planned on paper, tick off the scenes one by one and go home. In an ideal situation this is more or less what happens, but since this is an art form it is natural to assume that the creative process continues throughout the project, through planning, shooting and editing (even through to marketing, but more of that in Chapter 9). So, you should expect to encounter obstacles and temptations along the way. Obstacles in the form of challenges to your plans and temptations in the sense of other seemingly better ideas that come up, possibly deviating from the original one. Great planning for a film is about giving you the confidence to know your idea inside out, giving you the commitment to get round problems and the confidence to know the good from the bad when new ideas come up.

Another important point to realize about filming is how nothing ever works out the way you imagine it will. Every good filmmaker needs to have a plan B available constantly, followed by C and so on.

Figure 1.1 Acclaimed animator Phil Dale on the set of his short live-action film *The Census Taker*.

When working on a low budget this is more likely because you have to rely more on goodwill, on people helping you out and lending you equipment. But you will also find that a shot that looks perfect on paper just isn't possible for real. You may want the bank to be seen from the telephone box and it may be really crucial for the scene, but when you get there it becomes obvious that that tree in full leaf is going to get in the way. The answer is improvisation: the ability to think fast and clearly on set so that you stay on track with your plans, coming up with ideas that can solve a problem. If you don't do this, your crew and actors will quickly realize there is a power vacuum and start arguing about the best way forward. So, plan to improvise.

Stage 3: Editing

Priorities

In editing a film you will add a further layer of development to the whole creative act as your footage – all those tapes accrued over days or weeks of filming – is cut together in a way which best resembles your plans. Editing brings your film out of the uncertainty that is the initial idea and out of the scramble that is filming. It is about order, priorities, structure, pace, timing, accuracy. But it is also about play, spontaneity and creativity. Knowing how to place your clips in the right order is perhaps a triumph of instinct over expertise and, given the range of technical trickery on offer even in mid-level editing software, one of the hardest skills to learn is knowing when to stop editing. If you know what you want you are less likely to get side-tracked by the powerful influence of all that wonderful technology.

Skills you need

When you look back over the process of making your first production you may find that the skills you thought were essential to filmmaking – those centring on the technical aspects of the medium – were secondary to the more esoteric. Some filmmakers talk about the ability to remain both in control and open to new ideas; to negotiate your way through problems; to see all aspects of the process, however mundane, as having some creative contribution to the project, that nothing is purely technical; to think of a low budget as less a hindrance to realizing your imagination than a way towards doing so more artfully, more ingeniously.

The Crunch

- Know what it is you want to make clearly
- Planning the film will save you time and money later
- Enjoy surprises
- Handle the pressure – it's worth it to have your name at the end of the film
- Improvise to get you out of trouble
- Be prepared – your footage will always disappoint you straight after filming because you are tired and it's late and you just want to go home
- Postpone any rash decisions made after viewing your rushes – footage improves with time
- Look forward to editing – you are in charge again.

3. Low-budget filmmaking

'Thank God for FireWire and DV. The revolution will be televised after all.'

Chris Allen, founder, The Light Surgeons

Big money vs small money

In industry terms, there is a specific level below which you are considered to be a low-budget production. A standard budget in Hollywood terms can be somewhere in the region of $40 million to $100 million; low-budget is seen as anything operating on less than around one-tenth of this. But these figures are losing their relevance now that DV has brought the general cost of shooting and editing a movie down to something most people can afford. Many costs that served to exclude filmmakers from the business are now invisible or absent. For instance, rather than hiring an editing suite it is quite likely that you have the right level of hardware and software on your home PC or Mac to edit a movie. Similarly, short films have seen a huge boost to their numbers, evident from the large number of movies on the web and the growth of local screenings. One indication of the amount that costs have plummeted is the rise of filmmakers competitions aimed at making movies for $50, where similar events only a decade ago would have aimed at adding three zeros to that figure.

Increasingly, as the cost of filmmaking goes down, more and more directors find that they, by default, are low-budget people. The medium-budget movies of yesterday are today's low-budget. But while medium-sized productions will see their money go further than before, many will simply aim higher, trying previously expensive genres like science fiction and period costume drama.

Did you know?
Genre refers to a type of movie, such as the thriller, the western or the war movie. Movies within a certain genre tend to have similar characteristics, such as style, structure, story and so on. Sub-genres exist within these, such as the prison camp escape sub-genre, part of the war movie genre.

Micro-budget: even smaller

Below this level of low-budget filmmaker there has now emerged the so-called micro-budget filmmaker and the no-budget filmmaker – the film equivalents of freestyle climbing. The micro-budget filmmaker is operating with no funding, relying on private income or local arts centre grants, loans, and the investment of friends and relatives. Films are made for the cost of a DV tape, using whatever they own or can access as props, and running on borrowed cameras and a home computer.

On the positive side, however, although they have a dispiriting ceiling to their budgets they have no floor, almost no absolute minimum amount of money needed to begin a movie. A film shot on DV and edited at home will have costs primarily in front of the camera, in the form of props, actors, locations and so on. The traditionally high cost of filmmaking has usually been based on behind-the-camera items such as film stock, expensive cameras and edit units. You can wipe away other parts of the standard film budget if you write, direct and produce the film yourself, deferring your fee until, or if, someone buys the film and you make a profit.

Low-budget means 'different'

For many people working in the micro- and low/no-budget sector, these categories represent more than a total on a budget sheet. They mark a film as being innovative, different and challenging to the system. Low-budget is like a tag that says 'I do things my way and since I am not in anyone's pocket I can try anything I want.' You are prepared to make a movie with a different sort of commitment to those people getting percentage points from a blockbuster. It means you are prepared to put in unpaid time, your own money, and rely on networking and dealing within the filmmaking community to get your film made.

Figure 1.2 Shooting with little or no budget is not impossible but does present challenges. Director David Casals consults crew members on set.

Interview

'I think that is the beauty of a lower budget and these kind of formats that you really can do something different and tell your own story in a different way. You can experiment where you can't on a bigger budget. In a way, I was doing that on *Slacker* years ago, narratively speaking. I think that's why that caught on, because it was sort of its own animal. It wasn't a genre film trying to get bought into Hollywood; it just sort of existed on its own terms. I think people admire that because it didn't seem like it was trying to be anything. It wasn't a calling card to Hollywood.'

Richard Linklater, director of Slacker *(1991)*

DV technology

In terms of technology, too, you are challenging the industry. Making a film on DV is as much a cultural statement as a technical choice. When Michael Mann shot *Collateral* in 2003, he used both film and DV, allowing him to make a choice later as to which he preferred. With no CGI (computer-generated images) effects to handle, Mann had a straight choice between the look of film celluloid and the look of video. In what may be a crucial turning point, he chose video for the way it dealt with city lights in his nocturnal thriller.

DV has also entered the theatre. Many cinemas are converting to digital projection, using digital copies of films or showing movies beamed digitally by satellite. The pan-European CinemaNet agency beams new movies from emerging filmmakers direct to over 180 theatres across the continent.

Weblink
www.cinemaneteurope.com/   Home page for CinemaNet.

Being a filmmaker today

In many ways, the changing nature of filmmaking is becoming more and more geared towards the short movie. Features remain – and probably always will – the most profitable pinnacle of the industry, but are quickly being outgunned by the sheer volume of other forms of moving image. At the centre of being a filmmaker today is the number of ways the moving image can be viewed: on mobile phones, on laptops, palmtops, on portable DVD players, in screenings in local pubs and bars, on the web, on satellite TV and – most infrequently for many people – in theatres. In practical terms this means that the steps toward making movies involves working in one or all of these various outlets. It could be that seeing a film in a cinema is soon a specialist activity.

The effect of all this is to influence the way that filmmakers use their art. Filmmakers increasingly see features as a chance to experiment further with ideas developed in their day jobs in promos, motion graphics and ads, and it is quite likely that their reputation is sustained and enlarged by this work. Filmmakers going to see *Eternal Sunshine of the Spotless Mind* (Michel Gondry) were overheard recommending the movie on the basis of his experimental music promos. The same could be said of Jonathan Glazer after his groundbreaking Guinness ad and Spike Jonze after his energetic and surreal shorts.

Not long ago, the short movie was a stepping stone to making features and had almost no exposure beyond specialist art centres. Now, filmmakers still expect to launch themselves into feature-directing careers, but the level at which the short film gets seen has massively expanded. The web and phones have made sure that films of just a few minutes or less get potentially huge audiences. The good news for low-budget filmmakers is that this is precisely where most people have to start their careers.

So what?

What does all this mean for the emerging filmmaker? Low- and micro-budget are no longer places to escape from, but places where opportunities exist on a greater scale than before. The net effect of this is that the filmmaker with radical ideas, who wants to try new ways of telling a story, or of showing us the world, or simply wants to place before us issues that those at the top would rather ignore – these people have a greater chance than ever to take their ideas directly to audiences. In such a profit-driven industry as filmmaking, this is dangerous territory for some as it threatens to let new trends float straight to the surface without first being intercepted (and marketed) by the middlemen (studio bosses, film distributors, television programmers). But what is easily forgotten is that the history of cinema tells us that radical ideas are what it needs to thrive, that independent directors – independent in means and spirit – enable filmmaking to grow and evolve. Join that club.

The Crunch

- You have a valuable skill – the ability to make cheap films
- DV technology is helping low-budget filmmakers more than anyone else
- Break down the gates – do something new, make films your way.

2 Inside video

1. What is digital technology?

To some people the so-called DV revolution spells the end of a certain kind of movie: the end of celluloid and all the associations that we have with it – projectors, rolls of film and the romance of Hollywood. To others, though, it is more than a revolution or a change in the industry – it's year zero. To filmmakers who could only dream of committing their ideas to moving images, the DV age is the start of a career, not just a change in one, as the affordability of cameras and editing equipment makes it possible to get involved.

DV is here to stay, is reaching far wider into the mainstream of filmmaking than people thought possible and, in a few years, has affected every part of the video and film industries from Hollywood down to indie features, and finally – and most dramatically – the low-budget emerging filmmaker. In most revolutions of the technological sort (and maybe the political) it is those at the top that seem to benefit most financially, but the DV revolution is one that bucks the trend; big money producers agree DV makes a difference to the costs of a film, but to the filmmaker at the bottom it is the deciding factor in being able to make one at all. But before we run off with our winnings, it is worth looking more closely at this gift horse and trying to understand why it works so well and how it offers us what it does.

Digital video

Digital is called digital because it records information by the use of numbers: ones and zeros, which correspond to 'on' or 'off' commands. It has no variables as does the wave of analog; a signal is either one or the other, black or white, yes or no. This means that when the tape signal degrades after copying or playing – which happens however hard you try to avoid it – it alters only the strength of the yes or no, the on or off, the one or zero. It still gets read as one or the other, regardless of the strength of the signal. This is why digital is a better method of storing and reproducing information.

It is the reproduction of it that is crucial, since the ability to edit and distribute without loss of quality is to remain true to a director's original intentions.

Filmmakers used to rely on 16 mm film for their first forays into movies, and VHS tape never really caught on as an acceptable replacement. Filmmakers care about the way a picture looks and digital

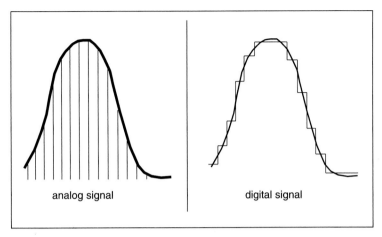

Figure 2.1 The digital signal on the right works by attaching a quantity to the wave. Each step of the curve is recorded as a number and this can then be reproduced more accurately than the analog signal on the left.

offers what many are looking for at the price they can afford, while VHS was neither quality nor did it have a specific 'look' as did 16 mm film. Why was VHS analog so bad? If you take a picture and photocopy it you produce a version of the original. But if you want to re-copy it you lose some information and the resulting copy is less clear than the original. Repeat this process several times and you end up with a muddy, unclear image. With digital, you are approaching the picture wholly differently: imagine breaking the tonal values and colours of that photo down into numerical values, in turn represented by ones and zeros. You have then got a set of instructions for the make-up of that picture and can send these instructions anywhere. All that it requires is that the receiver has the same information as the sender in order to be able to reassemble the image from the numbers it is given. With the right decoding knowledge it will reconstruct the image. Furthermore, because it exists in terms of numbers, it can be manipulated more easily, so that a picture can be turned black and white by exchanging one set of numbers for another, while keeping the rest unchanged.

Why choose DV?

Picture resolution

In general, the resolution of a picture on DV is about 25 per cent better than a comparable image on S-VHS – the best consumer-level tape for analog – and has about twice the horizontal resolution of a VHS recording. Low-priced mini-DV offers about the same quality as Betacam, previously the highest level analog format, which is a remarkable leap forward for the low-budget filmmaker.

Colour rendition

This refers to how well the format reproduces colour accurately. Analog is prone to vision 'noise' or interference, which smears and blurs colours. With DV, colour rendition is more true to what the digital camera first recorded. Edges are sharper and shapes more defined. But, as with analog, a lack of adequate light in DV filming quickly reduces quality. When you go up to better quality cameras – three-chip camcorders – things improve as the range of colour that can be recorded is larger, with each chip accommodating one of three colours rather than one chip having to cover all three.

Copying

DV offers greater quality control when copying. Since digital loses virtually no information each time it is copied, images can be transmitted or stored and the image that is read by the player is as good as the one on the master copy. The image is limited only by the quality of the playing instrument. Storing a film on any digital format guarantees greater longevity too. Magnetic tape is vulnerable to all sorts of environmental change, including heat, humidity and other magnetic fields, but digital tapes are very hard-wearing compared to previous formats.

Compatibility

Digital is 'backwards compatible'; in other words, all digital is compatible with itself, whereas other formats such as analog were not so interchangeable.

Broadcast standards

Most countries have very specific guidelines about what kind of picture quality is acceptable for broadcast. Pictures have to measure up to a set of standards and failure to meet these consistently may lead to the licence to broadcast being revoked, so broadcasters reject material from filmmakers which don't meet these standards. Some digital camcorders meet these specifications, but at the lower end there is an important difference. But broadcasters will accept material, in fact whole programmes and movies, which have been shot on cameras that are not actually broadcast standard. The Sony PD170 range, for instance, is a favourite with filmmakers, particularly documentary makers, and yet it should not really be good enough for TV in terms of its technical characteristics. Yet it is close enough to do the job, while other cams such as the Canon XM2 are well regarded by TV commissioners across the board.

Weblinks
www.ee.surrey.ac.uk/Contrib/WorldTV   Information on broadcast standards.
www.3dresearch.com/video/Countries2.html   More on broadcast standards.

However, beware of the term 'broadcast quality' if you see it on the shop window at your video store. The term has changed considerably since DV became a consumer item; in terms of the consumer it has become a loose term, often simply referring to a quality far above that offered by analog but not necessarily meeting broadcast technical quality guidelines. Whatever the publicity blurb says, check with an independent advisor first (don't even trust a manufacturer) before committing yourself to an expensive camera that claims to be broadcast standard but stops your programmes being accepted by television companies.

Audio

The CD format in music offers superior quality to analog and almost 'lossless' copying. As you would expect, then, audio channels on DV video are comparable to CD and when recorded on 16-bit stereo offer unparalleled quality.

A brief history of digital technology

DV has grown in the last decade from a corner of the video industry into a mainstay of the consumer leisure industry. Developments have been rapid in this early stage of the DV revolution, so it is easy to confuse the passing fads from the long-lasting major changes to the industry. But you could chart the advance of digital video in two simple words: Apple and compression.

A brief history of digital video

It was the arrival of the Apple Computer in 1984 that heralded the start of the multimedia age 'for the rest of us', as the company logo read. The big leap forward was the 'graphical user interface'; in other words, a more user-friendly way of dealing with computers, by having windows instead of glowing green letters on a black screen. This windows layout is the only feasible way for creative programs to work because you need to be able to work with several different kinds of commands at once – palettes of colours, video timelines and so on. The use of Microsoft Windows on the vast majority of the world's computers is a direct result of the pioneering work done by Apple's founders and by companies such as Lotus, Adobe and Digital Research Inc. Apple supremo Steve Jobs crops up again later in our short history lesson as the pioneer of another big step forward.

The important breakthrough in thinking was the view by Apple that computers could be creative tools, as Apple's early Macintosh home computers came equipped with painting software as well as spreadsheets. Rather than adopt a passive, consumer ethos for its products, Apple foresaw the Mac as something owned by makers, users and creators.

Weblink
www.apple-history.com/frames   Apple history timeline.

We used to edit in a very long-winded way, piecing together bits of film with tape or glue. Video was not much of a leap forward as you simply had two VCRs hooked up and you copied your good stuff from one tape onto your blank tape on the next VCR. It made sense later to call this 'linear' editing, since you laid down the bits of good footage one after the other and, crucially, there was no going back. Once you had copied them to tape you couldn't revisit an earlier section and re-edit it without having to redo all the following clips too. On the plus side, editors had to be more decisive than today.

So, when Avid, a leading multimedia company, unveiled its non-linear editing system it was the biggest shake-up in editing since Melies played around with time and sequence in the early 1900s.

Weblink

www.tvhandbook.com/History/History_timeline.htm   Broadcast history timeline.

We called it 'non-linear' editing in the professional arena and desktop editing for the consumer. Working on a computer, clips could be endlessly switched about and played until the perfect sequence was found. You could work on various bits of the movie all at once, building it up in a more organic fashion. Actually, it has more in common with the old scissors and glue method of celluloid, since you used to go back and add bits of film and work on any part whenever you wanted. Certainly, the kinds of visual devices common to us today, such as montage or flashback, are a result of being able to access any part of a film.

1994 saw the next big step, with the patent of Apple's FireWire cable – patented as IEEE 1394, or the Institute of Electrical Engineers' 13th patent in 1994. The big problem with video is its sheer size and here was a cable which didn't baulk at the huge amounts of data it had to conduct. Transferring at a huge 400 kb/s it avoids drop-outs of frames when you transfer footage from camera to computer. To use the analogy of traffic on a road, FireWire is like a freeway/motorway, while other cables like USB 1.0 are like quiet back roads; send too much traffic and it gets clogged up. The need for FireWire arose because new digital cameras were hitting the market which could send data direct to a computer, whereas analog cameras had to first translate their analog data into digital code. Like translating a document from English to another language, this process added time and expense.

Weblinks

http.developer.apple.com/devicedrivers/firewire/index.htm   All about FireWire from Apple.
www.ieee.org/portal/site   Keep up to date with FireWire technology.

With manufacturers putting cameras into the market which recorded in digital, FireWire made it possible to make the most of them on the home PC. The biggest problem next became what to do with the movies once you had edited them. The available storage disks were insufficient – floppy disks – and the modems of early Internet users were not nearly capable of downloading video files.

MPEG, Pixar and projection

Which brings us to the development of clever ways to squash down video into manageable files. Once again, Apple stepped in with QuickTime technology in the early 1990s, again placing it firmly in the consumer market rather than expecting it to have purely professional uses. A group of international experts called MPEG had been working for some time to standardize the issues around compression and made it easier for the expanding consumer PC market to agree on the kinds of software needed. The Motion Picture Experts Group developed the standards MPEG-1, used on much early compression; MPEG-2, the standard for DVD compression; and later MPEG-4, used for web-based video and gaming.

Weblink
www.mpeg.org   Home page for MPEG news.

Once you could edit digitally, it was a short step away to manipulate each of those digital frames using other software. In 1986, former Apple boss Steve Jobs bought Lucasfilms computer graphics division for $10 million. Renamed Pixar, their early films went one stage further by creating images wholly on computers, and this process of computer-generated images (CGI) has since made its way into almost every kind of movie today, whether it is to paint out an errant catering truck in the corner of a frame or the wires holding up an actor, or creating entire objects to interact with live action, such as hurricanes (*Twister*) or aliens (*The Abyss*). By 2004, films such as *Sky Captain* and *The Polar Express* pointed to a whole new method of making films, where real action is captured on computer and used to animate objects and people.

In 1992, a theatre was hired by Sony Pictures and used as an experiment with Pacific Bell to give the world a first view of digital cinema to an audience of several hundred. Rather than having to make a celluloid version of a digital movie so it could be shown on celluloid projectors, a digital projector introduced the idea that films could be digitally shot, digitally edited and finally digitally exhibited.

The web

In the mid-1990s, the idea of connecting PCs together took off when the Internet, formerly a system for hitching up university computers to share research between institutions, became the must-have addition for home PC users.

Advances in compression had been swift and by 1998 the compact disc was being used to hold entire feature films, using enhanced dual-layer discs and MPEG-2 compression – more of which in Chapter 3:2.

By the turn of the millennium, digital cinemas were becoming a reality for audiences in North America. On 19 June 1999, Fox and LucasFilms staged *Star Wars: Episode 1 – The Phantom Menace* in four theatres using digital projectors. A few years before, a low-budget movie called *The Last Broadcast* became, with no irony, the first to be broadcast by satellite to a theatre in a move that could yet pose the biggest threat to the mighty distributors.

Weblinks
www.digitalcinemareport.com   Market information about digital cinemas.
www.digitalcinema-europe.com   Forum for European developments.

High definition

Into the millennium, high definition (HD) video has pushed the boundaries of what filmmakers can use, doubling the lines of recorded video and kick-starting the possibility of HD-TV for consumers.

But filmmakers have found out that recording HD is one thing but getting it to squeeze onto tapes is quite another. Video compression may have to take another huge leap forward before consumers and low-budget filmmakers can use this new format. It also asks filmmakers to consider the question of whether picture clarity is the holy grail after all.

All this talk of technology can lose sight of what it was that these pioneers in DV were trying to achieve. Ultimately, it was about the art and craft of filmmaking and of storytelling. Like the Gutenberg printing press, which placed the printed spread of information in the hands of the masses, DV technology has enabled more to be produced with less, and by more people.

For all its being showered with new toys and gadgets each year, filmmaking remains an art form, concerned with images and story.

The Crunch

- Become technical – most artists have to work at this bit, but it is worth it because you are in control
- Get to know about broadcast standards for your country or the place you might want to show your work
- Analog is long gone – digital is going to give you better results
- FireWire is good – you need it.

2. How the camcorder works

Before we look at the inner workings of the video camera, we need first to define what we are looking at. Not all cameras can record images; some simply pass them on to another device, which commits them to tape. In television, for example, cameras in the studio relay images elsewhere and so are not, technically, camcorders, just cameras. For simplicity, then, we will talk throughout this section about the kind that records images as well as seeing them, from entry-level consumer models through to those in the upper range used in filmmaking.

How images get onto tape

To understand how the image gets onto the digital tape, we could start at the beginning and follow the whole process. It basically runs like this:

- image through the lens
- image is sensed by a CCD chip
- gets translated into binary code
- then gets transferred to tape.

Surrounding this process are a range of features that help modify the image, making it clearer or more stable, if needed. Audio signals recorded simultaneously go straight from the microphone, getting translated into digital information and onto the tape, and are matched with the images accompanying them.

Weblink
www.video-business-school.com/Howcamcorderworks.htm   Feature on how the camcorder works.

What happens when the image hits the lens

Lens

The lens is the point at which the image crosses into the camcorder, using an iris which functions much the same as the human eye. Lens quality is crucial; the camcorder may have a perfect method of recording what it sees, but to make the most of it must see perfectly to begin with. Consumer-level camcorders will not usually have the lens quality of those in the semi-professional and professional range levels, although some manufacturers try to improve the lenses on cheaper models by teaming up with established photographic lens makers.

Iris

The iris in the lens controls the amount of light entering the camcorder and will quickly shrink if too much is entering or dilate if there is too little. The reason it must do this is to satisfy the amount of information required by the CCD chip situated near the lens. If there is too little light and the required pixels do not each receive instructions, then the chip steps in and starts adding its own default information. This is known as 'noise' and is read as tiny white dots all over the screen, which is why you get a grainy image if you shoot in low light conditions.

Shutter speed

The shutter and the iris overlap in their roles to some extent. When light passes through the lens it hits a shutter that is opening and closing 25 times each second (in PAL standard cameras for the UK), or 29.9 (NTSC) for North American cameras. Each of these images that gets recorded is called a frame. The camera can alter the speed at which it opens its shutter, even though it still opens it the same number of times each second. The minimum speed for many cameras is 1/50th of a second, with the maximum in consumer level cameras around 1/8000th of a second.

The difference between these is most evident when you record fast-moving objects. In 1/50th of a second, the length of time a shutter is open, the object (let's say a car) travels a long way in front of the camera in one frame (let's say 20 feet), and therefore blurs all the movement within that distance onto one frame. If you up the shutter speed to 1/1000th of a second, then the shutter is open for only a fraction of that and records only a fraction of the movement, say one foot, resulting in no blurring.

However, there is a knock-on effect in reducing the amount of time the shutter is open; less light can enter the lens. So it is kind of doing what the iris does in keeping some of the light out. If your camera has manual controls then it will be straightforward to adjust both the shutter and the iris to make sure that enough light gets in to give a full, clear picture. You can also use shutter speed and iris settings to give a darker and more jagged effect to a movie. In *28 Days Later* (Danny Boyle), a high shutter speed in this digitally shot film gave it a spooky look, in keeping with the post-apocalyptic scenario and helping the large number of action shots by preventing blur.

So far so good, but the iris and shutter can play other roles too. If you reduce the hole in the iris then the range of objects that are in focus is altered too – this is called 'depth of field'. If you think of a line of trees in an avenue with you standing with your camera in the middle of the road, not all of them are going to be in focus all the time. If you were to adjust the iris to let less light in, making the hole at the front smaller, then there would be more of the line of trees in focus. If you were to open the iris, then less of them would be clear.

It makes sense, then, to think about these three aspects of a shot – focus, iris and shutter – as being linked and needing a joined-up approach to dealing with them. When shooting, if you adjust one of them, think about how it affects the other two.

Zoom

Another function of the lens is zoom. Digital camcorders zoom in one of two ways: optical or digital zoom. Optical zoom is by far the better option, as it magnifies the image using two glass lenses and reads it more accurately. Digital zoom, however, is almost without merit, as it simply enlarges the image it saw, drastically reducing resolution.

How the camera deals with the image

When the image makes it through the lens it gets recorded in various ways by a small chip located near the lens, called the charge-coupled device (CCD). There are two sorts, determined by which kind of camera you have:

- *Single-chip*. These dominate the lower, domestic end of the market. It collects over 300 000 pixel bits of information, which sounds a lot but is considerably less than the three-chip.
- *Three-chip*. This one is found in any of the better camcorders in the mid and upper ranges. The big difference here is that there are three chips, each gathering 300 000 bits of information, but this time each chip gathers just one colour each: red, green or blue. The single-chip gathers all colours together and so has to squeeze all three groups of information into one chip. The additional quality of the three-chip is worth about an extra 20 per cent in terms of picture and colour resolution.

If you want to make programmes for broadcast then you need to get a three-chip. Most people will not notice the difference between single-chip and three-chip, but broadcasters will notice and do not accept certain quality of pictures. But if you intend to show only on the web, this difference is going to be reduced later, so it may not be useful.

Tip   The term 'broadcast quality' has changed considerably since DV became a consumer item; in terms of the consumer it has become a loose term and often simply refers to a quality far above that offered by analog, but not necessarily meeting broadcast technical quality guidelines. Whatever the publicity blurb says, check with an independent advisor first before committing yourself to an expensive camera that claims to be broadcast standard but stops your programmes being accepted by television companies.

At this stage the camera sorts out how much information can be stored and how much has to be left behind. Mini-DV tapes do not have the capacity to store all the information that a camera could record but are significantly better than VHS. In terms of a ratio of information kept to that thrown away, mini-DV is 5:1, compared to 7:1 for analog Hi8 and 15:1 for VHS. How well a camera squashes down its information is crucial. The new generation of HD cameras have suffered from a poor compression method. It remains a problem for manufacturers to convince the market about HD because the recorded picture is so reduced from what it should be, given the huge size of each frame of HD video.

What happens when the image gets recorded onto tape

Digital tape is much more rugged than that used for analog S-VHS or VHS video. It is made of an advanced form of metal evaporated (ME) tape. It consists of a double-coated magnetic layer, which is in turn coated in tough carbon. This enables stored digital information to be played back with minimal loss of quality and less picture noise, or interference. 'Bleeding' from the audio track to the video tracks is also unlikely, further reducing interference.

Solid-state cameras record onto discs but have to use a sophisticated form of compression to enable it to do so. In consumer models images are recorded onto a fixed hard drive or onto DVDs, though the latter have failed to take off in the consumer sector in the way manufacturers would have liked. Cameras using hard drive recording have become more widely used, possibly a result of the iPod effect, where consumers understand and trust mini hard drives. A further development has been in removable hard drives. For filmmakers using cameras such as the Canon XZ2 or Sony PD170, the favourites of many low-budgeteers, hard drive recording was not possible until large removable 80 GB drives such as Holdan's Firestore made it to industry shows.

Compression	Format	MB/second	How many minutes of video for 1 GB on your PC
1:1	Broadcast	18.5	0.5
2:1	Direct transfer	9.3	1
3:1	Digi-Beta SP	6.2	2
4:1	Beta SP Pro	4.6	3
5:1	Beta Semi-Pro	3.7	4
5:1 in camera	Mini-DV	3.6	4
7:1	Hi-8, S-VHS Pro	2.6	6
10:1	Hi-8, S-VHS	1.85	9
15:1	VHS	1.2	14

Figure 2.2 Compression rates of camera formats.

Recording standards

There are several other factors that are worth mentioning in relation to recording. If you intend to make movies or programmes for selling in other countries, you need to know about the differences in broadcast standards around the world. Ultimately, this affects anyone who makes films because few people can afford to ignore the potentially lucrative returns in foreign markets. None of these problems are insurmountable, but being aware of them before you start a project can increase your chances of selling your work to a wide range of markets.

PAL, NTSC and SECAM

Each country has its own specification for how many lines a television signal must produce and how many frames per second it should have. In Europe and Australia, the standard is PAL (Phase Alternating Line), which operates on a high level of quality in terms of pixels on screen but slightly lower frame rate. In America, the standard is called NTSC (National Television Systems Committee) and has a lower number of pixels on the screen, but operates on a faster frame rate of 29.9 (often rounded up to 30). A different system called SECAM (sequential couleur avec memoire, or sequential colour with memory) is used in parts of eastern Europe, some African countries, parts of South America and the former states of the USSR. SECAM is closer to PAL than NTSC, using the same bandwidth as PAL but transmitting colour information sequentially. Countries using SECAM can play PAL videos or DVDs more easily than NTSC.

To complicate matters, there is also a version of PAL known as PAL 60, leaving the old PAL to be known as PAL 50. The new version is intended to help address the problems of NTSC users viewing

Countries using PAL	Countries using NTSC	Countries using Secam
Argentina	Caribbean islands	Albania
Algeria	Canada	Bulgaria
Andorra	Chile	Colombia
Australia	El Salvador	Czech Republic
Austria	Guatemala	Egypt
Belgium	Japan	Former USSR
Brazil	South Korea	France
China	Mexico	Iran
Denmark	Peru	Poland
Germany	Puerto Rico	Romania
Greece	USA	Zaire
Finland	Venezuela	
Hong Kong		
Iceland		
India		
Indonesia		
Ireland		
Israel		
Italy		
Kenya		
Malaysia		
Netherlands		
New Zealand		
Norway		
Portugal		
South Africa		
Spain		
Sweden		
Switzerland		
Turkey		
United Kingdom		
Zimbabwe		

Figure 2.3 Table of international TV standards.

PAL movies. NTSC uses a frame rate of 30 frames per second while PAL uses 25, but the new PAL also uses 30.

Pixels

The number of pixels, or dots on the screen, is determined by how many vertical and horizontal lines the signal has. The NTSC ratio of 640 × 480 has roughly 307 000 pixels, whereas PAL has 720 × 560, giving it the edge with over 400 000. This will lead to greater clarity and sharpness in PAL, but it suffers when it comes to frame rate.

Frame rate

Frame rate (the number of individual pictures that have to make up a single second of tape) affects smoothness of movement. A film shot on fewer frames per second (fps) will look more jerky than one on higher fps. There are ways of easily transferring a recording so that a programme made for American TV (NTSC) will play on British or Australian TV (PAL), even though they use different frame rates.

Format	Advantages	Disadvantages	Suitable for:
HDV	The highest quality available for filmmakers. It records 720 × 1080 (interlaced) video on tape and is now being targeted at the filmmaker and semi-professional. All camcorders may use this format one day.	For filmmakers, the problem is compression, with images being so large that they need extensive reduction before recording onto tape. Editing can also be problematic – settings need to be adjusted. File sizes, however, are not that big, when compared to the size of the data they carry. But this is the problem: compression is too massive – for now.	All types of filmmaking. HDV camcorders are reasonably priced and within range of the low-budget filmmaker.
Digi-Beta	Successor to Betacam, it uses ½-inch cassettes, recording on a 2:1 compression ratio. Good for ENG (Electronic News Gathering) due to the high broadcast quality.	Expensive tapes for expensive cameras.	Broadcast work; documentaries.
DVCAM/DVC Pro	DVC Pro is Panasonic's version of DV, designed for professionals with double tape recording speed for better quality and fewer drop-outs. DVCAM is a similar version put out by Sony, but slightly lower in terms of quality than the DVC Pro. Both are almost broadcast standard.	Both are being superseded by HDV.	Ideal for filmmaking. Location and news gathering is also suitable. The near-broadcast quality means that most cable channels will accept work on these formats.
Betacam SP (analog)	An improvement on the broadcast standard – until DV – introduced in 1986. Was hugely popular in broadcasting, with many cameras still being used in this format in smaller networks.	Large cassettes: 14 × 25 cm for a 90-minute tape. Smaller cassettes are often used on location, but these are only 30 minutes long.	Used for programme-making in cable and local television. Good for student-level broadcast training.
Mini-DV (digital)	Most widespread of all DV formats in the domestic market. Tapes are small and long-lasting; camcorders record at 500 lines, giving high quality images.	Compression ratio is good but still far under that needed for broadcast standards.	It depends on the camera. If you use a single-chip camera it is not suitable for filmmaking if you intend to submit to festivals or cable slots. However, a three-chip camera will record excellent images to tape, which will be acceptable to many broadcasters, especially cable, and will pass festival panels.

DVD-RAM (digital)	Arrived in the middle of 2001 to much fanfare. Images are recorded on disc, so can be randomly accessed (no rewinding needed). Also allows basic editing by moving around footage.	Heavy compression means you aren't editing with master footage, having already been compressed with MPEG-2. Discs don't play in all manufacturers' players. Problems with image pixellation when panning.	Although the quality of the images is good (mini-DV level), the format is unsuitable for filmmaking as the footage is not captured via FireWire cable but is taken from a disc. You cannot output to tape, which means you can only make DVD copies, not tape masters.
Digital 8 (digital)	Sony's upgrading of its Hi-8 format. It is backwards compatible with analog 8 mm formats.	Digital 8 cameras tend to be bigger and heavier than similar DV cameras.	Useful if you have a lot of analog footage on Hi-8 tape and need to archive it or convert to digital. But it is probably better suited to domestic home movies than filmmaking.
MicroMV (digital)	Smallest cameras on the market, capturing 60 minutes of footage with MPEG-2 compression on tape. Tapes are 70% smaller than mini-DV tapes. Footage takes up much less space on your PC as it is so highly compressed.	Very few editing software programs can deal with it. Compression rate is high, affecting quality.	Useful for work where lightweight camera is necessary (for instance, in mountain climbing shots). Not suitable for filmmaking, if possible.
VHS/S-VHS	Cameras for these formats are exceptionally cheap, especially in the second-hand market.	S-VHS is the upgrade to VHS, but both are dying out under the relentless march of DV.	Completely unsuitable for filmmaking. Useful for educational settings, with children, but even here the better camera is the small hard-drive recorder, such as the Bluemovie camera.

Figure 2.4 Video formats explained.

Timecode

Another, more complicated factor in frame rate is timecode. In terms of frame rate, timecode is more of a headache with NTSC than with PAL. PAL, with its nice, easily divisible numbers (25 goes into 100 neatly), presents no problem for accurate timecode. The 29.9 fps of NTSC, however, needs to operate with something called 'drop-frame timecode', in which certain frame numbers – not your actual hard-won frames themselves from the footage – are dropped out to keep everything in round numbers. It gets rid of two frames every minute but skips every tenth minute. Thankfully, you no longer have to worry about drop-frame timecode as many edit programs offer you the chance to work in this method. But it is essential if you intend to work in productions of 60 minutes or more, as you would end up with an error rate of 3.6 seconds every hour. If you are intending to sell broadcast material to zones with other broadcast standards, check what they use and edit the movie with this in mind.

The Crunch

- You need manual override on your camera
- Get a three-CCD-chip camera if you can
- Understand the way cameras record so you can use them creatively
- OK, maybe you don't want to know all this technical stuff, but make sure someone in your next crew does.

3. Operating the camcorder

Every model of camcorder is different, but there are certain ways of handling camcorders that make the best of what you've got. From the point of view of the filmmaker, as opposed to the tourist or home movie maker, some features need to be looked at a little closer.

Camera support

Digital cameras are so lightweight that the problem of camera shake is more pronounced than with previous models and the need to support the camera in some way is crucial. Even hand-held work is going to be vastly different for digital cameras than for film, so whatever your preference in films you will need to make some plans for reducing camera shake. Check that your camera has a universal tripod fitting on its base. Many tripods offer a quick release plate that locks the camera onto the tripod without having to screw the camera onto the tripod each time.

Zoom control

Using zoom on a subject does not always produce good results; zoom controls tend to move at a constant rate and this can look quite unnatural. It is considered to be a slightly redundant way of recording, except in non-fiction work, unless used as a self-conscious device. Use zoom only when a tracking shot towards the subject is not an option.

Focusing

Automatic focusing is useful for tourist movies, but in productions where artistic considerations are high, this is going to stop you from getting good compositions. Be prepared to use the manual override option to use your own focus on certain shots. In automatic mode, the camera senses the distance between itself and the nearest object, through the use of infrared beams bounced off its target. The problem with this is that it can't focus on everything within the frame, so it chooses only that which is in the middle of the viewfinder. This renders any slightly adventurous compositions out of focus. When interviewing a subject, for example, it may look more interesting to place the head to one side of the screen, improving depth. You will need to focus manually if you are to avoid getting the wall next to the figure in focus and the head blurred. To do this, use automatic focus on the subject but place it in the middle of the screen, let the auto focus find its optimum point after a few seconds and then switch to manual mode, freezing the focus at this. Then pan the camera to the right composition. Moving the camera closer or nearer to the subject will again render it out of focus and you must go through the process again. Deal with moving, unpredictable subjects like flames and running water in a similar way, but pan the camera to the side first so that you let the auto focus settle on a solid object the same distance from the camera.

Aperture and depth of field

Aperture refers to the opening or iris which allows varied amounts of light through the lens. Aperture affects both the light entering the camera and the range of the frame that is in focus, known as depth of field. Attaching other lenses also affects the range of your focus. For example, wide-angle lenses allow for a far greater range of focus, from objects far away to those near the camera, while telephoto lenses have very little depth of field.

Altering the iris

As we saw in the earlier section on how cameras record, the iris can be altered for creative uses, using manual controls:

- *Closing the iris* so that it is very small will let less light in and also enable objects in the foreground and background to be in focus – something that may look unnatural or could be just the effect you want
- *Closing the iris* can also result in well-lit sets appearing to have extreme contrast – the dark areas are unreadable and the white areas are strong and bright
- *Opening up the iris* will result in a narrow band of focus, so that objects or people moving towards or away from the camera are easily thrown out of focus
- *Opening up the iris* will also make normal lighting conditions seem over-lit – even an average lamp will seem to glow unnaturally.

If you manually operate the iris, beware of distortion at the edges of the frame.

Light and the camera

The automatic features of your camera are going to affect how you shoot. In auto setting, the camcorder thinks it is doing you a favour by removing some of the light on a bright scene or opening itself up to lighten a dark interior. This automatic light meter causes problems as it is going to stop you from using creative lighting effects. Video, in general, does not like to be deprived of light and will react badly if you try to work in conditions that differ from the norm. Just about all filmmaking involves using lighting in some creative way and your auto functions will do their best to cancel out any effects you set up.

To make sure you get a good image, light the scene well but try removing the lit areas and increasing shadow. You can learn a lot about lighting by trying to create shadow rather than create light. Any household lamps can be used for this as DV requires far less light to make an effective picture than VHS; 300 W lamps will be sufficient rather than the bigger 800 W common in many VHS low-budget shoots.

When you have the light looking good – creating the atmosphere that is right for your scene – avoid any fluctuation of the aperture during recording. For example, a tracking shot of a figure in movement between a desk with a bright lamp to a darker corner of the room will present problems because of changes in the level of light available. Moving between these two places, the camera is designed to step in and open up the iris as it gets to the darker corner. But that loses the whole effect, as the two places will appear to the viewer to be lit equally, with the uncomfortable moment in between the two places as the iris shudders around to get the aperture right. Again, switching off the auto controls will avoid this problem, but to find the right level of aperture, look through the camera at both the dark and light areas of the scene with auto switched on for a moment. Let the camera settle in one part between the two and find an aperture that is right for both areas.

White balance

White balance is a tool – usually automatic in most cameras – which assesses the temperature of light entering the lens and compensates to alter any inaccuracies in colour, to something approaching the mid-range in degrees kelvin. Colours seen in natural daylight are more true than colours seen under artificial light, due to the effect the different colour temperatures have on natural colours.

The automatic white balance feature filters out some of these colours to arrive at a more realistic light and should be used for each new take. As with other functions, you can alter it manually and use it as a creative tool so that, for instance, daylight looks bluer and colder than it should – by setting the white balance for indoor, household light it would assume there is too much orange and remove some from the picture. Get to know how your camera functions when you set the colour balance incorrectly. Don't forget to avoid altering the white balance setting while you are in the middle of shooting a scene.

Power

Batteries are expensive and don't last long, but cables are a hindrance. Think about how you can spread the use of your batteries, or hitch up to the mains as often as possible. Loss of power creeps up on you and almost always happens when you are about to shoot a crucial scene that can't wait. Some cameras in the upper range tell you when you are low on power or have a power meter to keep you informed constantly. Check whether your camera warns you when your battery is running low. If you are on location and have no access to mains supply, conserve power by restricting the amount you rehearse on camera or play with different camera set-ups and do not use the LCD display if your camera has one fitted. Try using a dummy lens, such as a still camera, to try out different compositions or framing, so that when you use the video camera you use less power looking for shots. If you do get stuck without power suddenly, hold the weak battery under your armpit for a short time; sometimes body warmth is all it needs to give you that last bit of power to finish the shoot.

Audio inputs

These will allow you to use external microphones for recording, or the use of audio mixing boards (on some models). Using external mics is strongly recommended.

Listening to audio

Most cameras have built-in speakers so that you can hear what is being recorded. These are no substitute for earphones, though. Make sure you always use earphones every time you shoot. Interference from power cables and mobile phones will affect the quality of your sound and if you have headphones you will hear this straight away.

Timecode

Most consumer-level models do not refer to timecode as such, but do have functions to allow you to start recording right after the last frame of the last take you shot, thereby ensuring that you don't break timecode. Models above this level will all allow you to record with timecode. Always 'stripe' your tapes before shooting – record continuously throughout the whole tape with the lens cap still on. This lays down a constant timecode track before you use the tape.

The Crunch

- Be in control of the camera
- Use timecode
- Learn how to move with it
- Get a tripod but don't overuse it
- Zooming in or out does not look great
- Always get the image in focus
- Always use an external mic.

Type of work	Lens type	Manual focus	Manual iris control	Manual shutter speed	Image stabilizer	Colour LCD monitor	Timecode	Format	Optical or digital zoom	DV input/ DV output (FireWire)	3-CCD	Head phone output	External mic output
Shooting for broadcast, cinema, DVD	Interchangeable lenses for maximum flexibility	Yes	Yes	Yes	Not essential	Not essential as you will use an external monitor	Yes	HDV Digi-Beta Mini-DV DV Pro	Optical	Both	Yes	Yes	Yes + XLR audio
Short films for more experienced filmmakers	Interchangeable if possible	Yes	Yes	Yes	Not essential – use a tripod	Not essential as you will use an external monitor	Yes	Mini-DV	Optical	Both	Yes	Yes	Yes
Short films to raise your profile or develop skills *(intermediate level of experience)*	Carl Zeiss lens or interchangeable	Yes	Yes	Yes	Useful	Yes	Yes	Mini-DV	Optical	Both	Yes	Yes	Yes
Documentary (any level below broadcast)	Any	Yes	Yes	Yes	Yes	No	Yes	Mini-DV	Optical	Both	Yes	Yes	Yes
Your first short films *(beginners)*	Any, fixed	Yes	Yes	Yes	Useful	Yes	Useful	Mini-DV	Either, but optical is better	Both	Not essential	Yes	Yes
Educational work	Any	Not essential	Not essential	Not essential	Yes	Yes	No	Mini-DV	Either	DV output	No	No	No
Web films	Any	Yes	Yes	Yes	Yes	Yes	No	Mini-DV	Either	DV output	No	No	No
Domestic home movies													

Figure 2.5 Camcorder buying guide: features needed in DV filmmaking.

Project 1. In-camera edit: hand-made movie

What this project is for: to learn about manual settings in shooting
Time: allow about three hours

What this project is for

The aim of this film is to encourage you to use the camera with complete control over every aspect of what it is doing. Cameras are easy: they do what you want, when you want, but they let you down when it comes to helping you be creative. Indeed, the aim of every camera manufacturer is to make life easier for you. But you don't want an easy life; that's why you are trying to make films, so we need to tell the camera to listen and do it your way.

To achieve this, we will make a short film that is made with the camera on *manual settings throughout*. If you have to resort to using automatic settings, it is so that you can deceive the camera, but more on this later. As with other films in this book, we need to make it short, lasting less than four minutes. The film is going to made in-camera, so you will be shooting each shot as you need them in the order they appear.

Stage 1

In this film, the subject matter is not the most critical element; it is no more than a vehicle for the actions and movement of the camera. The theme running through this film (it is too open-ended to call it a story) is titled *A Day in the Life*.

The film is going to follow you as you go through a typical day, encountering various situations and people. Since you have to keep the movie short, it might be useful to divide the film into sections, looking at different parts of your day. It may sound like a simple film, but many films are extremely neat in their ideas. Consider Kevin Smith's stunning debut feature, *Clerks* (1994), which was filmed entirely in the New Jersey shop where he worked. Smith manages to make one location and very little else go a long way, turning in a film which catapulted him into the big time. Richard Linklater's *Before Sunrise* achieves a similar feat in a few streets in Paris.

Stage 2

Spend some time getting to know what the manual features on your camera are there for. Look at the guide to camera features elsewhere in this chapter and look to see what yours has. Check:

● Where are the manual and auto buttons (if yours has manual override)?
● Have you got a manual focus ring?
● Have you got manual iris control (aperture)?
● Have you got manual white balance?
● How about manual shutter speed?

Stage 3

Choose a day and start filming. Shoot some shots of, for instance, what your house looks like in the morning, about who eats breakfast in your kitchen, where you have to go to work or study, who you meet along the way, where you eat lunch, who you meet in the evening and where you go, what it's like at night in your town. In all these situations, you will have to encounter environments that are very different to each other in terms of what the camera sees. Conditions will vary from place to place and from day to night, providing you with opportunities to encounter a wide range of situations.

Before we go further, let's take a look at how to handle sound in-camera. This project can operate on two levels: a basic level that looks at what the camera sees only, and a more advanced level for those who want to start using an external mic. Take the basic for now, if you prefer, and then come back to this project later when you have got to grips with sound recording in Chapter 5:3. But if you want to try using mics, go for a directional mic, which records wherever you point it. Try the built-in mic at least once so that you know how poor the quality is.

The aim of this film is not particularly to produce a great-looking film at the end, but rather to encounter problems. You won't be able to solve all of them and you may need to get some help from the automatic button on the camera, but at least you will know the limits of what you can achieve manually and what you need some help for.

Let's look at some of the problem areas you may encounter:

Light

Usually, you expect your camera to take care of 'exposure' when you enter a new lighting situation. Exposure refers to the amount of light that enters the lens: too much and it is too bright to see anything clearly, too little and it is too dim to see clearly. Let's suppose you start filming in your kitchen in the early morning. You may have a couple of fluorescent lights in the room and some semblance of daylight entering from the window. You have two problems to deal with here: the first involving the intensity of the light within the room and the second concerning the colour temperature of the light. A lack of intensity of light is easy to deal with on set simply by adding more light, but at home you are going to have to get the iris control and try various settings until you have what looks like a good image on the LCD monitor. Open the iris up a little if the image looks too dark, or close it down slightly if it is too bright. Go through all the manual options it gives you until you are satisfied with the image, then start filming.

Colour temperature (measured in degrees kelvin) affects the colour of the light we see. For example, a candle gives off a very orange, warm cast of colour, while daylight on a late afternoon in winter would give off a bluish cast. If you have standard household bulbs in the kitchen, they may give an orange tint to the film, while fluorescent strip lighting can give a greenish cast. However, none of this would be picked up as the camera removes some of the extra colour. But what happens if you want extra orange? How does the picture look? For this, you may have to resort to the automatic white balance if no other option is available, but at this point run through the manual options it gives you (if any). Some cameras suggest a few settings for the most common lighting situations: indoor, outdoor, bright day, cloudy day and so on. Try out some of these settings incorrectly. If you try, for instance, cloudy outdoor settings for shooting in your kitchen it will assume that there is a dominance of blue in the scene, which would occur in this kind of light, and balance it with taking away some of the blue. The net effect is a kitchen more orange than usual, as what little blue there was is turned down even further.

Shutter speed

If your camera has options for changing the shutter speed you can alter these to take into account different situations. Shutter speed refers to the amount of time it takes the camera to open and close the shutter. A fast car, at close range, will appear blurred unless a higher (or faster) shutter speed is used (for example, from 1/125 to 1/400). However, faster shutter speeds need higher light levels, so altering these settings can produce some effects. Try shooting a fast car on a slow shutter speed and perhaps you might enjoy the blurring of the image, particularly if a stationary figure is in the foreground to contrast against it. Then you might want to play around with how a fast shutter speed – requiring more light – records in a low-light environment.

Focus

Focus rings (a ring around the lens that you turn to alter the focus manually) are rare on most camcorders. Without any manual means to alter focus you will have to rely on using (or abusing) the automatic focus feature. Auto focus works by projecting an infrared beam at the nearest object in the middle of the frame and assessing from the speed of its return how far away it is. So far so good. But if you want to stop the camera from doing this constantly you will have to let it find one particular setting and stay there. For example, if you meet a few friends and decide to put them in this film, you can shoot straight at them by putting them in the middle of the frame, which is going to look dull, or you can get a more interesting shot. Home movies and tourist movies put people in the middle, but filmmakers want more in their shots and so may move these people slightly to the side so that we see a few other elements of the scene. So, set up your friends so that the arrangement looks less predictable; then set the focus automatically; then turn it off and see what happens.

The result is that your friends are going to be in focus most of the time. If they move a great deal within the frame that's fine, as long as they move across the frame rather than close to or further away from you. But if you had left the auto focus switched on continually your friends would be switching in and out of focus every time they vacated the very middle of the screen. So, in this case, you use auto to get what you want, then get rid of it. Now *you* are in control of the camera.

Evaluation

This project is unusual compared to the others in this book in that it relies very much on improvisation and on making mistakes. At each step of the way, you are wresting control from the automatic settings of the camera and seeing what happens when you shoot against the way it suggests. After all, the settings it gives are simply designed to give you what is considered to be the closest representation of reality. But in most filming you are trying to create illusions, to improve reality in some way, and so it becomes crucial to defeat these realist tendencies in the camera. You know where they are if you need them.

I want something more challenging

To stretch your skills further, try combining two or more manual controls – for instance, combine the iris with shutter speed, or focus with aperture. These combinations enable you to create new effects, such as the way increasing the shutter speed reduces light entering the lens in much the same way as aperture.

The theme in this movie is designed to offer an easy route, but you could try combining this with another project so that you make a film from elsewhere in the book but solely using manual controls.

4. Video safety and good practice

Treat your camcorder well

Water

A camcorder can be irreparable if damaged with water. Protect it from rain and wipe off moisture from the casing. Salt water is especially harmful, and can do damage to the outer casing as well as the inner workings.

Condensation

Some camcorders warn you if condensation is building up inside the camera and many will switch off automatically. To remedy this, take out the cassette, if the camera will let you. If it is not possible, switch off and wait two or three hours. Once you have removed the cassette, leave the cassette compartment open for two or three hours, to dry, in a non-dusty room at average temperature. Condensation is particularly problematic if you film in extremely cold places and the water freezes. If this happens, let the camera thaw naturally at room temperature and then go through the same process as for condensation.

Magnetized equipment

Any magnetic field can adversely affect recording. Television monitors, video games and loud-speakers generate fields that distort picture quality. No lasting damage is done to the camera itself but your footage could be ruined. Test how the camera performs if you are in any doubt and play back the results on a monitor. Occasionally, the actual mechanism of the camera can be affected, temporarily, but this is often solved by unplugging your power supply or removing the battery and then reconnecting.

Sunlight

Pointing the viewfinder at sunlight can do great damage to inner working parts. Worse, it can permanently damage your eyesight too.

Radio transmitters and power lines

If you have ever listened to radio near an overhead power line you will have heard an amount of interference. This noise badly affects your video recording, so avoid shooting near pylons or other high-voltage lines. Radio transmitters will have a similar effect on the sound and image. Mobile phones also cause problems with sound interference while recording.

Excessive use

Many camcorders are not designed to be used for excessively long periods, as for example in surveillance filming; the inside temperature of the camera can cause malfunctions.

Dust and sand

Take care when inserting the cassette that no fine dust or sand enters the camera. If you are using the camera in a potentially dusty environment, use a protective cover. If you don't have a cover, you can improvise with a black bin-liner, wrapped around the casing. But beware that the camera could overheat over a period of time.

Cleaning

Some camcorders react badly to being cleaned with benzine or thinners. The body casing can be deformed as a result. Use a soft cloth with mild, dilute detergent mixed with water. Wring out the cloth until nearly dry before use. Never clean the camera while the battery or mains supply is attached.

Clean lenses rarely, and with great care. Avoid getting the lens dirty. Try fitting a protective clear UV filter (semi-)permanently to the front of the lens if the camera has a filter thread fitted. You can always buy another cheap filter when it gets damaged.

Cleaning the video recording heads is advised, but with care. Sometimes, after a lot of use, dirt and tape particles build up on the video heads, obstructing perfect quality recording. Some cameras tell you when this is happening, with a display on the monitor. To clean the heads, get hold of a cleaning cassette, which cleans as it plays. But don't do this too often – the cleaning cassette is an abrasive cleaner.

Power

AC adapter

- When you charge your battery, make sure that the temperature of the battery is not excessively high or low. Charging when the battery is outside the right temperature will not adversely affect the charger – it will simply not charge. Some camcorder adapters will start to charge automatically once the right temperature is reached.
- When the battery is warm, charging can take longer.
- The AC adapter may affect radio reception, so don't charge near your radio antennae. One metre away from the charger is sufficient.
- Keep the terminals of the charger and the battery clean to enable maximum charging power.

Battery care

- Batteries for many camcorders work by generating electricity through a chemical reaction, using lithium. The reaction is easily affected by temperature and humidity, and impedes the amount of power you get from it. At very cold temperatures, a battery may have its life-span cut down to just five minutes, while high temperatures may cause the battery to switch off for some time.
- Protect the battery terminals from moisture, as this can cause rust to develop.
- If metal objects touch both battery terminals at the same time they may cause it to short-circuit and generate serious amounts of heat, even starting a fire. If you pick up a battery that is short-circuiting, you may receive burns.

Do not leave the battery attached to the camera for long periods when it is not in use, as this can damage the voltage level of the battery and affect its ability to recharge.

Weblinks
www.videomaker.com   Range of articles including battery care.
www.camera-battery.net/camcorder-battery.htm   Battery online store and information.

Using the LCD monitor

- Temperature will affect picture quality on an LCD monitor. When cold, the picture is darker than usual, even in reasonable climates. After a while the ambient heat of the camera is enough to rectify this, but bear it in mind if you use the monitor in cold environments. Over 100 000 pixels are used on these monitors but less than 1 per cent will be inactive, sometimes affecting picture quality. Don't worry about this as it does not affect recorded picture quality.
- Remember that using the LCD monitor will run down the power in the battery much faster than if you use only the viewfinder; a one-hour life-span is reduced to 30 minutes when using the monitor.
- If you have a touch-sensitive LCD monitor, avoid sharp objects touching it. Also avoid touching it if you have been using cleaning chemicals or other potentially corrosive substances.

Videotape care

Even though DV tapes are much more sturdy than VHS or S-VHS, they are still prone to problems from poor handling.

Storage

- Always store tape vertically, with the tape rewound, in its case.
- Store away from magnetic fields, direct sunlight or excessive moisture or dust.
- Avoid touching the tape.
- Avoid dropping the tape, or causing any other shock or impact to it.
- Cars are very bad for tapes; the temperature inside the vehicle rises and falls dramatically when not in use.
- If cassettes are excessively cold, let them warm up to average room temperature for a couple of hours.

- Do not leave the cassette in the camcorder for long periods.
- Rewind the tapes after use; tape stretching can occur.

Always label your tapes the moment you take them out of the camera, before you reach for the next tape. Every filmmaker has stories of having to trawl through numerous tapes looking for a particular lost piece of footage.

5. Video compression

Now that there are so many different ways of watching video – phones, the web, DVD, CD – it was inevitable that at some point we would have to find a way of reducing these movies to a size that our mobile devices can cope with. Video data is huge and it is inconceivable that it could be sent to any new format just as it appears on your master tape. To reduce this data, we use a process called 'compression'.

Over the last decade there have been big advances in the way we squash movies. There are now very sophisticated methods which present to the viewer a version of the movie that they would find hard to detect next to an uncompressed version. Much of this work is down to a group called the Motion Picture Experts Group (MPEG).

In this section we will take a tour through the basics of compression, as it is used by filmmakers on a day-to-day level. Compression is one of those subjects that gets rather involved and more than a little technical, but we will focus instead on the ways it affects a movie and how you can lessen these effects, utilizing the new mobile and web formats to the full.

How it works

In essence, compression looks at individual frames and decides which parts of them we would not notice if they were discarded. For instance, a blue sky that is the same over five frames doesn't need a new bit of information for each of those frames, so the whole group is assigned a code.

At its most sophisticated, compression works by doing three jobs: first to analyse the video signal, then to sort out which parts of each frame the viewer wouldn't miss if they were discarded, and finally by encoding this process. The best way of doing this is called discrete cosine transform (DCT), which samples a piece of video at regular intervals and figures out what an image can lose that the human eye would not detect. It is a complex algorithm that is behind the main methods of squashing down video that we use every day, including DVDs, Internet gaming, web broadcasts, CD-ROMs and cell phone movies.

The key to compression is that if you are going to squash something down, you have to be able to unsquash it again later. We could think of this as similar to sending a large poster to a friend via the postal system. The poster has to be rolled up so that the mail service can transport it efficiently. But at the other end, when it reaches your friend, it needs to be able to be unrolled again. We could call this process 'compression–decompression', shortened to 'codec', to describe the various ways we have of doing it. Many companies produce codecs for use with video and each use the standards that MPEG established. Some are good for one type of movie, others better for other types.

MPEG

The Emmy Award-winning MPEG group worked out several methods of compressing data for moving images and came up with a few different standards. Let's take a look at the main ones:

MPEG-1

This is a popular method used for encoding video for CD-ROM and for VCD, the format widely used in Asia. It is the main method used for web video with the suffix '.mpg' and also gave rise to the standard known as MPEG-1, layer 3, or MP3, which is the most widely used method for compressing music files.

MPEG-2

This method is a development of MPEG-1 which grew into the way we compress video for set-top digital TV boxes and for the DVD. It is probably the most widely used compression in the world, with the spread of the consumer DVD outstripping VHS, and the imminent digitization of TV broadcasting. At the moment there is no need for an MPEG-3 because this method is seen to perform well with high definition television, which will become more widely used in the near future.

MPEG-4

The need for this standard came about as we started to use moving images on the web and in mobile web devices. The format handles multimedia items very well and is ideal for gaming, broadcasting via the web and pages that contain media items. The best aspect of this method is that you can decide how compressed you want the video to be. This is called enhanced scaleability, and is popular with media providers because various options can be given for the user, depending on what sort of connection they have. They can opt for high compression for small bandwidth (a smaller file for 56k) or low compression (a bigger file for ADSL/broadband).

MPEG-7

This is another multimedia standard that enables the user to personalize and filter what they receive. It is ideal for web-based video, where it interacts with other media content.

How MPEG-4 and -2 operate

Let's now look at the most advanced way of compressing video to see what the most useful method does for your film.

To begin with, the codec looks at the information on several frames at a time, a group of pictures (GOP), in a process known as 'interframe compression'. It does this by breaking up a sequence into

I, B and P frames. I frames are 'index' frames and contain the entire information in a frame. The codec uses these as a reference to compare with the next few frames.

Even here the codec performs different levels of compression on different parts of the frame, so that the centre of a frame is compressed less than the outer, permitting about 15 per cent reduction in the size. Next, the B frames – 'bidirectional frames' – are noted. An analysis works out the differences between a B frame and the next or the one before. It discards any data that is repeated, keeping a code of where it was. It is like compressing a numerical sequence that runs 22222333366666 by expressing it as 253465 (the digit '2' is followed by a digit representing the number of times '2' appears, and so on). In this way, a 14-digit sequence has been reduced by half.

Finally, P frames are labelled as 'predicted' frames and reduce data by predicting where certain objects are going to move across a screen. Once there is significant movement or change – after a half second or so, perhaps – the whole process starts again with a new sequence being labelled I frames at the start, then B frames and so on. Thankfully you don't really need to know how this all works, but it does prove useful later when we look at DIY encoding.

The good codec guide

H.263 – use for video conferencing

This codec is a good choice for the business community. It's ideal for a video conference where you do not need high-quality pictures and where audio is going to take priority. It is best with low movement films, so a more or less stationary talking head is going to be just perfect. The data rate for this would be small, but much quality is lost. Perhaps the only use of this codec is if you wanted to send a quick version of a film for viewing by a co-worker; you may not worry too much about the way it looks as you just want quick feedback.

Cinepak – use for CD-ROMs

This is a good, well-established system which works best with small image sizes. This codec is outperformed by many others, even though its small picture size, at 120×90 pixels, is now getting bigger as computers improve. It is better used on low-end machines but is not usually the first option for web film, being more suited to CD-ROMs. A big advantage with this codec is that it allows the sender to customize settings throughout a film, so you can apply heavier compression to places where there is not much movement but lighter compression to where you need more detail on screen, perhaps during an action sequence. This process avoids 'data spikes', where sudden increases in data cause a movie to stop playing on the user's PC because too much data is needed.

RealG2 – good for web work, not for other uses

This codec is widely used on the web. It uses 'temporal scaleability', which means that the result for the user is smoother than others even on a wide range of computers or devices. This means movies encoded with it play at a high frame rate for fast processors and low for slow ones. This codec is hard to beat in terms of the number of users who may have access to it on the web and the ease with which the rest can download it (for free).

Sorenson – good all-rounder

This is a really good, high-quality codec and looks better than most at a screen size of 320 × 240. It's a good solution for movies that are going to be viewed over broadband connections, but some editions (notably the Developer Edition) cater for the other users by enabling scaleable streaming. One aspect which puts many people off using this codec is the length of time it takes to encode a movie in this way, but it remains the method of choice for most short movies, for the web and CD.

Intel Indeo 4 and 5 – good, but mainly for high power

With this method of compression you get a good result with high picture quality, but it is only viable for high-powered PCs or Macs. Version 5 allows for progressive downloads. Intel's codec is generally better than Cinepak, but cannot match the picture quality of the Sorenson.

Formats

There are various ways of decoding the information once it has been coded for sending over the Internet. Computer manufacturers have adopted different formats for codecs.

Video for Windows – short films and CD-ROM

This kind of file will have an '.avi' suffix at the end. The advantage of this one is that it comes as standard with Windows operating systems. This format is primarily aimed at the CD-ROM movie, for short films stored and viewed on disc. Reliability is an issue here, as this format is notorious for putting audio and vision out of sync. The preferred codec for this format is Cinepak, which has widespread use but is poor in picture quality, but for better quality it can use Intel's Indeo system, version 4 or 5.

Microsoft Windows Media – good streaming tool, flexible

This kind of file has an '.ask' after it and is designed to cope with almost any user, from the snail's pace 14.4 modem to the motorway that is ADSL. This format supports best the H.263, MPEG-4 and Intel's Indeo codecs such as Netshow. Netshow servers are designed to maintain speed of data delivery even if demand increases – what is known as true streaming. But it does so by reducing the quality of the images seen by the user, first visuals and then audio.

QuickTime – flexible, highly rated, free

This format is seen with an '.mov' or '.qt' after its files and is Apple Computer's answer to the format race. It is a flexible format, ideal as much for CD-ROMs as for DVDs or the Internet. Unlike earlier Windows formats, this also performs on Macs and best supports Sorenson, Indeo, Cinepak and

MPEG-1. QuickTime uses RTSP, or Real Time Streaming Protocol, which means that it delivers the movie in real time, as does RealG2 and Netshow.

RealPlayer – free and very widely used

Real Networks Real Media (with an '.rm' at the end of the file) format is by far the most popular on the market and has earned this degree of use by being accessible – it's free to download, as is QuickTime – but mostly by being able to alter its streaming level to suit the machine it is being viewed on. This means you don't have to create multiple versions of a movie for the user to choose from.

RealPlayer is a flexible format that copes well with content streamed live as part of a webcast or through a progressive download. The only negative point is that on low bit rates the film can start to look decidedly blurry and featureless, but compressing to this degree is to be avoided anyway.

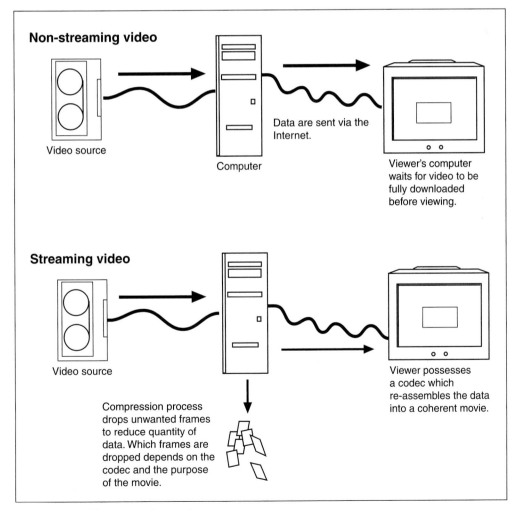

Figure 2.6 How video streaming works.

DIY compression

Most filmmakers who use the web regularly for showing movies tend to customize their compression settings. Co-ordinators of online movie cinemas will compress what they show themselves so that they can apply the right codec for the movie. As we have seen above, certain codecs are better for some movies than others. It is clear that a filmed interview with someone talking to the camera will have different compression needs to a sports film where there is constant movement, but where sound is less crucial. Customizing your movie yourself is not as difficult as it sounds, and there are software programs that will use the popular 'wizard' process to take you slowly through the decisions you need to make.

Decisions

The first task in customizing your movie involves asking which aspect of the movie is most important. Is it:

● sound quality
● picture clarity
● picture smoothness.

Let's see how this affects a few different films. As we saw above, a sports movie would prioritize picture smoothness first, then clarity, with sound lowest of all. A music video would probably want all three, but would have to settle for sound first, then clarity, unless there was significant movement in the movie. A film trailer may go for picture clarity (so you can read what it is and when it is released), then smoothness (for the action) and then sound.

Compression is available either in pre-set forms, whereby you simply choose from a selection on the edit program and in a few moments have performed the task, or you can use an additional piece of compression software to do it for you, which is slower but more exacting and more responsive to individual needs. If you choose the latter you need first to know something about the process to see how to get the most for your films. In practice, there are occasions when you will be able to send a movie straight to the web, with no complications and little work involved on your part, but it is more likely that you may need a separate method for each film you make, depending on content, style and where you want to send it. This gives you more control over quality and how people view the film.

Top ten tips for DIY encoding
1 Avoid recompression – do it only once, from the master copy each time.
2 For ease of use, compress using specialist software such as Cleaner.
3 If you know your film is primarily destined for the web or phone, shoot it with this in mind. Stand a couple of feet away from your camcorder LCD screen and see how the image you are filming looks. Notice how detail is lost and how close-ups are more necessary.

4 Compress just a single scene of your movie first before you commit to the settings you have chosen to save time.
5 Never capture video to your PC in compressed form. Always capture at uncompressed rates and then squash it down later.
6 Similarly, never compress a video before you edit. Don't store unedited footage in compressed form – on CD-ROM, for instance.
7 No codec gives very smooth video on the web, so don't be surprised by the results.
8 Always use specific settings for each film. Never reply on the general settings offered by a codec or compression program.
9 To test your compressed version always play back on a minimum target platform (a slow dial-up modem, for instance).
10 For unpredictable films where the content varies throughout, use a compression program to find the peak data rate. This lets you limit the data at specific places and avoids overloading the end-user's computer or device.

Encoding for the web

A good starting point is to use a Sorenson codec (part of Cleaner EZ) at 10 fps (frames per second), with a picture size of 160×120 pixels, with 8- or 16-bit sound.

If you are creating a copy on your website that is specifically for low-bandwidth users, aim to compress at smaller than the average dial-up modem of 56 kbps (kilobits per second) by going instead for around 35–40 kbps.

About data rates

We have talked a lot about the data rate, as it is one of the most important elements in compression, but there are some important facts to be aware of when talking about data. This is basic computer science stuff but has a potentially huge impact if you use the wrong terms. To begin with, there is a difference between a KiloByte (with K and B in capitals, represented as KB) and a kilobit (lower case, represented as k and kb). Multimedia and video tend to go with KiloBytes, where 1K is equal to 1024 bytes, but telecommunications tend to use *bits*, in which there are 1000 to the kilo. The byte consists of 8 bits, so you must adjust the way you calculate the downloading ability of a modem. For example, a 28.8k modem (notice the lower case) will provide 28.8 kilobits per second (kbps), but if we measure it in bytes we see that it is 3.5 KB per second when we divide it by 8 (the number of bits in a byte).

Working out how small a file needs to be

A useful method of working out what compression you need for delivery onto CD or DVD is:

Disc space (measured in KiloBytes (KB), not MB) divided by movie length
(in seconds) = KB of final movie.

For example, a film which is 10 minutes long, squeezed onto a CD-ROM with less than the full disc used up, say, 450 MB: 450 MB = 450 000 KB, divided by 600 seconds, equals 750 KB per second. This means that your data rate needs to be 750 KB per second to run safely on the CD.

The Crunch

- Compression is ideal for viewing a DV movie on the web or putting it onto CD or DVD
- Know what kind of movie each codec is best suited to
- Customize your own compression to suit your movies – use compression software
- View your movie when compressed to check quality
- You don't have to get involved with all the computer/data/technical stuff, just work out what aspect of the film is most important
- Compression is complicated – agreed – but it can help send your movie around more places.

3 | Films and how they work

1. Types of film and filmmakers

The aim of this section is to start thinking about what sort of filmmaker you want to become. Do you want to make films with straight stories, or are non-narrative films going to inspire you more? Does the music video allow you to be more imaginative than, say, a drama? Or do you ultimately want to make feature films?

Part of your task is to move as quickly as you can towards a position where you know what is out there and how you can break into it. Take your pick.

Narrative film

A narrative movie uses a story as its main motivation. Since the birth of cinema, narrative has been the driving force of the film industry, to the extent that other forms are described by how much or how little they address narrative. It evolved largely from the dominance of literary media in culture and borrows hugely from literature in the way stories are told, even down to the use of cutaways in editing. But as a primarily visual medium, film has other possibilities and many filmmakers have tempered the dominance of plot and increased the use of visual signs and symbols to develop the themes and meanings of a film, such as Stanley Kubrick and Andrei Tarkovsky.

Within narrative film there have arisen many conventions about how you tell a story. Largely due to the need to agree a common code with the viewing public which can be applied to each and every film, there are certain ways of shooting and editing that will disguise the actual process of filmmaking and draw attention only to the plot and the characters within it. Thus, film becomes a true escapist experience.

If you work with stories today, however, you need to possess some detailed knowledge of these conventions as if they are a set of signs that an increasingly knowing audience is going to decipher. This means that you can subvert conventions and can mix signs from different forms (for instance, by

Figure 3.1 Directing involves a range of skills from the technical to the artistic. Here, director David Casals sets up a shot for his short, *Time Cocktail*.

including parts of other genres, as in Tarantino's *Kill Bill*), but all the time you have to be aware of where you stand within the wider framework of narrative film. Audiences develop their awareness of these signs in narrative film simply by seeing lots of films, so as a filmmaker you are equally able to read the signs and then perhaps make up your own.

Narrative film may be the established dominant mode, but entering this area doesn't mean you have to follow film trends, making cliché-ridden films that only emulate other directors. Certainly this may be true within the profit-driven industry of Hollywood, but there are numerous directors who follow their own path by turning narrative into something that is their own.

The short movie

In the last chapter we heard about how short movies (average 10 minutes in length or less) have had something of a comeback as the new filmmaker's school. Almost all filmmakers have made several before going on to make successful features, the shorts serving as a place to try out ideas, road-test stories, and develop style and exercise conventions. The quick pace of short movie production also helps build confidence, as you can make one with very few resources or little time.

The micro-short

This development of the narrative movie is relatively new, resulting from the need for shorter-than-short movies that download fast over the Internet or to phones. The particular constraints of movies lasting less than a minute are invigorating, helping you to develop faster as a filmmaker. Straight narrative sits as easily as abstract movies in this form, although many narrative versions tend to be more successful because of the startling way they compress conventional storytelling into small spaces – temporally and spatially.

My kind of people?

The narrative filmmaker obsesses about films to the degree that relationships end (and start) over top ten lists of movies. For their own work, they ride a wave of adrenaline, enjoy stress ('I actually feel stressed now if I am not stressed, without anything to do.' James Sharpe, filmmaker) and stop at nothing to get a film made. Theirs is a guerrilla world where night-time raids are made to scale the walls of mainstream cinema, funded by credit card. Organized and skilled, they survive on little sleep but are sustained through their strong – and deserved – sense of their own talent.

Weblink
http://www.nokiashorts.co.uk/   Annual competition for micro-shorts.

Documentary

Documentary has a long and honourable tradition of seeking the truth and dragging it out from under a rock, so it has been an exciting and provocative place for a filmmaker to work. But as the ways of big business and government have become more wily and shrewd, engaging spin and marketing to protect interests, so filmmakers have started to employ new means of cutting through them. Pioneering filmmakers such as Nick Broomfield, Morgan Spurlock and Michael Moore, who mix polemic with fact and personal insight, have made documentary one of the most energetic and stimulating places for

Figure 3.2 Documentary filmmakers need resilience to work in extreme conditions far removed from the comfort of the studio. In this still, Franny Armstrong, director of Spanner Films, prepares for her film *Drowned Out*.

a filmmaker to work. Crucially, films such as *Fahrenheit 9/11* (Michael Moore) and *Touching the Void* (Kevin MacDonald) have convinced the industry that big financial returns are possible on what used to be a no-go area for Hollywood.

What these and other filmmakers have done is make documentary as creative and interesting as narrative film. It allows the chance to put together a narrative and employ the creativity you would like to use in narrative film, but without the limitations of conventional storytelling.

My kind of people?

Within the filmmaking community, documentary makers tend to opt for projects others would give a wide berth. If this was the world of sports, they would be doing the extreme end – hang-gliding while blindfolded above the sierras. Discomfort and obstacles are their bread and butter and they look for problems, war zones, trouble spots the way most of us avoid them. Documentary makers live rough, work alone and leave their critics at base camp while they go and chase the next story.

Non-narrative

This encompasses a whole range of work where other elements of the film are dominant rather than plot. Here, visual meaning is the dominant factor. If we talked about plots as happening in a linear way (this happened, followed by that and so on), then these movies are non-linear. You take in the whole experience and then try to figure out what it was all about.

Experimental/art gallery films

Even finding a label for this kind of film is hard – many films experiment in some way, and not all films seen in galleries are experimental, and in any case, can they be called films? It is probably the most intriguing area of film to look at and yet the hardest to find; it is almost impossible to find such pieces at your local store and many artists cannot afford to commit their work to DVD for commercial sale.

These kinds of works radically break outside of the normal viewing confines we are used to. Films can be minutes, several hours or even years in duration (Douglas Gordon's *The Searchers* slowed down the classic western to last five years – the duration of the eponymous search), may have no continuous action, recognizable events or places, and may rely on just a few essential images. What they do tend to focus on is a strong central theme on which everything rests. In Steve McQueen's *Wrestlers*, two men occupy a large wall-sized screen as they square up to each other in slow motion. Slowly they collide and fight, then part, and so the film goes on. In Bill Viola's recent work, using high definition video at ultra slow recording speeds, classical images are enacted such as group portraits, a figure walking in fire, being doused by a waterfall and so on. Probably the most successful video art relies on few images and on few themes for its impact. Editing is relegated to a secondary role, probably because of its artifice-inducing properties – editing lies, but the camera doesn't. Another crucial ingredient is the use of place. Where the film is actually seen is more than just an important element – it is

Figure 3.3 British-based group Blast Theory create stunning images by combining text, images and animation, as in this film, *Desert Rain.*

a central pillar of the work. Scale is often used in McQueen's work, and so is the arrangement of screens, as in Gary Hill's installations, where screens are arranged in sculptural shapes.

Weblinks
http://www.lissongallery.com/theArtists/Gordon/douglasgordon.html   Background on video artist Douglas Gordon.
http://www.tate.org.uk/learning/schools/stevemcqueen2436.shtm   Printable notes on Steve McQueen from UK's premiere modern art gallery.

To get a background to this kind of work, look at early Andy Warhol movies such as *Empire* (1964), the eight-hour stationary shot of the Empire State Building, or work by Korean-American artist Nam June Paik, who developed a more sustained approach to her work.

My kind of people?

Focused is an understatement – these people live and breathe their 'art' just as much as any Hollywood image of Michelangelo or van Gogh. They have to be, though, as the financial return from living as a video artist is low. Museums and galleries will show your work but don't expect to be paid, except in the more enlightened Nordic countries. The video artist is not a one-trick pony – they are adept at logistics, working with electronics and can turn their hand to most practical tasks. If not video artists they could just as easily run a military campaign – but would probably object to it, saying that the theme was not strong enough.

Figure 3.4 Music promo makers endure tough working conditions, but the stakes and rewards are high. This still is from Dominic Leung's promo for Moloko, *The Time is Now.*

Music promo

The music promo occupies a peculiar position in films in that it is more a marketing device and can be either narrative or non-narrative. The entirely narrative promo is rare today and most have slim narrative threads on which to hang a series of crucial images. The idea of a short film that accompanies a piece of music grew out of films including *A Hard Day's Night* (Richard Lester, 1964). This form has always been a primarily commercial one, since it is explicitly linked to the promotion of an artist for increased sales. But, as with the advertising commercial, there are increasing numbers of film directors who have found this form a place to define and develop their style. For many it is the freedom from narrative that is most liberating. It allows the director to focus purely on the visual aspects of a film and move far from the theatrical or literary aspects. For the emerging filmmaker, there are many reasons why this form is seen as the real-life film school: the fast production process means you make mistakes quickly and learn quickly, the tight budgets and strict client demands mean having to be creative with what you are given, and the short nature of the promo means having to grab a viewer's attention quickly and sharply. Beyond this, though, there are real benefits for filmmakers who would not normally make these kinds of films: narrative films gain greater depth of meaning when you allow non-narrative passages to coexist with the main plot.

My kind of people?

Single-minded, realistic to the point of being existential and with a skin as tough as old boots, the promo director can seem like the one most likely to succeed. On promo shoots stakes are high, with expectations

Figure 3.5 Advertising commercials demand production values as high as those seen in films, as in this shot from Neo's ad for Nike, directed by Jake Knight.

and pressure from artist and record label for 'the big idea', but the promo director takes delight in pushing their energies to the limit, taking pride in handing the client the movie on budget and on schedule. Nicknames are often variations on the 'Terminator' theme.

Advertising commercial

As with the music video, this form is also a training ground for new filmmakers. The fast output of commercials and the need to say as much as possible in the shortest space of time means that the practitioner has to master the whole panoply of non-verbal signs and symbols – both from the world of film language and from that of universal symbols. All of this helps with your more conventional movies by allowing you to practise saying what you want to say in the shortest time and in the most economical way. As a form to practise with, the commercial asks you to work within a narrow brief, but it is this very constraint that often encourages creativity and the development of new solutions. New ways of sending video mean that ad directors are being recruited for phone viral movies (brief movies sent from friend to friend via phone or email) and short web ads too.

My kind of people?

Ad directors can be hard-nosed about what they do – constant and occasionally dispiriting pitching for jobs leaves its scars, but it is this thrill of the chase that drives them. Many have features in development and see ads as being dirty and fast, but they pay well. However, most directors of ads will only find that they have control over their careers just at the point when they leave it behind to start on the big feature. Not for the faint-hearted.

Weblink
http://www.clipland.com/index_tvc.shtml   See the latest TV commercials online.

Polymedia

These are stylish, unusual pieces of work, often displaying new ways of combining animation, live action, text or still images, and pushing the creative possibilities of the medium to the limit. Meaning and content are less important than the visually arresting or innovative image, though these films tend to be in turns political, philosophical and entertaining. Practitioners make films that cross over into just about every form of the moving image, hence the 'poly-' prefix. They are like bees pollinating each form by taking elements of one into another and creating new works. This sort of work is at the front of the DV revolution, often mixing with scientists (Blast Theory), artists (The Light Surgeons), architects (Lynn Fox) and designers (Pliex). If you want to make fast progress while investigating the artistic potential of the medium and try an area that has no discernible rules yet, then this is for you.

Go to: Chapter 10:2 for more details on polymedia work.

My kind of people?

Increasingly, this sort of filmmaker works in animation, seeing the whole industry as part of an emerging 'motion graphics' field. Filmmakers of this kind don't call themselves filmmakers at all, preferring terms that hint towards the convergence of video, graphics, animation and text. They are likely to have a sideline in VJ-ing and animation for ads, and like to evangelize their medium in workshops. In recent years they have come in from the cold – no longer submariners in the video world, their skills are wanted in TV and on the web. If you opt for this career expect to be poached by the omnipotent – and deep-pocketed – games industry, where you should ask for a raise on day one.

Weblinks
http://www.blasttheory.co.uk/   Art and science meet in this innovative group.
http://www.lynnfox.co.uk   Watch Lynn Fox music promos online.

VJ (video jockey)

This form of video can be easily traced back to its birth – the dance music scene of the 1990s. The light shows quickly gave way to cut-up kung fu movies playing silently on a club wall. Later, cheaper video projectors and laptops enabled video artists to create a series of images that could be played alongside any music. But it is the ability to react instantly to changes in pace and rhythm that has let the VJ artist really enter the mainstream. With new developments in software, as a DJ plays a song, the VJ mixes spontaneously from a catalogue of prepared clips, using software to enable these clips to be cued and accessed without delay. Typically, more than one screen is used. New hardware has pushed VJs closer to the role of the DJ – the Pioneer DVD mixer allows a hands-on mixing of discs emulating the scratching of DJ-ing that makes it such a physical activity. There is a high turnover of clips; often, images last for only several frames or at most a second, but it is the repetition and mixing of these that VJ-ers use to add structure and give character to a piece rather than the content itself.

My kind of people?

The VJ is probably the most dextrous of all filmmakers but, like the projection artist, is reluctant to use the label filmmaker, preferring VJ or video artist. Films are called 'visuals' and artists often have a stage name or company name that is used as a pseudonym. Technical nerds but fashionable, VJs are amply rewarded at the higher levels of the field. A subtle shift in recent years means that the VJ is becoming more important than the DJ, so it is often refusenik DJs that enter the field. More often, though, these practitioners are coming from an art school background and are fascinated by images, shape, colour and form, seeing what they do as a kind of four-dimensional sculpture.

Weblink
http://www.vjcentral.com/   News and advice for VJ-ers from a UK-based site.

Projections

Many live music concerts now include large-scale video projections behind the band, utilizing everything that the medium can offer, from shaped projection screens to multiple, text-layered, spinning screens. Related to the music video form, these projections show images that relate to the ethos of the band in general, not necessarily for individual songs. Some bands employ projection artists as semi-detached members of the band, developing the visual impact of the band on tour. Many music labels have felt a sharp reduction in sales due to file sharing and have decreased the funding they give to music promos in some countries. Many now see the live tour as the best marketing tool they have, with a captive audience for two hours or more, and seek to fill the screen with images that can tie in with other marketing tools and relate to CD artwork and T-shirts.

My kind of people?

Crucially, these people are artists first and filmmakers last. They may have entered this field through art school, having experimented with Super-8 and light shows. Technically, they have a wide range of skills and prefer to push the envelope wherever possible, experimenting with every aspect of the medium. Leaders in this field will be highly paid and sought after by musicians. As a sideline, they will also be doing video installations for galleries, touring as a VJ and getting involved in whatever no one else has done yet.

The Crunch

- Get to know what area of filmmaking you prefer – maybe it's several areas.
- Feature films are just the tip of the film industry iceberg – other types of filmmaking are just as popular and far more achievable.
- Short productions help you develop more quickly.
- Try anything once – most forms are going to help you in whatever kind of film you prefer making.
- The more mistakes you make, the more you improve. Exercise your right to fail – at least you will do it your way.
- Invent, experiment, imitate, re-invent, do anything.

Project 2. In-camera edit

What this project is for: to learn about basic shooting and assembling sequences
Time: allow a few hours

What this project is about

In this project, we are going to use the camera alone to construct a film, without the need to edit. The purpose is to show in a very short space of time what you can achieve on camera and get through some initial skills fast. Before you can visualize how your ideas will look on the screen, we need to find out how the camera sees the world. It is better to work this out now than when you are starting to shoot a larger production. This project enables you to learn quickly about camera use, taking short steps quickly.

What's an in-camera edit?

The in-cam edit is a simple idea: it involves shooting each scene of a film, in the order in which it occurs. If it goes well then at the end of shooting you can take out the tape and play it as a finished film. This is the most basic method of making a film, but is an unexpectedly instructive way to learn about filmmaking and in a compressed way it takes you through the whole process of making a film, illustrating how the various elements interact. For example, while shooting this project you quickly realize that every movement of the camera counts, that you have to arrive at decisions fast and that there is little room for mistakes. One of the problems about video as a format is that it discourages decision making by allowing you to shoot just about everything and decide later what to use. The in-cam edit film asks you to work in a fast, concise way.

It also introduces a vital concept in a film: the sequencing of shots. This is an idea central to the whole filmmaking process, and the way in which you decide to order a sequence of scenes is best experienced for real, rather than as a paper exercise.

Finally, this method is a great morale booster; it takes you out of the still waters of paper development and into the fast lane, where you can discover quickly whether your ideas will work as you had intended. It also means that you can use this method for other films; an idea for a movie can be tried on for size before you go ahead and make it for real.

Stage 1: Find an idea

Although this film has a basic kind of narrative, it is simple enough to not lumber you with too much detailed storytelling. As with every project, simpler stories allow you much greater opportunities to focus on the way you are shooting the film, with less information to be conveyed.

As starting ideas, the following are examples of the mini-narratives you could choose:

- Escaping down a flight of stairs
- A short journey in a fast car
- A bad morning getting to work.

They each involve a direct progression in physical terms from A to B. These ideas may be simple but don't dismiss them just yet. By keeping the story to a minimum they enable you to focus attention on the way you tell the narrative; the fun (and the difficulty) comes in how and where you point the camera, what scenes you choose to show and how much you show. The multitude of choices is what makes filming stimulating.

To develop the idea a little more, make a list of the shots you think you will need to convey the action.

Stage 2: Visualizing

Follow the guidelines in Chapter 4:7, 'Visualizing your film', about sketching ideas for shots. List the shots you think you would like to shoot on one side of a sheet of paper, and then draw images that could represent these adjacent to them.

Stage 3: Shooting

With an in-cam edit movie, you will take the first scene on your list and shoot it. It may be useful to do a couple of rehearsals if there is action or dialogue. During a rehearsal, remain looking at the scene through the camera; this encourages you to stay on the lookout for new, better ways of shooting it. If the scene goes wrong, just rewind and tape over with a better version, but do so as accurately as you can, hitching the new clip seamlessly onto the last one. Carry on like this until you have completed the whole film.

> **Tip**   If an object or actor is static, the camera should be moving. If an object or actor is moving, the camera should be static.

Technical glitches

Cameras have their quirks and one of these is the tendency for some to rewind a couple of seconds once you stop filming. Manufacturers have good intentions with this, as it is designed to prevent 'snow' caused by the blank tape showing through between shots, so it rewinds slightly to overlap each piece of film onto the next. If yours does this, simply work out how much it is rewinding and build this into the length of the shot. If your shot is going to last 10 seconds, make it last 10 plus the extra, so it ends where you wanted it.

Evaluation

It is worth going over a few points to see what has been gained. First, don't worry if the final film differs often from the initial plans. A good film is not judged by how closely you have followed a pre-set path; if you have found better ways to shoot a scene while filming, use them. This is a good indication of the way your ideas are evolving about how to convey a scene, even during production.

1 Did you convey the brief plot adequately using the most economical shots? If you compress information to a smaller number of shots, the overall effect is more professional.
2 Did you manage to show more than one aspect, or view, of the action in a shot or did you find yourself having to constantly cut to close-ups to show what was going on? Maybe you moved the camera to new angles now and then to make the movie more interesting to watch.
3 Have you found it relatively easy to consider a number of different elements of filming simultaneously? Did you, for instance, find that you could think about the framing of the camera, the light on the subject and convey the right information at the same time?
4 The sequence of the shots is also important. Were you able to show the progression of events in order so it looked smooth and realistic?
5 You may also have noticed, when watching your movie later, that the length of each shot makes a difference about how the film works. It is very difficult to cut a shot correctly when using this sledgehammer approach to filmmaking, but you may have noticed how some of the more successful shots were the shorter ones. This is why cutting away to different views of the action is a useful technique.

In general, success for this film, however, is to be judged simply by whether you enjoyed making the film and found yourself with a short film that says what you wanted it to say. In a very short space of time, you have picked up some valuable skills in using the camera, telling a narrative and sequencing shots. And by planning on paper at the start, you help ensure that these areas work well before you pick up the camera.

2. How films work

The shortcut to making a film that lasts in people's minds lies in understanding the nuts and bolts of movies – not just the technical side but the mechanics of how you make viewers see and feel what you want. The tools you have learnt and the conventions and rules you have picked up now need to come together to add up to more than just technology and skills. In a sense, learning about continuity, lighting or composition is like learning about the anatomy of filmmaking. This section takes us into what we could call the soul of filmmaking – the meanings that lie within. Understanding how this inner life works means that you stand to make your next movie an experience viewers won't forget.

The tools

The basic building blocks in a film are:

- Image – what we see
- Sound – what we hear
- Space – what we think we see (perception)
- Time – when we think it happened.

Everything else in the movie is subservient to these basic elements. Story, plot and character are visible elements in the film, but are simply the result of the way the above are manipulated. If we look at how each of these elements are represented in your skills, we could identify them as:

- Image – camera framing, lighting, movement, colour
- Sound – diagetic sound (within the scene), non-diagetic sound (subjective, off camera), music
- Space – depth, focus, composition and sound
- Time – editing.

In different ways, each of the tools above are a way of expressing meaning in your film. Story and character are much less able to express meaning than they appear. An interesting way of throwing light on this is by looking at remakes, two films with identical stories but which have very different meanings through use of the camera, colour, symbolism and so on. The original *Cape Fear* (J. Lee Thompson, 1961) set up a moral narrative of how a decent family are targeted by a released convict, yet in Scorsese's 1991 remake, certain changes are made that radically alter the meaning. The convict is given a semi-religious motivation, while the family are deceitful and self-destructive. The first movie places the sinner as the convict, while the second places the family – and crucially, the lawyer at the head of it – as the sinner while the convict is the sinned against.

So what exactly carries out the meaning side of the film? The answer is in the fact that every element carries it – it is not separate from the film but is integral to every part of it. Confused movies are ones where no thought has been given to what they actually mean, while resonant movies are the ones where there is very clear meaning. But this has nothing to do with what kind of meaning you opt for. Successful films don't have to shout out an important message nor do they have to make the audience think something – they are not propaganda. In fact, many films today prefer to avoid sermons in favour of raising questions and ideas for us to take home and reflect on. Films such as *Sideways* (Alexander Payne, 2005), *Donnie Darko* (Richard Kelly, 2001), *Far From Heaven* (Todd Haynes, 2002) and *In The Cut* (Jane Campion, 2003) tend to nudge us towards outcomes rather than hand them to us on a plate.

We could refer to any emergence of the core themes and ideas of a film as signs. The devices that deliver these signs exist in layers surrounding the film. Some are easy to spot, others need a little work to uncover. Like forensic work at a crime scene, some signs are for rookies (the gun on the floor, the pool of blood) and others are for those who know how to look (the mismatched fingerprints on the trigger, the photos smashed on the mantelpiece). Like detectives, we try to uncover what happened and we look for a motive too – why it happened. Then we see how this makes us feel, what it tells us about people, life and the world today.

This hierarchy of signs is placed by the director so that we can experience the movie on different levels – it can be entertainment or it can be philosophy, depending on your choice. Sometimes, the philosophy side gets to be bigger than intended – for instance, in Hitchcock's films, where we get to know as much about the psyche of the director as we do the plot. Elsewhere, a film can become more meaningful through its relation to the zeitgeist – for instance, with *Terminator I* and *II*, where we can track the changes in masculinity in society as Arnie is all Rambo-style machismo in the first movie but by the end of the decade is able to look after children and even weep with emotion. It's easy to see why *Kindergarten Cop* was such an obvious next step. So, when watching a film, we need to look for signs at varying levels and look for others that may be attached later to the film.

Plot/story

Starting at the uppermost layer, we have the most visible elements of a film – the surface. This is like the shell of the film, containing the events that happen to make up the narrative. This outer surface is bigger than it needs to be – it contains not just the events and incidents that go together to make the plot, but also the entire fictional world that holds the plot. Signposts to this bigger world are strewn throughout so that we get a sense of where we are, what has happened to get us to this point, and what the norms and conventions are. Most films do this by relating the surface of the film to our own real world, and we imagine far more than is actually shown because it conforms to our experience. So, if we see two adults and two children eating together, we assume they are part of a family, because this is a construct we take from our world into the one on screen.

But films that don't relate to our world are peculiar and unsettling. David Lynch's second short film, *The Grandmother* (1971), creates an entirely imagined world in a dramatic departure from reality. This creates a surface or shell to the film that is unfamiliar and that straight away demands our forensic skills. We have to work hard to uncover even the most basic information. But it is rewarding if we stick with it, as we get to have profound and long-lasting ideas about life. These are films that people talk about long after they are over. This kind of surface has to draw in the viewer, however, just as much as the straight narrative does, but it does it by using other ways rather than recognition and identification. In Lynch's case, he uses juxtaposition of real elements with the dreamlike and with unexpected moments of cruelty or violence; you can't look away for too long as your curiosity gets the better of you.

Figure 3.6 A careful use of imagery enables filmmakers to create interest and meaning, as in this short, *Northern Soul,* from acclaimed director Shane Meadows.

In either case, the surface acts as a place where the events of the film are placed. Even if a viewer fails to understand the deeper parts of the film, they can't fail to see what is actively in front of them, whether or not this corresponds to real life or not. What goes on below demands another kind of viewing, however.

Subtext

If we imagine each of the events on the surface happening above us, we could also imagine that each of them has an echo below the surface. In practice, this means that everything that happens above has a corresponding meaning below; a car door being slammed loudly doesn't just mean that someone has shut the door, it also means the character is annoyed or angry. Scenes are not just descriptions of what happened (that is news reportage); they are imbued with meanings, all of which must lead back to the central ideas and purposes of the film. Subtext is about placing meaning at a micro level in the film so that each minor event adds something to the overall meaning of the film.

A knowledge of the craft of film means that the text (the surface) is not too heavy-handed in pointing us to the subtext. Subtle signs lead us in an unexpected way to what is below the surface through original scriptwriting, use of the camera or editing. Films tend to make the text explicit while the subtext is implicit, but in Woody Allen's *Annie Hall* (1977), an amusing scene lays out both for us. We see the two main characters (played by Woody Allen and Diane Keaton) having a conversation, with the subtext shown in subtitles. So, a simple response to a query is subtitled as 'Why did I say that? Now she will think I am stupid.'

Subtexts offer an added layer of meaning which make each moment more stimulating. Crucially, the way this is manifested is like this:

Text: Subtle and delivered in an elliptical way

Subtext: What the above really meant in explicit terms

$\downarrow$

Relates back to the main ideas in the film

As an example, we could take the scene in *Star Wars* when Leia, Solo and Skywalker are stuck in a corridor under stormtrooper fire.

Text: Leia grabs the gun from Skywalker and shoots an exit into the wall.
Leia: 'Some rescue.'

Subtext: Leia is capable and quick-witted. She is also sardonic.

$\downarrow$

Ideas: This is no fairy story, the princess is a hero too.

In this example, the better the line or visual clue, the bigger the subtext can be.

Weblinks
http://www.pubinfo.vcu.edu/artweb/playwriting/subtext.html   Concise university tutorial on subtext.
http://koreanfilm.org/trbic-oldboy.html   Insightful essay on subtext in the Korean film *Oldboy* (2003).
http://thematrix101.com/contrib/azilleruelo_arfn.php   Essay on subtext in *The Matrix* movies.

Theme

Further down beneath the micro-meaning that is subtext, we encounter the last stage that the director has total control over: the theme and ideas within the movie. The theme acts as an umbrella that brings together the individual micro-meaning of each scene. This doesn't mean there is only room for one theme, however. Films today tend towards a multiplicity of meaning, rather than supplying just one dominant meaning. These can be less dogmatic, and more ambivalent, allowing the director to deal with conflicting meanings and opposing ideas. In straightforward genre films such as *Armageddon*, the theme works without conflicting ideas. In this film, the idea of heroism and of a simple working man sacrificing his life for humankind is undiluted.

However, in other films, the themes are no less transparent but require more thought. In *The Virgin Suicides* (Sofia Coppola, 1999), a series of suicides of young sisters leads us to think of themes such as the power of fundamentalist religion versus the need to grow freely into adulthood, or the strange voyeurism of the narrators who witness all but cannot intervene. And we also think about their paradoxical awe at the courage of the suicidal girls. None of it adds up to any coherent philosophy or rhetorical message, but it does give us lots to chew on after we leave the theatre.

For the filmmaker, the theme has to be approached in two ways for it to successfully make it onto the screen. First, it has to be identified early on as a core idea, so that it can become a motivating factor in each part of the script. To this extent, the themes need to be easily described, uncomplicated and to a degree universal as part of something we all relate to. But second, the filmmaker also needs to allow for themes to develop in unexpected ways. During development or even in shooting and editing, it is likely that other ideas will emerge that relate to the central ideas but were unforeseen. It is almost impossible to avoid this, as the collaborative process throws up new ideas, the lighting or camera presents a further side to the ideas, and editing reveals other variations. In this way, a filmmaker can allow themes and ideas to float and collide within the film.

To take another good example, Todd Haynes's *Far From Heaven* (2002), mentioned earlier, uses a conventional appearance to throw up several ideas, all of which somehow go together but also collide in interesting ways. Set in 1957, it uses careful colour and design to suggest a technicolour period where values were uncomplicated and prejudices unchallenged, subliminally reminding us of film and TV of the time. Into this background, Cathy (Julianne Moore) uncovers the double life of her husband who is homosexual and, sensing the strict taboo on this subject in the suburban world she inhabits, can only confide in her black gardener, thereby breaking other taboos. In this movie, a series of ideas about whether the 1950s really were the golden age they appeared to be are revealed, colliding with others about the supposed tranquillity of the suburbs, which are portrayed as avenues of taboo and fear. Haynes then crosses all this with suggestions about film and TV itself, using clichés such as 1950s music and colour design to imply that we have continued to live in the world of *I Love Lucy* rather than the real one ever since.

In this level of understanding a movie, themes themselves often draw from the next level down in order to add complexity and – to a certain extent – interactivity.

Connotations: cultural and cinematic

This layer is the first to come from the audience rather than the filmmakers. Films can trigger references to parts of culture that we know already, that we bring with us to the theatre. This is like tapping into a grid of energy that can give the film extra life, where audiences hold reserves of interest in parts of culture that can be recognized in the film.

For several years, most audiences have been so sophisticated in their viewing habits and with their knowledge of films that it is now possible for a film to correspond less with the real world they inhabit than with the fictional world which other films have inhabited. The use of this has soared in recent years, perhaps more as a way of adding faux-depth to a film by alluding to a shared knowledge of culture, a safer bet in box-office terms than alluding to uncomfortable social truths. In some films this is more successful – Tarantino's subtler allusions to French New Wave films in *Pulp Fiction* places an unlikely waif-like refugee from films like *Jules et Jim* or *Breathless* in a modern LA setting. This later developed into the use of Asian-style references in *Kill Bill*, not just in the use of local star actors and storylines, but also in the use of the retro opening credits sequence, where the words 'Feature Presentation' are placed in scratched and gaudy tones, mimicking a faulty projector in a downtown Hong Kong theatre. The point of all this is that we, the audience, can relate to these references. It flatters us and also dislocates the world of the film in a way which we used to describe as post-modern – like seeing a character from one soap enter another. Two worlds collide and it's both amusing and unsettling.

Weblinks

http://www.livejournal.com/community/french_new_wave/   Discussion forum on French New Wave films.
http://www.greencine.com/static/primers/fnwave1.jsp   Primer on the background of French New Wave films.

Animation studio Pixar have become master purveyors of this method in recent years in films like *Shrek* and *Monsters Inc*. In *Shrek 2*, for instance, the movie taunts its more grown-up peers in Hollywood by lifting iconic scenes from films like *Titanic* and *Spider-Man*, replaying them in a comic setting and thumbing its nose at their status. It is hard to imagine a more complicated set of signs within any work of art. Perhaps the most head-spinning example of this appears in Pixar's *Finding*

Figure 3.7 In this still from Phil Dale's commercial for Mini Cooper cars, references are made to previous sci-fi films, such as *The War of the Worlds*.

Nemo (2003). A shark tries to butt his way through a gap, suddenly shouting 'Here's Johnny!' The reference was first to *The Shining*, where Jack Nicholson smashes his way through a door and says the same line, but also to the Johnny Carson TV show, which *The Shining* itself referred to.

Weblink
http://www.greencine.com/static/primers/fnwave1.jsp   Latest news on Pixar's post-modern empire.

Signs from wider culture

So these signs can be explicitly related to other films, or can be more subtle, drawing inspiration from an artwork rather than stealing it outright. When it is less obvious, it can be very rewarding, not least because not everyone in the audience will 'get it'.

David Lynch playfully uses cultural references in his films, most often from the 1950s. In *Mulholland Drive* (2001), Lynch places a very stylized 1950s lead character named Betty (what else?) in modern Los Angeles. The story she inhabits is melodrama, the acting more so. Film noir elements are drawn in, using conventions of storytelling and characters that we recognize from literature and cinema. Music helps set the scene, with opening credits of the jitterbugging characters. Elsewhere, Baz Luhrmann exploits our knowledge of hit records in *Moulin Rouge* (2001). Top-hatted Parisian men dance to Nirvana's 'Smells Like Teen Spirit' while a miniature Kylie Minogue, pop star and camp emblem, poses as a fairy. The aim is to collide our expectations by placing contradictory points of recognition in our minds. Whether this will work in much later years, when our store of cultural references has moved on (who's Kylie?), remains the only weak point in this method.

Weblink
http://www.davidlynch.com/   News and information on David Lynch.

Connotations: political and social

This stratum of a film is a fascinating one for the filmmaker to tap into. The zeitgeist – or spirit of the time – is a powerful pool of fears, prejudices and hopes. As we will see in Chapter 9:2, the zeitgeist can be used to add depth and resonance to a film, by building in references to world events. This layer of meaning acts in the same way as lighting a set – it changes what we see by revealing it in different ways. Just as a room can be transformed by lighting it differently, so a situation can take on dramatic new meaning when placed in the context of world events. In this sense we literally see it in a new light.

In the same way, the zeitgeist can throw light on a seemingly innocent story and some of the most intriguing of these are ones where the director has not obviously set out to tap into our current fears.

For instance, Shyamalan's *The Village* (2004) is a spooky tale in the best tradition of Ray Bradbury. Looked at 20 years ago, or perhaps 20 years from now, and that is all it is. But when you factor in the zeitgeist it takes on a wholly different complexion. The film's story concerns a group of people who fear the deadly creatures that are said to lie beyond its village borders, but which we later find out is a fiction to keep the inhabitants subject to its laws. The elders of the village have good reason to create the myth but find that it is ultimately impossible to maintain. On its release, it found an America in a similar state of fear – rightly or wrongly – of what lies 'out there'. Similar questions were also being raised of its elders' ways of keeping order in this climate of fear, albeit understandable after the tragedies of 9/11.

Weblinks
http://www.raybradbury.com/   More about the renowned sci-fi author.
http://www.futuremovies.co.uk/filmmaking.asp?ID=84   Interview with M. Night Shyamalan.

In this way, a film with prosaic genre starting points – and not especially original ones – became important for a time. In a more conscious attempt, Phillip Noyce's *Rabbit-Proof Fence* touched a nerve in Australia's soul-searching surrounding its treatments of Aborigines in the last century.

Weblink
http://www.iofilm.co.uk/feats/interviews/r/rabbit_proof_fence_2002.shtml   Director of *Rabbit-Proof Fence*, Phillip Noyce, interviewed.

The golden age of all zeitgeist movies was the 1950s, coincidentally when fear was at its highest in a climate clouded by fear of atomic testing (see *Them*, *The Incredible Shrinking Man* et al.), Russian invasion (*The War of the Worlds*, Byron Haskin, 1953), creeping communism (*Invasion of the Body Snatchers*, Don Siegel, 1956), and world war (*The Day the Earth Stood Still*, Robert Wise, 1951). Science fiction proves time and again to be the most fertile ground for this kind of movie to flourish, seen again in later zeitgeists. Does Ripley's discovery of the deadly alien growing inside her in *Alien 3* echo the AIDS crisis of the late 1980s? The director David Fincher's further fascination with the body in *Seven* suggests it was.

Weblink
http://www.awdsgn.com/Classes/Webl_Fall02/Webl-Final/JBusser/index.html   Brief guide to sci-fi films of the 1950s.

Often blunt, the best of these signs manage to catch the prevailing winds of the zeitgeist rather than the temporary storms, preferring to ask deep questions that don't go away rather than resort to cheap hits of passing fears.

In all of these layers there is a mix of both interpretation and intent. It is where the audience and the director join forces to inject meaning into a film. But the films with greatest interest are, perhaps, those where the director's intent is aware of the audience's interpretation and yet open to the possibility that a third element will enter the equation – the social and political climate of the era.

Film View

Five films to understand more about films:

The Cook, The Thief, His Wife and Her Lover (Peter Greenaway, 1989). Made at the end of the decade of strife in Thatcher's Britain, nothing else quite presents such a horrific metaphor of a nation.

The Crowd (King Vidor, 1928). Silent masterpiece portraying the life of an immigrant in depression-hit America. The man is everyone, while the eponymous crowd is – what? Capitalism? The tide of human aspiration about to wash away?

Chinatown (Roman Polanski, 1974). There were lots of films that used paranoia and corruption as their theme in 1970s America, but few have the prescience of this. Is the drought in the film symbolizing our dwindling supplies of oil and the corruption surrounding the commodity?

Dawn of the Dead (George A. Romero, 1979). It's not just highbrow films that can speak volumes about our world. In Romero's first version of the film, there are some of the most anti-consumerist visions ever to be screened.

Uzak (Distant) (Nuri Bilge Ceylan, 2002). Remarkably detached filmmaking that brings deep dividends. The theme that slowly develops through a series of comic and tragic scenes is one of isolation against a backdrop of Istanbul embracing new technology and rejecting the past.

3. Film language and how to speak it

We talk about film as being like a language but actually it is very different to spoken language. In spoken language the word is the smallest unit and from there we build it into sentences, and these into paragraphs and so on. So do we assume that the shot is the smallest unit in what we call film language and that from here we build it into scenes, and scenes into movies? It isn't that simple – and fortunately so because here lies the mystery of film. But if we can work out what actually makes up this complicated way of communicating we have a chance of mastering it – and perhaps adding a few new methods ourselves.

Let's take a step back a few decades to when we used to call film a language. In the 1950s we used to read film manuals which told us that this or that shot would say this or that: a tilted camera meant that the subject was off-kilter in some way. The way film was taught back then was like having an alphabet of how to shoot – you went on set, took out your ABC and shot exactly like it said, using the same device again when necessary.

By the 1960s, however, we started to think very differently about all sorts of language, largely as a result of French theorists like Saussure. Further ground-breaking work was done by his compatriot Christian Metz in looking more widely at all sorts of codes at work in a movie, not just the obvious ones of shots and camera angle. Metz talked about the multiplicity of signs that unfold in each shot, so that instead of a film language we have something like a cacophony. So editing had its own codes, as did the story, as did the setting and the use of the camera, sound, light and colour. All of these could potentially carry meaning and could be 'read' simultaneously. What's more, they borrowed many of the ways of doing this from other art forms, which themselves later borrowed them back (for instance, in the work of Cindy Sherman, photographer).

Weblink
http://www.cindysherman.com/   Information and gallery of the artist.

Syntax

The syntax of a movie could be said to combine all the elements of a film. But as we have seen, it doesn't lie in the use of the camera or the way a shot is edited, but in the space created by the pull of these two opposing forces in a film: the illusion of space (the images) and the illusion of time (editing).

The image consists of elements such as:

- *Camera angle* – how we view something changes what we think of it
- *Colour* – the connotations of certain colours affect meaning
- *Shape* – certain shapes in the composition can affect how we view a shot
- *Lighting* – elements can be highlighted and brought to our attention
- *Depth and focus* – where elements within the frame are placed affects how we view them; which is in focus further affects this.

Connecting these are the three-dimensional effects created by the camera in space by the movements of the camera or of its subject. Elements within the frame are altered depending on which lens is used (wide-angle, close-up) and by panning or tracking.

If we move away from this syntactic view of a shot we can see another set of elements waiting to add further meaning. As soon as we place one shot next to another – we edit the scene – then we include time in the equation. Which events are placed next to each other, whether we go backwards or forwards in time, and which events are highlighted and dwelt on, all affect the meaning of the film extensively.

In a sense, a film such as *Memento* (Christopher Nolan) is almost devoid of meaning when its editing conceit is taken away. If the movie is viewed 'the right way', as in the DVD version option, it is relegated to mere genre movie. Similarly, *Amores Perros* (Alejandro Gonzalez Inarritu) would be rendered an almost pointless soap opera if the events it told were placed chronologically or in parallel. Instead, their convergence to a central point in the middle of the film imitates the car crash that unites the various stories in a literal way at a literal crossroads.

Added to this two-way pull between space and time is a third force, the audience. This, however, is an unstable and unpredictable force that is shaped by locally shared perceptions (black is the colour of mourning in the west, while white denotes this in the east) and further skewed by personal perceptions. Perception is such a nebulous concept it is tempting for the filmmaker to drop it from the start. It is like trying to work out what to wear to an office party three years from now – you don't know who is going to be there, what your clothes will say about you then, nor what the climate will be. For most filmmakers, audience perception is seen as inhibiting the creative processes, reducing authenticity by forcing them to consider someone else's imagination outside their own.

But it can become liberating to consider perceptions. Once the film has left the filmmaker's hands and goes to the audience it then attracts layers of meaning and connotations brought along by each viewer. It snowballs, but while retaining the central meanings intended by the director. To ensure this happens, that the film grows in meaning, the filmmaker must include enough 'moments of meaning' through camera, symbol, motif, editing, sound and the other tools of the craft to kick-start the process.

Ways of conveying meaning

The main carriers of meaning – as detailed in the chapter on form and symbolism – are the many signs that populate a film. But we can be more specific about what these are, breaking them into two sorts:

1 *Signs* – where something is
2 *Symbols* – where something means other than what it is.

The first category is easy – it is a set of signs that we all recognize immediately. A building with a garden and containing a family is a house. Symbols go a stage further by including other visual clues that apply a meaning to what we see. So, the same building with drawn curtains, smashed windows, accompanied by tense music implies a certain sort of family, perhaps suffering. The signs it uses to convey this are something we can all agree on and recognize almost universally.

Symbolism

A symbol is a sign, a carrier of meaning in typically visual form, and is one of the most effective ways for depth of meaning to manifest itself. Its visual nature means that what it represents is not always

© MMIII, Onyx films - Iguana films - La Maison

Figure 3.8 Using dreamlike imagery, Juan Solanas's *Man Without a Head* was acclaimed at film festivals.

easily translated into words and its reception by the viewer may vary, according to culture and experience. This does not undermine the symbol, but may actually lend it longevity.

Being able to notice a symbol is less easy than defining it. In films there is such a wealth of visual material contained in every shot that we have to exercise some criteria if we are to distinguish a visual element which alludes to something else from that which is merely functional.

Where are symbols?

The key to doing this is in having some understanding of what a film's content is – often invoked in the film's first passages, but further clarified in the title, or in advance publicity. In Mike Leigh's *Secrets and Lies* (1995), the title gives us a clear idea of the theme that resides within the plot. From the outset, it is clear that plot is going to be less important than the themes and ideas in the movie. We become interested in what happens to the characters, but what we remember when we leave the theatre is the meditation on racism and family secrets at the heart of the film. *Independence Day* (1996) also tries to do this, with a title alluding to more than the simple events of the plot. It wants to be a film about big issues of patriotism and nationhood, but it fails to deliver further symbolism to satisfy its claims. Then, at the end, it has to hurry to get across its deeper aims with a scene of Bill Pullman's speech as President of the triumphant United States.

The key to finding symbols in a film lies in their being repeated often. We are led to their existence through particular composition or lighting, or can be reminded of them through sounds or musical motifs. A skilful director will place symbols discreetly but will reinforce them through using elements of the script. In Jane Campion's *In The Cut*, the symbolic lighthouse seen frequently in the film may refer to the location where the killer lurks, the literary lighthouse in Virginia Woolf's book, and perhaps hints at male power.

Weblink
http://www.symbols.net/   Graphics and explanation of literal symbols in history.

Know about the director

As well as the title of a film, we can find out more evidence for where to find symbols by looking to other examples by the same director, or other films within the same genre.

When watching Alfred Hitchcock's *The Birds* (1963), for example, we see broken crockery hanging on the dresser before we see the horror of the victim of a bird attack. Earlier in the film, after a previous bird attack, the camera lingered on other broken crockery and after a couple of these shots we can't fail to note it. Hitchcock has said that, for him, broken crockery represented disruption in family life, so we recognize allusions to his own experiences of family life and in turn our own. This symbol stretches beyond the original intention of creating suspense and preparing us for the appearance of the victim; it ripples outwards to the audience's own experiences. But we do not necessarily need to have prior knowledge of Hitchcock's own hang-ups here; by presenting this symbol repeatedly, we can start to look for it and it becomes a signifier of more than it would elsewhere. We add it to our canon of symbols and take it to our next Hitchcock experience.

Symbolism rests on more than just props. It can exist in any tangible object or set of objects within a film, and even as an unseen object. In Kubrick's *The Shining*, for example, the maze into which the deranged Jack enters parallels the labyrinthine layout of the hotel, and through careful presentation of this element of the set, we are led towards seeing it as a parallel of Jack's mind (for example, in a scene in which Jack looks at a model of the maze, or when we see him encounter different incidents in the hotel that his wife cannot be a part of – see Project 9 on subtext in the movies). When we later see him lose his way within the real hotel maze, the dramatic effect is magnified many times. The symbolism of these places, quietly generated throughout the film, and their resemblance to Jack's mind shifts this scene to one on a much higher plane, of Jack finally losing his way psychologically, of being imprisoned within his own mind – of finally losing his sanity.

Motif

A motif, according to a dictionary definition, is a dominating theme, but also a recurring design. In textile design, a motif would be a shape or design element that recurs throughout the whole design, carrying more of what the design is about than other parts, and its recurrence would confirm this. This helps us to understand how it is applied in the moving image, where a motif is also a recurring visual element that carries meaning.

Motifs are closely connected with symbols. Where symbols are immediate carriers of meaning, a motif can amplify this meaning several times over the course of a film, relating it closely to the main ideas motivating the film. In a sense, motifs are the parent of symbols and symbols are the parent of subtext; the resonance of their meaning becomes smaller as you move down one to the other.

To work effectively, motifs must be a tangible part of a film. In other words, they have to be something that we can see and may often be a central part of the plot. It will become a bearer of a film's underlying theme and, with skill on the part of the director, will be both specific enough to relate to the film's purpose, but broad enough to have some relation to wider experience.

Case study

In mainstream films, motif is perhaps less concerned with broadening a theme than with making it more explicit for the audience so that it is easier to get a grasp of the main message in the film. For instance, there is a difference between the eye motif in *Don't Look Now* (Nic Roeg, 1973) and the mountain motif in *Close Encounters of the Third Kind* (Steven Spielberg, 1977).

In *Close Encounters*, a recurring image of a flat-peak mountain is seen throughout the first half of the movie, serving to heighten the moment when Richard Dreyfuss finally sees it for real. But at no point is the motif held up to be anything greater than what it is – a plot device – and any further investigation is self-serving. With Roeg's example, however, the result of our delving further into the motif is rewarding and reveals much more about the film, but also stretches outside its filmic boundaries to offer a more reflective consideration of the issues raised by the film. Let's take one of those examples in more detail.

Motif in Don't Look Now

In *Don't Look Now*, we are primed to look for and reflect upon images outside of the immediate action. Roeg's skilful and systematic use of montage breaks down our reliance on the script and our need to maintain a chronological flow to the story. We start to decipher images which appear almost without reason and, together with our need to construct meaning out of what we see, we start to make connections. In other words, we infuse meaning into objects or images that normally would pass us by. Roeg makes sure, however, that this is no wild goose chase, but is actually pertinent to the scenes we see unfolding.

In many parts of *Don't Look Now*, vision is a part of the action. There are references to sight, seeing, second sight, blindness and so on. In the extraordinary opening montage, we see Donald Sutherland and Julie Christie enjoying a typical Sunday afternoon, oblivious (they can't see) to the danger of their small daughter at the edge of a nearby river. Sutherland then runs out of the house as if he has heard something within (has he got second sight?), but is too late to save the child. At the film's terrifying closing montage, his implied or partial second sight and his curiosity in terms of physical sight – to see the strange figure he glimpses throughout the film – leads him to disaster.

Between these two montage points, various elements reinforce the eye motif: the medium who claims to have seen the dead girl is herself physically blind and we get occasional shots of her eyes when

Sutherland is in danger. The overwhelming sense in the film is of seeing and not seeing, both metaphorically and physically. Shots that seem to momentarily throw our understanding of the plot in fact serve to clarify the film's meaning. The net result of these tangential moments is only realized, however, by Roeg breaking the rules of temporal and spatial reality, enabling us to see everything within the film as potentially important and potentially symbolic – rather than doggedly following the plot.

So what?

Where does all this leave the filmmaker? Without doubt, symbolism and motif can elevate a film when deployed sensitively. They can help make it more than just the sum of its separate clips, lending the film an inner life and helping to convey far more profound ideas than can be contained within a story. Nor is it restricted to any particular genre; a film that is not necessarily setting out to be insightful can benefit from the placing of elements within the film which hint at bigger ideas.

4 | Pre-production

Quick start guide: Pre-production

How to get to the part you need now

First choose your route:

Quick start guide: This is my first movie

First work out your story

1 Write your own script Chapter 4:4, page 100
2 Using a timeline Chapter 4:8, page 136
3 Action and pace Chapter 4:4, page 111

Then visualize your film

1 Visualizing your film Chapter 4:7, page 132
2 Sketching with video Chapter 4:7, page 135

Then storyboard the film Chapter 4:8, page 136

Quick start guide: I want to make a more challenging short film

First work out how much money you can afford for your story

1 Working out a budget Chapter 4:1, page 71
2 Devising stories for low budgets Chapter 4:6, page 124

Then write the script

1 Steps in scriptwriting Chapter 4:4, page 100
2 Classic structure Chapter 4:4, page 100

Then get a crew

Recruiting Chapter 4:2, page 80

Then visualize and storyboard your story

Quick start guide for documentary makers

First work out how much you can afford for the movie

Then recruit a basic crew of two or three people

Then work out how long it will take

Quick start guide for music promo/VJ

Work out what your video is about

Then visualize it

Then sort out copyright issues

Part 1: Logistics and crew

1. Working out a budget

DV is less expensive

The size of your budget should be part of the decision-making process from the start of the development process. How much or how little you have will play a key role in deciding what kind of film you make.

A DV film is going to cost far less than its conventional analog or celluloid forerunner. Moreover, getting high quality, or even broadcast quality, images is now within reach of most micro-budget film-makers, throwing up the possibility that a first movie by an unknown director will be of sufficient technical quality to find a buyer, leading to distribution. Until now, the best a low-budget director could hope for was to work on 16 mm film, which could be blown up to academy 35 mm at great expense should the film find its way into theatres. Soon, however, the debut DV director could be showing a film on digital projectors, beamed from satellite to theatres, saving huge costs previously spent on printing copies of the movie on celluloid.

Equipment

Getting hold of equipment also used to take some ingenuity. Expensive film cameras, rolls of film, lights and editing units were all guaranteed to take up a large slice of a budget, but digital camcorders are now getting cheaper with each new model and arriving with added features. Editing software is likely to have been bundled free onto your PC, while others still can be downloaded free from the Internet.

A common way of getting hold of equipment is to use facilities at weekends. Ask local companies or production houses whether you can borrow cameras, lights or other items when they are not being used. It sounds like a tall order but it is surprising how often it works.

Interview
'You should realize that film isn't all about money – it's also about time. If you give yourself more time to accomplish something you can mitigate the fact that you're doing it for very little money. In the time you give yourself you could have an idea that will add real production value to the film you're making, you could add finesse to a shot a couple more times resulting in a better scene; you could do another draft of the script when the film has been cast, honing it to actors' strengths. The possibilities are endless; all you need to know is that with enough time and imagination (and not money) there shouldn't be much of a limit to what you can do with the story you're telling.'

Richard Graham, director, Kafkaesque

Developing a budget

Once you have your basic equipment you can start to divide costs into the two main areas used in feature-film budgeting: above-the-line and below-the-line.

Above-the-line

Above-the-line refers to those people in a production who contribute to the main artistic aspects of the film. Therefore, the director, producer, writer and cast will be allocated a certain amount of the budget, often taking up one-third of the total above-the-line.

Below-the-line

Other areas such as design, props, lighting, consumables and all other production costs are entered separately, 'below the line'. In big-budget productions it is more likely that above-the-line takes up a disproportionate amount of the budget.

Tip Most features allow 5 per cent of the budget to the director and producer; 5 per cent for the script; 20 per cent for the actors; 20 per cent to the studio (independent movies don't have this overhead); 35 per cent for equipment, tapes and crew; 5 per cent for taxes; and 10 per cent for all the costs you haven't thought of yet. DV filmmakers will find equipment costs far below this figure.

In low-budget productions, however, it's likely that since you as director will occupy several, if not all, of the positions above-the-line and are probably giving up your spare time to get this together (in other words, you are not getting paid), you could find yourself with a budget sheet that has almost no above-the-line costs. In this case, it is the below-the-line costs that will be disproportionate since these are almost immovable, such as transport expenses, videotape, props and so on.

Weblinks
http://www.culture.gov.uk/moneymap/default.html   Map of funding opportunities for UK-based filmmakers.
http://www.afc.gov.au/filminginaustralia/azbudget/feat_faqs/fiapage_67.aspx   Australian resources for funding filmmakers.
http://shootingpeople.org/resources/index.php   Excellent resources, including free downloadable budget sheet.
http://www.bectu.org.uk/resources/index.html   Find out how much to pay your crew – rates from entertainment union.

Figure 4.1 Budget for stories that require few props or extra items, as in this scene from Neo's *Futureshock*.

Budgets influence stories

If you fall into the category of filmmaker who has little or no disposable income to invest in a film and wish to simply get what you can for as little as possible, then it would be useful to let your available budget affect the kind of film you are going to make. It's not too cynical to suggest that you centre a story around the props, locations and people you already have access to for free – in other words, objects you already own, places you can use as settings for the story and actors who will act for free or non-actors who may not expect to be paid.

Weblink
http://www.online-communicator.com/scriptip.html   Useful guide to how stories affect budget.

Certain types of film are going to cost more than others. If you take a look at the synopses of films currently doing the rounds at film festivals or online cinemas, it is common to find certain genres represented more than others. Epic genre movies are rare, but plots centring on relationships, road movies or crime all figure highly, as they involve few post-production effects or extravagant locations and props.

Perhaps even more noticeable is the originality of these films. An unusual story, an unfamiliar or quirky take on a subject, all result from a need to grab the audience's attention by means other than expensive special effects. In a sense, ingenious and creative ideas for films excuse you from the need to raise large budgets; the value of the film is in the way you have used the medium itself rather than what you have spent on it.

Reducing costs

The least expensive kind of film varies, then, according to what you have access to, but there are a number of other points that can help in reducing the budget of any movie. If we now look at the kinds of subheadings found in a typical budget we can start to look at ways that costs could be kept to a minimum.

Above-the-line

1 *Screenplay*. Write the film yourself, from your own original material.
2 *Producer*. On a larger production, a producer acts as business manager and administrator, pulling the various financial, legal and logistical threads together. Getting involved in these aspects of a small production yourself gives you an essential schooling in the business side of the industry.
3 *Director*. Direct the movie yourself. You can still collaborate with other people on a movie as long as you all forego payment.
4 *Cast*. If your story requires actors there are a number of ways of involving a cast while keeping costs low. Acting on film can be good experience, adding to an actor's résumé and many are willing to work on small productions for free provided they have no other commitments but may, entirely

reasonably, leave your production in mid-shoot if a paid job comes up. Deferred payment is another route, in which you say that you will pay everyone if the movie makes a profit. If your cast and crew believe strongly in the project's merits they will see this as equivalent to holding shares in the movie. But try to be as open as possible with people about the possibility that any money will be forthcoming; most independent movies, including successful ones, see little profit.

Film View
The low-budget feature *The Last Broadcast* (Steven Avalos and Lance Weiler, 1998) cost just $900. Peter Broderick, founder of Next Wave Films which supported the movie, said: 'When people ask me how much they need to make a feature, I ask them how much they have, because that will be enough.'

Below-the-line

1 *Sets*. Use locations rather than sets. For instance, if you need an interior set of an office, find a suitable real location rather than building the set yourself in a studio. Compromise in your aims so that you can use real settings; if a room is not quite right, it is still saving you much money.
2 *Props*. Build your story around props you have access to or can acquire cheaply.
3 *Costumes*. Again, follow the same ideas as for locations; set the film in the here and now, avoiding period costumes.
4 *Laboratory*. For films shot on celluloid, this is one of the largest expenses, together with film stock, while DV filmmaking removes this whole item from the budget.
5 *Stock*. Following on from the last item, however, the amount of videotape you need is greater than that used on similar-length movies shot on celluloid. Buy the highest quality you can afford and expect to shoot more than you will use. You should try to use tapes a limited number of times in order to keep recording quality high and consistent throughout shooting. DV tapes are built far better than previous analog tapes so should withstand re-recording many times. Reusing tapes no more than 10 times should be a reasonable aim.

When shooting you should try to keep all the takes you film, regardless of the amount of space this may occupy, and avoid the temptation to rewind and record over the bad take. In early projects, you may need up to an hour of bad footage for every minute that you will edit, but as you become more experienced in making movies this will fall dramatically.
6 *Editing*. Provided you have the hardware and software necessary to get your tapes onto your PC, edit them and put the finished film back onto tape or whatever format you need; you are making a huge saving compared to the budgets used in non-digital films. A typical film in the late 1990s costing less than $500 000 – classified as low-budget – saw editing costs take up 10 per cent of the overall budget. If you edit the movie yourself and do so using your own desktop editing unit, you are making big savings.
7 *Sound and music*. Use original material, avoiding complicated and expensive copyright fees. Try asking local musicians to collaborate with you in scoring your film. Or – as director David Lynch did – simply try creating your own music, which is infinitely more straightforward since the days

when Lynch devised the unearthly sounds for *Eraserhead* with the easy availability of music-making software.

8 *Insurance*. In larger productions insurance is a non-negotiable item. It is essential to protect the production company against claims from injuries or worse incurred by cast or crew during filming. It can also cover loss of tape or stock, delays in production caused by damage or illness to sets or people and damage to others' property due to production. In small productions where many of the roles are unpaid or filled by the director/writer/producer, it may not be necessary to set up such packages of insurance. Your own household insurance is unlikely to pay for equipment lost or damaged on location, so it may be useful to set up an extension to your existing cover. Actors receiving payment will expect some cover in the event of injury on set. It does not follow, however, that unpaid cast will exclude you from blame if injuries stop them from taking a paid job right after your production. If insurance cannot be arranged, try to come to some written agreement with crew and cast prior to filming.

Weblinks

http://www.ukfilmcouncil.org.uk/filmingUK/location/insurance/   Guide to film insurance.
http://www.dependentfilms.net/files.html   Huge range of free downloadable forms and guides for filmmakers, including budgets.

9 *Additional costs*. Just about every micro/low-budget film comes in over budget. It is almost a rule that the smaller the budget, the more likely you are to need to be flexible. This is mainly because of the notorious 'additional costs'. Notorious because they creep up on you and end up devouring half the film's budget on items such as extra gaffer tape, photocopying, petrol, parking tickets, mobile phone calls. One particular budget from a filmmaker who was aiming to bring in a 10-minute film for under £120 went far beyond this when the line 'additional costs' was added. End-of-shoot drinks and food alone added 50 per cent to the budget, while unforeseen petrol to ferry around unpaid actors and crew added 20 per cent.

How much money is needed?

As we have seen, at a certain low level of budget it is desirable to work out what funds are available and then look at what kind of film is possible. This is part of the creative process and to a certain extent plays a part in most directors' minds at whatever level they operate. Even on larger budget films it is usual to find the movie plot compromised by a lack of funds. However, to most filmmakers, if compromise is the difference between getting a film made and not getting it made, then most would rather make a few changes. If you know your film and what you are aiming at in the movie then it should be possible to make changes without necessarily cutting back on your ideas.

If you have managed to involve crew and cast without payment and follow the ideas listed above for reducing costs, the main immovable costs are videotapes and items seen in front of the camera – in other words, sets, dressing and locations. To be safe, add 20 per cent onto the cost to allow for unforeseen extras, but even then the cost of a short, self-made film can be less than a small family's weekly food bill (but with a greater lifespan). To give an indication of the kinds of figures we are talking about in short films, there has been a flourishing of movie challenges or competitions that throw down the gauntlet of making a movie for less than $100.

> **Tip** When we talk about cost of a movie, we need to think in terms of 'negative cost', which refers to the cost of making the movie before distribution and marketing. In Hollywood, typical negative cost is two-thirds of the overall budget.

Getting investment

Raising money for larger productions as a completely unknown filmmaker is complicated but not impossible.

Even unknown filmmakers can, and do, raise money from companies, charitable agencies, family friends and state arts agencies. If you go for this option, approach it as a business proposition. This means putting together a business plan, résumés, showreel, budget and screenplay. You can never be too professional about this, so think about devising a company name and get some headed paper and even a website domain name to demonstrate that you see this as a serious venture, reflecting your own commitment to it. Become professional: get yourself a suit, turn up to meetings on time and be well prepared, projecting the image of someone they can invest money in. Getting together a business package is going to need some investment itself, but many banks are very keen for the custom of the small business and will send free of charge a range of material showing how to put together a good-looking package, and some may offer discount vouchers from local companies for costs such as printing.

Compiling an investment package

The following should be included.

Résumés (curriculum vitae)

These should reflect the talent you have managed to coax into your project. Ask for detailed résumés from your crew and include any references that suggest that these people know what they are doing, or have studied somewhere to be able to do this, or have raised finance previously. Keep these short, summarizing the important information, and include photos where possible. If you or anyone in your team have received any publicity from any source, include it to suggest that you are, as a group, on the way up and are worth investing in.

Showreel

This is a selection of clips of the projects you have worked on so far, usually on VHS tape. Include those of your team as well. It is an extension of the résumé and is your chance to show that you do, indeed, know what you are doing and have picked up a camera before, that you have all the skills needed to finish the movie.

Tip   You may see postings on independent filmmaker websites offering to make you a showreel, including some interviews with yourself. These are generally regarded as something to be avoided, exploiting the desire of filmmakers to get themselves marketed.

If neither you nor your team have made any movies yet, then don't be shy about it. Include it if you have the material, even if it consists of half-finished drafts for movies and experiments, but don't worry if you have none.

Background material

A range of development material will help convince the potential investor that you have planned the film and have a hard-working and realistic approach to your work. Include a screenplay if you have one, a short synopsis describing the film in only a few paragraphs, artwork, sketches, storyboards, even possible advertisement designs for the film. Also include some indication of the assets you have that help in making the movie, such as editing software, mics or cameras.

Budget

Make your budget as detailed as you can, giving estimates at the conservative, upper end of the scale to be on the safe side. Investors will be more impressed by a realistic budget than a cheaper one with no hope of success. You should not have to seek extra funding halfway through production, even if much of Hollywood does exactly that.

Getting private backers for your film is not easy but there are enough anecdotes about well-established directors who have gone to great lengths to get cash for a first film to convince that it's worth a try. The young Sam Raimi, unable to secure funding for his first feature, sent investment packages to all the doctors and dentists in Michigan, eventually raising enough money to make *The Evil Dead* (1982), figuring they would not be put off by the amount of spilt blood in his movie.

Copyright

Be careful if you are sending out material that you feel could easily be imitated or copied by someone else. Your movie belongs to you even though you haven't shot it yet, so copyright the story or treatment and any other information or material you want to safeguard, including company name. Simply state at the foot of each sheet that copyright is owned by you and that this material cannot be reproduced in any way, including electronically. Doing this makes you look more professional, and therefore good value to a potential investor.

Weblink
http://www.bfi.org.uk/facts/legislation/ Details of copyright law for UK-based filmmakers.

Beware investment firms

You may also hear about companies that specialize in getting funds for new businesses. Such companies will invest in high-risk projects for gain, but even they often draw the line at getting involved in the notoriously unpredictable film business. There are, however, some who only work in entertainment and will advertise their services on Internet filmmaker sites, offering to raise finance for your film. Beware about committing yourself to deals if you are unfamiliar with this territory. It is common for you to lose 50 per cent of your profits – should there be any – to your backer, but this may be no more than what you would pay out to other private backers. To be on the safe side, don't take part in such a scheme unless you fully understand what you are signing and can repay any loans with or without your movie making a profit. And certainly avoid signing anything that puts your property or other collateral on the line if you can't repay. If you are keen to take this route, it may be safer to seek out someone from a law background rather than a credit/loans background. Many law firms have specialists in finding investment for entertainment projects, but this is more common in cities where the film industry is prominent.

Funding a movie on credit cards

It is now common to hear of films made at the low end of the scale that have been financed entirely on credit cards. But it is becoming more common still to hear of filmmakers saddled with insurmountable debt as they struggle to repay borrowed money and rising interest. The temptation is great: fill in a few forms and you get sent cheques for all the money to make your movie. But try to think of the long term; think of how you will finance your next project if you are having to work day and night to fend off the debt collector. Before you commit yourself to using credit, think first about the absolute worst-case scenario; consider what would happen if your film does not recoup any of its costs and you end up borrowing more than you first thought. If the figures you come up with look manageable then proceed, but exercise caution.

> **Tip** For further information, see *Film and Video Budgets* by Michael Wiese (paperback, ISBN: 0-941188-34-5, 480 pages).

The Crunch

- Make use of what you have free
- Some genres and stories are expensive
- Don't spend beyond your budget
- Avoid credit card movie-making

- Cover many filmmaking roles yourself
- If you want investment, plan well and make a package.

2. Collaboration and you

Billy Wilder's famous aphorism that making a film is 'a collection of creative people, in a profit-driven system' is apt; to many filmmakers theirs is a collaborative art form, involving a balancing act between various creative people and the commercial needs of the industry. Our culture has grown to expect a work of art or a cultural product to be 'authored' by just one person. This may be partly due to commercial demands and partly due to the cult of celebrity. Either way, it is misplaced. Film is and always has been a hugely collaborative effort.

In this section we are going to take a look at how to recruit a crew, how people can work best together, and what to do when problems turn up. If Chapter 3 was all about the machinery of filmmaking, this chapter is all about the relationships involved.

Options

First of all, we need to see what the options are in making a film in terms of crew. You are either going to work alone or as part of a crew, and between those two options there are a number of other possibilities, such as part-time crews, shared jobs and so on.

Solo

In practice, working solo is rare. Certain forms of work will be more suitable and others will be almost impossible unless you are solo. But in general, most filmmakers will work with others at least in a loose arrangement. Documentary filmmakers may find that working solo – actually operating the camera on location – is the best option, as it allows greater flexibility of movement, particularly if travelling. Artist filmmakers who work with video in an art gallery setting may also find that the personal nature of their approach demands a more intimate way of working that doesn't involve other people.

In narrative short movies, it is entirely feasible but exhausting to make a film alone and with no other production staff apart from actors. But this may become restrictive: as the ambition of your plans grows so too does the need to draw in other people who share your enthusiasm for a project. Sound may be especially harder to record. In this sense, the scale of your project is directly linked to how many people you need to include.

On the negative side, working solo has its own set of problems. It can be harder to stick to your plans if you are on your own. Filming has a notorious tendency to steer you from your intended route, with the result that you may end up with drafts for two or three films rather than finished footage for one. But like-minded people can be a steadying influence, restraining the more extravagant changes of plan you might have and acting as a sounding board for the testing of new ideas.

Figure 4.2 Working with a small crew can be effective. Spanish director David Casals discusses the next shot with the crew.

What sort of crew?

If you decide that you need to work with people to get the best results, then you next need to think about what sort of crew is right for you and how it is going to operate.

The small crew

A large crew can be cumbersome and unresponsive to changing situations, while working with a small number of people can be more flexible, almost as much as with a solo effort. But there is also a very different kind of working atmosphere when your crew, including yourself, can be counted on one hand.

Let's suppose you find yourself working with a camera operator (a director of photography), a sound recordist/mic operator and a runner. When you work with this size group the dynamics are very different to those when you are the director for 12 or 15 people. A small group will naturally want to be more involved in decision-making; its intimacy will mean that very little that anyone does is kept from the other members. You may also find that decisions are worked through together, and consensus is more likely to be sought by everyone. To this end, it is quite likely that members of a small crew will try to find a compromise when disagreements arise, again simply because they will feel more group ownership of the project. It could also mean that your crew will stick with you and will want to see the project through to completion, even if not being paid. It is possible that if you try to impose a different sort of dynamic on the small group then discontent may be more common, as members feel less a part of the route you are taking. So, if you opt for a small crew, bear in mind that you will need to operate in a less dictatorial manner to get the best out of everyone.

Medium crews

Working with larger numbers of people will place far more onus on you as director to be more organized and confident about what you want. Simply getting everyone to be in the right place at the right time and to keep within budget or to schedule is a huge feat. It is not uncommon to have unpaid crews even when on this scale and it may be possible to attract more professional or more experienced crew members if the project is larger. But, at the same time, all eyes will be on you as director to be in charge. You may also find that it is possible to have two or three people more closely associated with the film from its earliest stages who work with you in a more collaborative relationship and function pretty much as the smaller crew described above. But beware of excluding others on the fringes of the crew from decisions. You may make decisions alone, but make sure you talk to all your crew constantly, informing them of what is going on as plans change.

Interview

'For my movie *Crow* the crew was usually about a dozen people a day: aside from myself as director, there were the director of photography, first assistant camera (AC), second AC/loader, gaffer, electric, key grip, sound, boom, two assistant directors, line producer and two make-up artists. There were also people who were either around only for one or two days, such as assistant make-up artists who helped out when there was more than the usual amount of gore (and it's not a gory film by any means), and people who are in the credits but did not participate in the shoot, such as Nick, my co-writer, and the executive producer, Scott. For post we have an editor, composer, sound designer and a colour timer. The film was done on deferred fees. Not ideal, I know, but it was the only way to get the film made in the time available, and with the available money. Everyone understood that and really threw themselves into it.'

Sean Martin, director

Pay or no pay?

Other people can help you find fast solutions to many problems, simply because they share your aims and have a vested interest in your shared success. In a production where the costs start to exceed your monthly disposable income, sharing the costs can be a necessity. Working with other people does not necessarily mean adding to your costs, particularly if you adopt an approach where you see yourself as *collaborating* with other filmmakers rather than *employing* them. From this point of view, costs become shared rather than just falling on your shoulders.

In many low-budget films, including shorts and longer productions, it is common to have unpaid crew members. Within the filmmaking community there is a great deal of debate as to the ethics of this, with some filmmakers pleading that non-payment is the only viable way to get films made in a cash-starved and cash-hungry art form, while others argue that payment 'professionalizes' the low-budget sector, and therefore enables it to be taken more seriously. For most crew members – editors, camera operators

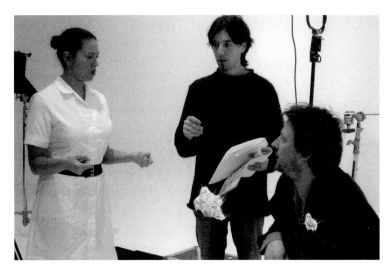

Figure 4.3 In any set it is important to consult and discuss decisions, even though you have the final say. David Casals with actor and crew member.

and so on – getting their first paid job is a major breakthrough in their careers. Jobs are few and hard to come by, and it is possibly a fact of low-budget filmmaking today that a small minority of directors exploit low expectations of crew members by avoiding raising funds for payment.

There are options for payment that don't need you to pay upfront at once. This is called 'deferred payments' and has attracted much notoriety with filmmakers, who call it a contradiction in terms. It works by offering crew members a fee when or if the film makes a profit. It could, for instance, get sold to a cable TV station or receive payments from web screenings. But it is highly unlikely that any short film will ever make money. Agents who travel the film festivals looking for new talent are keenly aware of this and will buy films to sell to agencies such as airlines or TV stations, while taking up to 50 per cent of the resulting payments. They know as much as anyone that the short filmmaker is not in it for the money and is simply looking to use their movie as a calling card to the next step upwards.

Being candid about your lack of funding and payment is better than promising cash that never turns up. At the lower end of the industry people will work for you for free provided you can convince them that your film is going to be of the quality that will help them get noticed and look good on a showreel or résumé. This doesn't mean you can presume non-payment. In fact, to offer something goes some way to making your production look professional. One posting on an Internet recruitment site for filmmakers was open about what was on offer: 'Editor needed, familiar with Final Cut Pro, for short film. This is a great-looking film and although I can't offer payment you will be blown away by the footage. It'll look great on your CV (résumé).' An editor was found, the film completed and all parties happy with the experience.

Paying your crew does, however, make it easier to expect 'performance' from the people you pay, easier to ask them to work long hours during bad weather and turn up on time, and easier to make sure that actors don't leave your production for a paid job midway through filming (and who could blame them?). Also, be careful about paying some members of the crew and not others, tempting if you have both experienced people and first-timers working together. It can split a crew apart when it is discovered that some are being paid for what others do for nothing, and your production could end unceremoniously.

The low-budget strata of the film industry is more dependent on mutual co-operation than any other and to a large extent has succeeded in producing a constant stream of new talent precisely because its participants are ready and willing to help each other make movies. Whether you can pay or not, the success of your production is likely to fall on how much respect and goodwill there is between all members of the production. Honesty and openness are integral to this.

How to recruit a crew

Recruiting people to work with you can be a time of self-discovery. You will find out as much about yourself and your skills as other peoples'. To get the most from the experience, be as honest and realistic as you can, avoiding the desire to 'talk up' a project or make yourself look more experienced than you are.

The most effective way to recruit is to use a bulletin board in a website or place an ad in one of the mailings that are now an essential part of the low-budget landscape. Mailings are the better option because they have an urgency to them and are targeted very precisely. It goes like this: filmmakers, actors, anyone involved in the business at whatever level – students, beginners and professionals – subscribe to a daily email. Under subheadings they can check out new productions that are recruiting, equipment that is for sale, or just look at general questions on technical or day-to-day issues of filmmaking. The people who place the ads leave an email address so subscribers can either respond directly (which is more common except for debates and general questions) or leave a message on the next mailing for everyone to see. In the UK, Shooting People.org has been the pioneer in this field. Its daily bulletin goes out to over 30 000 people, mostly in the UK. A New York version has grown steadily over the last few years and there are other plans to expand the service. Try also Talent Circle (UK), IndieWire (USA) or Australia's Screenhub.

Weblinks
http://crew-net.com/   Hire crew in US-based site.
http://www.screenhub.com.au/   Australian site for jobs and hiring.
http://www.indiewire.com/   Hire and get hired in US-based site.
http://www.ukscreen.com/dir/crew/Crew+Hire   UK-based crew hire site.
http://www.mandy.com/   International and comprehensive crew hire site.
http://www.film-tv.co.uk/   Directory of broadcast and film crew and professionals.

How to post a message

If you choose to post a message on a site, check first whether it will appear for one day only or whether it stays indefinitely until you remove it. Bear in mind also that the sites have certain rules that prohibit certain messages, so check out the main site if in doubt. If you get a good response to your message, post a follow-up message thanking everyone – this is good for the site and helps it continue. Follow these points in preparing a message:

- *Be specific.* How many people do you need? Do they need skills in certain areas or is this a collaborative film where each member needs general filmmaking skills? Give a clear outline of the film, a 'pitch', but don't be tempted to make the project sound bigger or more grand than it is.
- *Be honest.* If you are new to filmmaking, say so. Similarly, be blunt about whether you can pay anyone, about how much time you can commit and what equipment you actually have right now. And don't worry if your posting starts to sound too particular; just about any set-up will attract some response.
- *Timing.* Give exact details of dates you provisionally intend to work on and whether any follow-up dates would be needed.
- *Distribution.* Don't give false hope of where your film will end up. Avoid aiming too high or appearing to be unrealistic about your chances of success.
- *Contacting you.* In asking for replies, try where possible to use email addresses rather than land addresses or phone numbers. It is useful to set up an address specifically for a particular project that is terminated when you end the production. You could make this a remote access address, such as Hotmail or similar. On a note of personal safety, it would be advisable to agree to meet in busy public places rather than at your home address, taking the same kind of precautions you might expect in lonely hearts ads.
- *Budget.* Giving details of a budget is no longer an indication to the level on which you are working. Ambitious short films can be cheap, as can even feature films. Since DV has taken hold of the low-budget film world, budget sheets have smaller figures and more 'nil cost' entries than ever, without compromising too much on quality. Don't be worried about going further and describing yourself as a low- or no-budget filmmaker. Rather than put people off, this term now has come to denote a certain underground, maverick approach to the craft and with it the suggestion of something innovative and challenging.

Who are you looking for?

Ask yourself what skills you have and then look at what you don't. Go about recruiting people who are going to add to the production rather than those who are simply going to double up on what you yourself can already handle. If you are confident in more than one area, you may feel that placing yourself in one particular role is a better use of your time than trying to cover all bases.

Look at the roles outlined in the section on working with other people and identify which you want to work in and which you can hand out to others. In terms of numbers, as a broad guide, a crew of four would be sufficient for a small-scale, low-budget short film, not including actors.

This would consist of:

- A camera operator
- Director

- Editor
- Sound operator.

Not all of these people will be necessary throughout the project, but you may find people who want to be involved in all aspects of the project and who don't limit their time to their role. This sort of blurring of a job description is rarely seen higher up in the industry, as the inclusion of a pay cheque in the equation formalizes a person's relationship with a project. Your film can only benefit from involving people who want to be kept involved on a larger scale, but some may be uncomfortable spreading out artistic input among the whole crew.

What kinds of roles are needed?

Throughout the film industry a certain number of clearly defined roles have evolved within a film production. To a certain extent these have developed in line with the demands of the medium to emulate business, with a hierarchy of roles:

- *Director.* Acts as artistic controller, holding the project together with a single vision of the style and tone of the movie.
- *Producer.* Runs the production as business manager.
- *Assistant director.* Helps organize shots, does some additional shooting and schedules everyone.
- *Director of cinematography.* One of the most important roles on set, this person is responsible for lighting the set and the operating of the camera. However, in practice, the DP rarely operates the camera, but is responsible for every photographic aspect of the film, and for managing the camera crew.
- *Continuity.* Person responsible for the perfect matching of all elements in a scene, so that when edited the different takes work seamlessly together.
- *Sound mixer/boom handler.* These jobs cover, respectively, the correct mixing of sounds during filming and the adequate placing of the camera on set.

Weblink
http://www.skillset.org/film/jobs/   Guide to filmmaking jobs.

All about groups

In large productions managing sums greater than the turnover of many businesses, this hierarchy of roles is an essential way of remaining on target and within budget. But in the low-budget sector there are opportunities and benefits from doing it differently. Although this hierarchical structure remains the default method, for many it belies the reality where roles merge and responsibilities change. Many low-budget films work on a pared-down model that places the director (who has often written the script), the producer (who shares artistic commitment to the film and is rarely a simple business manager) and the director of cinematography on a more or less equal footing. One person may well have instigated the project, but each of this team must feel central to the decision-making process. Once a project is established, other members of the crew may be recruited.

At this level there is a lot of overlap in roles. After a couple of years of working on shared or low-budget productions, most people build up a sizeable range of skills – sound recorders become competent with a camera, camera operators become good editors, and producers develop a passing knowledge of it all. Indeed, it may be difficult to find skilled people who have no interest in any other part of a production than their own specialism.

A basic crew, by skill not job description

If you find that you can't hire all the people you need, look at what skills the people you do have can offer. At its most basic a small crew needs to consist of:

- Someone who understands cameras and lighting
- Someone who understands sound
- Someone who is good with editing
- Someone who makes sure everyone is pulling in the same direction
- Someone who others trust to make the final artistic decisions.

To find out what everyone can offer the production, ask each member to describe in order their top three skills so that you know what each person is essential for and what they can double as.

The kind of people you need in low-budget groups

The list above is based on technical needs of the production. But what about the group itself? If you are spending so much time working with a bunch of people, how you can be sure you are all going to get along, or more appropriately, that when you don't get along, it is for the right reason?

The need to operate without pay cheques and contracts requires filmmakers to renegotiate the power structure within a production. Without money greasing the wheels of production, you need to rely more on consulting and bargaining. Low-budget film crews have fewer members working as a crew and are therefore more flexible and responsive to new methods of working. They can devise new methods without having to worry too much about contractual implications and can encourage the spread of creative input across the film crew.

- The group needs one person who understands the idea behind the film better than anyone else, and this is usually the person who first devised it.
- It also needs several people who each understand and contribute to the overall creative drive of the film.
- These people must be able to cover each of the technical and artistic roles outlined in the more traditional model above, but it is likely that they will overlap in skills.
- Rather than placing the director at the top of a vertical hierarchy, this person may be placed at the centre of the group, having equal contact with each person and acting as conduit for the suggestions and contributions of each member.

- If there is a hierarchy in this model, it places the ideas and aims of the project as paramount and insists that all members agree at the outset what the aims are for the movie and abide by them; members are subordinate only to the general blueprint of the film rather than to an individual.

Groups that work well

There are particular mixes of people that work well together, quite apart from the technical or traditional roles that are seen in the conventional kind of filmmaking group. A bunch of reflective, ponderous people won't get a movie made, finding themselves stuck in the development hell of the coffee shop. On the other hand, a group of firebrands, hot-headedly chasing every new idea, will also find themselves trapped, this time by too many directions to go in. The artistic process of making a film is as reliant on the combination of various characters as on skills. If you are trying to find people to work with on a project, the list below may help in devising a group that works well and pitches in together.

Successful filmmaking groups have included:

- *The artistic warden.* Someone who is committed to keeping the film as close to the original plans and ideas of the film as possible. This person acts as a kind of earth wire, channelling all new ideas back to the main aims and checking that deviations from the film are consistent with the agreed plan.
- *The creative driver.* A person who thrives on generating new ideas and while sticking to the plans for the film is adept at devising new and better ways of fulfilling them. A creative livewire, this person is often one jump ahead of the other members, but does need reining in from time to time.
- *The sceptic.* This member sees the film from an audience's point of view, questioning whether elements of the film will work and applying a cooler, business-oriented view to the proceedings.
- *The technical perfectionist.* Although each member may possess more than adequate technical skills, this person acts as a technical quality controller and may have more understanding than most about equipment or software used in production.

The characters listed above are not exhaustive, but do suggest certain key types who seem to work well towards a successful outcome. If nothing else, observations of this sort tell us that dividing a crew by skill roles alone is only half the story, that other factors contribute to the 'good group'.

How to make sure your group works well: make ground rules for everyone

Aside from whether a filmmaker takes the traditional model or works in other ways, there are certain ground rules that may ensure that the group remains on good terms throughout production and that seem to bring out the most in each member. In 'good groups' these have included:

- *Everyone has an input.* Everyone involved in the production is part of the artistic process. No one's role is purely technical; everyone has something to contribute in terms of experience and technique.

- *Everyone is here to learn.* If it goes wrong in places, don't attribute blame. Don't exclude anyone from the opportunity to make mistakes and learn.
- *Only the best will do.* A belief that the production is going to be absolutely the best that can be achieved right now, given budget size.
- *The integrity of the initial idea.* Throughout production it is the ideas and plans drawn up at the start which were agreed on by all involved that are deferred to. When changes or problems arise, all members refer back to the original plans.

Weblink
http://www.wilderdom.com/games/gamesspecific.html   Guide to group ice-breakers and team leader advice.

What if other people change my movie?

What sort of person decides that they need to rope in other people to get a film made? Does it make you a realist or does it mean you are on the slippery slopes of compromise? Will it make the difference between making a film at all or carrying on dreaming about it, or will it mean that by the end you wished you had kept it just as you imagined it?

Maybe one of the better ways to approach these worries is to take a sideways look at the question of what happens when you bring people into that very private space where you develop your ideas and dreams. There is a school of thought which says that you somehow intuitively only learn what you need to know, derived from the ideas of Plato. We could take this a little further by saying that you perhaps seek out people who you need to know, that you intuit what they have and what they can bring to the project, and that you hone in on them, sensing that they can help you. In other words, you get the crew you deserve, in a positive way. Maybe, when you agree for certain people to work with you, you later can't imagine why you possibly let them into your dreams, such is their ability to trample all over them. But there could be a part of you which also senses that your dreams need a bit of pushing around

Figure 4.4 Actors need time to rehearse their parts fully, as in this shot of Rachel Rose Reid for *The Dark Hunter* (2002) by Jonnie Oddball.

and that you were drawn to this person because they are doing something you yourself can't do. It might be wise to expect that you will seriously disagree with people, long after you have agreed to have them on board. But perhaps what they are doing is acting out their role. If you can take the long view about your interactions with your collaborators then it may take some of the steam out of situations when they arise. For a start, try never to fire anyone – ever. By the end of the production you might realize why you hired them and congratulate yourself.

Why collaborating works

Sharing power on set

Working without payment, as is the case of most low-budget productions, does suggest certain rights in terms of how much one is allowed to contribute to the artistic route the film takes. There is perhaps an inverse connection between the amount of money you are paying a crew member and the amount of artistic input they can have. After all, if someone is going to work a 15-hour day in all weathers for no pay, it seems only fair that they should be listened to if they turn up with some interesting ideas on how the next shot should look.

Sharing power in a production means including the opinions and ideas of those you work with and increasing their sense of involvement in, and therefore commitment to, a production. The net result for you is greater quality of work from your crew and a commitment to see the project through to the end.

> **Interview**
> 'In terms of the hierarchy, with the director at the top, I prefer a more collaborative approach. I think it is good to get everyone's feedback whilst on the shoot … but you have to be careful as everybody can interpret the script differently.'
>
> *Mark Smith, filmmaker, Neon Films, UK*

Other people are good for your movie

If you work with even a small number of people on a production it is likely that your ideas will be tested and questioned. This sort of experience is crucial in pushing your idea to its most highly developed point and ensuring that the eventual film itself is the best you can possibly make. Some filmmakers prefer to be resolutely in charge of a film, but others recognize that almost no member of the crew found on a film set is purely a technician; most come with some creative ideas about each stage of production.

The process of pushing a project as far as possible is best done in a competitive atmosphere. Three or four people, each enthusiastic about a project and determined to prove themselves in an ultimately supportive group, can raise standards and lead to some highly original works, often to the surprise of each member.

Filmmaking can be a meeting of creative minds, but you don't have to lose control over the direction of your film when you start to involve other people; they can be as committed to the original idea as you. While it is possible to make films alone, the nature of low-budget filmmaking is such that you need all the help you can get and can only benefit from extending artistic input to include other people with other skills and experiences. Your crew need to agree on the basic aims of a project and the integrity of the initial ideas, but beyond that they may help push the movie higher than you could alone.

The Crunch

- Working solo can be tough
- Short and low-budget films use smaller groups, large budgets need large crews
- Treat everyone with respect
- Try to pay people you work with – if you can't, then be straight about this
- Crew working for free need to be consulted and included – share power on set
- Find people who work well together, not just with technical skills.

Project 3. Scene description

What this project is for: to recognize differences in individual imaginations
Time: allow around one hour

What this project is about

In this project we are going to see how much other people can offer you and your ideas. To prove it we are not even going to tell them what it is you are going to make yet. Also, the process of playing this sort of game is going to bring your group closer together. Certainly, the ups and downs of a production mean that you need to have strong ties if you are going to weather the storms ahead. Alejandro Gonzalez Inarritu, director of *Amores Perros* and *21 Grams*, starts each production on day one by getting everyone in a circle and releasing a bird. This sort of ritual seems to confirm the equal value he places on every member of the team through his very emotional and intense stories.

In this project, though, it is a lot less deep but you may find out some interesting ideas that get thrown up about your movies.

Stage 1

You might be working with between three and six people as the most common number, but more than that is fine for this project. Make sure everyone is relaxed and has a few sheets of paper and a large, black marker pen.

Ask everyone to write down ideas for a scene. These must consist of a number of characters, and a location. So, for instance, you could say there are two people and they are in a forest. Or you could say there are three people and they are at sea. In turns, go through each of these with each person drawing a personal interpretation of what an image from the scene could look like.

Don't let anyone discuss it or ask you questions; there is no more information than the few words used to describe the scene. Restrict the time to around two minutes. Make sure everyone indicates what time of day or night it is and what the climate is.

Stage 2

Take a look at everyone's pictures. It works well to ask everyone to sit in a circle and then turn them around so everyone gets a scan at them all at once. Even if you were born as sextuplets and raised together, it is unlikely that anyone's images match. One person might interpret the forest scene by setting the duo at night, another in the day, one in a safe clearing, another lost far from the path. In the sea scene, one person may have drawn a frail boat, another that the characters are on a luxury liner. There may be storms, it might be night, there could be sharks, there could be fireworks and flags.

What the process tells us is that each person has taken the initial very simple idea and interpreted it according to their own experience. For instance, if someone draws a forest path leading to a light, with dark images all around it, it is hard not to draw conclusions about where they are in life right now. Similarly, if someone draws a sea full of problems and danger. However, there are people far more qualified than filmmakers to take a pot-shot at a quick psychoanalysis of your crew, so don't be tempted. After all, they have to unwittingly bare their souls for a moment.

Ask everyone to talk about what each picture represents to them. The more everyone talks, the more they see the merits in other people's points of view. And you get to see the way people's minds work. In essence, what you are glimpsing is the architecture of their imagination, showing the tones, atmospheres, colours and shapes they think about.

Project 4. Collaboration

What this project is for: to enable a crew to work collaboratively and exchange ideas
Time: allow about one hour

What this project is about

This project is aimed at illustrating how a team can work collaboratively on a project. It will show how to work on other people's ideas so that you integrate your own ideas with theirs. In the low-budget world it is more common to work in an unpaid environment where everyone is getting something from the project, but not necessarily cash. To most, this is a chance to gain valuable experience and learn new skills. But this way of working means that you can't just resort to dictatorial orders to get work done; instead, you need to include everyone in the decision-making process and treat with respect ideas and suggestions from your crew. This becomes essential when working with those closest to you in the production – the cinematographer and writer. These people will have an equal stake in the film to you and suggestions they make need to be taken seriously. But everyone will know that this is your project and won't try to dilute it or assume power over it.

Before you start working with your team, this project will help set up methods of communication to enable ideas to be shared more easily.

Stage 1

Get your crew together and make time to have a relaxed and good-natured hour or two. Schedule it a week or so before your production actually begins shooting. Give everyone three sheets of paper and a black marker pen. Then brainstorm ideas on a narrative movie that you are going to sketch out. This process itself is interesting, as you will be able to see who is putting themselves forward and who takes a back seat.

Stage 2

Talk about the three-act structure outlined in Chapter 4:4 and make sure you all agree on what it is and how it works. Then ask everyone to contribute to devising a simple Act I describing character(s), situation and setting. Using a sheet of paper, each member then draws their own interpretation of that first act. Then take a moment to look at these – it will be interesting to see how far they differ. Each person started off with the same premise for Act I, but may have imagined it in widely varying ways. Everyone will have brought their own particular stance on the premise and put in their own experiences. This usually provokes debates about how varied they all are. It will enable each member to see what sort of visual references other people have and it will also prove that it is not enough to just have a script with a few lines of description – everyone has to talk about a scene and agree on your shared interpretation of it.

Stage 3

Now ask everyone – you will take part too – to draw a sequel to this act as an Act II. They will each take the characters in Act I and propel them forward into a perilous situation. Make sure that everyone draws their own ideas and isn't influenced by the next person's. Then ask everyone to pass their Act I along to the next person. Again, this can provoke discussions about differences – how your Act II fits in with their Act I.

Stage 4

Take a few minutes to complete the next stage, which involves each member completing the movie outline with an Act III to complement the borrowed Act II and their own Act I. They will be challenged to weave together the narrative from their acts with the crucial central acts from another crew member, prompting imaginative leaps that will prove how it is possible to take entirely random collisions of stories and fuse them together.

Evaluation

There are a number of interesting questions raised by this exercise. But the basic outcome is that your team members will have followed something through together and had fun doing so, improving your relationships. The ideas it investigates are displayed in a half-serious manner, but have a clear message. If you can make the ideas of entirely different people come together and work as a narrative, then anything is possible. When you want to make something fuse you can, suggesting that if there are serious disagreements in production it can always be resolved. Take note of the divergent ways people have of seeing passive descriptions – they project their own ideas onto it. Make use of these varied imaginations on set.

I want something more challenging

The idea of the three-act story may not appeal to you or your crew. If so, use the ideas in Project 8, which allows you to construct story paths that conform to different models. Ask your crew to make a branch model of a movie, devising it from a shared starting point. You will have to work together to make sure that the messages on each branch add up and forge a coherent idea. The model needs to be a group one, where each person is challenged to take the themes on each part of the branch further, and other people try to tie two or more together with more ideas.

Project 5. Developing stories

What this project is for: to generate ideas collaboratively
Time: allow one hour

What this project is about

The aim of this short project is to see how a group can develop a story more effectively than an individual. In a sense, generating ideas as a group is like hot-wiring up your imaginations – a web of experiences to rival the Internet. In this short exercise, we are going to develop ideas using photographs from any source, including magazines, newspapers and so on.

Stage 1

Before you meet with the other members of the team, ask them to bring along to this meeting a selection of random images that interest them. When you get together, ask everyone to lay out their photos in front of them and arrange them in a narrative. A photo of a person becomes the main character, while other images may become events, memories, locations, obstacles and challenges. Each person must make whatever connections they feel are appropriate to forge a cohesive story out of their images.

Stage 2

Ask team members to write down their story and keep it away from other members for the time being. Next, ask everyone to take just one image from their selection and pool it with the rest of the team's images. Give yourself a short time-span to make a complete narrative out of what you have pooled. It must be clear that you have no choice but to arrive at this story. A crucial obstacle is that everyone must agree. Consensus must be arrived at through discussion and argument, so that each person is either happy with the story or has been convinced as to its merits. It is a rule that everyone has a veto on the whole story until they are convinced by the ideas being generated.

This is a challenge only if you ask everyone to make plain their likes and dislikes and avoid having team members who prefer to shrink to the back. Discontent can become rife even in seemingly quiet groups – it is perhaps preferable to have regular arguments rather than simmering unhappiness.

Stage 3

In the last part of the exercise, ask everyone to take five minutes to talk, listen and argue to convince the rest of the group about their first idea, generated at the start. This is no competition – it is in fact the process of pitching the idea and having to field comments that is important. Avoid votes as to whose was best.

Evaluation

During this project your group will have practised several times the process of developing consensus. Each person will have contributed views and these will have been argued over. Each person has had a chance to be 'director' for a while, a few minutes to find out what it takes to listen, argue, reflect and make a decision about what idea is best for the group. And each person will also have found out what it is like to have to see their pet idea shot down so that the whole group can make the deadline.

In the part of the exercise where each person's favourite image was pooled, another aspect of collaboration is looked at. This is the idea of developing someone else's ideas, taking a single part of them and merging them with your own. It shows that your own ideas are strong enough to be heard through layers of other people's work.

The most important thing that will have been practised over and again is that the needs of the group are paramount, over the needs of the individual, and the needs of the movie over the needs of each person.

I want something more challenging

The aim of this project is developing consensus and learning how to listen, while at the same time not sacrificing what you feel. Ways in which this becomes harder would arise when the group is larger, when consensus is going to be harder to arrive at. You will be aware of the stage when this exercise becomes more challenging when factors like this, and shortage of time, budget and facilities, make themselves felt.

3. Making a schedule

In a feature film, the idea of planning how much time each part of the process will take is crucial to the smooth running of a production, and has a huge impact on marketing and subsequent profit margins. In short-film production and in micro-budget filmmaking, schedules are less rigid. The reason for this is the number of variables with which the micro-budget filmmaker has to contend, from the availability of non-fee actors, to the demands of day jobs. The smaller the budget, the more flexible, and changeable, the schedule.

Many filmmakers have made films over a number of years, filming at weekends while they earn the money to buy film stock or tape, reliant always on a complex set of timetables of each crew member as they juggle their commitments around the demands of the film. For many, the short film is more likely than longer productions to result in a piece of finished work. Actors are less likely to get called away to more attractive paid work and crew are more likely to be able to commit themselves if a shoot lasts just a few days. Morale can easily sink when you have a half-finished production and no way of knowing when you can get your crew back together to finish it.

Enough good footage

How much you need to shoot is one of the most important factors in working out how much time you will need overall. How much time will it take to get a shot right? Will you need to reshoot parts of your scene when you play it back over lunch? And will you have the confidence to go with what you have planned rather than try to cover all bases by shooting from all sorts of other angles, again and again? It all comes down to experience. How much a beginner needs to shoot will be different from a more advanced filmmaker. To work it out we could think in terms of a ratio – known as the 'shooting ratio' – of good footage (stuff you actually want to edit with) to bad footage (when actors fluff their lines, the mic is out, the camera wobbles and so on). For many people starting their first film, something like 10 or even 20 per cent good is average. After the first film, and indeed sometimes during production of the first, this rate rises in accordance with the quality of the actors and crew and the decisiveness of the filmmaker, but usually stays around the region of 50–60 per cent good footage after two or three short films. Short films allow you to learn more quickly than more cumbersome productions by letting you see your mistakes more quickly, so you may find that your ratio of good to unusable improves sharply.

How much you need to reshoot or redraft is a big factor in determining how much time your film will take, but is not necessarily a factor in its quality. Stanley Kubrick would frequently shoot up to a hundred takes for minor scenes, and it has been suggested that he used this as a method to push his actors further and get more out of them. To be cautious, consider that in one day's filming only a few minutes of final footage will be achieved, less if it is action, much more if it is simply-staged dialogue.

Interview
'Try to schedule things so that you don't have to go at a pace that's impossibly fast, or place ridiculous demands on yourself or any of the cast and crew. Shooting film is actually quite an industrial process once you get past the rehearsal stage. You can fiddle with a scene further down the line, but it becomes harder and harder. And if you're on a tight schedule it becomes harder still.'

Richard Graham, director, Kafkaesque

Length of each stage

In terms of overall schedule, the length of time to allow for planning, shooting and editing is never going to go according to plan. But it would be a good start to assume that it will take twice as long to plan as for shooting. Post-production may last up to four times the length of the shoot. So a ratio of planning, shooting and editing could be around 2:1:4. The editing stage is prolonged when working in digital editing with your own unit at home, as it allows you to play with alternative versions and tweak the final film, perfecting it to a high degree. However, to many editors schooled in the old analog methods, better editing occurs when you are pushed for time and need to make fast choices.

In between the stages mentioned above, there will be other tasks that need attention. These include casting, rehearsals, design, props buying, and viewing daily takes and rough assemblies during shooting.

Figure 4.5 Scheduling can be difficult in low budget films where unexpected obstacles occur, but good planning can keep you on time and on budget. Mark McDermott shooting a scene from *Jigsaw of Life* (2005).

Weblink
www.sag.org   US actors' guild advice on scheduling and working with actors.

Pre-production schedule

This stage is the most flexible in that you can wait until your film is prepared before you commit to a shooting date. However, the tasks to be covered need to be prioritized. Drawing up a budget is the primary task, as it dictates how much time you can spend filming, how many actors (if any) you can hire and what props you need to buy.

Make a continuity breakdown

To assess your budget you need to make a continuity breakdown. This is an outline of what is needed for each scene in the script, a list of what each demands and its associated costs. For example, a shot involving several cast members will require greater catering costs. It should also include for each scene:

- The amount of the script that is being covered by a scene. Note that each page of script is one minute of movie time. Partial pages are counted as eighths, so two and three-quarter pages would be two and six-eighths, running at about two minutes and 45 seconds.
- Details of location, including transportation costs, accommodation and catering.
- The time of the shoot, noting whether it is day or night.
- Any extra equipment or props that are required, such as cars, additional lighting, costumes.
- Which members of the cast and crew are needed for that scene.
- Any additional cast or extras needed.
- Set plans showing an aerial view of a location with details of where cameras, props and lights could be situated.

You don't necessarily have to stick to the above, but it is crucial to the smooth running of the production that others have faith in your organizational abilities or you may lose members of your crew. Plans that change, particularly as a result of the input of your crew, are better than no plans at all.

Shooting schedule

One of the logistical problems of filming is trying to arrange that all scenes set in one location are shot together. Ideally, you should try to arrange a schedule like a tour, placing locations together according to geographical proximity and shooting separate locations on separate days; try to avoid changing locations halfway through the day. Many low-budget filmmakers find themselves having to film at inconsistent times according to when the cast and crew are available, often weekends or evenings, and this can play havoc with attempts to maintain a smooth flow to the film.

It is also likely that your co-workers are simultaneously working on other projects and you may have to devise ways of reminding cast and crew about the key points of the film before each shoot. It is easy to lose track of the kind of film you are working on when you have several on the go and it is common for you, as director, to want to change and adapt the script between shooting dates. Make plans well in advance so that everyone – cast and crew – has the opportunity to place the schedule in their diaries before they get involved in other projects. If you have the choice, try to get everyone together for a condensed period of shooting over several days, rather than spread work over weeks. But as mentioned in the chapter on people, if payment is not a part of your shoot, be prepared for crew dropping out to take paid work. Be flexible with this as far as possible and they might drop back in again.

How long is a shoot?

Shooting times vary widely between different sectors of the film industry. Twenty years ago, a 90-minute feature film would take around 40 days, whereas now it is common for a film of that duration to take 60 days or more. Bear in mind, though, that this is studio production, where filming is in line with union requirements regarding working hours and breaks. In the independent sector union arrangements are not so common, and in short movies are almost unheard of. However, if you can't afford union rates and work arrangements, try to go along with the spirit of them if not the letter, as your crew will function more happily and efficiently on good rest, average food and a day or more off once a week.

In studio filming it is common to shoot slightly more than location filming – perhaps one or two minutes more of final footage – per day, although some directors will work more quickly if, for instance, working on television drama, which averages six pages per day. Clearly, some scenes will take longer, such as action sequences, scenes involving special set-ups or those with more cast members or extras than usual.

Bear in mind during the shoot that there will be enormous pressure on you to extend a schedule or to reshoot. Remember that footage of the day's shooting rarely looks good – it's messy and is interspersed with bad takes. Resist the temptation to reshoot without taking advice from others in the crew or people with a more detached view of the project, and try not to judge the daily takes of a scene too harshly without seeing them in the context of the shots preceding and succeeding them.

Using the script as a guide, and informed by the restrictions of your budget, it is possible to make a fairly accurate estimation of the length of time it will take to shoot your film.

The Crunch

● Be realistic: allow more time than you think – think of a period and add 50 per cent
● Plan in advance for your crew
● Make a continuity breakdown – be in control of the schedule
● Keep crew and cast informed of any changes – check their availability
● The size of your budget will affect how long it will take
● Avoid reshooting hastily
● Don't overspend by filming more than you have to.

Part 2: Scriptwriting

4. Story and structure

> **Interview**
> 'There is no substitute for a great story. Any script or film that seeks to go deeper than mere formula and throws some light on the human condition is going to get noticed because audiences are hungry for great stories. Especially in low-budget independent film, where there are no special effects budgets or major stars to hide behind, story must be king.'
>
> *Mark Innocenti, filmmaker, USA*

Story is indeed king. It has the authority to make or break a film. It can elevate it to higher levels and confer on it a rank that no other part of the filmmaking process can offer. A film with poor technical qualities can survive when hooked up to a wonderful script, but a film with high production values and all the budget it can eat is going nowhere if the script is poor.

In this section we are going to take a look at what makes good stories. And we will see that it is not what they are about that matters, it is the way they are laid out – what we could call their structure.

Plot vs story

Before we talk about narrative in detail, we need to look at the terms we use. A story refers to the whole sequence of events from the opening moment of the movie to its close, while the plot refers only to those events that take up the main focus of the action. For example, in *Taxi Driver*, the film concerns a semi-literate Vietnam veteran, Travis Bickle (Robert DeNiro). For the first section of the film we encounter daily life for Travis as he contemplates the dark side of New York street life. This is the story, but the plot only kicks in when Travis meets Jodie Foster, whom he wishes to rescue from prostitution, and Cybill Shepherd, whose rejection of him leads him to plan the assassination of a leading political candidate. In these and other cases, the plot takes on a slightly different pace to the rest of the film, increasing the tempo and providing a focus for confrontation and resolution.

Story structure

Classic script structure

Classic structure, as seen in many narrative movies, is the dominant force in storytelling and in the cinema. This particular model of film structure is based on a need to deliver a story that resembles what we grew up thinking of as a proper story: something with a beginning, a middle and an end, and which safely delivers us an outcome – for better or worse. We want to be moved, taken on a journey, and made to experience a distillation of the ups and downs of life in one condensed trip. Some of the most powerful films reject this in favour of something that is more provocative, and with success. But these directors – Stanley Kubrick and Terrence Malick, for example – have all been schooled in classic screenwriting forms and are then more confident to evolve them.

Classic structure operates along a three-act formula:

- Somebody is somewhere and everything's normal
- Something happens to this somebody, and normality is disrupted, prompting them to take action about what happened
- After conflicts and obstacles, normality is restored, but this is a new normality.

It consists of three events: the first and last are circumstances or situations, while the middle consists of action. So, a person is in one set of circumstances at the start of the movie and through a stream of action is taken into a new set of circumstances at the last section of the movie. This is often referred to as 'state–crisis–new state'.

Weblink
http://screenwritersguild.org/storystructure.asp   Screenwriters' resource on structure.

Classic structure in mainstream movies

The ultimate aim of this structure is to return the situation to the way it was before the event that changed everything. We can apply this structure to many films. In *Independence Day* (Roland Emmerich, 1996):

- We see the world on a normal day and focus on a particular character (Will Smith)
- Aliens invade and create mayhem
- Then we see how the main character copes with this and tries to return the situation to the way it was before the invasion.

In *Die Hard* (John McTiernan, 1988):

- Visiting cop McClane (Bruce Willis) goes to see his estranged wife
- The building where she works is hijacked by a group of terrorists, who take her hostage
- McClane tries to defeat the terrorists and release the hostages.

In this film, the narrative structure is very strong, with few diversions from the straight-line development of the action-based plot. We are taken from a quiet start, through endless near misses and cliffhangers, towards an upbeat conclusion in which all is resolved. There are clear stages in the action and we are accustomed to this kind of structure in this genre of movie.

In these films, good storytelling is about what methods you use to combine these stages of the story together and whether you can do so without the audience being too aware of it. This way of telling stories appeals to us because it takes us for a ride; we go from normality, through to struggle and difficulty, through to resolution and back to normality again, but we are meant to be changed somehow by the process. Like a good fairground ride, we are returned to the place we paid our money and took our seats, but we are altered in some way. So, Will Smith in *Independence Day* learns family commitment, while Bruce Willis in *Die Hard* enjoys a reunion with his estranged wife.

Use 'the three acts'

To a certain extent, we have to look at psychology to see why we desire stories to run a certain way. We could define the classic structure we have just looked at as one influenced by fairy tales and folk myths. Lessons are given in these stories and we learn something in the process as we watch. Even the most popcorn-friendly multiplex movies conform to our need for inner change and moral development. At whatever level of film you look at, the audience at the end of the feature are changed in some way – maybe they have laughed more, see the world more positively, or perhaps they reflect on some part of the human condition. Either way, a film takes you somewhere. Again, this doesn't mean every movie has to follow this route, but once you know this is the dominant way, you can break the rules and make your own way of doing it.

Let's take a look at this structure in more detail:

Act I

In the simple stories of myths, legends and fairy tales it was important to relate the sometimes fantastical events of the story to the real lives of the audience. That meant beginning in normality, in the natural state of the world that the listener lived in, or using elements of their world. This first act would typically involve the introduction of the main characters, the setting, the period in history and so on, but may have given some hint of the events to come. This state of normality can be a pleasant or unpleasant state, but it must be represented as normality. If this state can be presented as everyday and ordinary for these inhabitants, then the impact of the challenge in act II is all the greater.

Act II

In Act II, the main protagonist encounters an event which challenges the normal state of their world. This must involve some hardship, such as an invasion, the breakdown of a marriage, the loss of the loot or a false accusation. As far as possible, this event must be as hopeless and devastating as possible and, to take scriptwriting guru Robert McKee's advice, 'Thou shalt not make life easy for the protagonist.' Nothing in drama is going to advance without conflict; it is the fuel on which the story travels. This act is the most difficult, most challenging, full of cliffhangers, near misses and false hopes. Obstacles are heaped on the suffering protagonist. If it all seems rather over the top and unrealistic, this is because Act II is a distillation of real life, like compressing all the bad events we hear about into just one person's experience. Our protagonist is a cipher for us all.

Act III

Once the protagonist has encountered this life-changing event, it is then up to him or her to overcome it and triumph. This, the final act, becomes the quest and motivation of the movie's main character. In depicting this, it is important to show the audience what is happening rather than tell it. Exposition is cheap – important events can be described between two characters over a glass of beer – but to actually show is to truly make the most of what cinema can offer in visual terms. The protagonist will have gained something by this conflict, where the struggle and the triumph over it brings with it some reward in the form of heightened humanity or insight into the human condition; in short, she or he will be a better person. In the closing act of Hitchcock's *The Birds*, for example, we notice how the constant bickering between the characters gives way to family closeness as they survive wave after wave of bird attacks.

How the acts work together

The three acts are related in different ways. Act I does not cause Act II, but Act II causes Act III, through a series of choices and surprises. If Act II is the one with the most setbacks and surprises, the final act is often the one with the most action, and may alter the style of editing established throughout the movie. This act also possesses the most ups and downs in terms of crises. Early in Act III the protagonist may often encounter a crisis that threatens the entire plan. In *North by Northwest* (Alfred Hitchcock, 1959), the main character, Thornhill, finds out that Eve, whom he cares about, is in mortal danger. Thornhill has to rescue her, possibly jeopardizing his freedom.

At the end of Act III, there is often a climactic resolution to the conflicts of the film, referring right back to the initial aims of the film raised in the opening scenes. Script devices may be used to signal a link between the start and end of the movie, so that the audience feel that they have been returned back 'home' to the start of the narrative, back to normality.

> **Film View**
> As an example of the kind of climactic resolution or closure often seen at the end of films, in *The Birds* a pair of lovebirds are bought as a gift at the start of the film and act as a device to kick-start the plot. When the birds are brought out to the escape car at the end of the film we sense that some sort of closure is going on, that the end is near, even though other aspects of the plot are unresolved; it's a clever way of drawing the film to a close without concluding it fully. This kind of implicit closure is useful in this case, as Hitchcock stipulated that there should be no 'end' titles in this film, simply a fade to black.

Lengths of each act

It is hard to be precise about how much time should be given to each act, but a rough guide can be used if we take a look at the standard 90-minute film. Within the first 25 minutes or thereabouts, the main character needs to encounter the event that leads to Act II. Roughly midway through the film, the situation for the protagonist must be about as bad as it gets and does not need to improve until we get within the last 15 minutes. This is a very rough guide and applies to a very overused formula, but it does give some idea of the relative lengths of each act.

Pinch points

A useful device of classic film structuring is what are called 'pinch points'. A pinch point is a scriptwriter's term for a part of the story that pushes the action a little further. These are not huge leaps or changes in the action, but a nudge and push towards the next scene. You would expect to see several pinch points in the first two acts of the film and hardly any towards the end, when the action speeds up.

Film View

In *Apollo 13* (Ron Howard, 1995) we see many so-called 'pinch points'. The main crisis is the accident on board the spacecraft, but in addition to this we have further after-shocks, such as the reduction in oxygen supply, which serve to add to the tension and keep the audience engaged.

Write your own script

Writing the story and screenplay yourself is going to relieve you of a large item on the budget sheet and is, after all, probably why you started making films in the first place – the opportunity to express yourself. The ideas below apply equally to the standard 90-minute feature as to the short film.

1 Complete a brief paragraph outlining the story from start to finish. This avoids details and simply lists the events of the plot and your vision of the kind of film it will be. If you can't put it into one paragraph it may indicate a lack of clarity in the story. Reduce it to its main parts, as outlined above when we talked about *Die Hard*.
2 Write a treatment. This is a short story of the film, and would last for about 30 pages in a 90-minute feature. For short films five to ten pages is fine.
3 Draft screenplay. Using the treatment as the basis, write the screenplay with director's notes, dialogue and any other information that helps to describe the scene.
4 The final screenplay may not necessarily be the second draft; it is likely you will go into several more drafts before you are satisfied. In any case, the last draft will always be shorter than the previous. Each sheet on your screenplay will correspond to one minute of film time. In shorts, however, there is less pressure to cost out the whole film, so the one minute = one page rule is rarely observed.

Tip   Don't be tempted just yet by scriptwriting software – it may skew your judgement to see your words looking so much like a real script. Use pencil and paper to write the whole first draft.

There is not the space to discuss the finer points of screenwriting, but this is one of the most useful skills you can acquire as a filmmaker and puts you more in control of the medium than any other role. If you find that scriptwriting is not what you want to be doing or that you get more inspired by other people's stories, then you may want to consider how to get hold of that material, but more on that later.

Weblink
http://www.wga.org/ Writers' Guild of America.

Tip If you are writing your own script, limit the number of characters in the plot. Dealing with just two or three main characters simplifies the action and yet is enough to allow each to set off character traits in the other. Whatever you do, don't exceed seven main characters.

Developing good structure

There is no right or wrong way of structuring your film, only ones that are appropriate to what you are making. Narrative film as seen in mainstream cinema has a well-established way of structuring stories and this is seen as the default method for many filmmakers. Using this method does not mean you are working in a non-challenging, conventional way; you may use classic structure but delay it, subvert it or otherwise change it in ways that surprise the audience. To make it even more interesting for you, you can use the presumed knowledge the audience have of classic structure and use this against them by deviating from it now and then.

Using a timeline

To map out a good structure to a movie we need to use a tool called a timeline. As can be seen in Figure 4.6, this is a long box, horizontal on the page, subdivided into seconds and minutes. Along the line boxes are placed corresponding to the length of the individual scenes within it. So, a scene lasting 30 seconds takes up about one-tenth of the total line if the film is five minutes long. We can give each separate scene varying shapes or colours, enabling you to group them in terms of the three acts. You can now see the relative sizes of the scenes and notice which, if any, are dominating the film. Towards the end of the film you might expect to see the scenes become shorter than at the start. You can also use the timeline to map out the peaks and troughs of dramatic tension throughout, so you can see how to pace the story and deliver key scenes at regular intervals.

See the film at a glance

First-time filmmakers often talk about the problems they have in maintaining sufficient grip over the film throughout production, avoiding wrong turns and diversions. Many also talk about the effort in keeping sight of the main point of the film, rather than letting the action take over. The timeline allows

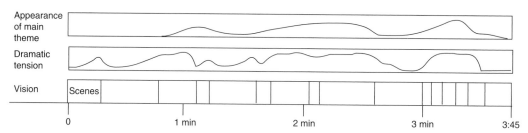

Figure 4.6 In this diagram, the timeline shows various aspects of the film. The first layer at the bottom represents the individual scenes, enabling you to see the structure of the film, reflected in the pattern created by the relative lengths of each scene. The next layer shows how the dramatic tension of the film will build in places throughout the film, reaching its climax in the final scenes, while the top layer shows how often the main theme is going to occur. For example, the theme could be good vs evil and this may become more and more a part of the story as the film progresses.

the director to see the film as a whole and, most importantly, see each component as relative to the rest. It is this ability to stand back and view the film from afar that gives many the clarity they are seeking in defining how to structure and pace the film.

The timeline in action

As a good structure starts to develop on paper, you may start to see a pattern emerging. We could take a look at *The Wizard of Oz* (1939) to see patterns at work. On a timeline, you would see a particular shape at the start representing Dorothy at home in Kansas, in scenes filmed in monochrome. Throughout the first hour you would see a pattern emerge of Dorothy encountering more characters to join her journey. At regular intervals we have a song and at further intervals we have interventions from the wicked witch. The structure changes in the last act, where we see the group enter the wizard's palace and here the action hots up, so we see a greater turnover in scenes. At the end of the film, Dorothy is returned to Kansas in monochrome scenes again, so we would use the same shape used to denote the opening scenes. Looking at the timeline we can see a very pronounced pattern, representative of a strongly structured film and typical of movies aimed at younger audiences, where the need is to conform to traditional storytelling forms. Even in later, more radical films such as *Reservoir Dogs* (Quentin Tarantino, 1991), we see a pattern emerge as we go to and from the warehouse to encounter various points of the story told in flashback.

Uses for the timeline

You can use this method to reveal the presence of just about any aspect of your film:

- Recurrence of characters
- Highs and lows of tension
- Possible dominance of types of scene, such as exteriors, interiors and so on
- Uses of flashbacks
- Recurrence of sounds or music

● Stylistic changes
● Points of action and points of reflection.

Further variations on the timeline could include drawing it as a circle, with degrees within it representing minutes and seconds of the film, in a clockwise fashion. There is also a variation using children's coloured building bricks in which a three-dimensional line can be built and rearranged to get the right structure. These various methods tend to appeal to the visual instincts of filmmakers.

Structure devices

When looking at structure in other films, it is easier to look at those that are more transparent; in other words, which have their structure and pace written all over them and which conform to some of the cinematic conventions. Films such as *Jurassic Park* (1993) and *The Day After Tomorrow* (2003) are instructive models because they do not attempt to alter the established formula and positively revel in living up to it, with the result that you can see the nuts and bolts and rivets of how these films are built after just a brief look.

Embedding the purpose of the movie early

The aim of this is to stake a clear aim of the film, apparent to the audience, right from the start. In the opening scenes you could suggest what it is that will drive the film forward. Separate this idea from the one described earlier, identifying the 'key scene'; the key scene is more likely to occur later and will go some way to resolving the questions and challenges raised in this early scene. This early scene may include some line of dialogue or some symbolic event that sets up the themes and aims of the film, while also giving us some important exposition. The difference between good and bad scriptwriting is whether the audience knows that they are being handed these points or whether this scene is fluidly and seamlessly embedded in the opening sequences. To use a restaurant analogy, this early crucial scene is like putting in your meal orders while the later centrepiece section is like getting the food.

Each scene should have conflict within it

This refers to the detail of the film and means taking a close-up look at how every scene works. Each scene needs to have a goal of which the audience is aware. This has to be something fairly obvious and solid rather than something abstract and ambiguous. The Indiana Jones series of films are masters of the art of setting minor tasks for Indy to complete in each scene – get the aeroplane, run out of the labyrinth – and then placing numerous obstacles in his path, such as pits of snakes, the armed guard and so on. This is a simple example and the more sophisticated the film, the more you may play with our expectations, raising hopes and dashing them.

In the Hollywood model, a typical scene climaxes as disaster strikes and the goal of the main character has been frustrated. This leads to an interruption of the way the overall action is heading. This is good for two reasons: it surprises the audience and it leads with neat continuity on to the next scene, with its own conflict and goals. Think of a particular scene in *Star Wars*, when the three main characters – Han,

Luke and Leia – cannot escape from an attack by the stormtroopers and bail out into the garbage chute. Unable to complete the goal of that scene, they have been forced to change direction. In the garbage pit they have a new goal – to get out. But they are again frustrated when the walls start to draw in.

Micro-structure within scenes

If we take a closer look at the structure of films we can zoom in on the individual components that make up each act. In Act II in particular we see how there are numerous small scenes that each advance the story. A useful model for these was put forward by creative writing teacher Dwight Swain, late of the University of Oklahoma. His idea was a cause-and-effect structure that applies as well to novels as to screenplays. Swain suggested a model in scenes in which there is a disaster or obstacle that the protagonist has to overcome and this then leads to action as the protagonist tries to deal with it, finally leading directly to the next scene as it resolves. This idea is summed up as: situation – action – sequel. It works by mirroring the larger overall three-act structure of the film.

At first, the main character must have some sort of reaction to the obstacle that has frustrated their goal. This reaction is determined by the kind of personality you have evolved for the character. To go back to the *Star Wars* garbage scene, Han delivers a sardonic comment aimed at the others, while Princess Leia tries to get a solution. We knew they would react this way; if we didn't, then the characters have not been built up into credible people. On this last point, the more your characters are like real people with real experiences informing their decisions, then the more opportunities there are for further conflict, as the individual personalities clash with each other.

The dilemma

Swain goes further and points to the need for a *dilemma*, something which causes the character to choose between two courses. In an action film this is usually the choice to fight or take flight. Prolonging this decision can add tension; there should be a clear difference between the two options and this must be apparent to the audience, so this is a good moment to show exactly how bad it would be if X happens and how great it would be if Y happens. The action taken to exit the character from the conflict of that scene immediately leads him onto the next. For example, in *The Fugitive* (Andrew Davis, 1993), the wrongly accused Harrison Ford escapes and is chased along a water outlet, hundreds of feet above a river. The cop closes in, Ford looks down at the long drop, then back to the cop, and so on. In a matter of seconds we sense his dilemma, between capture or freedom, and are made to wait while he decides which to take.

The protagonist

In your screenplay you should be aiming for a group of characters who are real in a number of ways but are, significantly, not human beings. McKee believes that 'a human being does not have the richness to become a protagonist'. This is because a film character needs to be a compression of lots of ideas and lots of people, a metaphor. The danger here is in making the character into a stereotype similar to other characters seen in lots of other films. The way to prevent this is to avoid the obvious, introducing elements that are counter to the stereotype (the piano-playing, art-loving serial killer, Hannibal

Figure 4.7 Annie Watson's short film *Knitting a Love Song* is able to project a strong sense of character through a carefully honed script.

Lecter) and make his or her aims unlikely (the poor boy who wants to escape the ghetto). Furthermore, add lots of contradictions. These surprise the audience and help you to add new elements into the story as it progresses in the form of skeletons in the cupboard, leading to people or situations that potentially obstruct the characters. They also help to make the characters more fallible, more human.

Finally, if you have secondary characters in the script, make sure that these are slightly less interesting than the primary characters. Secondary characters are there to draw out the qualities of the focal character by asking the right questions and setting up situations to which the main character responds.

Subplot

In thinking about pace and structure, it is useful to be able to have something that acts like a brake now and then, taking the audience's attention away from the main plot and into a diverting smaller story which simultaneously seems to help the main story. A subplot is a refrain, a time to breathe a little and reflect on the scenes in the main story. The James Bond franchise has managed quite well without this element but, to make up for its absence, needs to go frenetically from place to place, incident to incident. In *Star Wars* again, we see the subplot continue into the sequel – namely, who will win the heart of the princess.

Clearly, this is not the main plot and is not intended to be the well-hidden, true meaning to the film. It is absolutely secondary to the main story and in this case does a perfect job in taking us out of the fast action and into quiet exchanges, when the dogfights and light sabres become too much. These parts of the movie also serve to deepen our understanding of the characters and show another side of them.

Subtext

Many scriptwriters advise putting a subtext under every text. What this means is avoiding writing lines that mean what they say and nothing else. Your screenwriting should involve a kind of 'double-speak',

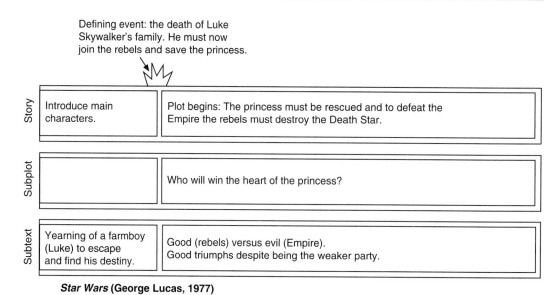

Star Wars **(George Lucas, 1977)**

Figure 4.8 Structure. In *Star Wars*, there are several levels going on simultaneously. The story is the most dominant part of the script, with the subplot appearing only occasionally. The subtext is the least noticeable part of the film and may shift as the story advances into the main plot.

where every line spoken represents other lines that expand the meaning in the scene. You could even try typing with double-spaced gaps between the lines for you to write your subtext.

Revealing the subtext is done carefully and only partially, allowing the audience to think about the implications of the script. Ambiguity is acceptable; if you are working with good actors, they will be able to reveal subtext through body language and the way they deliver the lines. The way Jack Nicholson's character talks to his son in the first few scenes of Kubrick's *The Shining* (1980) suggests a whole history of menace and familial tension in some very innocuous lines. This is good double-speak, saying one thing and meaning another.

Go to: Chapter 3:2, 'How films work', for more on subtext.

Pace in the script

Tempo and beats

Pace is also useful to look at here in relation to structure and scriptwriting. We can define it as being the tempo of the film, the rate at which the aims of the plot progress. The pace at which your film runs is determined by a number of factors, including the length of the movie, the subject matter and the style you have in mind. If we are going to talk about tempo it would be useful to have some way of measuring this, just as we can with music when we talk about beats per minute. With pace, we can describe scenes in terms of beats, which may be less confusing because actors will talk about scenes in terms of the

'French scene', in which each new entrance starts a scene and each exit ends it. In filmmaking, it is easier to talk in terms of 'units of time' and these could be anything from 20 seconds to a minute. If this sounds vague, think of each beat as like a footstep, advancing the plot, even slightly, towards conclusion. This analogy also helps us to think of these footsteps as rhythmic, determining the pace throughout the film.

How fast?

The pace or speed at which the film goes is entirely up to you. There are no rules that say that one particular rate of progression is better than any other, that sombre subject matter should naturally run at a slow pace nor that comedies should be frenetic. As with all aspects of the filmmaking process, and most arts in general, you need only justify it in terms of what you are aiming for. It is again all about good advance planning.

Action and pace

Pace determines the flow of information to the audience, how much they receive and how often. A dense storyline requires a quick pace to carry all the events within the film's duration. In *Die Hard with a Vengeance* (John McTiernan, 1995), for example, a series of encounters take place in the last quarter of the movie, any one of which would have served well as the main conclusion to another action movie, yet here they form part of a dense line of situations which pile action on top of action. This frantic pace is at odds with the slower, more measured pace of the first *Die Hard* movie, in which the subplot (of McClane's relationship with his former wife) and the subtext (in which a downtrodden man rediscovers his self-confidence through triumphing over conflict) both help to delay the action and serve it up in smaller portions, which leaves the audience keen for more.

Changing pace

In Kubrick's films, pace is often majestically slow, even in action scenes, but this is with a purpose. In these films, events can be seen to have more meaning and more implications if there are fewer of them. In *The Shining* (1980), this is illustrated where several scenes lead to false climaxes and where long, slow tracking shots take us relentlessly towards the bloody conclusion, hinted at in sparse, brief nightmare images. In this case, the viewer quickly becomes accustomed to the slow pace and it in no way deflates the action.

Terrence Malick, in all his films, also avoids the obvious and goes for slower pace even in action, plot-based films. In *Badlands* (1974), the murderous couple on the run seem more isolated from us, more in their own world, as the slow, objective pace shows them in a stark, cold light.

At the other end of the scale, Todd Solondz's *Welcome to the Dollhouse* (1995) uses a brisk, unsentimental pace to show the tragicomic events occurring in the life of the 11-year-old protagonist. This upbeat tempo belies the film's very poignant themes and rescues it from soap-opera cliché.

In all these examples, you can see how pace matches not the story itself, but the filmmaker's interpretation of the story; it can give a subtle new twist to an otherwise straightforward telling.

Weblinks
http://www.rocliffe.com/   Agency bringing together writers with industry.
http://www.firstfilm.co.uk/sfeedsvc.asp   Script evaluation for low fee.
http://www.moonstone.org.uk/intro.html   Highly regarded European-based agency aimed at helping writers.
http://www.awesomefilm.com/   Downloadable film scripts.
http://www.scriptfactory.co.uk/   News and advice for scriptwriters.
http://www.wcauk.com/   Protect your work by understanding copyright law.

The Crunch

- Write your own script
- Get to know classic structure
- Know other forms of structure
- Use the three acts
- Use a timeline to work out overall structure
- Get to know your core scene
- Use subtext throughout – it makes it more satisfying
- Use a subplot – give the audience a break now and then
- Think in terms of beats within each act – push the tempo up or down according to the action.

Project 6. Core scenes

What this project is for: sorting out priorities in your story
Time: allow about one hour

What this project is about

This very brief exercise is aimed at working out the priorities in your films, about which parts of it are more dominant than others, and can be done when you have a film outlined and planned up to visualization stage. To test it out, you can also apply it to a feature film you know well. The aim is to locate that part of the movie which is the centrepiece, on which the whole film pivots. When you find which scene it is, you can build the film around it and use it as a moment when some of the main features of ideas in the film come to the fore.

Stage 1

First, get hold of a packet of sticky stationery notes. On each note draw sketches of the main scenes in the film. If you can get to at least seven the exercise works more effectively, but it applies to shorts as well as to features.

Stage 2

Look at all the notes and try to find the one that you feel is the most important in the film, the one that you could not do without. This is usually not the big, climactic scene, nor does it have to be the one that explains the story. It is more likely to be the one that seems to sum up the film in that one, single scene by acting as a focal point for the dominant emotions, themes or aims of the film. This centrepiece scene is recognizable by the way it may connect, thematically, to all the other scenes in the film. Borrowing from the theatre, films tend to use a similar idea in which the revelation of the main purpose, theme or message of the film is buried in the middle rather than relegated to the conclusion, where it might be misinterpreted as a mere end-of-story sermon.

Stage 3

Place this image in the middle of a sheet of paper and draw a circle around it. You now have the core of the film, around which all the other parts will revolve.

Stage 4

Now try to divide these scenes into two lots: those on the inner band and those on the outer, drawing a circle between the two. Then take the others and place at varying points around the core scene, at various distances from it, depending on their relative importance.

Now you have a core scene, surrounded by scenes of primary importance, surrounded in turn by scenes that are of secondary importance, including those more functional parts that take the audience from one part of the story to the next.

Example of a core scene

A good example of the key scene that is not necessarily the most loud or impressive is one found in the Michael Mann film *Heat* (1997). The film looks at a gang of crooks and a police officer who is hunting them. The gang is led by Robert De Niro, while the police hunt is led by Al Pacino. Mann knew that the crucial scene of the film would occur when these two charismatic actors confront each other for the first time, although the scene itself is anything but turbulent, taking place in a dreary diner, and is more an oasis of calm in a sometimes violent film. But in terms of the main themes in the film, this scene is indeed the pivotal one, as it brings together the main opposing forces of this duel, while revealing their shared qualities and the more realistic ambiguity of the usual good versus evil equation. The whole film seems to run up to this point like two lines being drawn ever closer. Following this point, the film takes on a different tone, signalling the importance of this moment.

Knowing which scene fulfils this role in your film is important in knowing how to structure the film up to and after that point. Take your time deciding which scene occupies this place, since you are actually settling on the main thematic focus of the film in doing so.

Project 7. Silent movie remake

What this project is for: to learn about structure
Time: allow a few days to plan the movie. Shooting may be no more than one day. Editing will take around four to six hours depending on experience

What this project is about

As we saw right at the start of this section, screenwriting structure is like the skeleton of a movie. If we follow that analogy further, we could say that this next project is going to help us locate and identify the individual bones in a film. To do this, we are going to make a film where we have to take very specific decisions about what is a main scene, what is subplot and what happens within each scene.

In making a silent movie we will be forced to consider the structure of the movie more clearly through the use of caption cards to show the various stages of the plot.

Stage 1: Story

To begin with, we need to find a narrative. The film needs to have a very limited, simple plot with a straightforward linear progression that is obvious to the audience. A narrative action scene is ideal, such as escaping, chasing and so on. This is the easiest way to approach the project, but by all means make it harder for yourself by making the story more complex. In any case, make the movie short, perhaps five minutes in length.

Borrow a scene

A short way to arrive at a useful, action-led scene that involves simple progression of plot is to lift something from a film that you know well. Take something you have seen a number of times and that relies more on visual impact than dialogue.

A silent movie in three acts

The aim is to make a short movie that uses the ideas talked about in this chapter and consists of just three short scenes, corresponding to each of the three acts. So, as an example, a simple chase could have as Act I the main character before being chased, perhaps suspicious that something is about to happen; Act II shows the main action of the chase; Act III takes us to what happens when the chase reaches its climax in the capture of one character by the other.

Use a subplot

Don't forget, we need to include a subplot that will act as a diversion from the main film. If possible, try to avoid the use of flashback, as this may dilute the drama and tension in the film. For example, you could try introducing other characters into the chase who each serve to divert the pursuer from their task, or the pursuee from their escape. Break down the scenes in Acts II and III into small sections, after the action has kicked off, giving each scene:

- a clear aim (to swim across the swollen river)
- an obstacle (he can't swim)
- a dilemma (escape but possibly drown)
- and a reaction (finds a way of crossing without drowning).

In practice, it's going to be hard to cram more than just one or two of these obstacle-dilemma scenes into the short movie. As long as they serve the film's structure, as Act II or III, then you will have gone through the right sort of experience.

Title cards

For the titles it would be useful to have a text generator on your editing software. The vast majority let you do basic titles but there are one or two that don't, and in this case you could add titles by directly filming boards with captions written on, as was the method in the silent era.

Stage 2: Planning

Visualizations

Go through the process as we have seen in the previous chapters in developing the film on paper. Produce a set of visualizations that allow you to devise an overall look to the film and follow these through into storyboards.

Storyboards

At the storyboard stage you can start to consider the way you unravel the action. When you feel you have all the right scenes drawn on paper, cut these up into separate frames. Bunch them together into the beats or units of time we saw earlier in this section. Now you have chunks of the story laid out you can notice the structure of the film. Each chunk becomes a main structural piece, and within these will be smaller pieces involving the actions of the characters.

Stage 3: Shooting

When shooting this sort of film it may be useful to see the solutions that early cinema used to address the absence of sound. Actors tended to act a lot more with the whole body and more dramatically or extravagantly than today.

Tip: use strong lighting

Use lighting much more dramatically to focus attention on the important details in each scene. Rather than set up realistic lighting, try instead something more like what you may see in a theatre, with higher contrast between the dark and light areas, strong shadows and exaggerated colouring. You could even go the whole way and use the kind of devices used widely in silent films, such as the keyhole wipe (blackening the screen except for one small circle, and wiping out from this point or towards it), to draw attention to a particular part of a scene.

Go to: Chapter 5:2 for more ideas about how to get the right sort of lighting and how to avoid the camera reacting badly to creative lighting.

The result of all this is to allow the visual elements to do the talking so that you can more effectively put across the information the audience need. Use the camera far more as an 'explaining' tool, showing the audience clearly what is happening (without going so far that you hand it to them on a plate).

Stage 4: Editing

It is at this stage that we need to become absolutely sure about the structure of the film, which is not set in stone until you start assembling the movie. Paper preparation helps you some of the way, but there is no guarantee that you will get the shots you wanted. When you have logged the footage and assessed which are the good and bad takes, start grouping the footage as you did with your storyboard in the planning stage. It would be useful now to plan the editing of this film on paper, so you could prepare an edit decision list (EDL; see Chapter 7:3) or do a brief, shorthand storyboard. The latter is always preferable if you want to stay aware of visual style throughout the film. Certainly, you need to start to become familiar with the timeline as a tool for assembling the movie on paper and revealing the inner skeleton of the movie.

Where to insert caption breaks

This next stage involves the breaking up of the film into pieces. We are using caption cards which serve to hint what has happened or what is about to happen. These will require us to decide exactly where the *joints* in the film's skeleton are, as it were. In other words, where the key elements in the structure of the movie begin and end. These points will articulate between one scene or beat of the film and the next, but their use is going to have to be strictly rationed so that the overall flow of the movie is sustained.

Let's take this example:

Scene 1. Bob is seen sitting on his sofa, with beer and TV *(caption explaining where we are)*.

Scene 2. The door rings. Bob thinks it is his ex-wife, who he argued with that day, and we realize he has had a bad day, amidst a complicated life. He looks at the photo of a woman on the mantelpiece and we see that normality for Bob is not good *(caption explaining his thoughts)*. After a second ring, Bob casually looks through the curtains and, with a look of horror, steps back, turns off the light and searches for a blunt instrument *(caption as he tries to find something to use)*.

Scene 3. Cut to the figure outside Bob's door. He/it rings again and fingers a pistol held in his jacket.

Scene 4. Bob slams the back door and tries to exit quietly. He knocks over the bin and attracts the figure's attention *(caption articulates Bob's desperate thoughts)*.

Scene 5. Running along the street, Bob flags down a neighbour's car *(caption shows Bob's relief)*. The neighbour thinks he is drunk and drives on *(caption explains the driver's thoughts)*.

If we take the scenes above, we could agree that the first scene is slow and casual. A caption card establishes this scene as one of normality for Bob. Dragging out this scene a little by detailing the homely detritus of his small room allows the audience to sympathize with Bob, essential if we are to be cheerleaders for his journey and escape. The relatively sparse spread of captions indicates a slow pace at this stage. This scene also introduces a subplot as he looks at the faces in the photograph. Subtext, on the other hand, could be more challenging without sound and in such a short film, but is possible with carefully worded captions.

- When Bob finally breaks out of the house we are on to a whole new part of the film, a new structural block where suspense and tension are punctured slightly and replaced by the action of running. Within this block, we see a few encounters, one of which is with the disbelieving neighbour.
- A further caption appears as Bob encounters the neighbour and gets a chance to end the chase, but is foiled by some hint of a previous problem between the two men. Is he a disturbing element in the neighbourhood? Is the neighbour colluding somehow with the mysterious figure? These questions allow us a diversion for a moment and make us see another potential side of Bob, even questioning whether the house we saw at the start is Bob's at all or whether it belongs to his former wife. This momentary stillness in the action allows the film to pause before the next plunge.
- He carries on with his escape. A caption here could indicate that the nightmare is far from over.

At the end of the exercise we can see how the film has been paced by the caption cards, which have allowed the action to progress but have now and then slowed it down. Towards the end of the movie we see more captions than at the start, but these will have fewer statements and may be more punchy and precise.

Evaluation

This project has allowed us to see how a film can be broken down into chunks and that these pieces are precisely moulded and shaped to fit the purposes of the film. Some are short, some long, some fast, some slow, but all play a part in pointing the film in the right direction, but not taking us there so quickly and predictably that we can guess the next moves.

- Plot a timeline chart showing the peaks and troughs of drama throughout the film. Is the film too slow at the start? Is the action over too quickly when it gets going?

- How did you use the caption cards? They should not interrupt an event but should signal its imminent arrival. Did you find they were placed more frequently at some points than others, and how did the wording of these affect the way other people may read the film?
- Using a different timeline, map the appearance of each character in the film. Do insignificant characters take up too much time and is the main character on screen enough?
- Look at your editing. Does the purpose of each segment of the film match the kind of editing you adopted for that bit? For example, does a slow, introductory scene use fast, accelerated editing, or does a scene with lots of action have long slow cuts?
- Take a microscopic look at the film. Have a look at one particular scene and see whether it breaks down into the kind of parts we outlined earlier: goal, obstacle, reaction, next scene and so on. Produce a timeline of that scene and try to see how you have edited the different shots together and whether the purpose of that scene was served by the shots you included. Watch out for sudden diversions mid-scene, or interruptions that break the chain of cause-and-effect that you have set up. If this cause-and-effect seems unclear in the way you have recorded the shots or the way you have edited them, try to find out which shots are at fault or which are missing.
- Finally, as with every film, look for the way the various elements of your film synthesize into one artefact. Does the lighting reflect the mood of the film? Does the sound or music add or detract from the aims of each scene? Does your framing of each scene convey information or does it leave too many unanswered simple questions about the plot? In summary, is everything in the movie pulling in the same direction?

I want something more challenging

If this project didn't stretch you enough, try making a different version. In this one you could try a storyline that does not focus so much on action but more on character or situation. This will ask you to look more closely at the more subtle signs that tell us when different parts of the film begin and end. For instance, if you are trying to depict the stages in feeling of someone whose date didn't show up, you could show worry, anticipation, anger and then resignation. Each of these stages is a chunk of the film. You would show that a new chunk of the film has started by changing camera style slightly, or editing style. Consider how to signal each stage, in the way that the caption cards do, perhaps using a fade to black at these points.

5. Alternative script structure

The classic structure detailed above takes the audience on a journey and then returns them to a point at which the story started, albeit in an altered state. Like the protagonist, they will have learned something of value along the way. It could be termed a circular structure due to its enclosed shape. One aspect of this shape is that its predictability lulls the audience into a state of consciousness where they suspend disbelief readily as they lose sight of the mechanics of the structure – in short, they forget they are watching a film – and instead get involved with the characters. In doing so it lends them some control, in a sense, because they know what to expect and know the rules. But it isn't too restrictive either – it bends sufficiently to allow deviations now and then.

A different model of movie: the branch

A radically different model exists, however, which offers possibilities that the circular structure cannot. We could call this 'the branch', since it starts with a single thread and then divides, in a kind of Fibonacci sequence, as each new limb splinters, resulting in a branch-like appearance.

How it works

Act I

As we can see in Figure 4.9, the single limb starts our movie. We are given a thread to focus on but also see other seemingly unconnected branches. Limbs curve back from later in the movie and nudge up against these early stages. Their displacement causes us to remember them.

This model also uses the three-act structure, but in a different way. In the first act we are introduced to what we assume is the main branch in the film – the location and characters and their motivations. The plot, however, is not the central stem as it would be in mainstream films. Instead, we have to make do with the characters' motivations – but we may be given some unnerving displaced elements thrown in at this stage to keep us involved. These could be new characters who pose mysterious threats, or unsettling moments where there is the possibility of having to rethink what we have seen so far.

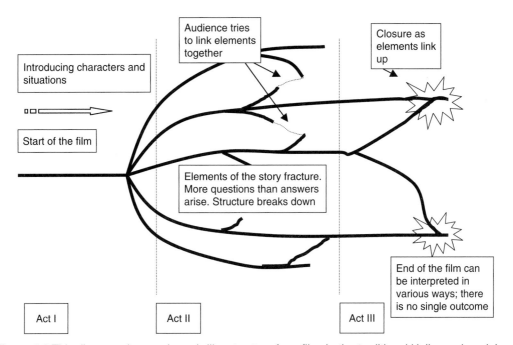

Figure 4.9 This diagram shows a branch-like structure for a film. In the traditional Hollywood model based on a circular structure there is little room for interpretation or for the audience to form their own ideas. In this model, not all elements of the film are explained, leaving clues that the viewer can piece together.

Act II

As we go on in the movie we approach the nearest we have to the crisis seen in the circular structure. In that model, the crisis exists within the fictional world the movie created for us: aliens invade, a marriage ends, a death occurs and so on. In this model, however, the crisis takes place outside this fictional world and is taken into the realm of the audience. In the mind of the viewer the film starts to break down, certainties dissolve and the film starts to lose its shape. We no longer know what sort of film we are watching as our ideas of genre, roles and story expectations are confounded. Sometimes this is achieved through a very sudden rupture of the plot: characters change names or we might shift to another point of view, throwing new light on the movie's events.

The effect on the viewer is internally traumatic and yet this is precisely the moment when they are wholly drawn into the movie. They are stuck with the conflicting signs and yet are determined to unknot them. They have a two-fold job: to figure out current events and to reorder the past events in the movie. In so doing, this 'hook' of rupture or disintegration draws them in. At the point when the movie starts to fall about around them they step in and do what we are all programmed to do: make sense of it. The trick for the director is to make an achievable task rather than an abstract wild goose chase.

You can only set this process up for the viewer if the individual elements – the separate branches – are clearly defined. Often, this is done through utilizing genre conventions so that elements are, almost literally, from different films. The case study of *Mulholland Drive* at the end of this section describes this. If the audience can clearly identify and label the branches, then they can start working on bunching them together. It takes a particular mind, however, to make each branch similar enough for links to be forged, but also different enough for clear identification. Again, this is where simple genre devices help, as they 'colour' each branch while allowing its form to retain continuity with other branches. In practice, this means using devices such as camera framing, style of shooting (the sections of TV soaps in Oliver Stone's *Natural Born Killers*) and use of genre-specific props or people (the French New Wave girl in *Pulp Fiction*) to differentiate sections while leaving characters the same.

By the end of this central crisis, the viewer has bonded with the film – or walks out of the theatre – and is then further challenged to step into the movie and influence its outcome. Again, this is not in terms of the internal story of the fictional movie world, but in terms of what is to become the main stem branch of the movie and which other branches pair up and form stronger elements.

This is a busy time for the movie and its partner, the viewer, as the branches break off thick and fast to form splinter branches. Ideas and possibilities appear and disappear. The job for the viewer is the forging of ties and connections between branches. Clues laid by the filmmaker explicitly help the viewer through motif and symbol. But the director purposely lays out more branches than is needed in order to increase the likelihood that there will be more ideas and themes than was intended by the filmmaker. In this way the film achieves an afterlife in which connections are made long after the movie has ended.

Figure 4.10 Arin Crumley and Susan Bruice's self-financed movie, *Four-Eyed Monsters*, was proclaimed as the best unreleased film of 2005.

Act III

By this stage, the fragmentary nature of Act II has given way to a more pruned structure, where the viewer cancels out certain stems of the branch and stakes a claim to others that are more important. But at no time is there a pointlessly loose stem; everything is there for a reason. But let's just take a look at what we mean by 'reason'. In the circular model we could say that everything is there for a purpose, suggesting that everything will lead *to* somewhere. This model offers the reverse. It suggests that everything arose *from* somewhere and this is what gives it a place in the film. Each stem arose from the same central stem but its direction is uncertain. In the first, you know where you are going; in the second, you know where you came from.

The trope

This rupturing of the movie also has its parallels in literature. In literary theory, a trope is a twist that suddenly gives all the signs in the movie up to that point a new relationship to one another. For example, Bruce Willis discovers he is a ghost in *The Sixth Sense*, we discover the protagonist's real gender in *The Crying Game*, or we find out that Norman's mother is actually a figment of his imagination in *Psycho*. In each case, everything is different after this point. It is a satisfying point for the audience, but more so if they did not guess it beforehand.

The trope in the branch model is brought forward to the centre of the film but is not, as we have seen, a plot element that can be explained fully and fits into the rest of the film. It is outside of the story and exists in the very structure of the film itself. To use a metaphor, a trope in the classic circular film model is like having a glass of water where the drink itself changes but the vessel stays the same. In this model, the vessel (the structure of the film) changes, requiring the water (the stuff that actually happens in the film) to flow in new ways.

Closure

Ultimately, the point of completion or closure in this kind of film comes when the audience successfully ties branches together and assigns meaning to the outcome. The director may have preferred outcomes but may be more positive about unexpected outcomes determined by the audience. This is the film's afterlife, as it mutates and grows in the mind of the viewer later.

Case Study: *Mulholland Drive* (David Lynch)

Mulholland Drive represents a high point in what could be termed David Lynch's mature period – a series of films which are the clearest manifestations of his ideas, as opposed to earlier films such as *The Elephant Man* or *Dune*, which played with almost a vaudeville style to provoke the dislocation he seems to seek. By the mid-1990s, however, he had started to place his characters in suburban settings, in recognizable worlds and with pulp stories. This breakthrough for Lynch meant that he had a foil against which he could use structure and genre-specific displacements to unsettle us.

In this movie, Lynch rises to the peak of his mischievous craft by employing daring devices such as changing actors and names as if on a carousel. In this way the crisis he provokes is sudden, within a single scene, halfway through the movie. We see that the actor is no longer who she was, names have changed and there are new relationships between the characters to understand. It is the structural equivalent of the jump cut in editing – a cut that disrupts space or time in some way. It is the very essence of the trope.

Elsewhere, Lynch lays the groundwork for possible red herrings. We are introduced to characters and events that seem unrelated to the main plot (such as it is), which seems to centre on the arrival in Los Angeles of Betty, a would-be actress. In film noir style, an amnesiac femme fatale hides out in her new apartment and both are drawn into a series of strange events. However, the supposed red herrings are actually central to the later disruption of the film. For instance, near the beginning a policeman recounts a nightmare of a creature who lives behind the café they are eating in. When we see the creature, we don't forget him but he disappears from the movie. It is only at the very end of the film, when he reappears, that the significance of this branch becomes apparent. Lynch suggests that we tie this branch to another completely separate one, in which an elderly couple help the newly arrived Betty at LA airport. In so doing, he radically reorganizes the relationships in the film one last time, leaving us mystified but also convinced that we can now assemble the movie. This search is rewarding and fruitful for the audience – all the more so when we see the next Lynch movie and see motifs from this and other films that suggest new ideas and relationships (for instance, the use of stage singers or curtains). Where Lynch succeeds is through his careful understanding of the need not to make us work without a prize – this isn't abstract Warhol-style cinema.

Ultimately, however, the audience manipulate the different branches in the film and whatever conclusions they come to, Lynch prescribes that each will have a certain flavour or tone. This effect is rather like a montage sequence of disparate images with no apparent connection (see Eisenstein or Walter Ruckman). We see each image, wrap one around another, try to make sense of it all, but end up with a flavour or atmosphere as the dominant result.

Project 8. New movie structures

What this project is for: to figure out how alternative movie structures work
Time: allow around two hours or more

What this project is about

In Chapter 4:5 we looked at alternative means of telling a story. In this case, the film was concerned with more than just the events going on in the plot; it was as much about the way the film is structured and about the ideas in it. The philosophical side to the movie was the main driving force behind it. To achieve this we saw how the shape of this kind of film could be described as like a branch, consisting of a central stem and several limbs leading off from it.

This project is about physically tracking the course of this kind of film and seeing how various stems can join up to create new themes and ideas. If you are working on a movie idea that needs this kind of structure, use it for this exercise. If you are not, try to map an existing film, such as those directed by David Lynch or written by Charlie Kaufman. For classics, try Luis Buñuel's *Un Chien Andalou*.

Stage 1

You will need several metres of thick string and about 20 card tags like those that you fix to your luggage when flying, usually a few inches square with elastic bands on one corner.

Take one long piece of string, about a metre or so. Label this as the main starting theme. Then tie further pieces of string to this stem and label these as story pieces which venture away from the main stem, or seem unconnected to it. Place each piece roughly in proportion to where it appears in the timeline of the film, with elements that appear early being tied near the start of the main stem and so on.

After a while you may have an intricate web of the film showing the separate ideas contained within it. It will then be possible to tie together certain of these pieces of string to make new connections. At these points, place more labels to show what has been forged by the new combination. For instance, in *Mulholland Drive*, we could have one piece of string that is tied a few inches from the start and is labelled 'elderly couple who help Betty on the plane'. This piece of string then stretches off to the side without seemingly going anywhere. Sure enough, it is some time before we see how to tie this piece up: at the end of the movie, the couple reappear and storm the apartment of the much reduced Betty, causing her death, so we could tie this piece up to the main stem of Betty's life at this point. We could also tie the 'elderly couple' string to the one labelled 'weird man who lives behind the diner'. Perhaps only a David Lynch film would offer this combination, so his work is particularly apt for this project.

Evaluation

With this sort of film it is not appropriate to suggest definite ways that elements of the movie tie up together. The whole idea is that it is a process which is open to interpretation, depending on who the viewer is. But this relativism only extends to how the different parts tie up together. What can be predicted is the fact that a certain number of these will tie up, that the new combinations they make can themselves tie up with others and so on, and in particular that there will be few, if any, loose ends.

So the only way to evaluate this exercise is by looking at whether ties have been made at all. If they have, then you have managed to create a structure to a film where ideas can be brought together in almost endless variations. You will notice how certain ideas (or pieces of string) were orphaned and did not manage to make connections. Try to work out what it was about these parts of the film that made them break away. Were they too divergent to the rest of the film or too similar perhaps? And what made the successful pieces of string so able to be tied up with other ideas? Was it the symbolism they carried? Or was it a small, almost unnoticed, link that let it mix with other ideas? It is all questions and few answers, but stimulating nonetheless. If you found it so then your audience may also.

I want something more challenging

This exercise is already fairly challenging but grandmaster versions could be made where you don't just restrict yourself to main elements in the film or 'story strands'. You could add another mental layer to it by making links with individual symbols and motifs, music, names, colours and so on. For instance, two very different strands may actually converge earlier than first thought by the shared use of certain symbols or locations.

With some directors it is also possible to push this further with links to other films, suggesting an over-all and unique artistic consciousness. Suitable directors could include Pedro Almodovar, Alfred Hitchcock, Roman Polanski or Jane Campion.

6. Devising stories for low budgets

Narrative is about telling the audience about a series of events and engaging that audience to sympathize with one or other party in those events. Questions of why, what, when, where and how are essential if the cog-wheels of the film are to turn correctly and if the audience are to stay with you. You are in control of the information the audience need to take part in the plot; give them too much and they will feel patronized and bored, too little and you lose them.

One of the most difficult aspects of narrative is the necessity to compress time as you juggle the wide-ranging elements of the story against your resources and the duration of the film. In most films, this is achieved through editing to suggest the passage of time or to suggest parallel events that were actually recorded weeks apart.

Film View

Biographical movies often have to deal with the passage of time on a large scale, such as *Raging Bull* (Martin Scorsese, 1980), in which details of the life of boxer Jake La Motta are compressed into 129 minutes. *The Godfather Part II* (Francis Ford Coppola, 1974) attempts to unfold two lives stretching 60 years in 200 minutes. Stylistic elements are commonly used to show that one scene is set in a different time from another, as seen in *The Godfather Part II* when a sepia tone colours scenes set at the turn of the century.

For the low/no-budget filmmaker, the most compelling factor in drawing up a script is what level of funding is available for the film. As we saw in Chapter 4:1, 'Working out a budget', it can actually be a source of creativity to be starved of funds. Many filmmakers are forced to be more ingenious than their better-salaried peers because they know they have to grab attention through good filmmaking craft rather than expensive props and effects.

Narrative costs

Regarding the actual story you choose, working with a low budget requires you to handle certain restrictions to the kinds of movies you can make. If you visit film festivals you quickly become aware of an absence of potentially expensive genres in debut films. Character-led movies are more common than science fiction; films set in the here and now are more common than period costume dramas. Don't immediately drop plans you may have which seem to contradict this; there are always ways around problems of resources, locations, costumes, but the low-budget filmmaker needs to be far more ingenious in finding solutions than their studio counterparts. Independent filmmakers are noted for their dogged way at working within a frustratingly tight budget. Imaginative shooting and editing will go some way towards this, and optical effects are increasingly viable through digital software. You may also find that when people find out that your film is a low-budget, do-it-yourself production, made outside of the normal production framework, they may be prepared to help out, give free access to locations, props and so on.

Potentially expensive story elements

- *Historical setting*. Costumes and dressed locations are expensive. Films set in the future can present less of a problem if you agree with the visions laid out in, for instance, the Mad Max movies, a post-apocalyptic world of decay.
- *Uniforms*. Anything official and realistic will need to be hired.
- *Stunts*. You should always use a trained stunt performer for any stunts, not only to prevent actors' broken limbs but because legal issues and insurance are easier to deal with if you employ an experienced stunt person. If you can't get a stunt performer, cut that part of the script.
- *Insurance*. You can't avoid it, but you can limit scenes which are high risk, avoiding potentially dangerous situations for actors or crew (most accidents on set involve crew, not cast). Check also what cover you have for equipment, on your existing personal insurance.

Figure 4.11 Stories set in the here and now present fewer problems for the no budget filmmaker. Test shot by filmmaker Chris Carr.

- *Heavy make-up and prosthetics*. Expensive, if you want good quality. If you need unusual make-up effects, try recruiting students from theatrical make-up courses, who may be willing to work for costs only.
- *Too many locations*. Transport and hospitality will add much to the budget. Stay local, where crew can return to their own homes. If you need to visit locations, don't plan to go to more than one each day.
- *Permission for street filming*. If you are working with more than a small (half a dozen or so) crew, you may need to get permission – and pay for it – for filming in public places, especially metro lines, streets, public buildings and so on. Smaller towns and cities can be much more co-operative than well-used main cities. For example, Scottish city Glasgow has tried to welcome filmmakers to the city, aware of the benefits of boosting tourism. Some cities have dedicated film officers at the local authority offices.
- *Extras (crowd scenes)*. Even if your production is rained off, you still pay the extras for turning up. Try recruiting local people, or place notices with amateur drama societies, some of whom may be willing to appear for more manageable fees.

Making the most of a low budget

Use what you have

Many low-budget films have taken shape purely in response to what the director has access to. *Clerks* (Kevin Smith, 1994) is a good example, made for less than $28 000. If this film was made entirely on digital equipment today, the budget could probably lose a zero off that figure. For this very successful debut feature, Smith was able to use the convenience store he worked in late at night and involved many friends as the cast. The action is entirely within the shop and it is the witty, sharp dialogue and perfect timing that make this such a classic of independent film. Using this approach should encourage you to make an inventory of the locations and props (and even people) that could be used to make a movie. It takes filmmaking out of the studio and makes it a more flexible ground-level art form; as one filmmaker said, 'My garage is my Hollywood.'

Low-budget ideas in action

To put this to the test, let's try a few examples of the very basic ingredients that make some movies:

- **Idea 1.** An empty warehouse available free for a couple of weeks, some (slightly mean-looking) friends and some suits. The result: *Reservoir Dogs* (Quentin Tarantino, 1991).
- **Idea 2.** Two people, a script which they helped to write, the streets around your city. The result: *Before Sunset* (Richard Linklater, 2004).
- **Idea 3.** A bunch of interesting-looking friends, but not much else. The result: acclaimed independent movie, *Happiness* (Todd Solondz, 1998).

This exercise may be half-serious but it does reveal that underneath quality filmmaking with great ideas the actual potential cost of these movies is minimal. Clearly, with 90-minute films, expenses are going to rise no matter what you do, but compared to a large studio you have the ability to turn in a film like those above on a very small budget, and that is a skill the large studios would pay you dearly for, so nurture it.

Write your own screenplay

As we saw in Chapters 4:4 and 4:5, many filmmakers prefer to use stories they have originated themselves, enabling them to maintain more control over what they make. Free software is available on the Internet to help you compose a screenplay in a conventional format.

Acquire a published story

It is not really advisable in the low/micro-budget sector to use published work, but if you are determined there are many people, as you can guess, who will help you part with your money.

Optioning

It is less expensive to take what is known as 'an option' on a story than an outright acquisition. Optioning means that you have said you are very interested and need to go away and raise the finance. Options usually last for 18 months and you will need to engage an entertainment lawyer to handle the contractual side of the process. Working with a story will usually be far cheaper than acquiring a finished screenplay, for the reason that you are not buying a finished, ready-to-shoot product.

Out-of-copyright stories

But don't forget the ultimately cheap option: older stories may be out of copyright under the 100-year rule, but before you commit yourself check with the estate handling an author's work if you are unsure whether copyright has expired; such estates can be highly litigious.

True stories

Again, this option is more expensive than simply coming up with stories yourself. If you have read an article or heard about a true story that you would like to use as the basis of a film, you need to tread carefully. There is no doubt that such stories can and do make fascinating – and award-winning – films including *Erin Brockovich* (Steven Soderbergh, 2000) and *The Insider* (Michael Mann, 1999). But beware of the subjects of these stories taking action against you during or after production.

Film View

In the seminal documentary *The Thin Blue Line* (1988), director Errol Morris pursued a death-row convict's story, eventually proving his innocence, only to find himself being sued for the return of the life story rights by newly freed Randall Adams. Stories told second-hand, where the original protagonist is masked in some way but the general thrust of the story is retained, include *Taxi Driver* (Martin Scorsese, 1976) and *Rope* (Alfred Hitchcock, 1948). But you cannot guarantee that the participants in the real-life events will ignore the potential reward from following you through the court should the film make large profits.

The Crunch

- Narrative films need careful handling so we know what is happening
- Build a story around props or places you have available for free
- Write your own screenplay
- Small-scale stories are low-budget stories
- Avoid expensive genres – make films about people, not falling asteroids
- Use the close-up to learn about telling a story.

Project 9. Revealing subtext in your movie

What this project is for: to learn how to get hidden meanings in your films
Time: allow about two hours to view and note the movie

What this project is about

The aim of this project is to investigate subtext and to see how to find it. It is in just about everyone's movies, but if left unidentified will point in several different directions at once, so the meanings will be all over the place. It is also useful to see how hidden meanings can form threads in your work, highlighting ideas or themes you didn't know you were interested in.

Stage 1

Take a copy of a storyboard of a film you have made recently. This can be a drama or non-narrative; documentary work is less easy to use in this project.

If you have no films suitable, take a clip from someone else's movie of around three minutes in length and storyboard it briefly.

Stage 2

Watch the film that you based the storyboard on and note below each image in just one or two words what you think the subtext is. For instance, a sequence showing a man gathering possessions and preparing to move out from an apartment could be summarized as 'change, regret, hope, anticipation' and so on.

Stage 3

You will have ended up with a list of descriptions of each scene, summarizing each scene and saying what is really going on beneath the action.

Evaluation

Go through the words you came up with to describe each scene. Circle those that appear more than once. What do these words tell you about the kinds of ideas you have in your films? From all these subtextual pieces, can you see a single thread that connects them? To find this, try to group words together under general headings. For instance, a series of words such as 'moving, leaving, going away, starting, ending, finding new places', all could be grouped under the word 'change'.

I want something more challenging

Take the same movie and try looking next for symbols and motifs. In this exercise, you will need to arrange your ideas in columns on paper, so that in the first column you have the scene described, the second column shows the subtext, the third symbols and the fourth motifs. To push yourself further here, try adding a new drawing after these columns to show a better way of showing what you have identified. For instance, in the words listed above, could the general summary word of 'change' be shown more succinctly or in a more subtle way?

Project 10. Symbolism in the movies

What this project is for: to look for symbols and motifs in movies
Time: allow around one hour for the paper version, three hours for the video version

What this project is about

This project is designed to help identify where the meaning in a film appears. It is easy to talk about what a certain film is all about, what its themes are or underlying ideas, but less easy to say exactly where these are on screen at any given moment. This project allows you to do just that. And if you can do it with feature films it will be possible to reverse the process and place symbols in your own films for the audience to find. This project allows you to see that certain symbols such as colours, objects, shapes or places can have significance for the story and can be easy to identify. It also shows how recurring symbols of a more general nature can be called motifs.

Stage 1

Find a movie you have seen and have found fascinating. There are no restrictions here and you don't need to choose especially art-house movies. There are several classics that are particularly useful, outlined below. Find a particular scene that you feel is pivotal in the movie; it is less likely to be a scene with lots of action and probably a quieter moment of suspense or heightened emotion.

Stage 2

Read Chapter 3:2, 'How films work'. Try to see how to spot the difference between a symbol and any other part of the picture, based on what is described in the chapter. Notice how symbols reinforce the themes that underpin the film and how motifs can be strong presences in a film, taking us straight to the heart of the film's ideas.

Stage 3

You have a choice here – you can either load the clip you are analysing onto your PC or work on it by analysing on paper. The video version is more fun and helps develop ideas of using text.

Go to: Chapter 7:6, 'Working with text', for help on using text.

For the video version, place the clip onto the timeline and splice the clip into separate cuts so you can see where the film is edited.

For the paper version, storyboard the movie clip over several sheets of paper. But make sure the individual frames are no smaller than a CD box.

Stage 4

For the video version, isolate individual frames that you think contain interesting symbols and freeze them. Then use the text tool to write directly onto each frame. Look for visual symbols and motifs and circle them, writing next to them what they really mean. Use colours to highlight them so you can distinguish one from another more easily.

By the end you should have frames with scribbled words and shapes highlighting the visually significant parts of certain frames.

Good examples for analysis

Blade Runner (Ridley Scott). Try the scene where Deckard (Harrison Ford) gets escorted from the rainy city streets to the police captain, or blade runner's, office. It's about five to ten minutes into the film and includes shots of the streets, the flight to the office, the discussion with the captain.
Look for: images of eyes; signs of far eastern culture; signs of technology; references to film noir movies; origami.
The Shining (Stanley Kubrick, 1980). Try the scene where Jack (Jack Nicholson) plays ball in the foyer of the deserted hotel. Danny and Wendy enter the maze outside and Jack watches a model of the maze in the foyer.
Look for: labyrinths; one-point perspective; fire; Jack's expression. Where else is there a maze in the hotel – is Jack a maze? Is the hotel itself a maze?
Elephant (Gus Van Sant, 2003). Look for the scene where the two boys who later become killers meet at home. One plays video games while the other plays Beethoven's Für Elise on the piano.
Look for: the landscape of the video game; the revolving 360-degree camera shot; the juxtaposition of video game with music. Does the game look like a real one to you? What about the landscape of the game, all frozen wastes and emptiness? And aren't those people too easy to shoot at?

Evaluation

In either version you will have emerged with a complete translation of the film into simple terms. All the hidden meanings will be revealed and the specific ways they have been placed in the frame highlighted.

This may enable you to then use symbols more freely in your own work.

I want something more challenging

Try taking a clip from more challenging films where you need to see the whole movie before symbolism is revealed. Concentrate on one small part of the movie as you did above. Choose a movie with less obvious meanings such as *In the Mood For Love* (Wong-Kar Wai, 2000) or *Dogville* (Lars von Trier,

2003) (really tough without props – can camera and composition convey what we need?), and even documentaries such as *Bowling for Columbine* (Michael Moore, 2002) or *Capturing the Friedmans* (Andrew Jarecki, 2003), for the use of symbolic imagery (for instance, the archive footage of the young girl dancing in *Friedmans*).

Part 3: Visuals

7. Visualizing your film

Planning a film is different from director to director. Some will insist on a very clear idea of what they are making before production, others will opt for the more risky approach of letting some elements develop on set. At one end of the spectrum, some directors find that the actual process of committing a story to film is less interesting than the long gestation period, over a year or more, when they are able to invent and re-invent the film, subtly changing it and deepening it with layers of meaning. Other directors prefer to organize the film as a set of bases to touch, leaving the precise look and detail of the film until shooting.

The process of production for most art forms is centred on the personal; the artist is in direct control over a painting, as the writer is over a novel. The absence of people or technology to get between the artist and the artefact allows much greater freedom in how such works are developed. In film and video, however, the number of people involved, even a very small crew, can depersonalize the work. If you are not careful, the resulting film can be the sum of several individuals working with their own ideas rather than several people with one idea. This is not to say that working creatively with other people is unwise; on the contrary, it is the involvement of others that forces a film towards its highest peak of development. But at the tip of this pyramid of creative people and ideas there needs to be one single vision to carry the film forward. This can be the result of one person's efforts or several, but it does need to be fixed in advance of production, on paper, as a blueprint.

Interview

'On any low-budget film, planning is crucial to the success of the project. Every second the camera is running it is costing you money, so you do not want to waste valuable time and money reshooting. It is no good simply turning up on the day and making it up as you go ... if you try that it will only lead to stress and a bad film.'

David Norman, filmmaker, UK

Translating words into images

One of the most difficult aspects of developing a film is trying to translate the words you may have that describe your proposed film into images that can be realized on camera.

This inevitably involves much compromise and change as the ideas form themselves into a workable, practical list of shots. This aspect of development is one where you partly make it up as you go, noticing the shape your ideas take as you commit them to paper. It is only later, when you have studied the visualizations, that you come to select the shots that will go into the final storyboard.

Visualizing involves sketching ideas. You do not have to feel confident about being able to draw; the aim of sketching in this context is to communicate information as clearly as possible about the angle of the camera and the arrangement of objects within the shot, so you need only draw as you would for diagrams.

Visualizing methods

- Begin by being as precise as possible about the ideas you are trying to convey.
- Find several words that describe the scene you are trying to visualize; these can be as abstract or descriptive as you like.
- From these words, sketch images that show how you see that scene in your mind. It is better to sketch without first drawing a frame; just freely doodle on paper, as you might when your logical mind is otherwise engaged on the telephone.
- When you have finished a set of sketches regarding a scene, add rectangular frames that show what you would leave in the frame if you were shooting.

The advantage of drawing first and adding boxes later is that it allows you to toy with several ideas for frames on the same sketch, as can be seen in Figure 4.12.

The key here is being relaxed and not hurrying the process; you need to filter the idea for a scene through your subconscious, allowing it to pass out with a shape unique to your particular view. Your drawings will show where your preferences lie and indicate what you could call *style*: the particular way that your ideas manifest themselves, unique to you. As we will see throughout each project, it is this pursuit of self-knowledge as a filmmaker that will characterize your development.

What do you draw?

When sketching, you are trying to depict a range of elements in the film. These include:
- The arrangement of the various props and actors in the scene
- The intensity of direction of light cast
- Colours that may dominate a scene
- The amount of contrast between light and dark
- Possible camera movements, such as sideways (tracking shot), rotation from a fixed point (panning shot) or zoom
- Images or text layered over the main image.

You may not be aware of each of these as you draw, but may go back to sketches later and add to them to include most of the above.

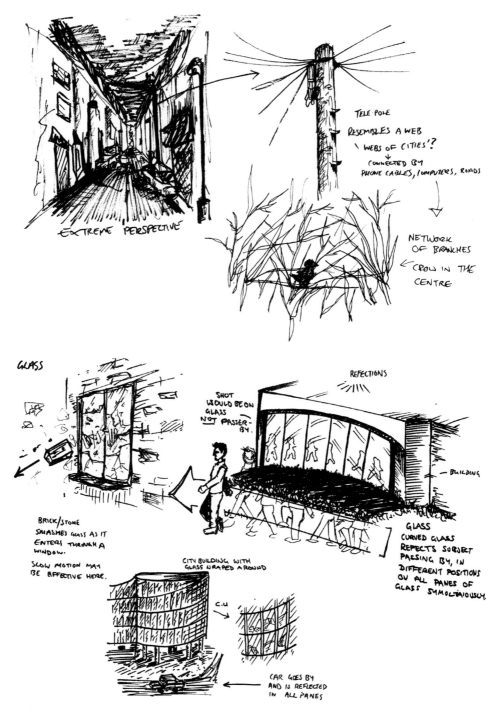

Figure 4.12 These sketches from the early stages of a short movie, *Crow's Vanity* (Jon Price, 2001), detail the filmmaker's attempts to develop images to match a poem. See more of Price's visual work in Chapter 4:8, 'Storyboards and visual tools'.

Developing ideas into pictures

When visualizing, the aim is to take fast steps towards the very best ideas you can come up with. It is rare that these are the first ideas you have and there are ways of getting from that initial blunt idea to a more defined, less predictable one.

This process rests on the route of going from a first, obvious idea through to a more advanced version of it, working out your ideas on paper as you go. The following is an example of one filmmaker's thought processes on a particular scene. The scene required that a man enters a house, intending to steal whatever can be found. It's very straightforward, but the filmmaker did not want to film this sort of overused scene in a predictable way.

- **Idea 1** (most predictable idea, thought up in a second or so). This suggested that the camera is placed outside, looking at the man, recording in a fairly direct way.
- **Idea 2** (less predictable). A second drawing suggested that the camera instead looks from inside the bedroom, as the man attempts to force it open.
- **Idea 3** (other ideas are rejected in favour of something more unusual). The third drawing takes it a step further, suggesting that, instead, the camera dwells on something else to cut to occasionally. In this case, the filmmaker thought of someone preparing a meal in the kitchen. Besides showing the prospective thief, we also cut to and from images of cooking. When the thief breaks the window an egg goes rolling off the worktop; when he later leaves the house we cut to an image of a meal in an oven burning. This disrupts something – the meal – we can all relate to and suggests the disruption to the house rather than actually have to show it.

The aim of developing an idea further is to get into the habit of a more advanced way of communicating.

Tip   Another good way to develop your visual ideas is to use a small artist's wooden mannequin and arrange it in the way you would want your actor to move. Photograph it using a digital stills camera. You can then use a program like Adobe After Effects to roughly composite the stills together to make a rough outline.

Sketching with video

Although development on paper affords you the chance to think wildly and come up with diverse ways of shooting a scene, there are other ways that can help you to visualize. Try using the camera as a sketching tool. This means losing the idea that each frame you take has to have some purpose and simply seeing how locations or people look on the screen. It is difficult to imagine how a scene will look until you shoot it and by that time you have already invested heavily in time and money. It would be more useful to have produced some rough video shots of the place where you will film, under certain lighting conditions, with or without the actors, to see in advance how it looks when viewed on the rectangle of the screen. In many cases, a place or person can seem mundane until viewed through the lens;

they then reveal their cinematic qualities. Video sketching in this way enables you to experiment with new camera angles which you could not necessarily sketch on paper.

Play with the camcorder

There is also a great deal to be gained from simply playing with the camera, seeing how the world looks through the lens. The more you get used to the way filming alters the world, the more you are able to recognize locations, settings, people that work well on the screen. A location such as a train station is a good example. Seen as a participant in the chaos and movement, standing on the platform, you may be deluged with visual information coming at you from all sides. But when you look through the lens on your camera you order that environment and you start to notice, for instance, how the roof structure of the station helps you form a good composition or how the perspective lines of the track look good with people standing alongside.

The Crunch

- Planning is crucial
- Don't let the film stay in your head until shooting – you must see it on paper early
- Sketch basic images without thinking about scenes
- Develop words into images
- Progress your ideas further by more sketching
- An hour of planning is worth a week of shooting
- If you start filming and have not done enough planning, your crew and actors may lose faith in the production.

8. Storyboards and visual tools

In the last section we noted how a film needs to be visualized first on paper before you pick up a camera. In this section we need to see how to collate these visuals together into a coherent whole.

Why plan at all?

Planning helps to devise ways to show the events of a film more clearly. It is aimed at presenting the audience with the highest possible development of your idea. In so doing, chances are you will represent their world back to them from a fresh point of view. It is rare that images arrived at on set with no prior thought can achieve a level of interest and meaning of images conceived on paper, rejected and superseded by better images.

Why plan visually?

In making a film you are making a piece of art, just as much as if you were doing a painting or a sculpture. But it might be tempting to think that since you are making a moving image you should get straight down to working with stuff that moves. Why bother doing still images when the art form you work in seems far removed from drawing or painting?

The quick answer is that movies are nothing but lots of still images strung together. But that is not the whole story. Movies are far more than just movement and action. The illusion that they so successfully create depends also on convincing us of the reality of what we are seeing, and this is often done through visual phenomena like depth, space and colour. It gets more complicated immediately you bring these into play. For example, if you show a long shot of a street disappearing into the horizon, you can amplify the importance of whatever action is about to take place there (see the opening to the riot scenes in *Pleasantville*); if you show a wide-angle shot with lots of space around a character you suggest that they are isolated and vulnerable or perhaps a maverick (see the prelude to the crop-spraying attack in *North by Northwest*); and if you subtly include a red scarf in the corner of the shot when a murder is being discovered you heighten the alarming effect (see the body in the river in *Don't Look Now*). Each of the scenes mentioned here would be vastly different if different visual tools had been used. But the master filmmakers of each one incorporated their knowledge of what looks good in art to make their films look good.

The kind of resonance they achieved is possible because they are making us see the world differently. Film professor and writer Haig P. Manoogian suggested that:

> 'It is often remarked that people listen but do not hear. What is true of our hearing is also true of our sight. We see, but do not perceive. The successful filmmaker must see for us [and] must open our eyes, provide meaning for what we see and thereby break through our isolation.'

Different ways of preparing

A film needs a sense of overall design if it is to become a fully developed movie with its own inner logic, structure and style. How this design is arrived at has many variations, from a detailed plan to a sketched outline of images. We could think of this sort of plan as consisting of various elements similar to a map, depicting the route between the start and end of a journey. If we take this analogy further, some people would prefer a very detailed map on a small scale, showing not only the overall route but also where the possible problem areas are, and get to know exactly what the journey will look like. They will then be able to reassure themselves that the journey will be successful before committing time and money.

Interviews

'I find storyboards essential – I need to see how my story is looking. Drawing up the shot list and having a storyboard means that you are beginning to see how your film looks. I work out quite a lot in the storyboard stage, but with no budget it does mean that as ideas change these aren't necessarily reflected in the storyboard.'

Debra Watson, filmmaker, UK

'It's a really good idea to get a great storyboard artist so that you can create the film on paper before shooting to see how it might look. This gives you time to plan the shots to get the most from the camera.'

Paul Cowling, executive producer, Starving *(2000)*

On the other hand, there would be others who would prefer a map showing only the main points on the journey, the must-visit places and general compass direction of the route. This person would be more likely to make the journey precisely for the reason that it is unknown territory and would provide surprises. They work in terms of the overall direction rather than the precise route; they know they can deviate from the route now and then, safe in the knowledge that they are generally heading in the right direction.

How much planning is right for you

These two approaches could represent two very different ways of approaching the movie planning stage. You need to find out what level of planning makes you comfortable, and it could be argued that you should strive to reduce this level of planning to its minimum, asking yourself what aspects you can live without. Certainly, there is no right way to develop a film and it is to the benefit of the film that the creative process does not stop at the planning stage. Each stage of filmmaking presents its own opportunities for creative decisions, ones that affect the entire purpose of the movie and its overall success. The pressure that goes with this informs you that you cannot afford to run on automatic when shooting and editing, merely following the orders you drew up on paper. If the film sticks too closely to its plans, the result may be artificial and contrived, with the realization of the filmmaker's ideas made too literal.

To arrive at the best method for you, try working with varying degrees of looseness from the initial plans. However, no filmmaker can afford to depart on the journey of making a movie without reference points. How much detail you include between these points is up to you.

Storyboards

A storyboard is the blueprint for a film. It is not the final look of the film but it is the best you have right now and it provides a list of all the information you need to include throughout the film, including sound, music, images and the effect that each of these have when juxtaposed with one another. The example storyboard illustrated in Figure 4.13 shows a typical page layout. Three or four frames are drawn on the left side of the sheet, in accordance with the aspect ratio you will work with. These may each be the size of a credit card, with similar dimensions. On the right, linking to each frame, information is given about that shot, concerning sound and music, dialogue, camera movement, and any other elements that cannot readily be depicted in the diagram.

You don't need to be an artist

In drawing the storyboard you do not necessarily need to be a good draughtsman; it is enough to show the image clearly and precisely to the extent that you could give the storyboards to someone else and they could go ahead and make your film.

2 CAN PLAY AT THAT GAME - STORYBOARD

Page: 3

I	SHOT No............SCENE..................ACT..................... LOCATION:.. ACTORS:.. SHOT TYPE: 1. LS STATIC 2. CU STATIC CAMERA-INSTR: STILL ON TRIPOD ....
DESCRIPTION: PLAYER 1 DEAL THE CARDS FOR HIMSELF AND PLAYER 2	PROPS: CARS DIALOGUE.................................
	SHOT No............SCENE..................ACT..................... LOCATION:.. ACTORS:.. SHOT TYPE: MS STATIC CAMERA-INSTR: STILL ON TRIPOD ....
DESCRIPTION: PLAYER 2 RECIEVES CARDS	PROPS: CARDS COSTUME CIGARRE DIALOGUE.................................
	SHOT No............SCENE..................ACT..................... LOCATION:.. ACTORS:.. SHOT TYPE: CU STATIC CAMERA-INSTR: STILL ON TRIPOD ....
DESCRIPTION: THEY EXAMINE THEIR CARS	PROPS: CARDS + COSTUME DIALOGUE.................................
	SHOT No............SCENE..................ACT..................... LOCATION:.. ACTORS:.. SHOT TYPE: MCU STATIC CAMERA-INSTR: STILL ON TRIPOD ....
DESCRIPTION: PLAYER 2 DEALS HIS MONEY	PROPS: MONEY COSTUME DIALOGUE.................................

Figure 4.13 Storyboards from *Two Can Play At That Game* (Jon Price, 2001).

2 CAN PLAY AT THAT GAME - STORYBOARD   Page: 5

	SHOT No............SCENE...................ACT................... LOCATION:... ACTORS:... SHOT TYPE:........STATIC M.S. CAMERA-INSTR: STILL ON TRIPOD
DESCRIPTION: PLAYER 2'S CASH LANDS. 1 HtS HIS GLASSES	PROPS: CASH / GLASSES DIALOGUE...
	SHOT No............SCENE...................ACT................... LOCATION:... ACTORS:... SHOT TYPE: PAN CAMERA-INSTR: PAN SLOWLY FROM LEFT-RIGHT, GIVING TIME FOR ACTOR TO SNEAK BEHIND CAMERA INTO 2ND SEAT
DESCRIPTION: A PAN FROM PLAYER 1 TO PLAYER 2.	PROPS: GLASSES (CAMERA, CASH DIALOGUE...
	SHOT No............SCENE...................ACT................... LOCATION:... ACTORS:... SHOT TYPE: STATIC M.S. CAMERA-INSTR: PROFILE, STILL ON TRIPOD
DESCRIPTION: PLAYER 1 SHUFFLES AND DEAL CARDS	PROPS:.. DIALOGUE...
	SHOT No............SCENE...................ACT................... LOCATION:... ACTORS:... SHOT TYPE: STATIC C.U. CAMERA-INSTR: STILL ON TABLE
DESCRIPTION: HE TAKES CARDS	PROPS: CARDS DIALOGUE...

Figure 4.13 continued.

If you are not confident with your drawing skills the tendency is to use pencil, but this serves only to reveal skill weaknesses. Try using a bold, black marker pen to give the image more impact and help you to show shadow and light.

Make images with meaning

In your storyboards and visualizations you can also develop a sense of what each image means. Every scene must show more than just the passing of the events that make up the plot; the shot must lead the audience to the view that this is not just an image but that it has meaning, revealing more about the central theme of the film. For example, if you have a shot of a figure sitting in a chair in a room, you can alter the meaning of what we are seeing simply by changing the lighting from dim to bright, or from changing the actor's expression from passive to agitated, or by including objects or colours in the shot that suggest meaning. All these subtle variations in one simple shot are the result of what the camera sees; there is a whole other set of opportunities for more meaning when we look into sound and editing, but for now it is enough to realize the impact you can make with imagery. Every element forms a set of signs which the audience are cued to look for and which they will assemble into meanings whether you want them to or not. When planning and storyboarding the film you place yourself in control of this process of reading signs, giving the film more depth and pointing the audience towards a certain interpretation of the movie.

Get in control of the images

The successful filmmaker knows the power of the image and judges what information can be used in a scene and how to temper it for effect. Unfortunately, there is no opting out of this. When an audience see your film they will read into the information they are given and attach meaning to it whether you intend it or not. Being a participant in this dialogue between you and the audience is better than being a mute presence. This does not mean that you have to dominate this dialogue, by prescribing how people should read the film, and some of the alternative planning methods mentioned here will all encourage sequences that allow the director to relax control now and then.

Interview
'I storyboarded some scenes, though not all. I regret not doing them all now, it would have sped things up. I wrote a detailed shot list for each scene, noting the action and dialogue being shot, the shot size and also the choice of focal length. Comparing the finished film and the shot list they agree about 90 per cent of the time, which isn't bad. The next film I make is already fully storyboarded and this is something I think I'll continue to do – they don't have to be a Bible, and if you see something more interesting on the day, and you've got time, then shoot it – but they aren't half helpful when you're scratching your head to figure out which set-up to go to next. They also save a lot of time explaining your plans to cast and crew – instead of saying "I want a hand-held tracking shot holding the actor medium wide," you can just show them a drawing.'

Richard Graham, filmmaker

Alternatives to the storyboard

The storyboard has evolved as one of the best methods for seeing the film as a whole before you start shooting. Although you can rarely afford to leave anything to chance if you are working with a large budget and large crew, in low-budget digital video you can allow more flexibility and use chance and improvisation now and then to give the film some spontaneity and spark.

Reducing control

Various directors use techniques which allow them to reduce their control over the film while still retaining an overview of it. The benefit to these directors is that they feel the resulting movie is a better product, that it is less artificial and more vibrant than the more thoroughly planned. Making a film in this way becomes a risk-laden business, but also has a thrill of uncertainty that can bring out the best in some people, like some kind of extreme sport. For many, it is about getting the kind of buzz described by those who work on live television, where the knowledge that anything can happen, and you are not always prepared for it when it does, forces the director to be more ingenious in responses to problems.

Use a timeline

One way to prepare is to use the timeline chart, and a more advanced version could resemble the timeline used in editing packages. Several tracks are used to depict images and audio, including simultaneous clips such as text or layers of image. This method uses blocks to show where certain scenes will occur and presumes that you have first developed an idea of the images you want to use in sketches and visualizations. The development of images is purposelessly left only partially resolved so that the rest of the process can occur during filming.

The timeline is useful in showing how the tone or atmosphere of the film evolves, or how subthemes or meanings evolve throughout. More important is the main, underlying theme of the movie, whether this is 'betrayal', 'escape' or 'triumph over evil', and without this it is not just a case of not having a map for your journey, but of not having any starting point or destination – a true definition of being lost.

'Key frame' method

A second, less risky, method involves the use of what could be called key frames. In this approach, you lay out 'signposts' showing the route the film will take by devising a series of scenes that you want to include, roughly in the order they will appear, but with gaps allowing for the inclusion of further images and scenes. This originates in animation techniques, where the overall movement for a character would be sketched out by an artist with the main movements, or key frames, shown, and this would then be passed on to animators who would fill in the movements in between.

In practice, this means drawing storyboard frames depicting the main parts of the film and cutting them out to resemble a deck of cards. For example, five frames could show the development of a thriller showing a terrorist train plot from:

1 Man receives call
2 Man takes suitcase to train station

3 Man boards train
4 Man leaves suitcase on train
5 Man jumps off moving train.

You may only have five main scenes but would place these on a sheet of paper with large gaps between each, allowing you to make notes of the kind of shots and atmosphere you want to use to connect these key scenes. You could show what encounters the man has on the train, what obstacles he has in jumping off the train and whether he is seen; all of these allow improvisation on set and yet do not detract from the main plot.

Image circle method

This method takes a completely different approach, designed to suit the needs of the more theme-based, non-narrative movie, including music videos. In this sort of film the linear arrangement of scenes is not too important. Instead, you need to be able to see the whole set of images at once and look for connections between them.

Prioritize your images

To try this method, draw a set of visualizations depicting the scenes or images that will appear in the film. Take a large sheet of paper – at least 24 inches square – and draw a large circle on it. Place the images around the circle, placing the most important ones, most central to the film's theme, towards the centre. The less important ones are placed at various points around the circle, indicating their relative importance to each other.

This method allows you to arrange all the scenes from the film without regard for their linear appearance. You are prioritizing the clips, instead of showing the order in which they appear, allowing you to treat this in a more intuitive way when you start editing. This form of movie doesn't sit comfortably with the traditional arrangement of shots in a storyboard, but with this method the film can be built by seeing the way all the shots react with each other.

Image circle in action

For example, a particular filmmaker was making a music video on the theme of jilted love. Rather than show just a simple narrative, the filmmaker wanted to have various scenes in which this theme was developed: loss, betrayal, love and hope, all of which play a part in the overall theme and were reflected in the soundtrack. Using this method of planning allowed each part of the film to develop equally, but allowed the filmmaker to see how each element affected the rest. It's an organic way to work which may not suit everyone, but if you find that the usual way of doing storyboards seems to restrict your thoughts, then this may help.

The Crunch

- Find the amount of planning that is right for you
- Visual planning carries on sometimes during shooting

- Plan to improvise
- If you can, do visual planning yourself
- Visual planning and storyboards help you develop structure
- ... and they help develop meaning in the images
- Try different methods of planning (storyboards, key frame, image circle or timeline)
- OK, you know a lot of it is going to change when you start filming, but without a base to start from you can at least keep track of these changes.

5 Production tools

Quick start guide: Production tools and aesthetics

How to get to the part you need now

First choose your route:

Quick start guide for documentary makers

First record sound professionally
Sound recording techniques   Chapter 5:3, page 150

And look at other documentary filmmakers to get ideas
Documentary background to revival   Chapter 6:3, page 221

Quick start guide for music promo/VJ

First shoot so that you can work with the clips on any screen
Shooting for compression   Chapter 5:5, page 188

Then avoid clichés
Ingredients of VJ work   Chapter 6:4, page 238

1. A condensed guide to shooting

This chapter is going to help to get you filming quickly, taking you through the basics of filming so that you can start working on the projects detailed in this book. Refer to this chapter before you start each project so that you go shooting with more confidence, aware of the various obstacles that could arise.

Preparing yourself

As we saw in Chapter 4, much of the filmmaking process is about how to deal with problems – minor and potentially larger ones. Every day you may encounter some obstacle to your plans, some person or rule that puts everything on hold. The sorts of skills you need to overcome these problems are the kind that you use every day to deal with many situations: those transferable skills that have enabled you to negotiate a pay rise, calm a distraught friend, sort out a problem with your bank – or all three at the same time. All these hurdles are the kind that have been secretly preparing you for the process of shooting. You already have the most important skills needed to accomplish the task of making a movie, and when you put these to work with your technical knowledge of cameras and your ideas about what you want to express on video, you are on your way.

Equipment

You need:

● *Video camera.*
● *Power supplies.* Batteries or mains connection cables.

- *Videotapes*. Take four or five for a day's work, although it is unlikely that you will accomplish this much shooting.
- *Camera support*. Take a tripod.
- *Microphones*. A boom or shotgun mic should cover most situations, but take a unidirectional cardioid mic as well if you have one. A lavalier or clip-on mic will help with close-ups, or if you want to exclude other noises when recording dialogue.
- *Lights*. If you only have one lamp, make sure it's a strong key light such as a Redhead (a brand name, but people will know what you mean if you refer to it). But you don't always need high-powered lamps – DV copes with less light than previous formats, so a 300 W should cover you for all eventualities. But you can make great-looking films using just one strong, purpose-built lamp. Avoid using lamps that clip on to the camera. If you have the budget to use a good range, see the list in Chapter 5:2 (the ideal kit-bag), but also refer to this list for the extras you will need, such as gaffer tape.
- *Monitor*. If you want to be sure that the film you are shooting maintains the highest technical standards throughout, consider using a monitor, a small television hooked up to show you what you are recording.

Interview
'One real "must-have" is a monitor, and one that you can calibrate [colour, contrast and other settings]. You will then be able to see what your picture will look like on a screen, not down a grubby viewfinder; £30 a day is well spent on a small unit with full controls. Once it's calibrated, get some camera tape and stick it over the knobs with the legend, "anyone who twiddles here dies".'

John Wildgoose, Filmmaker, UK

The camera

- *Focus*. Don't shoot constantly with automatic focus as it plays havoc with interesting compositions. Use manual focus and check that the frame looks sharp and in focus often, even after the slightest movement of camera or actors.
- *White balance*. See Chapter 2:3 for details of white balance.
- *Aperture (iris control)*. Automatic settings will again affect your best laid plans with lighting. See Chapter 2:3 for more about this.
- *LCD display*. But it uses more power to use the LCD display than the small viewfinder – often halving battery life.
- *Timecode*. See Chapter 7:5 for more details about timecode.
- *Continuity*. Keep notes, take Polaroids, use video shots – anything to make an accurate record of the location of props, the arrangement of costumes, the kind of light, the costumes and so on.

Using audio

- Record sounds separately if you want to be able to manipulate them later in the editing stage.
- Use a mixing board if you have one.
- Don't record with the built-in camera mic, but if your mics fail and you have no choice, go ahead and use the camera mic, as you can use this as a guide track if you need to dub sounds later.
- Look at the hierarchy of sound recording techniques in Chapter 5:3. Use this as your default guide to every situation.
- Use headphones to be sure that you hear the levels of audio correctly.
- Use XLR adapters on the mic cables to minimize interference.
- Always record at the highest possible level before the sound starts to distort.

Working with actors and crew

- You may get far more out of actors if you treat them as part of the team – involve them in discussions about the direction in which the film is headed.
- Don't skip on good, plentiful food on set – for actors and crew. Aim for cheap, filling food that suits everyone: pizzas, fried food and so on ('I was nearly fired for taking two donuts when it was made clear that one was the maximum per day per person' – Harrison Ford on the set of *American Graffiti*).
- Listen to your actors – they may have as much or more experience than you about filming.

Interview

'Share your ideas; some of the best ideas came as I was telling people what I was doing and then a little brainstorm would happen and things would develop a new layer. Also: write everything down; trust your crew to do their jobs; but when recruiting, make a back-up list of every member of the crew, even two or three. Don't make new decisions on set without taking a two-minute break to think things through, and don't hesitate to ask for help when you are stuck – there were a few points when I was in a tight corner and one of the crew came up with a really elegant solution.'

Debra Watson, director, Animal–Vegetable–Machine *(2000)*

Getting help

What happens if you are filming and you come up against a technical problem you cannot solve? The downfall of many filmmakers is a lack of experience of technical issues – it stops a production in its tracks and undermines your confidence.

- *Get to know the retailer where you buy your filmmaking gear*. They make a living working out what each bit of equipment does, how useful it is and why you need it. They may help with your questions to make sure you come back and buy more goods.

- *Get involved, in advance, with local filmmaker networks.* One of the strong points about the independent sector is that people help each other, on the whole. Exchange of information and help is the commodity it thrives on, as much as Hollywood does on dollar bills. Cultivate contacts with other filmmakers and don't be shy to ask for help.
- *Use the Internet for quick advice.* If you can wait 24–48 hours, post a notice on one of the excellent filmmakers' notice-boards, such as Shooting People (UK) or IndieWire (USA), and wait for a response. It's common to see urgent ads asking for replacement actors, legal queries or technical problems. No question is too stupid and, in any case, answers are often posted on the site and benefit everyone.

How much to shoot and how long it will take

This one has no answer but it deserves attention because it is so frequently asked.

- Shoot as much as you like, but bear in mind that economical use of your tape helps focus your mind. If you shoot everything and anything, you may end up with 10 slightly interesting, unfinished films. Limit what you film and you make better decisions. But also remember that some of the most useful shots that add spontaneity to the movie are found by being more relaxed about how much you shoot.
- If you want to be able to compare what we could call the success ratio of useful to useless footage, it would be good to aim for something like 1:10. When independent feature films are being shot it is common to try to complete shooting of about two minutes a day, or two pages of script, but will vary according to the complexity of the sequence.
- If you work a whole day you might get in about four hours of shooting solidly. Short films tend to overrun more than features because there is the tendency to make each scene perfect.
- Build a good, fair schedule that reflects both your experience and the amount of available time you have and you will remain on time and, consequently, on budget.

But bear in mind that some schools of thought recommend gathering far too much footage, leaving the shaping of the whole movie to the post-production stage. George Lucas took this route on *American Graffiti*, and the result is a vibrant drama with a documentary feel.

Insurance

If you can stretch to the cost of this, it could be the one outgoing that enables you to carry on making movies. Ask your insurer about large-item cover for your basic equipment and check to see how you are covered if you borrow other people's gear. If one of your actors breaks a leg during work and cannot take the next acting job, you need to be sure that you are covered either by written, legal mutual agreement or insurance.

Permission

If you are shooting in public you may (perhaps inadvertently) film someone who objects to being filmed, or would not like their image to be broadcast. A written consent form will cover you and save you from costly recutting or shooting later. Prepare a form that you can use on set should the need arise. Children will need the consent of their parents or guardians. In general, you can film anyone in a public place provided that footage is not improperly used, or shows them in a derogatory manner.

Emergency funding

What happens if you run out of money during filming?

- Credit is one option, but investment from people who believe in your project is better. Credit has the potential to stop future projects, even if it helps your current one.
- If you run up against the possibility that you cannot finish your film, don't consider abandoning the whole project. Shoot certain key scenes and consider applying for completion funding.

The Crunch

- Plan the shoot well and you will achieve more
- Remember – power, batteries, headache pills
- Listen to advice
- Don't rush – be confident and calm
- Be bold and decisive
- Improvise and think around a problem
- Be calm and relaxed
- Make the shoot fun for you and the crew – warm food, music and mutual support.

2. Lighting

Digital filmmaking is a double-edged sword: on the one hand you are going to be able to make a movie for less than you ever thought possible, but on the other you are going to have to be much more creative with very basic equipment. You don't just need to make the best of what you have, but make what little you have look like the best. In the area of lighting, this is certainly true; good lighting has the ability to lift a film out of the limitations of its budget and into another league.

Basic principles

Purpose of lighting

Lighting helps to do the following.

Pick out relevant details and figures in a scene

At its most basic, lighting can pick out like a stage spotlight a significant part of the frame for us to focus on. But it goes beyond this to the use of shadow and light together. How we use shadows is similar to the way we use composition – it is another way of directing the viewer's eye towards a certain part of a frame. We could simply zoom in on the important element, but the use of composition would then be limited. For instance, if you want to create a feeling that someone is isolated, we need to see space surrounding the figure, to suggest emptiness. We may also want to see the figure in relation to other objects, to suggest that the figure is smaller than the surroundings, and therefore vulnerable. So, shadow is a compositional tool as well as a visual direction, helping assign a meaning to what we see.

Reveal shape and form

How we use space is crucial to a frame. It is tempting to think in terms of the space within the four 'walls' of the camera frame as being all that we have to play with, but there are two other planes in the illusion we want to create. Three-dimensionality is central to creating the illusion of total space and the main way of revealing it is in variable lighting of parts of a form. By throwing light at just one of those planes of space we throw the others into relief. So a figure sitting on a chair can be lit by throwing strong light on the side, with less light reflected on the front, and none at all on the other side. In this way we see the differences in each aspect of the form and start to believe it is no longer flat. Two-dimensional shape and three-dimensional form are each made apparent to the viewer through variations of shadow.

Create mood and atmosphere

This brings us to the core of what lighting is for most filmmakers, an aid to creating a layer of meaning to a set of objects in a scene. A simple living room can be made to take on human characteristics of emotion simply by changing the use of light. A light bounced around the ceiling to create a flat, all-over look will suggest inertia or odd calmness. The same room lit by soft small lamps with warm orange colour casts will suggest a pleasant and attractive place. Again, strong lamps creating shadows of objects out of proportion to their size may create unease. There is no shortcut to knowing how to set up a certain look, despite what some film manuals will suggest with the outdated three-lamp technique, but one starting point is to use the accumulated wisdom of how we light for mood at home. From here, experiment with lamps to moderate or amplify moods.

As an aid to the camera

On a more prosaic level, this is probably the most important in the list. Without a basic level of light a camera will perform badly and even the most carefully set-up shot will not create the effect you want. DV cameras are more capable than VHS or other analog of picking up light, so you can get away with less powerful lamps. You probably don't need to use the old 800 W Redheads that were common with low-budget filmmakers (see lamps guide below) but you will still require at least a 300 W lamp illuminating the subject. In almost all situations extra lights are preferable to ambient light.

Go to: Chapter 2:3 for details on how the camera reacts with light.

Allow you to create a style for the film

This is a less crucial function of lighting, but can help create a design for your movie that cuts across the entire film. It is essential to plan this before you turn up on set as any changes will seriously affect continuity and have a drastic effect on narrative. The most effective way to begin is by listing a few descriptive words which summarize the style you want. Sketch locations you have earmarked for the film and try them in different lighting set-ups until you get the effect that closely matches your description. Then experiment with lamps for real to see how it translates into reality.

Maintain continuity between takes and shots

Assuming that continuity is what you want for your film, lighting is an important factor in enabling continuity during production. Much of your work towards continuity will take place during editing, but lighting (and sound) is going to make this process much more straightforward. Use notes during planning and production to maintain a consistent quantity of light throughout a scene. You can change lighting effects for the next scene, but any lighting within a single scene (defined here as a sequence within a single time-frame and place) needs to be carefully adhered to.

Attributes of light

To describe how light functions in relation to a camera we need to understand first how we can measure it, what its attributes are. This is useful in figuring out what light is actually in a place (the objective light) and what we are seeing (the subjective light). The subjective light in our perception will always be what we are aiming towards in creating a lighting effect for a scene, but in order to set it up we need to think entirely in terms of objective light.

Hue

Hue is what we normally think of as colour. In technical terms colour is the reflective waves not absorbed by the surface of the object.

Saturation

This refers to the strength of that colour. We can describe a colour as being diluted or pure, using percentages to assign a measurement to this: 100 per cent would be described as pure colour, while 50 per cent would be half the saturation.

Brightness

This is a tough one to adequately describe, since it involves looking at what is both subjective and objective. We talk about light as being bright or weak, but this gets confused when other lights come into play – for instance, when a torch is shone directly at the eye we see it as being as bright as a car headlamp. It is confused further when colour is included. A green surface is perceived as being less bright than a red surface because the brain perceives red before other colours. For extra clarity in talking about brightness, a few extra terms have come into use: 'luminance' refers to the actual brightness of a surface, while 'luminosity' refers to the perceived brightness we think we see.

Good practice

Nestor Almendros, director of photography on many acclaimed movies, including *Days of Heaven* (Terrence Malick, 1978) and *The Last Metro* (François Truffaut, 1980), often preferred just one light source, rejecting the traditional key, fill and background light technique. 'The result [of this traditional method] has nothing to do with reality, where a window or a lamp, or at most both of them, normally provide the only sources of light.' (*A Man with a Camera*, Faber & Faber, 1980, p. 8.) He used the key light as a functional source, taking his cue from the light that would be cast from sunlight or from an interior lamp. 'Once the key light has been decided, the space around it and the areas that might be left in total darkness are reinforced with a very soft, gentle light, until what is reproduced on film is close to what the eye would see.' (Ibid., p. 9.)

Almendros's approach is to match reality through as little intervention as possible. And yet the three-lamp technique of placing a hard lamp, a smaller filler lamp and a background lamp at specific places around a subject has become a staple of many film schools. Other cinematographers also bemoan its use, blaming it for films where everything looks as if shot in a controlled studio. It does, they say, prevent the human eye from seeing places as real, whole environments – instead portraying them as theatrical stages.

High contrast

Film noir made a virtue out of using lighting with high contrast and unusually placed shadow. For example, a scene with a detective standing in a doorway, looking ominously at a figure he is tailing, may be lit with just a few puddles of light scattered around, some of which is strategically placed on the detective's face but, by and large, the scene was under-lit, relying on darkness to evoke a feeling of menace and uncertainty.

Did you know?

Film noir refers to a type of movie dominant in the post-war era of Hollywood. It is often seen as a sub-genre of the gangster movie, but it is more a visual style than a genre and is frequently picked up by today's filmmakers as a self-conscious style choice.

Softening contrast

Contrast is badly used, however, if you use it without regard to whether it suits the film you are making. Although its effects are to make compositions look stronger, it can flatten three-dimensional objects by removing the shades of grey that show form. At this extreme, it is as destructive as flat, low-contrast, all-over lighting, which also has too little shadow to reveal three-dimensionality. Use contrast to a degree, but also add softer lights within the scene to make sure that the tonal values of objects are not lost. Use contrast as a tool to solve problems associated with composition or to help show depth and texture in a shot. But avoid using it simply as a style option, as it can take on too prominent a place in your film; use it as a tool to reveal atmosphere in a scene and to mask an absence of expensive props and sets.

Use lamps

Realism is often the aim of a filmmaker. But you don't get realistic lighting by using just what is around naturally. If the camera was as sophisticated as the human eye then you could do this, but you have to help a camera to see as we see. This involves using additional light, whether you are outside in natural daylight or in what seems to be a well-lit room. The level of light is not really the issue here; it is about directing the light, altering its intensity and removing it from some areas. Lamps will help you with this, but you don't necessarily have to go out and spend half your budget on the full range. Like everything, there are ways of using fewer.

Natural light and ambient light

Natural light varies considerably moment by moment and as such is a problem for continuity in any outdoor shooting. Certain parts of the world experience more settled weather and have a quality of light that varies little throughout a typical day. For instance, in Europe light is bluer (see colour temperature below) than elsewhere, weather is unsettled and frequent changes in cloud affect the intensity of light and its direction, and change it from hard light to soft and back again within minutes. In warmer countries nearer to the equator than Europe, light is less refracted through the atmosphere due to the sun's position on the equator being higher, and can be harder, warmer in colour and more predictable to work with.

Ambient light refers to the kind of light that is present in a location without any additional artificial light. In a room, for instance, the light that is generated by a single bulb in the ceiling and that which is coming through a window would be the ambient light for that particular place. But for most camcorders this would be insufficient and would need boosting to a certain extent.

All of which points towards natural light being less useful for filmmakers than artificial. But many cinematographers highlight the effects of light at certain times of the day that are unmatched by artificial means. The so-called 'magic hour' of dusk or dawn presents colours that are extremely captivating, creating atmosphere through unusual shadow colours and glowing horizons.

Film View

Terrence Malick's *Days of Heaven* is perhaps the most audacious use of the 'magic hour', the period just after dawn and just before dusk, when colours and light are different to the rest of the day. Malick filmed at these times of the day for much of the location shooting of the film, sometimes keeping crew and cast waiting for just the right kind of light.

The master cinematographer Gordon Willis pushed natural light to its limits in films such as *The Godfather* (Francis Ford Coppola, 1972) and *Manhattan* (Woody Allen). Nicknamed 'the prince of darkness' for his disposition towards under-lighting a shot, Willis won many awards – although never an Oscar – for his technique. It is useful to look at because it relies far less on hard, studio-style lighting and places more emphasis on the use of the camera to pick up light. In *Manhattan*, an ambitious opening scene connects a series of images of New York, in strong black and white and with high contrast. It runs like a series of photographs in an art gallery, displaying the attributes of a good cinematographer: the ability to use light and composition together. Celluloid is more suited to this kind of work given the range of film stock to enhance the absorption of low levels of light. But video users can also try to limit their use of light, using natural light extensively, with a small and efficient use of artificial light. He once said, 'Sometimes I think the more tools you have, the worse it gets; I'm an eliminator, not an adder. Your point of view is what's important.'

Figure 5.1 Working in low lighting conditions requires skill. In this still from David Flemholc's *House of the Tiger King* (2004) there is just enough light to illuminate the scene. In a documentary such as this, additional lighting could have looked too dramatic.

When you assess a location, look for the level of ambient lighting present. Record tests on camera to see whether the existing light is sufficient or can be aided by bouncing natural light around with reflective boards.

> **Tip** To see the effects of natural light and its possibilities for creating atmosphere, look at the paintings that have inspired the great cinematographers, by the Dutch painters van Eyck and Vermeer, and the Italian Caravaggio, whose style is remarkably cinematic.

Colour temperature

Something else that video cameras, particularly at the lower end, are not good at is balancing the colours they see, which is why they have a white balance feature that helps take out the 'cast' of a particular lighting condition – that is, the particular colours given off by most artificial light. The human eye performs a similar routine every time you enter a new environment. A room lit by a domestic light-bulb, for instance, will not give off true light in the way we think of daylight, but instead is tinted by orange. Your brain can automatically compensate for this, but the camera will need your help. We need either to use light that does not give off unwanted colours or adjust the camera to offset what it sees. On the other hand, like everything about filming, there are creative uses to colour imbalance, such as setting white balance incorrectly in outdoor daylight by altering it to remove the orange cast of indoor lamps, resulting in a cold, blue tint to the scene. The worst of all worlds is where daylight and artificial light are mixing in the same frame.

To understand this, we need to have a look at colour temperature. All light has a temperature, measured in degrees kelvin. In film, we refer to daylight as normal light – light giving a true reading of

Candle	1900	Warm, orange red
Sunrise/sunset	Between 2000 and 3200	Orange red
Household lamp	2800	Orange
Tungsten lamp	3200	Yellow, close to daylight
Daylight in Europe	5600	Clear, white
Cloudy day	Between 6000 and 8000	Cold, blue

Figure 5.2 Colour temperature.

colours – and it resides somewhere in the middle of the scale, at 5600 degrees. This applies to sunny afternoon light in Europe, but in places where light is stronger, such as in California, colour temperature will be lower, whereas an overcast day with poor light will have a higher colour temperature. The point of looking at this is to be able to use certain lamps to light your scene effectively, with colour as true to daylight as possible. To this end, use tungsten lights, which have a colour temperature of near daylight, and avoid household lights for movies.

Tools

When you are on set there are certain shortcuts that will help you to make the best use of lamps, to trouble-shoot and to use your time more efficiently. In an area of filmmaking that includes physics, electronics and perception, these are going to seem complicated at first but make real sense when you try them out.

The cosine law
This refers to the difference made to light when it is reflected. It is usually the case that when you shine a light at a surface it bounces at an angle to that surface and in doing so it covers more area than the original source. To put this into practice, suppose you have a figure in front of the camera, requiring lighting. You could bounce light from a white surface so it illuminates the figure. It would be useful, then, to know how much the light is reduced when it is reflected.

At a 60-degree angle the area of light is doubled, while the light actually reaching the figure is halved – it is covering a broader area but is less intense. At a 45-degree angle there is a 30 per cent loss, while any light bounced at less than 25 degrees loses a negligible amount of light.

The inverse square law
This law is as useful in sound work as in light, because both deal with the loss of energy over distances. In terms of light, it follows that since light spreads out (diverges), the further you move the lamp away the more it spreads out. The effect is that it becomes less intense as it covers a wider area. The basic idea is that when you move a lamp double the distance from a subject, the illuminance is halved. The practical

value of this is that, when lighting a set with few lamps, or even just one, you can define how to reduce light more exactly simply by measuring how far you move a lamp to or from a subject. So if a lamp is one metre from a figure, and you feel the light is too bright, moving it two metres away will reduce the brightness by 50 per cent.

The camera and light

The video camera reacts to light in much the same way as the human eye. It has a sensor behind the lens, called a CCD (charge-coupled device), which converts light entering the lens into digital information to be stored on tape. But unlike the human eye, if there isn't enough information coming into the lens, it compensates, resulting in bad quality, grainy pictures. Today's cameras are designed to see in almost any lighting conditions, but you cannot rely on this to give a clear picture. To keep picture quality high we have to feed the camera lots of light. This doesn't mean blanket lighting, but rather enough strong light in spots for it to maintain quality.

Most video cameras are less able to distinguish between shades of light or colour than traditional celluloid film. Film is about 10 times more able to see the various subtle tints or hues in a shot than video. To make matters worse, the chips embedded in lower-end cameras are less able again, and need particular attention. You will eventually get great results with any camera as long as you know the limitations of the camera you are working with. Be aware that video – at least at the low to mid range of cameras – does not read subtle light to the degree you might like; what looks good to the human eye may not reveal itself through a camera lens. This means lighting your sets in a certain way that will exaggerate natural light.

Automatic camera features: why you don't need them

Your biggest enemy on the camcorder is probably the automatic setting. This is useful for some conditions, but on the whole you cannot rely on it to deliver when it comes to creative filmmaking – it's the fast food of lighting. Since the camera fills in the frame if it doesn't see the amount of light it would like, it is better to have a camera with manual override to switch off this feature – which the vast majority do. This means you can set the lighting yourself and be more creative about what you record. As an example, you may want to shoot a scene in which a group of people are in a room, with windows behind them with bright sunlight flooding in. On auto, the camera simply cancels out some of the sunlight, rendering the figures dark beyond all recognition, the sunlight just about right. But you may want the scene to be overexposed (too much light coming in) in the windows because that gives a certain feel to the scene, and in any case is the only sure way to still see the figures. Automatic will do it the way the manufacturer's handbook says, but manual allows you to do it your way.

The iris and light

Just as with the human eye, the camera has a small hole at the front of the lens that controls how much light is allowed in. In bright conditions, it closes slightly to block some out, while in darker conditions it opens to make more of what little light there is. On a technical level, the iris is important in stopping the inner workings of the camera from being damaged by too much sunlight, just as does the human iris. Too much light also stops the camera from reading colour correctly. But like other features on the camera, we can use the iris creatively. Allowing too much light, or restricting light, can be useful ways of adding atmosphere to a scene.

Depth of field and light

Furthermore, the iris performs a quite separate job of adjusting how much of the frame is in focus. This is called depth of field and refers to the aperture of the iris. On some cameras these are expressed in numbers, such as f/2, f/8 and so on, the larger numbers corresponding to the smaller hole openings. As we have seen, the higher the f-stop number (or the smaller the opening of the iris), the greater the depth of field. Greater depth of field means that you get more objects in focus before and behind the main focal point. In some conditions, then, you may want to open up the iris for other reasons than just light.

Go to: Chapter 2:3 for more details on depth of field.

Lamps

When using lamps we can break them up into categories, serving different functions. In different ways, each lamp will affect both the technical aspects of your production – for instance, by exposing too much or too little – as well as the artistic aspects, such as dramatic mood and atmosphere.

For each lamp, we should look at its:

- *Quality* – or the harshness or softness of the light it throws. Hard light refers to a light that is not diffused and creates strong, crisp shadows and reveals texture. Soft light is more diffused and reveals form but less texture.
- *Intensity* – that is, how bright it is. This is determined partly by the amount of power going in and by the type of bulb it uses, such as halogen, fluorescent or tungsten.
- *Colour temperature* – that is, what kind of colour cast the light gives when picked up on non-white-balanced film. Ideally, you should stick to lamps that do not have any inherent colour of their own, allowing you maximum freedom to add your own, with the use of gels, a transparent coloured film that is placed over the lamp (don't use anything but a film manufactured for use with lamps – something that can't stand the heat could be a fire risk).
- *Direction* – that is, the degree to which you can point the light at the places you want. For many lights, however, you will have the option of shutters or barn doors, which allow you to let the light diffuse outwards in many directions or fill just a small area of the set.

Further to this, you need to consider how simple each lamp is to use in exterior shooting in terms of how easy it is to move about and how much power it consumes.

- *Redhead.* A good workhorse and very versatile, this 800 W tungsten–halogen (quartz) lamp is named after the colour of the lamp top, although actually a kind of orange. It is the brand name of Ianiro, but its popularity has made it a generic term for this sort of lamp. Use this for hard light as your main lamp; it is too strong to use easily as background, but you can direct away from the subject by bouncing light off other surfaces to get adequate fill light.

- *Blonde*. So called because of its gold painted head, it is a 2 kW lamp from the same company as the Redhead. This is a versatile, strong and reliable lamp with uses for key and fill lighting.
- *Pup, Mizar, Inky-Dink*. These trademark names are all at the lower end of intensity and power. These are useful for lighting very small pockets of the set, with direct, focused beams. Use these for picking out specific parts of the set.
- *Dedo*. A set of lights probably out of the price range of most low-budgeteers, these are actually a set of lights that are small and versatile and designed to add complexity and variety to a set. The name comes from the company, Dedo Wiegart Film.
- *HMI*. Using a special, high-pressure metal–halide bulb, this lamp is much more economical in terms of power use, and is brighter than a similar wattage Blonde. It has the colour temperature of daylight and so can be used to fake sunlight in interiors, or to just maintain good colour balance.
- *Sun-gun*. This is a term referring to any battery-powered, hand-held light, available in tungsten or halogen.

You should be able to find any of these lamps through specialist suppliers or via photographic retailers.

Film View
Five films with great lighting:

The Cabinet of Dr Caligari (Robert Wiene, 1919). No other film looks like this – sets are painted so shadows are literally thick and black. Light is made to curve and cut jagged shapes against the crooked townscape.

Days of Heaven (Terrence Malick, 1978). Nestor Almendros's cinematography is perfectly judged for the elliptical storytelling of Malick's second movie. The movie shows what can be accomplished though real light, rejecting artificial lamps in favour of what creates the most atmosphere.

Cat People (Jacques Tourneur, 1942). For Martin Scorsese this film proves that an understanding of light is crucial to creating atmosphere: 'Tourneur had practically no budget and none of today's technologies. But he knew that dark has a life of its own.' (*A Personal Journey Through Film*, Faber & Faber, 1997.)

In The Cut (Jane Campion, 2003). Shot by Dion Beebe, the film portrays its urban setting as intensely drained of life, but somehow manages to find colour and tone everywhere. Beebe is a rising star of this kind of work, having shot Michael Mann's *Collateral* (2004).

Wisconsin Death Trip (James Marsh, 1999). An exceptional debut by the British director now working on features. This documentary is a gothic reworking of a dark past as told through daily newspaper stories of death, suicide and madness.

Lamps: the ideal kit-bag

Whatever your budget, you need to still work with the same kind of range of lamps. Some of these lamps can be supplanted by those not specifically made for the film industry, but the range should be about the same as that used in a well-resourced production.

If you can, get hold of:

- Big, versatile lamps such as the *Redhead*. Get three or four if you can. Anywhere between 300 and 800 W is sufficient.
- A battery-powered, hand-held lamp: the *sun-gun*.
- At least two small, highly *directionable lamps*, such as Mizars or Dedos.

On top of this, you should carry:

- Many metres of *extension cable*.
- Some *distribution boards* or multi-sockets.
- A large flat, white, *reflective surface*, such as card or polystyrene, or a folding, reflective panel called a Lastolite, to bounce light around or complement lighting without too many smaller lamps.
- Some *coloured gels*, especially blue, so that your tungsten lamps will not upset colour balance in daylight.
- A few sheets of *tracing paper* to diffuse light but make sure it is heat resistant.
- Lots of *bull-clips or pegs* to attach gobos (opaque pieces of board to obscure light and make interesting shadows) and gels. Wooden clothes pegs are also good for this.
- *Spare bulbs*. You could change these more often than you need, to avoid a lamp blowing just in the middle of a crucial, one-off scene.
- *Gaffer tape*, to bundle wires out of the way and make your set safe.

If you are a no-budget filmmaker, try:

- One strong lamp of up to 800 W

or

- A starter kit of three smaller 300 W lamps.

The Crunch

- Get to know how your camera reacts to different lighting conditions
- Keep control over your camera – avoid automatic features
- Use high contrast for web films
- Say no to the three-lamp technique – it will turn your films into stage sets
- Use a small selection of good lamps
- Use lamps as near to daylight in degrees kelvin as possible

- Avoid at all costs a scene where both daylight and artificial light meet
- Look at alternative methods of lighting – try lamps you already have, but also look for cheap alternatives for halogen (household security lights, for example)
- Feed the camera what it wants – strong light.

3. Sound recording

Video filmmaking is cheap, enabling you to make movies at a fraction of the cost of those on traditional celluloid film. But for most filmmakers using basic, consumer digital equipment, picture and colour resolution are poorer than high-level digital video or film. In one particular area, however, you can compete with the very highest quality: sound. The sound quality of your movies can equal the best by using a 16-bit digital stereo signal and an interesting layer of sounds. If you can master good quality sound recording, you can give your film the best possible start in life.

Interview
'Often people don't consider sound as an important factor – it is. Design the sound fully before the shoot. One or two badly framed shots will not ruin a film but bad sound will – it will lose its audience. Sound and image work together to create the film's atmosphere, as well as giving the audience dialogue to listen to.'

David Norman, filmmaker, UK

Reasons not to use the built-in camera mic

The easiest way of recording sound is by using the mic that comes built in with your camera. But sooner or later you will see the limits of the camera mic and need to invest in an external mic to plug into your camcorder. For almost all filmmakers, inbuilt mics are too inflexible, whether for creative work or documentary. The essential aspects that you need to be able to control are the level of sound (how prominent it is on the video), which part of your location you record (which actor, for example) and the background sounds.

Cam mics boost sound levels unnaturally

The problem with built-in mics on camcorders is that they boost sound levels automatically, even if there is not much to hear. This is very frustrating when encountered for the first time and results in costly reshoots or extensive post-production cleaning up. For example, if you film a quiet room with whispering voices, the camera will push up sound levels and end up recording the background, ambient sound too loudly. This doesn't mean that it records low-level voices at perfect volume, but that it pushes up the whole range of sounds in the room, and not just the one that you actually want to hear.

You can't tell if the sound levels are correct

The problem with camcorders is that they do not usually offer any way of viewing the sound levels. This means that you have no visual way of accurately telling whether sounds are being recorded at the right level, which should be as high as you can get it without the sound distorting.

Your basic aims for sound skills

1 Record sound cleanly
2 Get to know about external mics
3 Know how to record ambient sound
4 Record any sound anywhere
5 Match camera with sound
6 Create a sound environment
7 Consistency and continuity in recording.

Clean sound

Recording sound with DV is not very different to any other format; the crucial placing of the mic is the most important factor in the quality of the sound you record, just as it always was. Even the best mic in the world will perform badly if used in the wrong context, but the worst mic will perform far better if it is used exactly in the right way. One of the most fundamental skills is recording sound as cleanly as possible and knowing how to use the mic is the first step in achieving this.

Clean sound is a track that is free from interference, free from background or unwanted sounds and recorded at the maximum level.

The reason why clean sound is needed is because it opens up wider possibilities in post-production. Post-production sound technique, as we will see later, is concerned with how you mix and layer sounds to create an aural environment. Sounds that can be isolated and treated separately are much easier to edit with than ones where parts of other sounds are audible beneath.

To do
- Learn how to use mics.
- Always carry a variety of mics.
- Use headphones to hear immediately if problems occur.
- Plan a scene in advance so you know what sounds to expect.
- Place the mic correctly to record only what you want to record (see 'Know about ambient sound' section below).
- Always record sounds at the highest level possible, which will appear as zero on a sound meter. This is the last point before clean sound becomes distorted through excessive levels.
- Watch out for interference from power sources (cables or concentrations of hi-fi or computer equipment). Mobile phones will also cause problems. Note that you can't always hear interference on headphones and you need to play back to be sure your sound is clean.

Get to know about external mics

Different mics react in different ways and it is essential to find out which is best for which job. Go through the list below to work out the uses for each one. In basic terms, mics tend to accompany the shots you are familiar with on your camera and can be considered in a similar way: some mics will pick up a whole room or environment, just as in a long shot; some will pick up a smaller area, as in a mid-shot; and others will pick up only very close subjects, as in the close-up shot. Within this range are many varieties to accommodate different conditions.

To do

- The best way to learn what each mic does, once you know the general purpose of each one, is to play with them.
- Take them out and shoot in a range of locations. See how they perform in big spaces, tiled rooms, noisy train platforms and so on. Only through applying a hands-on knowledge of each mic does a good working knowledge of them take root.

Weblink
http://arts.ucsc.edu/EMS/Music/tech_background/TE-20/teces_20.html   In-depth article on microphones.

Know about ambient sound

Ambient sound is one of the most underrated aspects of a shoot. If used badly or ignored it can ruin a scene, with little chance of correcting it. But if used well it has the potential to make editing a smooth process. It helps with continuity and with enabling consistency in recording, all of which are next on our list.

Figure 5.3 The overhead boom mic will give the most natural recording of sound and should be the first option for most scenes. Spanish director David Casals and crew in production.

Ambient sound refers to the background sound in a certain location, containing sounds that are indistinguishable from each other much of the time.

When you shoot in a room or other location there is a constant sound reflecting the environment unique to that place. Each time you move the camera and microphone position for different shots, the ambient sound will change slightly. Also, every time you record a new take, perhaps if an actor has missed a line, the ambient sound has changed slightly. If you then edit these shots together, those sound differences will become very apparent. The audience won't know exactly what is wrong but it will immediately remove any sense of illusion, which is why the radical Danish group Dogme 95 insists on *not* using ambient tracks.

To do

- To add an ambient track, record a few minutes of background sound for every scene while on location and loop this on the film later, at a constant but low level.
- If you are filming an interior scene, simply empty the room of actors and hold the mic steady, pointing at nothing in particular, but not too close to anything giving off sounds that could distort the overall track, such as computer fans or air-conditioning.
- When doing this, don't fall into the trap of recording it quietly – in other words, down on the decibel register. If you have a digital recording device, such as mini-disc, you may be able to alter the level at which you record, but you may have to use the camera itself for these sounds, and most midrange or consumer-level cameras record on an automatic level.
- As with everything, record as high as you can go – usually $-8\,dB$, or zero on a meter. Reduce the volume at the editing stage later.
- For a more professional feel, record two presence tracks to add depth and to aid in creating a transition between two clips.

Record any sound anywhere

In just about any recording set-up it is necessary to add extra sounds in post-production to create a 'sound environment'. This means that you need to be able to use the right mic to record anything you need. CD sound effects are going to sound nice in isolation, but really do not compare with sound you have recorded yourself. CD collections tend to be extremely sterile in their sound, somehow making atmosphere hard to create for a scene. Avoid them as far as possible.

Use the guide below to the hierarchy of sound recording techniques to get a starting point for just about any situation. For best results, a hand-held unidirectional mic will pick up most sounds cleanly, but it is important to experiment widely with recording sounds so that you are aware of distance from the subject as a factor in both clean sound and good levels.

To do

- Carry a lavalier mic, a unidirectional mic and a contact mic if you are recording sounds, as opposed to recording an entire situation, where a boom would be necessary.

● Try recording a range of sounds, such as a washing machine, cat purring, taps pouring water, fire crackling, car exhaust, telephone conversation, footsteps, door unlocking. This list may then enable you to feel confident in situations where sounds are quiet, sudden, via transmission, at a distance or variable in levels.

● As mentioned above, always record at maximum level. And use headphones.

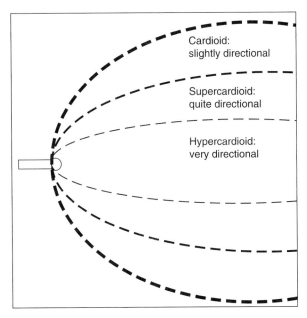

Figure 5.4 Types of unidirectional mic showing pick-up range.

Figure 5.5 Recording dialogue in a car presents many problems, but in this case the sound of the car is prevented from drowning out the sound of the actors. From Jo Price.

Match camera with sound

This is another essential which will inhibit an audience's belief in your scene if used badly. It refers to the process where the level of sounds matches what we see on screen. So if actor A is close to the camera and actor B is further away, we would expect A to be louder than B. To a great extent this relates to the use of the boom mic; placing it accurately – in other words, close to whatever is nearest to the camera – will ensure that certain parts of the frame are heard more prominently.

A central part of this skill is the idea of 'sound perspective'. This refers to those sounds coming straight from the source itself, or direct sound, and those that are reflected by surfaces on their way towards the mic. We usually hear direct sound when the camera is in close-up. We may see a face near to the camera and expect to hear it as if we were standing close to the figure in place of the camera, because the sounds are hitting our ears – the mic – before they hit the walls or the floors or any other reflecting surface.

With reflected sound, you help to create a sense of the place in which the actor is speaking by recording the way the words bounce around the room. Hard surfaces such as stone, tiling or glass produce a strong reflection as they bounce the sound back, whereas soft surfaces such as upholstery and curtains will absorb sound waves, thereby deadening the sound and reducing echo.

Recording this sort of sound is difficult as various surfaces at various distances from the subject reflect in different ways but, if recorded correctly, the effect of using this kind of spatial awareness in sound can add a real sense of three-dimensionality.

To do
- Make sure the boom handler is in close contact with the camera operator, or use a camera monitor to show which parts of the scene are close and which are further away.
- Let natural sound reflections carry. Don't try to eliminate the way sound bounces around a room or is reflected more harshly off hard surfaces.
- It is hard to notice sound perspective, even with headphones. Try closing your eyes in rehearsal time to get a more realistic idea of what it sounds like.

Create a sound environment

This skill is related to both ambient sound and sound effects recording. With low-budget films in particular, it is necessary to create illusions of space, place or situation by adding sounds that were not present at the time. For example, in Ridley Scott's *Blade Runner* (1982), Scott managed to create the sense of a city crowded and polluted with dense layers of sound. The restrictions of his budget did not affect his ability (or rather that of the sound designer) to suggest scale and density of population. Seventeen years later, a similar dystopian sci-fi film *The Fifth Element* (1999) would employ every visual trick to emulate this kind of city, but still does not seem to match the claustrophobic effect achieved through sound environment in Scott's film.

Planning is essential both in determining what sort of environment you want and how to record it. Use the script as the starting point for this. The notes in italic, the direction notes, may suggest a certain atmosphere or place.

To do

- Use timeline charts (see Chapter 4:4) to plan the sort of environment you want the viewer to believe is in front of them. In most cases this is concerned with enhancing elements that are already present – for instance, by adding extra street sounds of sirens or crowds to create a more metropolitan feel, as in *Blade Runner*.
- Use your knowledge of clean sound recording and use of the right mic to capture sounds free of interference from other sounds, as far as possible.
- If using sound effects as loops to create a section of sound environment, make sure each sound has no sound 'spikes', where sudden and noticeable parts stand out. Audiences will become aware of the existence of a loop.

Did you know?
The 'sound environment' refers to the different layers of sounds that make up the soundtrack, not just those that are present on location. When editing, these are arranged in order of priority. A simple sound environment could consist of dialogue as the loudest, clearest sound we hear, followed by sounds relevant to the setting, followed by music, followed by ambient sound.

Consistency and continuity in recording

Good sound recording will not be noticed by anyone outside Academy voters, but bad sound recording will be noticed by just about everyone in the audience. Each of the ideas above contributes to sealing a soundtrack that supports what we are seeing on screen. To connect these together, we need to look at the uses of sound in continuity. As we will see in Chapter 6:2 on continuity filming, the aim is to ensure that editing does not disrupt the illusion we want to create. As soon as two shots recorded separately are placed together there is the potential for sudden changes in sound quality. With ambient sound we have seen how a background track can iron over the creases created when two shots are edited together. This creates a feeling of simultaneity so that events can be seen to be occurring at the same time. But it is important not to rely on ambient sound too much beyond what it is meant to do. Sound recording must be consistent throughout a scene, first and foremost, and throughout the film in terms of quality, levels and style. In this case, 'style' means any way of recording that is particular to the film, beyond the basic rules described here. For instance, a film where you want certain levels of tension and claustrophobia may require a foregrounding of most sounds, so that the viewer hears everything intensely and hyper-realistically.

To do

- Ensure that sound levels are consistent for an entire film. Agree at the start what level you will be shooting at – usually at the maximum on the sound meter, or zero – and stick to it.

- Sloppy recording will be apparent when sounds are recorded too low and need to be boosted later in post-production – a background hiss may become heard.
- Make a note of the quality of sounds recorded on location and re-record if necessary – don't wait until post-production to examine them.
- If you have to dub dialogue over later – known as ADR, or automatic dialogue replacement – make sure you carefully revisit your notes on how sounds were recorded and what mic you used. ADR is notoriously difficult to do and it is better to reshoot rather than risk badly synchronized voices. But you might want off-camera voices, where lips don't need to match sounds, and these present similar problems.

Tools of recording

Recording with external mics

Recording with a slightly more expensive camera may allow you to alter the levels at which you record. Loud sounds can be reduced and low ones omitted. These kinds may also allow you to plug in a mixing board so that sounds are recorded at a maximum and at clearer levels. Mixing boards are good for filmmakers; they enable you to have far greater control over what you record and how it is mixed, so that different mics can be used simultaneously for the situation.

The constant aim, regardless of what equipment you have or what production you work on, is to get the strongest possible signal without getting distortion, so any device that allows you to boost or reduce signal is going to make life much easier on set. One of the best principles of sound recording is to get the microphone as close to the subject as camera framing will allow. This way, you will get more of the sound you want and less of the sound you don't.

High quality mics usually use what is called XLR as connectors, which gives it a balanced signal – so you hear no interference – even over long distances of cable. It works by having two opposite wires – one positive and the other negative – and when electrical interference is picked up on the cable, that noise is heard by both wires. Because they are opposite, they each cancel out the offending signal. Don't get hold of a cable that has XLR at one end and a mini-plug at the other; a transformer on it to convert the signal is superior.

For the professionally minded filmmaker – even if not professionally funded – external mics are going to be a necessity. There are basically six common types:

- *Personal mic.* Also known as a lavalier, clip-on or tie-mic, this is a discreet small mic that can be easily hidden from view, clipped onto the actor's clothing. For dialogue these give great results, as they pick up a full, deep, resonant sound from the chest.
- *Hand-held.* A common mic used in close proximity by on-camera interviewers.
- *Boundary effect.* These are used to pick up reflected sound bounced from hard surfaces and are sometimes known as PZ or PZM mics.

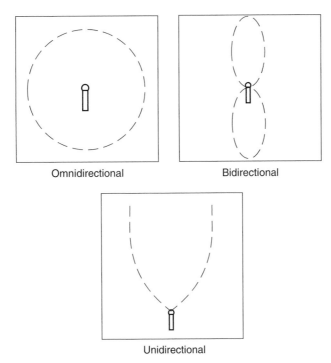

Figure 5.6 Mic ranges.

- *Contact mics*. These are used for attachment to musical instruments or the picking up of any other sound in physical contact with a surface or object.
- *Shotgun mic*. A very useful mic for location shooting, as it picks up sounds at a moderate distance from the camera.
- *Studio mics*. These encompass a range of mics used for studio filming, including television work.

What to use and where

Let's go through the uses of these mics and look at what sort of mic you will need and what you can manage without.

Basic level

If you are working at the most basic levels of equipment, you need a *dynamic microphone*. This is a rugged type often used in news reporting and can cope with a wide mix of recording situations. A really useful feature is that it does not need a power supply, unlike the next category we shall look at. If time is at a premium and you don't want to be reshooting, you need to avoid the mic battery running out during a scene. Dynamic mics don't necessarily give the best quality but are easy to manage and will give you clear sound if you are not sure what to use.

Mid to experienced level

Once you get more experienced, you can start using the more sensitive and vastly smaller condenser/ capacitor mics. These are not so good outside in poor weather and do need a small power supply coming through the mic cable itself, from a mixing board or an AC power supply. They also run off batteries, which can be a more flexible, convenient option but will, to the fury of you and your crew, run out of power without informing you.

Which microphone?

Within the categories above there are a number of types, for situations ranging from recording all sound in a given area to that just within a small range. We refer to mics according to their directional characteristics – in other words, the range of the angle they will pick up. This is similar to lenses, where a wide angle will see everything within a wide range whereas a macro lens is better at picking up small, close objects. There are three types: omnidirectional, bidirectional and unidirectional.

- *Omnidirectional.* These mics are sensitive to sounds that they hear all around them. They will pick up these sounds equally, so they record what you want plus all the other sounds going on around. This may sound good for busy, crowded scenes where you want the actors to be heard amongst a crowd, but it is rarely as clear as that. These mics will not distinguish between sounds and will record everything as an even mix, which can be adequate in some situations if there are no other sounds around to interfere with what is your main sound. You are almost always going to want to avoid this kind of mic because control of sound is your primary aim and this simply gives free rein to whatever happens to be around, including sounds behind the camera.
- *Bidirectional.* These mics are open to sound coming from two directions and can be used in two-way interviews or, occasionally, when working with stereo. But achieving clear stereo is not easy to accomplish using these mics without some skill, and in any case it is better to play with directions of sound in the editing process, when you can alter the track of all sound sources (when recorded separately).
- *Unidirectional.* These really are the ones you need for your DV movies. If you go into a store and ask for one, however, you will be asked what kind you want from a range of four types. They all pick up sound coming from one direction, in decreasingly narrow ranges of sensitivity. With movies shot on digital video, unidirectional affords you the most control over what goes on to the soundtrack.

Tip   Bringing sounds forward can affect the story. In *On the Waterfront* (Elia Kazan, 1954), Marlon Brando tries to explain himself to Eva Marie Saint and excuse his earlier actions, but the rising sound of a boat-horn drowns him out at precisely the point when he apologizes, with bad results. Using a separate track brought forward at the right moment, the result is impressive, portraying the protagonist as clumsy and unlucky.

Types of unidirectional mic

Unidirectional mics involve a wide range of types and we need to look at these in some more detail:

1 *Cardioid*. The least narrow unidirectional mic is the cardioid. It is named after the heart-shaped look of its range pattern. It picks up sounds in a relatively wide range in front of the mic, but is less sensitive to sounds from behind the mic. For many situations even this is too wide, as it will pick up reflected sound bouncing off the walls or other surfaces in addition to the original sound. You can reduce this by moving the mic to within five feet (one and a half metres) from the source of the bounced sound.

2 *Supercardioid*. These mics record sound on a narrower range than the cardioid. The shotgun mic described earlier is an example of this type and is widely used on location shooting. They are useful because you can stand back from the source and point the mic from a distance of up to 13 feet (four metres) – safely recording sound of an actor while avoiding placing the mic in view of the camera.

3 *Hypercardioid*. This is even more narrow than the supercardioid and is useful for some work where distance is required and you may have lots of off-axis, or unwanted, noise to avoid. These do need careful handling; move a little to the side – or if your actor moves – and you lose pick-up.

4 *Parabolic*. These are the most directional of this range of mics. To be exact, this is not exactly a type of mic but a way of using other directional mics. You can fit a parabolic reflector, which allows the mic to pick up only those sounds along a very narrow line in front of the mic. If you use one of these reflectors, running from 35 cm to a meter in diameter, you will have a very accurate angle of recorded sound. But, as with the hypercardioid, any movement of source or mic needs to be closely accommodated and headphones should be worn to notice unwanted changes. There are not many situations when you need a parabolic mic for movie location work, so you can skip on these unless you intend to shoot a remake of de Palma's *Blow Out*, or record field sports.

Good sound recording on location: the hierarchy of microphone techniques

There are ways of achieving good, clear sound from all your diverse sources on the movie set. Knowing how to get this when working at a fast pace is going to make your production move smoothly. In larger productions, there is a concept known as 'the hierarchy of microphone techniques' and this model can be used as your default method for recording a scene and then altered only when you encounter unusual recording situations.

In this technique, the top method of recording – number 1 – is going to work most of the time in most situations, while the method following it can be used when the first won't work and so on.

1 Overhead boom/shotgun mic
2 Shotgun from underneath
3 Shotgun mic placed in one position
4 Lavalier (personal) mic in one position
5 Lavalier mic on the actor
6 Lavalier mic without cords.

Overhead boom/shotgun mic

If you want good quality sound with minimum effort and minimal mixing later, and if you want it to sound natural and not over-produced (in other words, artificial or too clean), the shotgun mic is the best option. This elongated mic is held, typically, above the heads of the actors, out of view of the camera. This is even more helpful when you start working on a scene that has more than two actors speaking. Actors can move about, enter or leave the scene, stand up or whatever they need to do and still be heard, the mic operator adjusting the angle of the boom to focus on the right person. Furthermore, there are no cables to get in your way. This approach will work in almost any scene and allows for great flexibility in what you record, depending on how close the mic is to certain sounds.

Shotgun from underneath

There are times, though, when obstacles on set get in the way of an accurate reading of all sounds and you may need to hold the boom from beneath the actor. This does alter the tone of the sound, as the lower, bass sounds are located in the lowest parts of the chest and are nearest to the mic. It is less common to do boom recording this way, as you are more likely to get the mic in shot and it reduces the freedom of movement of the actor, but it does have its uses because it is quick and easy to set up.

Shotgun mic placed in one position and lavalier mic in one position

There are occasions when it may not be convenient to hold a mic above an actor – for instance, if the camera is recording a wide angle – and it is easier to secure it to a stationary part of the set. You can secure a large boom mic or a small lavalier at a given point in a room, set or location to pick up a particular sound. There are times when this is the most favourable method when a boom is not feasible – as in a car – or when you need to pick up a sound on one part of a set only occasionally, allowing you to hold the main boom mic over the main action or dialogue.

Lavalier mic on the actor

Although not your first choice, a lavalier mic, or tie-mic, situated on an actor's body offers a good method for recording dialogue. Some people prefer this mic as it gives a strong signal with lots of bass when using a standard consumer-level camcorder. These cameras record high quality sound but do not always allow you to alter the tone of the signal – something that can, in any case, often be achieved in post-production with very basic sound software. Attaching a mic to the body gives you deeper sound but is prone to interference when clothes rustle or other objects or actors obscure sound. On the whole, if you want natural sound it is better to record with hidden rather than attached lavalier mics. Bear in mind that if you do use lavalier mics a lot in your dialogue, the result will be clean but maybe a little too clean, and you may need to add ambient sound later to create a more natural effect, as achieved by a boom or shotgun.

Lavalier mic without cords

If none of the above work, then you can resort to the radio mic. These bring a disproportionate amount of problems with them, despite their usefulness in capturing a fast-moving, unpredictable source. These mics use a weak FM signal, as weak as possible to avoid contravening national guidelines, and so tend to attract interference from other radio transmitters. Local taxies, security walkie-talkies and other radio users near your location can often cause disturbance. Many radio mics allow you to alter the channel you use for transmission and it is usually possible to find a clear path free of interference, often in the UHF (Ultra-High Frequency) range, but you may still have problems with metal surfaces obstructing transmission. There are two types of radio mic: hand-held and clip-on. Radio mics are getting better at eliminating interference and some camcorders have built-in antennae for picking up this sound. The convenience of the radio mic is obvious, but it is the method most prone to causing problems.

Line feed levels: getting the mixture right

If you can invest in a mixing board to combine the various sounds being recorded you will achieve high quality results. As we have seen, one of the main advantages is being able to see the levels – the power – of the audio signals and adjust accordingly.

Using an audio mixing board

An audio signal entering a mixing board is boosted above that coming in from a standard mic, usually at the 600-ohm level. However, most camcorders can't function with sound this powerful, so you will need to reduce the signal by about 30–50 dB, although some mixing boards have a simple switch to set the levels at the right point for camcorder mic inputs. Again, make sure you check for interference on the signal the camcorder picks up, not just that which the mixing board hears. Testing is crucial to see whether your levels are correct and whether you are experiencing problems with interference, so record a test scene and play the sequence back using headphones. Don't rely on what you hear on headphones as you record, as sometimes you may hear a buzzing sound on the tape that you couldn't hear when recording.

Location recording troubleshooting

To summarize the ideas we have covered so far, it may be useful to look at a few different situations and see how you would use mics and how you would record the signal. There is no typical scene; every film has different needs and will present different problems.

Example 1: two figures, interior
A scene involves two actors, A and B, situated in a room. They talk and at a particular point a third actor appears at the door, after which the scene cuts. For this sequence you can assume that the dialogue is important and needs to be clear and audible. As the two actors are sitting in the same position throughout the scene, you could use a stationary shotgun or boom mic, which picks up their voices. Actor C appears later and we will need to pick up what is said by all three. Actor C will stand at the door entrance and say a few lines before departing, so we can safely attach a hidden lavalier cardioid mic to the side of the door frame.

You will also need to record the extra sounds to be placed behind these tracks later, when editing. You would first record ambient sound or presence, which acts as a continuity device, smoothing over the subtle alterations in background hum as you film each part of the sequence. Record just a few minutes of this using omnidirectional or cardioid mics, and loop it when editing. Each of the other separate sounds are recorded including, for instance, street sounds outside the room, footsteps of actor C coming up the drive and a slightly exaggerated door opening and shutting.

Example 2: several figures, street scene

The scene is set in a narrow street with several actors, all of whom are talking simultaneously. There is a strong sense of atmosphere as the rich sounds of a street market, traffic and cathedral bells in the distance combine. To record this complex scene, use a shotgun mic mounted on a pole or boom, situated a little higher than usual above the actors' heads. The shotgun is good for giving you a sense of sound perspective (sounds far away are less powerful) and will pick up other background sounds to give a more natural sound, but will not drown out the main voices. If one actor above the others needs to be heard at one point, you can direct the mic the right way. Even though you are recording good, natural sound with the voices, you still need an overall ambient track to iron out the differences in the various takes later. You will, don't forget, be shooting over a period of time, during which the sounds of the street may change. With this scene, you could use a dynamic mic to record everything if you want to stick with basic equipment; it should pick up sounds in all the various conditions present, but may compromise quality.

Example 3: two figures, a car, exterior

A scene involves two people in a car. A third is to talk to the others as they arrive at their destination and get out of the car in one continuous take. This is tricky, as it involves different situations, dialogue and potential problems with situating the mics.

To begin the scene, place lavalier mics in the car. Hide one each on both driver and passenger sun visors to pick up dialogue clearly. Attaching it to clothes would cause problems with seat-belt or clothes causing rustling sounds. If you can't attach it to the sun visor (a soft-top with the roof down?), try attaching to clothes but soften the clothing and take out the starchiness that causes the noise by damping a small section of cloth, out of view.

When the two reach their destination, we need to have one take in which they get out of the car and talk to a third actor. Record this by using an overhead boom mic angled to pick up all three at the same time. The noise of the car engine will also appear in the background of the shotgun track, adding realism. The lavalier will pick up the last of the conversation in the car, while the shotgun picks it up from there outside. In this case, you actually need a difference in sound to reflect the move from interior to exterior, so the alteration in what you pick up is satisfactory. If you want one continuous recording, try a radio mic attached to the actor's body, but switch to a more reliable mic as soon as you can in the scene.

Example 4: three figures, exterior, sea front

Continuing on from the scene above, let's assume the three actors then walk down to the sea front and talk further. Recording this scene presents problems because of the need to keep crew and cameras well back from the actors as they walk further along the beach and the potential of wind noise to interfere with quality. Although parabolic mics are going to do the job more cleanly, a hypercardioid may be easier to use as it does not have to be so pin-point accurate, and if your actors are moving around this is going to be crucial. If you are restricted by your equipment, and do not have an accurate long-distance mic, you could consider overdubbing voices if you cannot actually see clearly the actors speaking their lines. You may still want natural sound, with all the ambient sound of the beach location, but this could be more easily handled if the actors are close to the camera. This would be a better option than radio mics in some ways, since the latter will tend to give sound that is too clear and neat, requiring you to lay over much ambient sound to 'rough it up' sufficiently to convey the location.

Sound effects

If you have relatively little experience of sound work it is better to record all your sounds on videotape at first and then, in the editing stage, import and alter sound clips in the same way as you would for vision clips. This method for recording background sound or particular effects, such as footsteps or telephone rings, is straightforward because you can simply use your existing editing software and don't need to yet get involved in specialist sound software. The timeline in most software offers a useful visual guide to the layers of sound on the soundtrack. On the negative side, capturing these clips at the editing stage is less than economical, as video clips are far larger than sound files, but you can, of course, delete vision from these files as you use them.

There are two formats available if you choose to record sound separate to the camcorder: mini-disc and digital audio tape (DAT).

DAT

Digital audio tape was created in 1987. The quality of the DAT format is such that professional studios very quickly adopted it and made it the digital standard for recording. It offers three hours of digital sound on a tape half the size of an analog audio cassette tape, with the same format as a CD (44.1 kHz sampling frequency and 16 bits). While both digital compact cassette (DCC) tape and mini-disc use data compression, DAT is the only consumer recording standard that does not, meaning that the whole signal is held on the tape. DAT is easy to use on location; indexing of the tape and rewinding are extremely fast (50 seconds for a 120-minute tape), so you can quickly access any place on the DAT tape. For clarity and purity of sound, DAT rivals the compact disc (CD).

Mini-disc

Mini-discs were created by Sony in 1991 as a disc-based digital recording medium that is as near to CD quality as possible. There are two types of mini-disc (MD): pre-mastered MDs, which can be recorded on once only and are similar to CDs in operation and manufacture; and recordable MDs, which can be recorded on repeatedly and employ magneto-optical technology.

DAT vs mini-disc: which format is better for filmmaking?

Bear in mind that while DAT and MD are both digital formats, MD stores audio signals using a data reduction or compression technique and there are data quantity differences between the quality of a

CD recording and an MD copy of it. But this doesn't mean that anyone listening will hear the difference; most people will assume the CD and the MD recording are the same. So, for filmmaking there is going to be a negligible difference between the high-data DAT and the compressed MD. However, the one disadvantage of MD is that differences from the original increase with each generation copy, even though it is recorded digitally. There is a build-up of 'artefacts' (picture disturbances caused by technical limitations) as data is recompressed.

The Crunch

- You may not have the best model of camcorder on the market, but you can have sound quality to match big-budget productions
- The camera mic is almost never a good solution to your sound needs
- Use good quality mics with XLR transformers and adapters to attach to your camera mic input socket
- There is no need to buy the whole range of mics unless you can afford to right now; a good shotgun cardioid and a lavalier will cover you for most situations, while a hand-held cardioid mic will help record individual sounds
- While you are building up experience of how to record sound in varied situations, use the hierarchy of recording techniques.

Project 11. The chase

What this project is for: to get better at sound recording
Time: allow a few days for planning, two days for shooting and a few days for editing

What this project is about

This film is going to put into practice a few ideas we have covered so far. This doesn't mean it is necessarily harder than other projects, just that it starts to challenge you on several levels. Here's how.

This project asks you to make a film in which we don't see the main aspects of the narrative. We are going to use the powers of suggestion in sound to imply what is happening rather than showing it directly, allowing us to make a drama that relies less on a big budget and more on what comes free – namely, your skill and imagination.

The film centres around a figure running through a series of dark streets, running into different obstacles, possibly being chased by something we cannot see. We only hear what the figure encounters throughout the film. In addition to your use of sound, we need to use the ideas brought up in the earlier parts of this section, on using the camera. Use the whole range of camera angles in this one, and go as far as you need to suggest the tension and drama of the events of the plot. In order to keep your options open as to what the figure encounters, try to avoid complicating the plot in any way. It's enough to use the figure's journey as our sole purpose of watching the movie.

Stage 1

Since we have the story worked out in its essentials, you need only at this stage to think of what the figure will encounter in its path. The specifics of this are down to you: you can make it a comic film, a serious scary movie or a futuristic fantasy. Indicate what the character is going to run into – for instance, 'wild animal sound' or 'weird flying object'.

The kind of movie you make may be influenced by the locations you have access to. If you know of a place you can film with a labyrinthine set of corridors, or a series of narrow streets, or an industrial site, then let that be your deciding factor in where it is set. Add to the air of mystery by keeping several facts from the audience. Where are we? What year is it? Who is the protagonist?

Stage 2

Complete a set of visualizations and storyboards that detail how your film is going to look. Since we have few details to go on, it is going to be easy for the audience to become lost, so we are going to have to remain in control of continuity issues. This means making sure that the lighting you use is constant throughout, so that we get a sense of the chase taking place in one continuous flow of events. Keep the costume the same throughout and make sure that the direction of the figure running is maintained: this means he or she will probably go from left to right, exiting right but reappearing left and continuing on right. This will help to show that the movement of the figure is in one main direction: away from whatever is threatening.

Stage 3

Shooting this movie may feel artificial, or at least more artificial than it usually does. It's going to be like Keanu Reeves dodging on a film set from a hundred imaginary, but soon to be computer-created, Agent Smiths. But bear with it. Indicate to your actor points on the set when particular reactions are required and, since we don't have to use sounds recorded actually on set, you can shout as much as you need.

To maintain continuity of lighting, choose a set-up you like and stay with it. If you are unsure what to opt for, choose a strong single lamp stationary on the set, casting a light that the actor can enter and leave, revealing facial expressions and yet keeping the majority of the set in shadow, allowing us to fill the shadow, as it were, with sounds. Now and then, step back and take a few shots of the overall scene, showing off a particular part of the set that looks good. These covering shots, displaying the actor in full and allowing us to notice the left–right direction they are going in, are going to be useful later in the editing stage, helping to stitch the whole film together easily.

Stage 4

Editing this film is relatively straightforward. But before you start piecing it together, we need to put into place some way of the action getting more intense as the film reaches the end. Keep the individual cuts on the longer side at the start, perhaps four or five seconds or more, while the last quarter of the film sees the cuts get quicker, indicating a speeding up of the action and an imminent conclusion.

At this point we can start to think of the sounds that indicate what the figure has encountered. This is a time to have some playtime with the microphones. Spend a few days investigating and recording sounds. Go into this with an open mind; it really is a revelation how something very ordinary sounds when taken out of context. For example, try recording how a cabbage sounds when cut in half; the crunching sound was often used in horror movie scenes of a guillotine. Record washing machines, dripping water taps, a cat howling, and make use of whatever you can do with your voice. The aim is to find raw sounds that can later be layered to create a full and menacing soundscape.

Stage 5

When you begin the process of inserting sounds, try layering few together on the timeline. Import sounds directly into your editing program and play around with them on the timeline, listening to how they sound in conjunction with others. Look for the available tracks you have on the timeline and create as many as you need. Place the clips down first and make a complete silent movie. Many editing programs enable you to place visual markers on the timeline, so that you can tie-in certain sounds later to particular shots. Also make sure that you adjust the sound levels of each clip.

Make sure that you have:

- A constant noise that will indicate to the audience that we are in one place.
- A suggestion that there is a 'something' pursuing the figure, again by sounds alone. Try footsteps or a howling.
- A particular sound that we associate with the figure, maybe a musical watch or panic-stricken breathing. We need to associate the pursuer and the 'pursuee' with two very distinct sounds.

Film View
Look at the closing scenes of *Blade Runner: The Director's Cut* (Ridley Scott, 1991) for a chase where we often hear Harrison Ford's pursuer.

Evaluation

This project requires much more work on the post-production side than shooting. You may well have shot everything in one evening but then had to spend many days perfecting the sounds and the way they match the visuals.

How was the sound layering? Success in this area can be measured by how you have managed to take the sound out of its setting and given it a new life. So, if the sound of dog growling layered with a child's rattle, for example, is like nothing else, then you have hit the right mark. As you may have found, the plot of the figure being pursued and encountering different events along the way is no more than a vehicle to allow us to play around with sounds.

Beyond this, however, look at how you handled the potential continuity problems. Play the movie to your friends, ask whether they noticed any unnatural jumps in action, as if a section of time had been removed, or whether it seemed as if the events of the film flowed realistically.

When looking at your use of the camera, make a note of the kinds of shots you used. Did you use shots which resembled each other too much? Or was the range of shots varied, maintaining our interest in the film?

Whatever you managed to achieve, the main purpose of this film has been to see in this very extreme example how sound can be just as powerful as images, but at a fraction of the cost.

I want something more challenging

We focused in this project on action-oriented scenes, which make it easier to include sounds because there are specific objects or places that need them. But if you wanted to try a more difficult version, opt for a scene where there is little discernible physical action and where the real action is going on in the mind of the protagonist. Refer back to the scene from Hitchcock's *Blackmail*, earlier in this chapter. Can you devise a scene where simple sounds are used to create a metaphorical feeling? For example, in a scene of a simple family dinner, can you suggest what is going on in the mind of one person, who may be experiencing some terrible, traumatic period? Could sounds be amplified, altered, layered or new ones added to suggest feelings for this character?

Project 12. Sound environment

What this project is for: to look at how to change a scene simply by using sound
Time: allow around four or five hours for editing

What this project is about

The aim of this project is to find out exactly how far you can manipulate a scene by changing the sounds we hear. It is surprising how much of the total information we receive from a scene is derived from sounds. Some estimates put this at around 60 per cent from sound and 40 per cent from visuals. Put this to the test by replacing the sounds from an existing clip and altering how we perceive it.

Stage 1

Find a clip from a movie. This needs to be around three minutes long and centred on one location. A clip without dialogue is far easier to manipulate because the sounds of the environment are foregrounded, but it will work just as well with dialogue.

Stage 2

Watch the clip a few times and note the sounds you can hear. List these in order so that the loudest or most noticeable is at the top or your list, with other sounds placed below. Next, figure out how you could add to these sounds to alter the situation. For instance, can an interior scene have wartime noises outside, with sirens, bombs and crowds? Can you transform a city street into a futuristic one by adding sounds to suggest flying cars, futuristic talking billboards and so on (look at Jean-Luc Godard's classic sci-fi movie *Alphaville*, a big influence on *Blade Runner*, to see how a contemporary street can be sent 50 years into the future).

Stage 3

Place the clip on the timeline of your editing software and gather sounds from other sources, such as other movies, sound effects CDs and your own recordings. Layer the sounds and mix them until you get an environment you feel matches your plans. Remember to always reduce the volume of the sound layers if you want another layer to be foregrounded, rather than simply increasing the volume of the main one.

Evaluation

The key to success in this film is a naturalistic sound environment which convinces the viewer that the sounds were always on the clip and do not seem out of place. To test this, watch parts of the movie before your clip and then watch your new sequence. There will be an obvious jump in the way it appears, but this is exactly what you want; the movie should seem to have moved to another entirely different location, even another genre or time. The more you have changed the movie, the more you have unleashed the power of sound to affect what we perceive.

I want something more challenging

To push this project further, try recording the sounds yourself, giving you good experience of foley work (sound effects). It will restrict you in what you can record, but will ensure that you also find out more about how microphones work.

Another challenge is to try using very diverse sounds to mix together and make new ones. Collect and merge sounds, using edit settings to alter the speed of them, perhaps to create entirely new ones. For instance, some spaceships in *Star Wars: Attack of the Clones* (2002) are a mixture of sounds including what appears to be hydraulic machines and World War II Spitfire aircraft.

4. Real world guide to location shooting

In this section we will road test what we have talked about so far and talk to filmmakers who bring their own experiences of location shooting to bear.

In each case, they highlight the way that what goes on while shooting on location is different to what is expected, and how knowing this can help prevent problems large and small. All the filmmakers have been making short films for several years and were interviewed by the author.

Matt Sheldon, James Sharpe, Liz Crow, Jon Rennie, Richard Graham, Sean Martin, Nick Ball, Max Sobol, David Casals and Carl Tibbets all make short films. Gurchetan Singh is a music promo director. Phil Grabsky is an award-winning documentary director. Jonnie Oddball is founder of 48-hour Film Challenge and a feature-film director.

How the shoot went

Liz Crow: I shot in daylight and for the days leading up to the shoot conditions were perfect, but just as the shoot got underway the sun appeared and spent the whole time dodging in and out of cloud, so my exposures were all over the place and the shots didn't match. A reshoot was out of the question, so it had to be made to work. What it did was force me to experiment wildly in the edit. In the end, I think the resulting images are more interesting, more beautiful, than the pictures I'd thought I was trying to make.

Richard Graham: I've just finished post-production on my second short film, *Kafkaesque*. We shot over six pretty relaxed days and that included two nights of shooting in the supermarket location when it was (supposed to be) a bit quieter. The really hard part was shooting two nights in the middle of the schedule and trying to keep everyone energetic at three in the morning, with 15 set-ups left to shoot. I planned the shoot as meticulously as I could. During prep I made the decision to shoot one continuous week and not break the shoot up into smaller chunks.

Jon Rennie: Bad weather caused me to postpone to the weekend, thus costing me my actress, who had to be replaced at short notice. However, the shooting day was bright and clear, and it took us about five hours to get all the shots.

Worst moments

Liz Crow: We were up against the clock, the make-up guy had a terrible cold, the actor's back was hurting from crouching under the tripod for too long and I was balanced on a stool trying to peer through the viewfinder. My main job then was trying to make people laugh.

Richard Graham: The worst moment occurred on the first day of night shooting. We'd just shot the pivotal scene of the film with an actor who was about 60, a real thespian, whom I had convinced to work for nothing, so we tried to make the whole night shoot in a supermarket as pleasant as possible for this chap, shooting his scenes quickly so he could go home early. This meant giving preference to his set-ups and saying we'd go back later and shoot the stuff without him in. I missed one really crucial set-up because of this. Every time I see this scene now I wince at the lack of the set-up I missed. Also, when we went back to pick up the shots we'd purposely missed we only had a single-chip JVC camera which didn't have manual colour temperature controls and produced some pretty weird colours under fluorescent supermarket lighting.

Sean Martin: The shoot went very well. It was very quick – all done in two weeks. In fact, the whole film was very quick and unexpected! Things got a little tense the week before we were due to begin shooting, as there was almost no money in the bank and we couldn't track down the investor. I remember having to rehearse the actors as if nothing was wrong and having chest pains throughout the day due to the stress. Then, at the last minute, Doug, our producer, called me to say that the money was finally in the bank.

By the last day, exhaustion was really kicking in and we still had to somehow shoot the remaining scenes set in [main character] Cade's flat, despite the fact that we no longer had access to it. The final scene we shot was of Cade throwing up. I felt like doing the same by that point, but again there just wasn't the time.

The best moments were those wonderful times during rehearsal where a scene that's only half working suddenly comes to life, and somehow what you end up with is much better than what was originally in the script.

Phil Grabsky: The most difficult thing on a documentary is lugging all the equipment through endless security checks at airports. Once I arrive at the location, I'm so relieved! Apart from that, I also spend a lot of time cleaning and maintaining the kit.

Jon Rennie: Worst moment was when it began to rain. It was also very cold, but because I was well prepared, shooting went very smoothly.

Nick Ball: It was our first shoot, so we hadn't really got anything to compare it to. The worst moment was probably on about the third day of what was a four-day shoot. Your time is incredibly pressurized on a schedule like that. Nick and I were standing discussing a shot, thinking we were doing quite well, and Dan Bronx – our DoP [Director of Photography] – came up, put a friendly arm around us, smiled and said 'Lads, we are drowning.' He was basically saying that if we didn't pick the pace up we were going to be left with half a film.

Guchetan Singh: My last short film *Ned Warking* worked out really well, but the shoot was terrible. It was probably one of the most stressful things I have ever done. Everyone working on it was paid nothing and did it for the credit, and we were all quite novice filmmakers. It was my fault to the extent that I hadn't scheduled the shoot. Although it was kind of clear in my head, it wasn't so clear to our DoP. This is a must: always, always schedule your shoots. This is something your production manager or producer will do, but when it comes to no-budget or low-budget filmmaking, you sometimes find yourself taking these roles on yourself, which can be very stressful, as you're trying to think logistically and creatively.

We also worked long hours, 12–16 hours, which again could have been controlled with decent scheduling. Again, try to avoid this, as people start to become stressed, and when people are stressed it becomes a pretty sour set. Also, our DoP did not get on with our sound man, which created problems as the set became pretty intense. All this said and done, the set might have been terrible, but each evening when I would go to bed, a little smile would come to me as I knew I was getting a little closer to achieving my goal, which was to make a great little short.

Also stressful is people letting you down, which will happen because people are rarely being paid. The best moment is when you hear the positive comments from other people, because filmmaking can be

Figure 5.7 Director David Casals co-ordinates a complex location shoot for his short, *Time Cocktail.*

very personal and lonely. If it's your idea, your script, your direction, then you're exposing your most personal thoughts to the world. So it's great to hear the positive voices because it means that all that hard work and stress has paid off.

Carl Tibbetts: The worst thing I think for any indie director is not being able to get that one all-important shot because the kit's late back to the hire firm or the light's gone or something else to do with the a non-existent budget.

Nick Miles: One of my most recent location shoots was an all-nighter, to produce a two-minute short worthy of showreel material. I had worked on many night shoots before, from being outside all night with the crew working in torrential downpours to split days where half of the day was spent at night on one stunt. But this was different; it was written, directed and shot in one night from concept to returning the equipment to the hire company the next morning. The problem with working in this environment is that everything takes twice as long; at night you are tired because you are out of sync with your usual working day.

James Sharpe: The shoot was planned for two days; it was only just done in time. I was dead lucky with not having rain as there's quite a bit of stuff done outside. There were difficult moments. For instance, there was a scene outside shot at a bus stop. James Fisher and 'Marielle Dreier' were seated saying about five lines each. Although it's on screen for 30 seconds it took about two hours to get a clean take of sound, as there was a building site just behind us and as soon as I shout action 10 cars decide to come past. When I cut it's so quiet you can hear a pin drop. I then used sound from the good take and then wild it over close-ups from a bad sounded take. I sync'd it perfectly then cleaned the audio up in Adobe Audition.

Equipment choices

Liz Crow: I prefer a Sony VX2000 on fixed tripod, plus a mini-disc. I used the mini-disc because it gives a much better sound quality than the camera mic. I edited on a Mac using Final Cut Pro.

Richard Graham: We shot on a Canon XL1 and for shots where the Canon was too big and heavy to put it where I wanted, we used a single-chip Panasonic. We also did a few pick-up shots of a scene using a JVC single-chip camera which, compared to the Panasonic, was quite frankly rubbish. The project was edited on Final Cut 3 and 4.

Phil Grabsky: It depends on the project, but right now I am married to my Sony PD150. I was a late convert from super-16 mm film to Digi-Beta, and then from Digi-Beta to DVCAM (where appropriate), but the PD150 (now PD170) is extraordinary; I couldn't have made my Afghan film if I hadn't have had the PD150. My Australian cinema distributor thought I'd shot it on HD [high definition]. I think the most welcome compliments I've had for the film have been for the photography.

Jon Rennie: I took the opportunity to use a Digi-Beta camera for the film so that I could get a high quality anamorphic image. Although I'd considered using a [Sony] PD150, I wanted to get as good an image as possible so that the rendered special effects would not look out of place. It pays to use the best possible quality equipment – that's where my money went.

Carl Tibbets: Get hold of an HD camera (go to your local facility house and beg or just go and look and learn the kit); lots of companies will lend you gear over weekends if it's just sitting on a shelf otherwise. For editing, Final Cut Pro 4 – it's right for this level of filmmaking.

Nick Miles: The camera that I would recommend to any filmmaker starting out is the Sony DSR PD170. It has great functionality and when shooting DVCAM stock with good lighting practice can produce

Figure 5.8 Preparation on the set of *The Dark Hunter* by Jonnie Oddball.

outstanding results. I have pushed this camera to its limits both technically and physically, like when I door-mounted mine to the door of a car to get a brilliant two-shot whilst the characters were driving along.

The PD 170/150 gives a very cold broadcast look, great for TV and documentaries (that is why the BBC endorse it as a camera for their journalists), but if you want to achieve a more film look, I tend to white balance off a blue-tinted white card to give a warmer cinematic feel usually only achieved by film.

James Sharpe: I saved up £3000 and really wanted an XL2, but thought the extra £500 wasn't worth it. I know that some BBC documentaries are shot on [Sony] PD150 or 170. I went for that and am not disappointed.

Essential tips

Liz Crow: Plan all the details and brief the crew and actors thoroughly. It leaves room both to be spontaneous and to problem solve. I storyboard the full film beforehand and, because I'm new to shooting my own footage, I try to have test runs before the day of the shoot.

Sean Martin: Try and keep a clear head. Take deep breaths. Focus. Be decisive, but always remain open to suggestions (just because you're the director, it doesn't mean you have a monopoly on all the best ideas). Always remain calm. And always make it seem like you know what you're doing, even if you don't. Once a director has lost their authority through being indecisive, difficult, rude or just plain wrong, it's very difficult if not impossible to get that respect back.

Jon Rennie: When you're making the film, don't just leave the camera on a tripod or set it on the widest angle. Think about your shots and storyboard in advance. Rehearse your actors so that you don't have to keep directing them all day when you should be dealing with the camera and sound.

Jonnie Oddball: One of the biggest things I learned is what can be done when you really focus on what you want. Take a die-hard attitude and do whatever it takes. I asked the cast to improvise the scenes, but only told the actors the scenes on the day of filming. I found writing a film around what you know and what you have around you works and that goes for locations as well; with no budget at all it's amazing what you have around you that you never think about.

Gurchetan Singh: You will always hear people talking about how you should only work with people who are on the same wavelength as you; this is great but if you're starting out then that network isn't always accessible, especially if you don't live in a film/media-orientated world. So as a director you have to become very clear about the style you like, about the shots that inspire you. Dabble in some editing, try and put footage together and make stories. Try and experiment with ideas and techniques, and by doing all this you can start to realize what you like and what you don't, so when that network isn't so strong at least your vision will be, which will often help to carry a film.

Nick Miles: The single most important piece of advice I would give to any first-time producer, director of photography or filmmaker is visit your location again and again and again, as many times as possible, before your location shoot. No matter how many times you check the location and prepare for anything, something will always throw you. Unexpected building works is one, parades through city centres with loud bands, adverse weather conditions another, e.g. snow in May/June. Owners of buildings/land can also be quite unpredictable. Also, always take more than you need – it is better to have a car loaded with too many chocolate biscuits, AAA batteries and umbrellas.

Matt Sheldon: Time is the worst thing. There is never enough time. It's OK if you have lots of money because then you have time, but otherwise it is your worst enemy. I started off well because I decided that to get the crew on my side I would shoot the first scene in two takes. But 13 hours later, I thought it was getting out of control. After that I learnt to keep the days short.

James Sharpe: Make sure you are familiar with exposure and focus. If you don't have an outside monitor be sure you're used to the viewfinder and LCD monitor, otherwise what might look OK then could look totally dark or overexposed when you get back.

Always have belief. There's nothing worse than setting up as a beginner and having people you know saying you can't do that and laughing at you. I had that and I just blocked them out. If you have the burning desire to do it you will do it. *Living with the Dead* was screened to these same people and now they eat their words in style.

Crew

Jon Rennie: There were seven people on the shoot. You don't need a large crew to make a film – just enough so that no one is standing around and you don't have to wait around too long. It wasn't paid, apart from food and expenses, and in all it has cost me about £400 to make.

Jonnie Oddball: Amazingly, yes, every single person I got for the film was wonderful and helped out any way they could; I was trying to keep everyone happy in −2 degrees in woods in the middle of nowhere. You have to really respect everyone on your no-budget movie more than anything else, as they paid their own travel expenses and brought their packed lunch.

Carl Tibbets: I think at this level of micro-budget shorts you should not push people too far – it's a fine line getting the most out of what you have without annoying everyone left, right and centre! I think crew and actors working in a good atmosphere, not stressed out, with plenty of food and water on tap is the best way to get the most out of your shoot.

David Casals: For location food, hot meals are the best. Pizza is a classic that always works. In our last short film we had Chinese food and it was a success. People also appreciate home-made food, but that also depends on how many people can help you out preparing it.

Max Sobol: Crew will always like fat sandwiches, stuff like bacon butties, and an almost constant stream of coffee.

Figure 5.9 In this still from Richard Graham's *Kafkaesque*, the scene requires a shot in a moving bus.

Figure 5.10 Graham uses a tripod to overcome the shake of filming in the bus.

James Sharpe: To get the best from actors, make sure you screen test them at the audition, as they all appear different on camera than they do in real life. Make sure there's a few rehearsals so they know exactly what to do when you go to shoot. This is good practice and helped me shoot a 12-minute film in two days. On location, I made sure they weren't cold – make sure there's plenty of tea and coffee and at least feed them and pay their expenses. Make sure the actors stay fully charged. Sometimes I shoot the same thing from several angles and sometimes after several takes you have to make sure they keep the same enthusiasm as they did in the first.

5. Shooting for compression

There is no doubt that the web opens up new possibilities for the filmmaker. But like any new medium, some films look good when shown on the Internet and some don't. The same is true of the difference between showing films on a television or a cinema screen. The small scale and intimacy of television means that shooting for this medium imposes certain restrictions; television is described as a close-up medium, requiring the filmmaker to bring the viewer close to the action and avoid large-scale panoramic scenes. The aspect ratio also changes between theatrical and video release to make use of the maximum amount of screen in the smaller medium.

Web movies are different

Filmmakers work within these restrictions to obtain the best results for a production. It should come as no surprise, then, that the web has other restrictions that you need to bear in mind. These are useful only when your film is going to be seen primarily on the web and you don't expect to show it theatrically. However, the results of these guidelines on non-web films are not without merit; many films can benefit from the ideas suggested here, such as a simplification of image.

The effect of altering the movie or the way you make it, to accommodate the limits of the web, is a little like working with live music. Studio music is always going to sound clearer, neater and more subtle, but playing live requires a band to make a song understood despite the poor acoustics of an auditorium. Usually, this means making it more explicit musically and less subtle.

Modem type	Data rate in bits/ second	Data rate in bytes/ second
28.8 k	20 kbps	2.5 KB/s
56.6 k	32 kbps	4 KB/s
Dual ISDN	96 kbps	12 KB/s
T1, DSL and Cable modem	300 kbps	40 KB/s
WAN/LAN	160–800 kbps	20–100 KB/s

Figure 5.11 Data rates for video images via the Internet.

Shooting web films

Length of the movie

Short films fare better on the web, for obvious reasons; anything less than a few minutes in length is going to be more suited to the extremely slow connection rates most people still have. If you want to make something more ambitious, try dividing the movie up into small sections and turning it into an episodic series in which viewers can download a few minutes and watch it as part of the whole series.

Audio vs video

Bear in mind the choices you may have to make about the priority of audio or video. If a film needs both very smooth, clear images and a complex, layered soundtrack, you may run into problems.

If you decide to lose some picture quality in favour of sound, then the Internet is going to be kinder to your film. Fantastic sound quality is far easier to compress than pictures and you will get more quality for your data bits with sound rather than vision. If sound is not a priority, avoid relying on stereo as it will be flattened into mono in most compression methods. This won't get rid of any sounds but, together with the overall reduction in quality, it will make them harder to distinguish from one another. Avoid complex layering of sounds. Keep interference or excessive ambient sound to a minimum. If you think in terms of sound perspective, in which sounds occupy various levels in terms of foreground and background, webfilm offers you less depth, so keep sounds obvious and clear. In general, use lavalier mics for clear, if slightly unnatural, sound. Imagine playing the movie to someone over the telephone; you would need strong, obvious sounds.

Go to: Chapter 5:3, 'Sound recording'.

Clear-cut stories

As a whole, the story and/or themes must be more apparent, lucid and defined. Think of the live music analogy: subtlety may be lost by the time it reaches the viewer. This is not to say that you must hand the film to the viewer on a plate, but you will have to make the information more obvious, given the reduced size of that information.

Beware of text

Credits are still going to be legible but should be placed on straight colour, which should not be too highly saturated. Place credits one at a time on separate frames rather than bunched together and with a slightly larger font size than usual, maybe set at 24 point, at least. Text within the film, either as subtitles or as a design element layered over images, is more problematic. It is likely to be lost if the frame starts blurring, and the reduced screen size is going to make it blend with the background images.

Simpler imagery

This is going to mean making your compositions sharper and better, but this applies equally well to all your movies, not just those intended for the web. Try to eliminate extraneous parts of the frame, so that it shows what we need to see and virtually nothing else. Use plain backgrounds to lift out from the screen the elements you want the viewer to pick up on. Compositions should be bolder and more 'blocky' – in other words, with greater use of larger shapes and fewer details. In most instances, this is going to bring us back to the idea of dominance of the close-up. One way to define the kind of clarity we need is to look at design. There is a rule of thumb sometimes used by poster designers which says that a good poster needs to still make an impression viewed in passing through a dirty bus window, and this applies equally well to webfilm.

Go to: Chapter 6:1, 'Better looking films', for more help with stronger compositions.

Use close-ups

The film is to be seen on a small screen, at roughly 5 cm across, so you need to radically alter the way you depict action. The close-up will need to be utilized much more frequently than in other productions. If a scene requires some depiction of the expression on an actor's face, an extreme close-up is necessary, perhaps even focusing on parts of the face in turn.

Go to: Chapter 6:2 for more help with using the close-up in your movies.

The right lighting

Celluloid film has better resolution than video, and straight, uncompressed video films have better resolution than webfilms. Being at the bottom of the heap can be resolved somewhat by a certain use of lighting, offsetting some of the detrimental effects of picture clarity. Strong contrast is crucial; flat, vague lighting is going to enhance detail but heightened shadow and light will make a frame more easy to read, while improved composition may also enhance a sense of drama. Use a key light to pick out the main subject and use some fill lighting to separate the figure from the background, but above all avoid fluorescent lighting, as this flattens the picture. To test how your scene will look, take five paces back from your camera and have a look at the LCD monitor showing your movie.

Go to: Chapter 5:2 for more detail on lighting techniques.

The right colours

Some colours don't travel well. Just as website designers use what are called 'web-safe colours', so films can also suffer from colours merging into one another that are similar in hue or saturation. You will, on the whole, be safe with colour as long as you do not rely on it to convey important parts of the film; subtle differences between colours may be lost. This would have an impact, for example, on text, if the text and background image colours were not dissimilar enough. Note also that strongly saturated colours cause some problems with some formats or players regardless of the image, though this is decreasing as an issue as software codecs become more advanced.

Use of the camera

Since clarity is a constant requirement, one of the biggest obstacles is camera shake. Despite the creative possibilities in shooting with a hand-held camera, the results on the web could be disappointing. By dropping the frame rate, the video becomes slightly more jerky and anything that increases this is to be avoided. A stationary shot is going to look better than pans, tilts or tracking, as these all increase the blurring or make the picture more blocky.

Aspect ratio

As with normal video movies, try at all times to shoot in the aspect ratio (screen shape) you want to edit in. This means that if you want a widescreen look, shoot in it. In practice, you should choose the aspect ratio best suited for your film, perhaps because a television broadcaster wants it a certain ratio. Try to avoid using widescreen as a style choice – it rarely improves poor images and usually simply heightens the bad result, cropping the frame unnaturally. However, if you film from the start in this aspect ratio then it is embedded in your compositions and looks natural and well suited to the film. Web movies are usually shown in screen shapes resembling television screens, a 4:3 ratio. If you film in widescreen, no matter how natural it looks, you lose a portion of the screen at the top and bottom. Unlike the cinema, the web broadcaster doesn't stretch its screen to accommodate your aspect ratio.

> **Tip** Aspect ratios for video are measured in pixels. The standard 4:3 PAL picture is measured in 720 × 576 pixels for video monitors, but for computer monitors a slightly different ratio is used to take into account the computer's square pixels, resulting in 768 × 576. You won't notice any difference; the different pixel ratios are there to maintain the same aspect ratios between television screens and computers.

Creative web movies

Looking at the list above, the don'ts far outweigh the dos and it must seem as if there is little artistic point to using the web for making films. But part of the progress within the medium of film over the last century has been the result of filmmakers pushing the limits of what can be achieved. Hitchcock pushed the very limited resources of sound when he made Britain's first sound film, *Blackmail*, in 1929. Even earlier, Georges Mellies devised the first special effects by accidentally using the camera for multiple exposures.

Push technology

Part of the task of the low-budget filmmaker is to look at what can be done with the available technology, work with it as far as possible but at the same time push it further by experimentation, discovery and, basically, doing what the manual says you shouldn't. A quality that many independent filmmakers possess is that of being able to see possibilities within a tightly restrictive framework, whether this is budgetary or technological. Given that the web offers a filmmaker a direct way of reaching the viewing public, the constraints of this route are worth working with.

Some of the innovations seen in movie websites are testament to the fact that the filmmaker is a lateral-thinking, irrepressible artist. Many films make direct connections to early film experiments, conducted in the first decade of cinema. In that period, the theatrical movie was not the dominant form; people also wanted to see events they would not normally witness, like a train rushing overhead, filmed from the track, or burning barns crashing down. The pioneering spirit within film was a result of the desire of filmmakers to push the limits of this new form of communication and steadily turn it into an art form. That process was happening within a tightly confined space, in technology terms, yet produced a launch pad for generations of directors.

The Crunch

- Web movies are an evolving form, but they are still in their infancy – get in on the history of them from the start
- You're an artist – you like new ways of working and new forms of movie
- Watch your movie through the camera LCD monitor from a few feet to check how it will look
- Decide whether you sacrifice picture resolution, frame rate or sound
- Keep it short and simple
- Use strong lighting
- Use steady camera
- Avoid small text
- These restrictions imposed by web movies are good for your other movies too
- Be experimental
- Don't let it sit on the shelf – send it to a broadcast site.

Project 13. New format movie

What this project is for: to learn about shooting for the ultra-small screen – phone and web
Time: allow one hour to shoot and another to evaluate

What this project is about

Until new formats of communication evolved in the web and cell phones, filmmakers showed their work in only two ways: on the big screen (theatres) and on the small screen (TV). It was commonly accepted that shooting for these demanded different approaches to using the camera, editing and even the way text is used. Television needed close-ups more frequently because of the small size of the screen, while wide-angle shots and panorama shots could work more easily in the huge screens in theatres. Now we have other ways of watching films it is essential to figure out how this affects your movies.

In this project we are going to try making a short descriptive piece which addresses the demands of the web, phone viewing and hand-held devices.

Stage 1

There is no need to plan this film as it is not one that demands much forethought about structure or narrative. This is going to concentrate on a simple description of a commonplace event like making a cup of coffee or washing the car. It sounds like low-level material but the advantage of shooting something so simple is that it enables you to concentrate on the images rather than on symbolism or any meaningful stuff.

Choose a situation that you are going to film.

Stage 2

Shoot this film in-camera, so the movie is ready to play as soon as it is finished. This approach is good for morale as you can track your progress fast and see results quickly. The aim is to show every stage of the event – getting a cup, switching on the kettle, grinding the coffee and so on. Be as descriptive as possible so that it is absolutely clear what is happening.

For shooting for the ultra-small screen, make sure you shoot bearing in mind that the eventual movie will be seen at something like the size of the LCD monitor of your camcorder.

- Place the camera close to the action
- Use compositions that focus on the important elements of action
- Avoid rapid pan or tracks of the camera, as these shots will blur when compressed (see Chapter 5:5, 'Shooting for compression')
- Avoid detailed shots where we need to see small objects – make sure really crucial objects fill at least 30 per cent of the screen
- Avoid text that is less than 25 per cent of the height of the screen (if a screen is about 3–4 cm high)
- Light the images clearly, using hard light and strong shadows.

Evaluation

Look at the resulting movie on your camcorder monitor and assess which shots are clearly defined and which are vague. Look out for shots that are overly descriptive and uninteresting; possibly the use of light and shadow will have balanced the effects of too much description by adding atmosphere.

I want something more challenging

As a final task, try to re-edit the movie on simple editing software as a series of still images. Under the heaviest effects of compression your movie may need to appear as a slide show, or reduced to a jerky five frames a second or less. See how far you can push your movie by selecting only the most essential descriptive shots as still frames. Try selecting one for every five to ten you erase.

6 | Production aesthetics

1. Better looking films

You've spent a while looking at how to stretch the potential of your camera without spending any cash on the film itself. Now you need to look at what kind of 'feel' you want in your film and how the overall look of it can be achieved. Working with a small budget, you may not be able to rely on well-known actors or sets to make your film stand out from the competition, so you need to become more confident about what you can achieve with those tools that don't cost anything: what the camera sees.

Make your camera work harder, make your film look better

The aim of this section is to go through some of the basics of getting the most from the camera; how to get the right shots and how to find those elusive, special shots that will make your film rise above the rest. But as well as knowing the shortcuts to getting these kinds of shots, we need to look at how you can depict something in a professional way, to industry standards. This doesn't mean you are going to produce dull, uninspiring images; we are just going to concentrate on learning a few rules in camerawork so that later you can feel free to break them.

Use the rules and bend them

It may seem that if you know what kind of film you want to make you shouldn't need to know how other people work. It's true that no one knows better than you what kind of film you want, but this next step is not about copying how other filmmakers do it, it is about learning how to get your preferred shots more quickly. When you know how a certain shot is often filmed it gives you a starting point – you can either go with the norm or reject it. It can make you think faster. Furthermore, if you find yourself working with a crew of other people also committed to making films, they will expect you to know what works when filming – and what does not.

Conveying mood

Mood is a nebulous concept, but to attempt some definition, we could say that it is the integration of the various style elements of a film with the core theme of that film. Lighting, music and camera angle are the main tools behind the camera helping you to achieve this. It may shift throughout the film, but a pervasive atmosphere will dominate if the film is to be coherent and consistent. Mood is something that is evoked rather than described explicitly, so you have to rely on subtle methods to add a particular slant to a scene. Being able to manipulate mood is useful because it enables you to specify what sort of emotions are dominating a scene and how we as the audience should interpret it.

Let's suppose you want to shoot a scene in a drama. There is a character who is afraid of something; he is in a dark room and is apprehensive about something that is about to happen. You decide you want lots of tension and you want to increase the sense of drama. Now your job as a director is to shoot that scene in the most effective way, conveying clearly the *atmosphere* evoked by this character in this room in this situation. If you know some of the ways other people have produced tension or fear in a shot, then it immediately gives you something to start with. When you know the rules you then start adding something of yourself to them; indeed, your own personal style is the way you respond to the rules and in what particular way you break, bend or stick with them. So, in this instance, you may use lighting with higher contrast and with the camera may use close-ups to exaggerate the facial expressions of the actor, or long, wide shots to emphasize the sense of isolation and vulnerability of the character in the room.

Composition

Let's concentrate now just on what the camera can achieve in showing the plot and conveying mood. We can look at how shots are more effective if you think about how you are arranging the objects within the frame. The position and angle you select for the camera relative to the subject and its surroundings is called the 'composition'.

Figure 6.1 Setting up a well-composed shot takes time. In this production shot, director Carl Tibbets tries to use the mirror to give pictorial interest.

Composition in filmmaking has developed mainly from the ideas of painters in Renaissance Europe; many cinematographers will freely admit to being inspired by great paintings of this time. But the great filmmaker Eisenstein has suggested that we need framing for all our art because we tend to look at the world through windows.

> **Tip** Try looking at Renaissance works by Masaccio and Giotto to see where classic, epic staging originates, or look at the sumptuous attention to light by northern Renaissance artists such as Jan van Eyck or, later, Vermeer.

> **Tip** Sergei Eisenstein is credited with having established some of the fundamental ideas behind montage in his ground-breaking films such as *Battleship Potemkin* (1925) and *Strike* (1924).

Composition helps a low budget

Going back to our scared-man-in-the-room scene above, it is quite likely your budget averages your monthly disposable income and you definitely can't stretch to dry ice or a specially composed score. The lower your budget, the more you must try to get your camera to work harder. It's no coincidence that directors making their debut feature will display quite high levels of ingenuity with the camera, showing off a number of different compositions to make up for a lack of expensive props or effects to point the camera at.

But don't show everything

You are also going to rely on the audience to imagine some images. A good director would not have to display all the action or spell out the whole narrative and will use imaginative compositions to suggest and evoke, allowing the audience to fill in the gaps. But this sort of filming is quicker and more successful with a good grasp of the basic rules. If you watch *The Haunting* (Robert Wise, 1963), you can see how a small budget was somehow irrelevant. The film's scariest moments rely on clever composition, pointing the camera at a certain shape, shadow or object and at a certain angle to give a feeling of unease. As if to prove the theory that what we don't see is scarier than what is spelled out for us, the remade film in 1999 (directed by Jan De Bont) made much of the implicit horror explicit and was widely condemned as not scary enough.

Basic starting points in composition

- The clarity of the objects in view
- The amount that is not in view
- The use of shapes to denote particular theme or mood
- The angle of the camera.

Within this there are certain kinds of composition that are more suited to certain situations. The eminent cinematographer Nestor Almendros used a lifetime of experience to describe the following principles:

- Horizontal lines suggest serenity and calm
- Vertical lines denote strength or authority
- Diagonal lines suggest action or movement
- Curved lines suggest fluidity and sensuality
- Moving a camera forward to enter a scene suggests 'bringing the audience into the heart of the narrative'
- The opposite movement, away from a scene, is often used as a way of ending a film.

(*A Man with a Camera*, Faber & Faber, 1982, p. 14.)

Placing action in the viewfinder

To get to grips with composition, start by looking at the way you use the whole. Try a short exercise: get a sheet of paper the same shape as the screen you intend to work with.

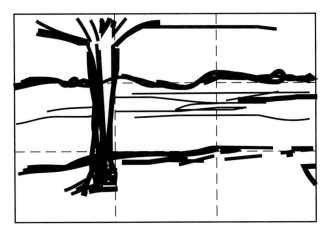

Figure 6.2 Use the division of thirds on the paper to place objects within the composition. 'Hooking' them onto the verticals or horizontals gives rise to depth in the image.

The shape is what is called the 'aspect ratio' of your screen. Aspect ratio refers to the height and width of the screen. The common standard for European television is 16:9. Most filmmakers like to work on a slightly rectangular screen because, in terms of composition, it is easier to get a more interesting arrangement than using a square. This shape has evolved over time as one which will most help you in finding a good arrangement.

An A4 sheet of paper is as good a shape as any to start. Fold it into thirds both horizontally and vertically so you have nine rectangles. Try to imagine the sheet as your viewfinder on the camera and look at any shots you have so far on your camera, noticing in which rectangle the action tends to be in each scene.

Lazy parts of the screen

If we number the rectangles from 1 to 9 across the rows, you might find that most of the action in your footage takes place in the fifth box – the centre of the screen. Whether you are shooting a very still scene such as a conversation, or a running chase scene, it is common to find that the focus of attention is in the middle and all the other boxes are unused. This is easy to shoot – you just place the subject in the centre of the screen and stand back – but it makes for bad composition. It's predictable and boring, but your job is to grab an audience's attention as much as possible, even in quiet scenes. Have a look at some of your own images on your films: is box no. 5 doing all the work or are the others pulling their weight too? To encourage you to find new camera angles, keep moving the camera around until the action is spread throughout the nine boxes. Every box doesn't have to be used in each shot, but there should be a spread throughout the film. After trying this method for a while you will soon find that you naturally want to compose the frame rather than just shooting into the middle of it.

You can be aware of this during the planning stage, so that when you do storyboards you can stop the bad ones in their tracks and redo that frame. But if you find that you have poor compositions when you are actually filming you need to rectify it on location, under pressure. If you have an LCD viewfinder you could place a sheet of clear acetate with a grid over it to keep a check on how you are dividing up the screen.

To assess how you use the screen, you could shoot a simple scene (such as making a cup of coffee), but avoid putting the action in box no. 5, in the middle. Avoid the tendency to depict the action squarely in the centre and try constantly to be aware of the whole screen. Although you would not want to avoid the centre box all the time when making a movie, this exercise of abstaining from the centre does force you to give added weight to other areas of the screen.

You can then try watching feature films and notice how much of the screen is used. You might start to notice some of the conventions that filmmakers use. For example, placing a character to the edge of the screen can heighten the dramatic content of that scene and tilting it can give a sense of unease. Don't forget, however, that there are many times when a centrally framed shot is just right for your film. The director Stanley Kubrick made this kind of shot his trademark, as he found it gave some shots a kind of claustrophobic feel.

Film View

Watch *Paths of Glory* (1957), Stanley Kubrick's film set in World War One, to see how a one-point perspective shot can work as he takes us around the trenches. In other Kubrick films we often see shots where we look down a corridor or narrow space. *The Shining* (1980) is full of long corridors with unknown horrors waiting around the corner. In the earlier *Killer's Kiss* we see a similar clip of moving down a narrow street, as the main character has a nightmare.

Composition dividing lines

With a bit of practice you may now see separate areas when you look through the viewfinder, dividing up the image. But the four dividing lines that separate the boxes can also be very useful. You can start to use these as 'hooks' to peg your actors or action on. Let's use an example of, for instance, a simple dialogue between two people. When you watch other films you start to notice the most common

Figure 6.3 The right framing can create an atmosphere out of the least inspiring places. In this case, director Jake Knight shot an underground car park as part of his short, *B3*.

Figure 6.4 In this image from director Jo Price, the two actors are placed to the left, in line with the golden section, leaving room for depth in the background.

composition for placing the face within the frame. Heads can be very difficult to place because you need to make sure the mouth is visible all the time and the eyes are prominent. Try putting the eyes on the upper line (see Figure 6.2) – don't worry about how much of the forehead you have to lose – then place the nose on either of the vertical lines.

Feel free to break this rule, but it is a good place to start for a well-composed shot. Avoiding overusing the centre of the frame works because it moves the focus of attention away from the place where we lazily and automatically want to look and allows other objects or people to occupy the spaces left over, adding more interest to the film.

The same goes for landscape shots: place the horizon on one of the horizontal lines and any distinguishing features such as trees or a building on the verticals. You are making the audience look at different parts of the screen and this makes for a less predictable experience. If you make the audience look around the screen constantly it starts to work in your favour, as they will then start noticing everything in the shot. Of course, if it is done badly it is distracting, but every kind of filmmaker tries to make his or her film more interesting to look at. In fact, now that Hollywood has discovered computer-generated images, directors can also achieve unusual, daring shots in large-scale action sequences such as the extraordinary city sweeps in *Spider-Man 2* (Sam Raimi, 2004).

Using depth in your shots

We have looked at how to use dividing lines to help you get good compositions. One of the things created by these compositions is something called 'depth'. Don't confuse it with meanings in your film;

Figure 6.5 John Sealey's short film, *The Greatest Escape,* raises fascinating issues of race while dealing with the Second World War.

this is *pictorial* depth. Basically, depth is your way of inviting the audience into a scene. If you follow the ideas in the last chapter about dividing up the screen you will almost certainly have put some depth into the shot without trying. Depth is achieved where one object or person is close to the camera and something else is further away. The space you create in the middle is called depth. It is disarmingly simple, but if you are conscious of it when setting up your camera then you are going to get a much higher success rate in terms of getting great-looking shots. Once you've understood it you can then start to use it to your advantage, putting greater depth where you want a more dramatic scene.

Using tripods for composition

The tripod is a very useful, essential piece of equipment, but it is expensive. It can be very restrictive, but on balance it's probably a good idea to have some sort of support for the camera occasionally. If the cost puts you off, try a mini-tripod, which is a shorter and smaller version but does need a tabletop or other surface to rest on. Some wildlife filmmakers use a beanbag on which to rest the camera, as this enables the user to move quickly to various camera angles and doesn't require a flat surface. It also helps you to get a range of steady shots without having to fumble around altering the tripod constantly. Alternatively, you could get rid of the tripod altogether. There is a school of thought which says that the tripod stops your film from having vitality and spontaneity. Filmmaker Robert Rodriguez suggests that, 'If you have a tripod you are going to leave the camera stuck on it. It looks nice – and your film is going to look dead.' Good advice for the lazy filmmaker, but remember also that filming without a tripod requires skill. Keep the camera under control, giving us a view of the action from one viewpoint, just as if it is another actor, watching rather than participating in the action. Feel free to alter this viewpoint throughout the scene.

> **Tip** Watch out for 'hosepiping', which occurs when the filmmaker waves the camera around without providing the audience with a firm place from which to view the action. Apparently, when watching *The Blair Witch Project*, more people felt ill from the violently moving camera than from the violent events it showed us.

Tripods can inhibit good composition

The idea goes that as soon as you have placed your camera on a tripod you effectively close the decision-making process, removing the possibility of other ideas coming up which could improve a scene. So, if you are using camera support, you need to be certain that you have got the right shot before you get out the tripod. Try setting the composition to begin with without any support, looking continually through the lens to make sure you try out every conceivable angle and then, when you are sure you have found the shot that works best for you, set it on a tripod. This method ensures that the camera angle does not have to compromise to suit the tripod's limitations.

> **Tip** There are many other filmmakers who reject camera support. The Danish group Dogme believes that any use of tripods adds further layers of artificiality to a film and takes its audience one step further removed from it.

Finding and using unexpected shots

It is reasonable to suppose that if you have planned a film properly you should never need to find extra shots. Many filmmakers, however, believe that the combined energy and input of a lot of people on set can throw up unforeseen opportunities for quite unexpected shots. It is already accepted that actors may ad lib in a scene, only to find that the director keeps their off-the-cuff lines and removes the written part of the script. It is the same with filmmaking; you have to be aware that there are many shots you are not getting because you are sticking rigidly to your storyboard.

It is poor practice to shoot endless amounts of footage that you have then to trawl through in post-production, but try to strike a balance between letting new ideas enter into your plans while shooting and sticking to the plans worked out earlier. Many first films look too precious in their choice of footage, as if each frame was a life and death decision, while some of the most captivating are those that let less well-considered shots into the final edit. In writing terms this would be the equivalent of communicating solely in formal language, as in legal small print, where each sentence is perfectly chosen and in perfect English. But less formal language can be more affecting sometimes and may enable you to communicate more directly to the audience. In both the editing and shooting stages, look for and keep footage that veers from your plans. Let these 'slang' shots enter into the language of the movie later.

Spare shots

There is another good reason for allowing more footage to be gathered than first intended. When we look at editing in Chapter 8:1, you will see how useful it is to have spare shots with which to patch over parts of a scene now and then to add interest and keep the audience watching. The kind of shots that turn up when you are simply experimenting to find the right angle or lighting effect can add variety and spark to a film.

What kind of shots?

Inevitably, preparation work is capable of preparing you too well; you end up knowing exactly what you want and will probably end up making a good, honest movie. But filmmaking remains an art form as well and as such needs to have some allowance made for the unexpected during shooting. It is this that marks the line between the average, workaday movie and the one that grabs the audience and makes the movie a more dynamic experience. The kind of shots you can use to sprinkle over the movie later are the ones that you would usually discard, either because they don't fit in with the rest of the scene or because they have some slight fault in them. You might stumble across some of the most unusual compositions when you have occasionally departed from your plans and might have considered the result a mistake. But when you get to edit the movie later, revisit these unwanted parts of your footage tapes and give them a chance.

Let's take our earlier example of a straightforward scene with dialogue between two characters. Filming this scene will be relatively easy as you have to show only two actors, but after a minute or so you could start inserting the occasional shot of the two from a distance, or a shot taken in close-up as the actors were rehearsing earlier. However, don't show faces on these 'patched' shots if the actors are speaking, as the new shots would be out of sync with the rest of the scene. Try to film shots of the actors' hands moving; this can emphasize drama in certain scenes and is vital for covering up the join between two takes of the same scene.

Film View

In *American Grafitti* (1973), George Lucas made his first full-length feature by filming virtually everything from every angle and leaving decisions about how the film would look to the editing stage. The result is a drama that has the realism of a fly-on-the-wall documentary.

Figure 6.6 In this still from Amma Asante's *A Way of Life* (2004) the characters stride towards the audience – and the action.

Figure 6.7 In this still from Lisa Gornick's *Do I Love You?*, the main character is framed by two unseen hands and we are left with the impression that plans are being made for her.

Camera language

Camera language is something that is going to apply as much to narrative films as to non-fiction work. We have seen what good composition can do for a film, but here we need to know how the camera can convey certain meanings and use these as part of a repertoire of shots to say what you want without having to use words. Take a health check, however, on any slide into thinking that camera language is like verbal language. In film, there are so many other variables which alter the meaning of a shot that it is impossible to ascribe definite meaning to a certain sort of frame, track or tilt. Just use the ideas below as starting points to which you can add more meaning in your own way.

Camera framing

Camera language is an important way of conveying your ideas. Subtle changes in camera angle, height or movement all affect what you are showing. Over time, a broad vocabulary has been established in which certain angles of shot correspond to certain feelings or views of a subject. Much of this has been developed by the early masters of narrative cinema, such as Hitchcock. Being aware of this language is useful in being able to adhere to, or subvert, convention.

For example:

- *Close-up shot*. This kind of shot will often raise the dramatic tension in a scene. It evokes intimacy and sensuality, but also suggests enclosure or claustrophobia. Directing the viewer's attention so tightly to one aspect of a scene also makes clear your own interpretation on the subject.
- *Tilt*. In this shot, the camera is tilted so that the viewer sees the world at an angle. The general effect is to suggest imbalance, a situation not quite right, a character unable to find his bearings. A slight tilt of perhaps 70 degrees (where 90 degrees is vertical) will give a more subtle indication of this state, while more exaggerated angles increase this feeling.
- *Camera looking down on the subject*. This can suggest vulnerability in the subject. It indicates that the viewer is higher than the subject and is therefore more powerful than the subject.
- *Camera looking up at the subject*. As the reverse of the above, this shot can suggest that the subject holds power by placing us below.

Camera language is similar to spoken languages in that it evolves and is a result of its usage rather than being formulated in advance and adhered to. Certain devices are seen to work but change considerably over the years, partly as a result of the increased sophistication of the audience. So-called 'Hollywood grammar', popular in the middle of the twentieth century, has evolved so far as to be unrecognizable.

Multiple meanings in camera language

As with narrative film, non-fiction film takes full advantage of the uses this kind of camera language brings and enjoys subverting one sign with another. For example, a happy, optimistic image can be altered slightly, suggesting some underlying unhappiness by slowly withdrawing the camera from the subject to reveal an isolated subject. One way to illustrate this is to look at spoken language. When we listen to someone, we take on board what they say but also watch the way they move their arms, their whole body language. Interesting juxtapositions can be made when one form of communication contradicts the other.

Film View

Some films use cinematography as a significant way of conveying meaning. In *Paris, Texas* (Wim Wenders, 1984) every scene seems like there is an extra actor present – the landscape. It carries the weight of the theme of alienation and loss like an Oscar winner, but only does so because of the judgement of the cinematographer. Many filmmakers use the American landscape to show similar themes, focusing on the deserts and midwestern flatlands to throw into relief the feelings of the protagonists. See also Terrence Malick's *Badlands* (1974), *Napoleon Dynamite* (2004) and David Lynch's *Wild at Heart* (1990). Australian landscape develops similar themes in films such as *The Adventures of Priscilla, Queen of the Desert* (Stephan Elliot, 1994), *Walkabout* (Nic Roeg, 1970) and *Rabbit-Proof Fence* (Phillip Noyce, 2003).

How we read images

Another factor is that the image the camera gives us is read as both a mental and optical phenomenon, hitting the brain in two ways. When we see an image, we read it as (1) a simple array of patterns on a mental or cognitive level and (2) as a cultural reference point. Take, for example, a shot where a character is standing in a doorway with strong light on the face, the door framed by black shadow. We can track how we perceive this image by focusing on both the mental and optical.

Optically, we see the figure before we see the blackness, and we respond strongly to the impact of the bright light shining on the face and the high contrast of black and white. We feel a need to decipher it and will pursue whatever little information we are given, and yet our interpretation of what we decide the image is saying is influenced by the impact of the optical effect the image has on us. This is why some camera compositions and lighting effects are particularly useful for the filmmaker.

But the image of the figure in the doorway will strike us for other reasons, on a cultural level. We have preconceived ideas regarding shadow and others regarding faces lit in the darkness. An air of mystery may surround it, or a sense of something spiritual or perhaps menacing. The face may also have a particular expression, drawing in our memories and feelings about the particular emotion we are seeing; one section of the human brain has the sole function of analysing every other human face we see, for recognition of the familiar tribe or family, so we also search for anything that resembles a face, also linking into the optical view of the image. Our response is determined by our culture, affecting the significance of certain signs in the image.

It is the combination of both cultural and optical that work together to come up with a single idea of what is being signified. The signifier is nearly always visual, while the signified is necessarily a mental picture.

When you frame a shot, you are therefore setting up a range of responses in the viewer. Being able to control all of these responses is outside anyone's reach, but it is possible to manipulate response to a certain degree.

Tip   For more reading about the area of visual perception and art, try art theory classic *The Hidden Order of Art*, by Anton Ehrenzweig.

The Crunch

- Make your films look good
- Get to know the rules of composition
- Know when to use the conventional approach and when to try something new
- Good composition can give a low-budget film a high-budget look
- Be aware of the whole screen when shooting
- Use composition to allow for pictorial depth
- Try unexpected shots, found during bad takes
- Show you are a master of conventional filmmaking and a master of doing it your own way.

Project 14. Close-ups

What this project is for: to improve camera technique
Time: allow a day to plan, another to shoot and two to edit

What this project is about

This project concentrates on the use of the camera and how it can help you in conveying narrative. In this project we will be making a straightforward movie using a simple plot, but will be doing it with a particular restriction: the entire film will be filmed using close-up shots only.

If narrative is concerned with information then the purpose in working with close-ups is to focus attention on what is important in a scene and prioritize the various elements within. In conveying the story you develop, you should be able to see in the final film a positive linear progression of the plot through the use of this device. The close-up enables the viewer to see what is important in the shot and demands that you determine this in advance of shooting, with implications for the way your story is conveyed. As an example, in filming a dialogue between two actors, some people would be inclined to show more of the human reaction to a set of events, training the camera on the faces and hands of the actors to show the emotion behind the story. Others may prefer to focus on the mechanics of the action, with more emphasis on how the actual events are occurring and perhaps delivering a simpler reading of the action.

Controlling information

Visual and stylistic aspects of filmmaking are described in Chapter 6:1 and help in describing the means with which we convey the story. This project, however, focuses entirely on the ability to control this drip-feed of information making up the narrative to the audience and, when used alongside the previous projects, may help you deliver not only the plot, but also much more.

Stage 1

In preparing the plot for this film, it would be more effective to find something simple, a familiar plot that an audience can relate to. But if you want to try more advanced versions of this project, make the narrative more complex. Use simple linear stories, taking the audience from event A to event B, such as a delivery, a heist-and-getaway or a confrontation between two people.

Stage 2

Developing this film is going to be slightly different from other projects. When you have completed the visualizations stage and are ready to move on to the storyboard, work instead on much larger frames. Draw a frame the size of CD box or larger.

When you have completed a first draft of the storyboard you will then need to start drawing smaller frames around certain parts of the image, trying to home in on the essential parts of that shot. To do this, you could try making a number of window frames out of paper, at anything from one-quarter to one-sixteenth of the frame size. The aim is to see if you can isolate images within the frame which convey the primary information in that scene. Look at what is the most important section of that frame, what is the next most important, and so on.

Multiple shots in one frame

As can be seen in Figure 6.8, the single frame here contains several frames that are telling different parts of the story. The primary source of information is probably the gun on the table and the hand resting on it. But a close second are the two frames showing the faces of the actors. After this, you could look at the foot tapping nervously under the table and the clock ticking on the wall. All these sections of the frame give portions of the overall information contained within and it is for the director to prioritize each part when deciding how to point the camera. Does the hand on the gun need to be centrally placed in the frame? There are infinite ways to order the shot depending on what you want to show the audience and how much you want to 'spoonfeed' them the plot. Bringing unlikely elements to the fore now and then can add layers of meaning to a scene. Hitchcock demonstrates this many times as he draws our attention to a minor part of scene, often showing human quirks and frailties in the process.

Figure 6.8 Close-up frames. One frame can contain many pieces of information. In this example, a frame of two figures with the suggestion of confrontation has within it six frames that could be shown in close-up, each of them telling the audience vital parts of the narrative.

Stage 3

When you have completed this exercise with all the frames in the original storyboard you are ready to begin sorting the new images taken from the larger frames into some kind of order. We need to build a new storyboard out of these images, paying careful attention to the order in which the close-up shots appear and the frequency with which they recur. It is likely that you will need to have more shots of shorter duration than in a similar film made without this device.

Stage 4: Shooting

Shooting this film is going to take slightly longer than other narrative films. Although you will be setting up more shots than in other films, you can make your task much simpler by asking your actors to play a scene several times while you take various shots from different angles. If you have access to additional cameras this would save time and make continuity problems less evident by shooting different parts of the scene simultaneously.

In obtaining the close-up, it is better to move the camera closer to the action rather than rely on the zoom control. Zoom tends to increase camera wobble and removes the opportunity, to a certain extent, for you to track or pan the camera.

Shooting tips for this project

Focusing

Like just about every aspect of filmmaking, even something as technical as focusing can be a creative tool. When working in close-up, the aspect of focus is even more emphasized due to the laws of optics. You can choose which part of the screen the audience look at when you decide which area will be in sharp focus; the focus tool is like an arrow pointing to the crucial part of that shot. But there is no reason why you should not challenge this convention by settling attention elsewhere in the scene. The director Kieslowski has some memorable images in his films obtained through a creative use of focusing.

Film View

Near the start of *Three Colours: Blue* (Krzysztof Kieslowski, 1993), we see a doctor enter a ward containing the victim of a car crash. From the point of view of the victim we see a close-up, focusing on a few feathers on her pillow moving with her breath, while the doctor is a blurred figure in the background. This tells us that the victim is alive but also conveys something of the sense of bewilderment felt by her. The next shot is equally impressive: the camera fills the screen with her right eye and we see the pupil contract as a reflection of the doctor appears in the iris.

You may also find that some camcorders are designed to focus the object in the centre of the frame and reject your attempts at creative focusing, particularly if you want something on the side of the frame in focus and the main object in the centre not. If you do have a manual focus option, see the instructions in Chapter 2:3 for getting round this problem.

Camera wobble

When shooting close-ups you will find that the camera is going to reveal more shakes and wobbles than in other shots. Although a tripod is advisable for many shots, it would be useful to devise a more flexible solution that did not restrict the range of angles available to you, such as using a beanbag or similar movable, soft support.

Lighting

When you are working close to the action, lighting becomes an important factor. There are some lighting conditions that will aid you in trying to convey information and some that may confuse the scene. Avoid flat, dispersed light from fluorescent lights and household bulbs. Use light that is sharper and more directed at the action, so that the shapes of the subject are revealed and contrasting shadows are thrown. This will help to reduce the amount of extraneous information we see and draw attention quickly to what is important in the shot.

Extra shots

Finally, when you are shooting, it would be useful to get additional shots you had not previously planned for. When you feel you have shot all the parts of a scene you needed, look around the scene for anything else that could be used to break up the rigidity of the final edit. If we are constantly given crucial information the film becomes hard work, but if you can occasionally cut away to something not so crucial it may make for a more rounded, less frenetic film.

Stage 5: Editing

There are a number of points to consider when editing this sort of film with its dominance of close shots. As well as having a greater number of shots than other films, these may be shorter and you may find that it is useful to use cutaways – cutting to and from a shot repeatedly. For example, if we consider Figure 6.8, you may cut from the hand on the gun, to the face of actor 1, to the face of actor 2, and back to the gun. You will need to avoid bewildering the audience, however, and include regular longer cuts: too many short, sharp edits can be physically hard to cope with. To vary your shots when filming, you could try tracking and panning to link two close-ups together.

Evaluation

Much of the evaluation for this project can be seen as assessing how you told the story and what you emphasized. This project reveals your individual preference in how a story can be told, as well as encouraging you to focus on the essentials of a scene, simply by asking you to draw our attention to what you feel is the most important part of it. This sort of self-knowledge is worth a lot in helping you towards a personal approach to the medium.

- When you were shooting, were the shots you filmed close to the storyboard you prepared? You don't lose points for deviating. It is more useful to assess which is the better document: the tape or the storyboard. For many filmmakers it is the former, since the camera shows you what you can achieve while the paper version only shows what might be achieved.
- How did your use of light alter? Did you become more aware of where you were placing lighting to reveal certain parts of a scene? Did the use of strong, directed light help you in simplifying the frame and making better compositions?
- Focusing will also have been a useful tool for composition – did it prove useful in close-up?
- When you were editing the movie, how did you feel the flow of the story was interrupted by the need to cut between the elements of the scene? You may have found it useful to use one particular shot as the dominant one and insert others now and then. The length of each shot itself tells the audience something about your priorities for the story and determines how they will read it, according to which shots are dominant. You may have decided to dwell on a particular, seemingly less significant, part of a scene in order to challenge the presumed priorities for that scene, changing the way we expect a scene to be shown.

I want something more challenging

To push this project further, try turning your attention to non-narrative ideas rather than action-orientated ones. You may find that you are then having to focus more on symbols and other signifiers of meaning rather than just signifiers of action. Expect to have to work hard on suggesting significance in each shot because the action in the frame won't do it for you.

2. Continuity

Continuity in narrative filmmaking refers to the way shots go together to create a seamless chain of events. It is going to be the invisible tool that helps you bind your film together and link it as a single, whole experience. It is going to hide the nuts and bolts of filmmaking, creating an illusion of reality and merging separate pieces of film – sometimes recorded days apart – into one stretch of fictional time.

The need for continuity arises because the audience does not see everything. Time is compressed and space is shown only selectively, cropping the imaginary world we see. To illustrate this effect, try a test where you look only through a small tube. You start to feel the need for more information to tell you about your environment. If someone leaves your small frame of view, you want to know whether they have left the room. It is unsettling if there is a gap in your internal map of the room you are in. Watching a film is very much like this test, so one of your tasks is to provide the viewer with a complete sense of where we are, who is there and when any part of this changes.

Good continuity keeps the audience with you. The audience's dependence on you for information is made more acute when you factor in the editing process. Now shots are broken up into small pieces and it becomes essential that some way is devised of maintaining the smooth flow of events on film.

Continuity is disrupted easily: the slightest object out of place, a confusing camera angle or a shift in the style in the film can all break the audience's involvement with the illusion. The effect of broken continuity is unusually shocking; it momentarily drops the viewer from the fairground ride experience of watching the film and sends them back to earth with a knock. Of course, with such a noticeable effect, discontinuity is just one more trick for the filmmaker to utilize. If you are aware of the positive and negative effects of keeping continuity and disrupting it, you can choose when and how you employ these tools. To use the fairground ride analogy again, you can choose when to keep the ride smooth and when to give an unexpected jolt to the passengers, without risking the whole ride falling apart. In other words, maintain continuity closely and you then have the option of editing against it for sudden effects.

Narrative continuity

In narrative film, continuity is crucial. Various elements have the potential to cause problems during shooting and editing, including:

- technical factors such as changes in picture quality
- plot factors such as omitting crucial explanatory scenes
- prop and set factors such as clocks out of sync

- style factors such as a shift in the look of the film
- unexplained implausible moments such as exaggerated compression of time.

Know the rules, know how to break them

It is worth noting that bad continuity is not necessarily good discontinuity. In other words, simply ignoring the rules of continuity will not automatically lead to a ground-breaking film that has its own innovative look. Every film needs to have an internal logic where any disruption of the basic ideas of continuity is planned and incorporated into the film as a whole, so that it corresponds to its own rules. This may sound vague because each film has its own individual needs but, in general, rules are broken in a planned way rather than arbitrarily.

Go to: Chapter 4:5 to see how to plan effectively for an alternative approach.

Figure 6.9 In any location shoot, continuity of action is crucial, especially when dealing with several characters, as in this still from David Casals's *On Off*.

Avoiding bad continuity

How do you set about ensuring that continuity is under control? The range of issues outlined below need to be considered.

Tape quality

This is less of an issue for digital tape but is important nonetheless. Use the same quality of tape throughout production, new ones if possible. Digital tape degrades far less than analogue tapes through reuse because it is built very differently, but there are other ways in which tape can be affected through length of use, so it is safer to buy new tapes and use a consistent number of times, usually less than 10.

Camera features

Make sure you remain with the same camera settings throughout production. If you start the film using, for example, an aspect ratio of 16:9 (sometimes called 'cinema' on the camera), stay with it throughout unless you have a scripted reason to change. Set the white balance to the same values each time you shoot. White balance is often automatic on many models but check before every shoot; any unknown changes in lighting and you could end up with one shot having a warm, orange cast to it and the next having a cold, blue cast to it. Altering the white balance on purpose can be a valid tool, of course, allowing you to change the look of a scene.

Plot disruption

Even the minor absence of some small part of a plot can be baffling for an audience. For example, a shot showing a character in one location, a beach perhaps, followed by a cut immediately to the same character in an entirely different location, perhaps back home, needs some explaining. We have soon assumed that the character jumped in a car and drove home between the two shots, but we need to be shown it or told it with a subtitle, even if it is just a glimpse of the car speeding on the road for a couple of seconds or a title saying 'later'. A narrative is like a ladder; its upward, linear progress depends on having all the rungs in place. Miss out a few rungs and the ladder still works but requires considerable effort to climb, and eventually you lose faith in the overall structure.

Closure: the viewer fills in the gaps

However, before we start handing the audience everything on a plate, there is a concept called 'visual closure' that refers to the ability of the mind to fill gaps in a narrative to make it into a coherent whole. If you draw a circle but leave out a few degrees of it or draw one with dotted lines, you will still recognize it as this shape, but the crucial point is that enough information has been given for us to conclude that it is a circle. Just a few lines *in the right place* and we can fill in the rest, just as in the example above we needed to see only a fraction of the car journey to see that it had taken place. Leave out the scene that connects the two locations and you risk losing the shape of the film as a whole.

Sound

One of the more subtle but still noticeable continuity problems is often in the soundtrack. Ambient sound, or sounds that are recorded in the background to each scene, will differ greatly, even those recorded on the same day in the same place. The reasons for this are looked at more fully in Chapter 5:3, but bear in mind that ambient sound has the capacity to make or break continuity. The use of devices to smooth over the changes in presence are one of the hallmarks of professional filming.

Go to: Chapter 5:3 to find out more about sound recording and Chapter 7:4 for ideas about editing with sound.

Style disruption

Style is something that occurs naturally as a result of the numerous decisions you make about camera angle, composition, music, editing and so on. Once you have noted the constant elements in the film, such as the kind of shots you use, dominant colours or style of acting, you need to nail these down and stick to them. There will be times in the film when you want to disrupt this conformity of style – for instance, in dream or fantasy sequences and flashbacks or to denote a radical change in the film's pace. At these points you will certainly devise a very different look to the film, but it is a constant style throughout the rest of the film that allows you to lift other sections out of it so neatly. Try to establish the look of the film early on in the planning stage. Use a timeline to indicate the dominant style and where it is to be broken.

Figure 6.10 Over-the-shoulder shots like this help preserve a sense of continuity in dialogue scenes. Still from *Crazy* by Noel Stephens.

The action line

Among the devices we have looked at to ensure smooth continuity, one of the most useful regards the placing of the camera. This rule is also known as the 180-degree rule and has evolved to ensure that the fictional space created by a scene is sustained throughout. Both shooting and editing play a role in this. Every new shot has the potential to suggest that we are in a new location or at a new point in time. The purpose of the 180-degree rule is to reassure the audience that we are in the same place and that the events are happening in the same short space of time.

How the action line works

It works by drawing an imaginary line between characters in a scene and drawing a semi-circle that runs 180 degrees around them, on one side only. The camera must shoot from one side of the line, from

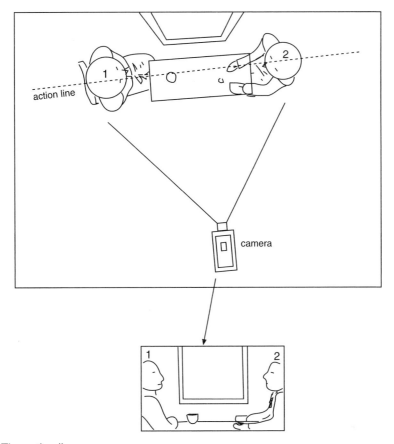

Figure 6.11 The action line.

any position. If we look at Figure 6.11, we can see what the camera records if it stays on one side of the line. In this shot the two actors are on opposite sides of the frame, actor 1 on the left, actor 2 on the right. The audience notes the position of the two actors and sets up a kind of internal map of the room accordingly. But if the camera goes onto the other side of the line, near the window, the actors seem to have changed sides, with 1 on the right and 2 on the left. The audience then ask questions: Did an actor move? Or did an edit go missing?

The action line and the jump cut
A further use of the line is in avoiding the 'jump cut'. A jump cut is an abrupt cut between two clips when the camera of each gives a slightly different angle or view of the subject. When framing a figure we will notice a disruption of our view by moving the camera slightly to the side and cutting between the two shots. It is as if you had filmed a tracking shot and left out a small piece of tape as the camera moves, as you may expect to see in badly preserved old silent movies. The effect does not destroy the scene but does introduce some hiccup in the flow of the film. As with all discontinuity, this is also a useful tool as it produces dissonance against the harmony of the overall continuity and, as anyone working with music will tell you, dissonance is a valued element in music composition.

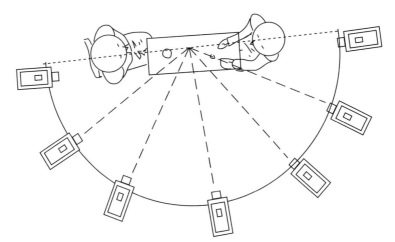

Figure 6.12 The 30-degree rule. In order to avoid a jump cut, cameras are placed at least 30 degrees apart.

The 30-degree rule

To avoid this effect, however, cameras are placed at certain locations around the action. Imagine a semi-circle radiating around the main action, as if the camera is in the auditorium of a theatre looking at a stage. Cameras can be placed *at least* 30 degrees apart from each other around this semi-circle, but no closer. If cameras are closer than this and the two resulting close shots are edited together, the effect will disrupt the space of that scene. Cuts to new angles have to be sufficiently different to justify their occurrence.

Motion within the screen

The rectangle within which we see the film, whether it is a television or projection screen, is also a tool in achieving continuity in that we construct a map of the invented world of the film. Movement within and off screen needs to be handled particularly carefully. Explaining this gets a little complicated, but here goes.

There is a difference between scenes that are stationary and scenes involving forward movement, such as a chase or journey. Let's take the first kind to begin with. Say you have a scene involving, for instance, some people within a room or in a particular defined space. If a figure walks off the screen we adjust our internal map of the scene and place a mental marker regarding where they are now. If they go left, we expect them to return from the left; if they exit right, that's where they should re-enter. Ignoring this makes for an unholy mess in continuity. At worst, your audience are going to lose faith in the whole movie and start watching for more such continuity errors. Even a simple plot is then in peril, as now nothing the filmmaker is offering to the audience can be relied upon.

The other kind, and you were warned it gets confusing here, involves the reverse of this. Suppose you have a scene in which one character is chasing another. Maybe a policeman is pursuing a villain, or a *Tyrannosaurus rex* is chasing a jeep. In these kinds of scenes the participant will exit right (usually) and re-enter left, showing us that the journey or chase is constantly in the same direction, left to right, left to right. If you follow the piece on the action line earlier, then much of this problem is solved.

There is a convention regarding the direction actors will be moving when filmed. If a figure is going forwards or onwards *metaphorically*, in the script, perhaps to a new location or new part of the plot, we expect the figure to travel consistently from left to right across the screen, and the reverse when seen to be returning from somewhere. There are times when you need to imply onward or returning motion and this device becomes even more useful when you have few location landmarks to help orientate the audience. In David Lean's *Lawrence of Arabia*, the exhausted Lawrence is journeying across a barren desert, and we see him go from left to right. When he later learns that one of his party has fallen from his camel many miles back, he returns for him and we see him go from right to left across the screen. With no landscape elements to help us to judge which direction he is going in, this becomes essential.

Film View

An interesting example of how movement from left to right is used can be seen in David Lynch's *The Straight Story* (1999), in which an ageing and car-less man travels hundreds of miles on his only mode of transport, a lawnmower, to visit his long-lost and ailing brother. In many shots, Lynch places him travelling from right to left, thereby hinting that the man is returning home, travelling back to the place he needs to be.

Light quality and intensity

Since light is one of your tools for showing the passage of time, you need to ensure that light is constant throughout a scene if the audience are to view the events of that scene as contemporaneous. This means light should reflect only those changes to the scene that the audience can perceive – for instance, the approach of dawn, a car headlamp moving past and so on. Lighting used in a scene should be maintained at predetermined levels; if you are unhappy with the lighting of your scene, do not change it halfway through, redo the whole scene. If filming takes place over days or weeks, make careful notes of the position and intensity of lights. Similarly, daylight is notoriously unpredictable; a temporary cloud can radically alter the colour and lighting of a scene. The weather may influence the day you shoot a lengthy scene. Hollywood grew up where it did because it enjoyed near-perfect clear, blue skies almost every day. Continuity becomes easy, even if two parts of the same scene are shot days apart.

Continuity in non-narrative movies

Non-narrative movies demand a very different approach to narrative. They require that you embed continuity as a part of the whole structure of the film, not as an afterthought during filming. Non-narrative movies such as music videos, abstract movies and multimedia projections used in live concerts are particularly susceptible to looking fragmented. At their most out of control, they look like you are channel surfing, looking at a number of clips of movies by different people. Of the following ideas, the more effective ones are those that are part of the planning and shooting stages rather than those placed over the film in post-production.

Methods of ensuring continuity in non-narrative

Single filter effect (edit software filters, not camera filters)

If your editing software has special effects that you can use to alter the look of clips – for instance, to make them change colour, stretch or change contrast and tone – you could apply one of these to the whole film, or at regular points. Restrict yourself to one filter only.

Tracking

A tracking shot – where the camera moves while it shoots, tracking the action – can make a good way of connecting shots. Decide on a constant speed of tracking and stick with it throughout the film. To enhance the effect, keep to one direction in the screen – for example, left to right. For example, you could show a slow, left-to-right movement of the camera along a beach, cutting then to a similar constant shot along a busy street.

360-degree movement

This device is particularly effective in linking shots. Decide on the height of the camera and the speed of the camera as it moves, then shoot everything while moving 360 degrees around the subject, at every location, throughout the film.

Common space

This involves including an object or space in the background that is present in each shot, and could be as simple as a fireside with picture frame. This is commonly used in scenes with dialogue where it is useful to be able to locate two actors within the same space by showing some common space or object in each actor's frame. In a non-narrative film you could choose a single prop that is present throughout.

Transitions

At the editing stage, you will need to decide how you cut between scenes. The most common – the straight cut and the cross dissolve – could be developed by trying something a little more noticeable. An example could be to fade fast to white as the picture cuts, suggesting flash photography.

The length of the shot

A style of editing that uses short cuts, with a high turnover of clips, will encourage the viewer to see these clips as linked in some way, even if the subject matter is not. Therefore, we tend to see a montage sequence consisting of a lot of quick images because the diversity of images needs to be balanced by speed of perception. But what is a 'long cut' or a 'short cut'? In this case you could think of a quick cut as half a second or less and a slow cut as anything from three to five seconds, but your subject matter will dictate how fast your cuts will be.

Motif

In non-narrative films, a motif can be used with some thought to what kinds of objects or colours add to the overall theme of the movie. For example, in an interpretation of the word 'anger', we could justifiably use the colour red as a motif in the film. To stand as a motif you would have to see the object or colour recur often enough to be noticed. Alternatively, you could use images of a clenched fist or a brick hurtling towards a window, letting us see more and more of it as the film proceeds.

Linked imagery

For this idea we could take a look at Kubrick's *2001: A Space Odyssey* (1968). After a lengthy start where we see ancient pre-human apes, Kubrick needed a way of jumping tens of thousands of years into the future without disrupting the flow of the movie. If ever there was a time to use a continuity device, this was it. His response was to have the camera follow a bone thrown high into the air, and immediately cut to a similar-shaped, bone-like spacecraft, occupying the same space in the frame. This is a daring way of connecting two shots that could not be more dissimilar, visually. While shooting, you could look for parts of the scene that visually resemble a part of another, with the aim of linking the two later.

Sound

This is a last resort method of connecting shots and is not the most effective way. A single piece of music is dubbed over the whole film as with a music video. If you want to use sound in this way, try to use a particularly noticeable home-made soundtrack of sounds, rather than music, and one where you have altered the sounds or looped them, producing a repetitive, rhythmic effect.

The Crunch

- In narrative, continuity is crucial
- In non-narrative, broken continuity can be a useful tool
- Get to know the rules of keeping continuity and break them wisely
- Continuity is developed both in the script stage and *also* while shooting
- In non-narrative movies, beware that the movie doesn't look fragmented – use continuity devices in editing or shooting
- Get to know the action line and the 30-degree rule
- Use good quality sound and take care of ambient sound.

Project 15. Urban legends

What this project is for: to create a narrative movie
Time: allow a week to plan, another to shoot and two weeks to edit

What this project is about

This project enables you to put into practice many of the ideas looked at in narrative storytelling. Continuity, camera work, lighting, sound, scriptwriting, genre editing, all contribute to this short film.

The inspiration for it rests on the many urban legends or myths that are present in every community. These tales may or may not be true, but are certainly spooky and tend to be atmospheric, tense, with occasional spots of action and delivering certain veiled messages – in other words, perfect for narrative films. They also tend to play on the audience's fears, phobias and nightmares, engaging spurious moral codes – for instance, in *Final Destination* (James Wong, 2000), *Scream* (Wes Craven, 1996), *A Nightmare on Elm Street* (Wes Craven, 1984), *Halloween* (John Carpenter, 1978) and *My Little Eye* (Marc Evans, 2002). More original movies rely on mythical events where fantasy and reality can be merged to dramatic effect.

Stage 1

See Chapters 4:4 and 4:5 to help work on a story. For ideas, look in local newspapers, paranormal journals such as *Fortean Times* and weblinks to urban legend sites. Look for:

- A strange event that took place near where you live
- A supernatural tale
- A myth from indigenous peoples (Native American, aboriginal, for instance) that could be updated – see *Whale Rider* (Niki Caro, 2002) for a good example
- A cautionary tale (most horror films today tend to have such moral overtones).

Weblink
http://www.forteantimes.com/   Journal of the weird and unlikely.

Stage 2

See Chapter 4:7 for help with developing a visual style to the movie. Look at Chapters 5:1 and 5:4 on location shooting, Chapter 5:2 on lighting and Chapter 5:3 on sound recording to help with technical aspects. When shooting, make sure you stick to what is available – use friends as actors, props you already own and your own house as location. Close-ups are going to help in this movie more than any other kind of shot; they obscure imperfections in your non-professional actors' performances and also heighten tension and drama.

Stage 3

Make sure you stay within genre editing as outlined in Chapter 8:1, but feel free to experiment with a looser narrative style similar to the kind seen in music promos with simple stories. After the first cut, leave the film for a week or more and then come back to it with a more objective eye; you will then be able to do a re-edit where you try to reduce the length of shots. One of the most common faults of short films is shots that have not been cut enough. Try shaving off a few frames and watching the results, although make sure you keep a master copy of the first version safe to return to if necessary.

Evaluation

It is important with this movie to let it have an outside life beyond your friends and crew. Take it to local screenings and get comments from other filmmakers. If you get good responses, send it further afield to festivals or cable TV slots.

Go to: Chapters 9:10 and 9:11 to get more details on getting your work seen.

I want something more challenging

Option 1

To stretch your skills further, try writing a script that adds layers of meaning to the film. Look at Chapter 3:2, 'How films work', to get ideas about this. Stretch the cultural and social connotations more by offering connections to bigger world events. Urban myths by their nature tend to be localized, but some have engaged wider fears about the world, such as the fear of Native American ghosts in *Poltergeist* (Tobe Hooper, 1982), which perhaps reflected a wider awareness of historical and current political issues about Native Americans.

Option 2

Alternatively, try making a silent movie – one where there are sounds but no spoken dialogue. It will push your skills of storytelling to the limit, resting all information on what the camera can show rather than the cheap shortcut that is dialogue. It is also a great way to learn about sound environments (see Chapter 5:3 for details on sound environments).

3. Documentary

The current period of documentary is arguably approaching a kind of golden age. Factual films have earned huge receipts in the global box-office in films such as *Fahrenheit 9/11* (Michael Moore, 2004), *Touching the Void* (Kevin MacDonald, 2003), *Super Size Me* (Morgan Spurlock, 2004), *Capturing the Friedmans* (Andrew Jarecki, 2003) and *The Fog of War* (Errol Morris, 2003). The industry and critics have responded in the awards ceremonies, most controversially by awarding Moore the Cannes Palme D'Or in 2004 for his searing look at post-9/11 America. But it wasn't just his partisan view that caused a big stir – it was the point at which it broke through the $100 million barrier in box-office receipts, a return not seen before in documentary films. Suddenly, fact could be as enticing as fiction.

At some point it became acceptable for a documentary to be entertainment, but it is the filmgoers who have driven this change rather than the distributors, who failed to see that audiences were receptive to films that looked at social or political issues. Andy Glynne, director of the London Documentary Group, acknowledges the change:

> '*Touching the Void* is a great documentary, has done incredibly well in the cinema and has helped to change what people think of as a documentary. This idea that it had to be really didactic and straightforward has gone. Now you see dramatic reconstructions, animation, drama documentary, music video sequences, and you see it getting into feature films like *American Splendour*, which uses fake documentary-style footage and archive footage as part of the film.'

Documentary on a low budget

The low-budget sector is seen to be dominated by the short film, the calling card of the future feature director. But equally vibrant in this level is the documentary filmmaker. To a certain extent, this kind of filmmaker is more self-sufficient than others due to the size of the crew needed – the one-person self-shooter and editor is common. They also have few opportunities for funding, with many television companies cutting factual budgets before more popular dramas. The political nature of some documentaries – but by no means the majority – is also an obstacle. For award-winning documentary maker Phil Grabsky this is a problem, but not one without a solution.

> 'Generally speaking, there has been a general lack of nerve of TV people as well as a slavish rush to secure the highest possible audience, even if that means the lowest possible standards. But things are starting to change – and largely because digital technology has allowed filmmakers, including myself, to say "Hey, we can make the films we want with much less reliance on TV." At the same time, audiences are seemingly less happy with TV and are now going to cinemas to watch docs.'

Often, filmmakers seek other routes for finance so as to continue making the films they want to make without interference from outside agencies. Britain's Spanner Films, for example, runs a successful training company to help other filmmakers, and sells DVDs direct to the market. Its 2003 movie *Drowned Out* told the story of Indian villagers refusing to leave their land to make way for a hydroelectric dam. A version was sold to an American cable TV company, which helped fund more work. A later movie, *Baked Alaska*, focusing on oil drilling in the northern state and global warming, raised finance by asking for small donations from viewers of their previous films.

Figure 6.13 Director Franny Armstrong of Spanner Films shoots her film, *Drowned Out*, portraying the fight by Indian villagers against the destruction of their homes by a reservoir.

The severe financial and physical obstructions (the extensive travelling and research) would suggest that this field of the low-budget sector should be diminishing. But the very particular survival skills of its exponents have created an industry shaped by realism and able to overcome these obstacles.

> **Interview**
> 'I attended NYFA and mostly went on sets and observed the director at work, visualizing myself as the external director working on the same film because my ambition was to be in his position. I have worked in different positions on small productions that have not made it on TV – basically showreels. I read a lot of practical filmmaking books till I felt that it was possible to make my own documentary and believe me it is possible.'
>
> *Amaru Amasi, documentary filmmaker, USA*

Background to the revival

Documentary started its revival in the mid-1980s. Errol Morris's *The Thin Blue Line* (1988) made a great impact by incorporating dramatic devices usually seen in fiction movies. Its production values were high, it had a classy soundtrack by Philip Glass and it used narrative reconstructions to illustrate what had happened. The film told the story of the wrongful conviction of a man currently serving a sentence. The film attracted attention by meticulously laying out the evidence against the conviction, leading to a successful appeal after the film was released. Morris himself preferred the term 'non-fiction' to describe his film, reflecting his sense that it signalled a departure from previous documentary films. It also allowed him to enter the film for festivals where the documentary tag would have barred his entry.

The term 'non-fiction film' itself was first coined by a group of influential documentary filmmakers of the 1960s, Drew Associates. Within this group, working primarily for television, were the brothers Albert and David Maysles and Don Pennebaker, who made the Bob Dylan portrait *Don't Look Back* (1967). Prior to this group we could go back further to a group of French filmmakers in the early 1960s who for the first time admitted that the presence of the camera made a difference to what was being filmed. This '*cinéma-vérité*', as it was known, changed the way documentary was perceived and led towards the form becoming more subjective and perhaps more honest about its capabilities in that it could not claim to be entirely impartial and dispassionate.

Broomfield and Moore

A further step was taken with the work of British filmmaker Nick Broomfield and American writer/filmmaker Michael Moore. They have placed themselves firmly within their films, showing how the presence of the filmmaker affects the subject of the documentary and positively trading on this fact. Antecedents in this can be seen in the books of Hunter S. Thompson, such as *Fear and Loathing in Las Vegas*, which sparked a whole new kind of news reportage called gonzo stories, where the writer was firmly a part of the subject.

In Moore's *Roger and Me* (1989), the director tries in vain for three years to track down General Motors' chairman Roger Smith in order to confront him with the human consequences of GM corporate policy of redundancy in Moore's home state. Moore jumbles chronology and places his own feelings about the subject at the heart of the film – both these ideas would have once been outside the parameters of documentary. Moore's motivation was the sense that facts don't adequately portray the situation, that they need illuminating somehow by meeting human response. In successive films since then he has sought to display the human consequence of his subject matter in what may seem to some like headline-grabbing stunts or to others like original ways to pierce a cloak of secrecy.

In *Bowling for Columbine*, Moore took a teenage victim of the high school massacre referred to in the title to the headquarters of the store where the bullets that were still lodged in his body were bought. The store then promised to remove the sale of these bullets from local stores. In this sequence we could see the transformation of the documentary from detached observer to slightly subjective view and finally to subject of itself. It was less a description of the situation than an attempt to intervene and make a new situation. Less successfully, Moore's *Fahrenheit 9/11* asked senators to sign up their grown children for Iraq tours of duty in the armed forces. Documentary filmmakers remain divided about Moore's tactics, with many suggesting that his films remake the documentary form too radically.

Nick Broomfield deserves a place in this chart of the changes within documentary as a filmmaker who has sought out subjects which say something about wider society and avoided explicit political aims. As a result, films such as *Biggie and Tupac* and *Aileen Wuornos: The Selling of a Serial Killer*, with their subtle exposition, result in highly charged political statements, without having to resort to rhetoric.

Documentary convergence

Although much used in media circles, the term 'convergence' has something to tell us in describing the emergence of documentary in its newest incarnation. It has begun to sprout offshoots that are clearly documentary but incorporate other elements we normally expect to see in narrative film, including montage editing, the reconstructing of events to show what happened rather than simply tell it, the use of unusual and challenging structure, and imaginative use of the camera.

Go to: Chapter 10:2 for more ideas on what convergence means to the film industry.

Music video-style sequences are now common devices for breaking up less easily digested facts into more audience-friendly chunks. Animation has also crept in, allowing the filmmaker to use satire and metaphor to illustrate points, as in *Super Size Me*, which uses brief animations extensively throughout. An extended sequence in *Bowling for Columbine* made by South Park creator Matt Stone (a former resident of Columbine) combines a set of ideas that would have tested the attention span of most filmgoers if presented in any other form. By using cartoon characters and an offbeat narration the sequence can raise complex questions, in this case the relationship between American history, a state of social fear and gun culture.

These animated or music video sequences allow the filmmaker to state clearly that this is a very separate part of the film, thereby allowing a new set of rules to come into play. In much the same way, a narrative film uses montage to denote that certain sequences are to be seen as separate to the rest of the film, perhaps as flashbacks or intimations of the inner state of characters.

A further significant movement has seen the documentary form spill out into narrative, creating a hybrid movie. Jonathan Caouette's accomplished *Tarnation* (2003) uses archival footage to tell his own turbulent story, a strange combination of documentary and drama in an entirely new variation.

Film View

Made for $218 and edited with Apple's iMovie software, Caouette's movie *Tarnation* moved documentary and drama beyond the constraints of either form, and was a correspondingly big hit at the Cannes Film Festival in 2004. Caouette started making films at the age of 11, borrowing a neighbour's camera to document his turbulent childhood. After 20 years of hoarding tapes and photographs, he embarked on a rough cut of the footage as a side project. After a festival director saw the movie, the tape was passed to director Gus Van Sant, who signed on as producer, calling it 'a brilliant and devastating biographical documentary'. The official website is http://www.i-saw-tarnation.com/

Figure 6.14 Jonathan Caouette's debut feature *Tarnation* (2003).

Other films have also obscured the division between forms in this way, such as *American Splendour*, highlighted at the start of this chapter, while other films appropriate documentary devices for narrative ends, exploiting the unpredictability and rawness of the form, as in *The Blair Witch Project* or *My Little Eye* (Marc Evans, 2003).

Interview

'My advice for first-time documentary makers? I now have what I term the Nike mentality – just do it. Look out on the streets, question yourself about things you don't understand and find out the answers on camera from different societies. You don't need to go to film school or have a rich uncle, just have film passion. Research your subject, sometimes you don't need to because it unfolds before your lens into a story. Pick up a camera like the Sony or the Canon and start shooting. If you are not ready yet, read books on filmmaking or magazines like this one that's the only way you can get advice on what to shoot with.'

Amaru Amasi, documentary filmmaker, USA

Figure 6.15 In the forests of South America, documentary filmmaker David Flemholc worked in particularly adverse conditions for his film *House of the Tiger King* (2004).

Where next?

To some extent, the non-fiction film is becoming more challenging and provocative than the narrative film, stealing from other forms but doing so with the aim of a truer representation of the events it is portraying. The difference is that we now question what the meaning of truth is, and how to locate it. Filmmakers agree that once you point a camera at a subject, it stops functioning as itself and becomes a part of film rather than a part of real life, something that anthropologists and sociologists realized years ago. If the camera makes the objective subjective, then the filmmaker is only following the logic of this by presenting a film that uses elements from fictional and factual forms.

The result is a form that is more attractive to the aspiring filmmaker. The low costs and opportunity to be as creative as with narrative film means that this form is a valid place for a filmmaker to work; it can teach a great deal about all forms of filmmaking.

The Crunch

- Documentary film has evolved into other forms
- This is a great place for the filmmaker to build knowledge about filming – try it out
- Non-fiction film often requires you to use narrative filmmaking methods, so it's going to help your narrative movies too
- Always tell the truth (at least your own interpretation of it, anyway)
- Get to know how to convey ideas and opinions through images, through the way you use the camera
- Use non-fiction as a low-budget method of making movies (no actors, no sets).

Tip   For further viewing, try the following, though they are not easy to find in video stores: *Medium Cool* (Emile de Antonio, 1969), about the 1968 Democratic Convention; *Hearts and Minds* (Peter Davis, 1975), about the US involvement in Vietnam; *Italianamerican* (Martin Scorsese, 1970), a portrait of the director's parents; *Day of the Fight* (Stanley Kubrick, 1953), a portrait of preparations for a boxing match.

Project 16. My obituary

What this project is for: to investigate documentary filmmaking
Time: allow a few days to plan, a week to gather all the footage and another week to edit

What this project is about

The aim of this project is to try making a documentary which focuses on a mixture of fact and opinion and which offers opportunities to include other kinds of filmmaking within it. The inspiration for this comes from movies such as *Super Size Me* (Morgan Spurlock, 2004) and *The Thin Blue Line* (Errol Morris, 1988), and documentaries by Nick Broomfield.

The project centres on the slightly morbid premise that you are making your own obituary, but in a slightly light-hearted way. Friends and family members give their opinions about the life and times of you and offer anecdotes, some of which can be dramatized or re-created as music promo-style interludes. The aim is to create a documentary that is both entertaining and intriguing. The movie will be around five to seven minutes in length.

Stage 1

Begin by creating a rough chronology of the main points of your life, including first dates, accidents, high points at school and work, and so on. List those people you think could contribute and devise questions or starting points to jog their memories. Ask current friends to take part, contributing ideas about who you are, who you think you are and the gap in between.

Stage 2

While shooting make sure you keep the tone of the film constant; maintain a light-hearted look at serious subject matter, aiming for a kind of black humour or irony. While shooting the interviews maintain a constant approach to camera style, so that framing is similar throughout. Close-ups may suggest seriousness and may alter the tone of the film, so avoid anything too intense. Note how in many documentaries the interviewees are situated in similar positions in the frame, with certain colours in the background. Or you could opt for placing interviewees in locations which add to the story they are relating. Use props, too, to add symbolic elements to the image. For instance, in *Capturing the Friedmans*, a central person in the story is revealed to be a professional clown, and the director cunningly lets him talk in full costume, suggesting a level of pathos and poignancy impossible to achieve otherwise.

Stage 3

Take a look at the footage when you have finished gathering the interviews and look for places where it can be expanded. Look for moments which can be punctuated by cutaway shots to other images, or which could be dramatized. These dramatized sections need only be seconds in length, interspersed with cuts back to the interviewee, or could take up longer sections of the film.

Stage 4

In editing this film aim for a consistent pace, avoiding throwing us off guard with sudden changes in style or rhythm. Keep it steady and maintain a solid and strong structure, similar to that discussed in Chapter 4:4.

Keep interest sustained by, for instance, cutting from one interviewee to another or by mixing timelines, so that we go through your life by themes (love, career) rather than by chronology. Use text to emphasize points, perhaps for irony (for instance, an image of a younger you standing alone at the school dance, with the ironic caption: 'I had great success with the opposite sex').

Take a look at early Woody Allen films for some wry self-deprecating moments where Allen puts his life under the magnifying glass. Try *Annie Hall*, *Manhattan*, *Husbands and Wives* or *Hannah and Her Sisters*.

Evaluation

The success of this movie is in how it manages to tread a line between morbidity and entertainment. It is a typically unusual subject for documentary and so is good practice for devising similar ideas that combine real life issues with other forms of filmmaking, such as music video and drama.

When you watch the movie, look for threads of themes that appear throughout it. Can you learn anything about yourself through the way you edited the movie rather than what people said about you? Perhaps you emphasized certain characteristics above others, or glossed over other issues. As a filmmaker, if you can handle working with such close subject matter – it doesn't get any closer than this – and still maintain a relatively objective approach, then you can handle any documentary idea and remain focused on your plans.

I want something more challenging

To push this project further, enhance the dramatizations, bringing them to the fore. Focus on three or four events and plan them in a similar way to other narrative movies. Aim for high production values, where lighting, sound quality and composition are treated as if you were working on a normal narrative film. Also, try to arrange the narrative chronology in a different way, so that certain themes dominate.

4. Music video and the VJ

The non-narrative movie that we call the music promo has become a central feature of the video landscape. The idea of putting together images to market a piece of music is not new and has probably already experienced its golden age as it gives rise to other forms such as VJ-ing and viral movies. Meanwhile, today's promos have earned the right to be viewed as movies rather than ads, with festivals dedicated to them and cinema screenings for the best.

Figure 6.16 Members of British VJ group Addictive TV performing in Paris, 2004.

Today's music video is in hot pursuit of new technology and has a keen appetite for anything new – new styles, new gadgets, but most of all new ideas. The promo is at the centre of the film industry in an unexpected way. More film directors are schooled in promos than in any other form; they take the techniques they learn – most usefully, how to stick to budget – and make some of the most original and ground-breaking films.

Graham Daniels, co-director of UK-based VJ company Addictive TV, sees promos as having travelled from commercial tools to art films:

> 'The whole visual aspect to promos is now a thing in its own right, not just a part of a campaign. It's kind of like the backing singers have come to the front and formed their own band – what used to be a commercial product to help a band's sales has now become an art form itself.'

Beginnings

In a whistle-stop tour through 100 years of music promos, one thing is certain – it was never about the music. In fact, for some directors the music got in the way of a good movie. The history of the promo has always been dominated by the images rather than the music. Even the earliest photographic shows in 1900, where photographs were projected with music, were concerned more with how the images looked than whether the music was well served. By the time we get to MTV in 1981 the promo has developed into an entirely separate art form. If MTV execs thought viewers might also switch on and just listen, like a radio, they were quickly proven wrong, as it became more common to watch with the sound turned off, the music videos acting like a visual digest of the new, the cool and the soon to be mimicked.

Interview
'It really frustrates me that people only see Britney Spears or P. Diddy spending £7m and you think, how can you possibly have spent £7m on that three-minute piece of nothing? But there's this new stream of genuinely talented people doing stuff that knocks your socks off.'

Jordan McGarry, creative director, Shots *magazine*

Timeline

If we take a step back from the current whirlpool of change in the promo, we can see that it has had a surprisingly long life. The earliest use of image and music was created by American George Thomas, in Minnesota. His 'Live Model Illustrated' shows kicked off with a series of photos to accompany turn of the century one-hit wonder *The Little Lost Child*. Thomas's shows became a phenomenon, with over a hundred being staged at one point in his state. But for the first use of music with moving image we have to go to Sergei Eisenstein's 1938 movie *Alexander Nevsky*, with long sections to music by Prokofiev. This is seen as the first music 'video' because of the way the music led the cutting and rhythm of the movie, rather than having to fit around it. Before this, animation had started to investigate abstract cartoons set to music, with Oskar Fischinger's surreal, and oddly psychedelic, short movies.

Disney's experiments with music and image led to early cartoon shorts which made it plain that music was as crucial as image by naming them Loony Tunes or Merrie Melodies. From these successes arose the extended music video which is *Fantasia* in 1940, a bold and bewildering movie that has more than a little connection with 2004's animations by award-winning Lynn Fox or Pliex.

The first performance promo arose with blues singer Bessie Smith's short *Saint Louie Blues* (1929). By the 1940s, another way of viewing sound and image was patented by jukebox-style 'Soundies', coin-operated boxes that showed reels of performances of popular songs, mostly by jazz musicians or crooners, a development that echoes the web-based 'jukebox' of many online promo sites.

The early 1950s saw the first wave of music videos as we would recognize them in Lou Snader's Telescriptions, jazz/blues clips produced for local TV as fillers and for jukebox-style machines. The leap forward was the use of sets to illustrate the music rather than just performing to camera – these started to be interpretations of the music. But a series of allegations and rumours led to its early demise after just a few years, just missing the birth of rock 'n' roll by a whisker.

Breakthrough in movies

The landmark in the 1960s was not so much the films but their purpose – now we get to see films specifically designed as marketing for a band. Richard Lester's Beatles vehicle *A Hard Day's Night* (1964) is acknowledged as the first movie that took this approach; it became a marketing tool to reach out to fans and help crack new territories. Essentially, this and the later *Help!* were music video sequences contrived to fit together in a narrative that would be comprehensible to any viewer in any language without subtitling.

But the idea stuck that a band could present an image, beyond even a marketing concept, with music sequences. It wouldn't be long before The Monkees' TV show took this concept to its head-spinning conclusion and created an image but no real band. Meanwhile, the late 1960s saw the first forays into what would grow up 30 years later as the unruly offspring of the music video – the VJ. The first light shows at parties and concerts used Super 8 projections and lava lamp-style effects to create disorientating sensation events, where images created atmosphere – you didn't actually watch them, just stayed in the same room as them. Chris Allen, of VJ pioneers The Light Surgeons, followed much the same route in the 1990s with celluloid and music, and used video to create half party, half art exhibition environments.

The modern promo

It took a performer with a wholly conceived image and identity to make the first promo that we would recognize as such today in 1972's *Jean Genie* by David Bowie. An eclectic mix of location images made by photographer Mick Rock, it was shot for $350 in just three days.

By 1975 the promo voted one of the most popular was made by director Bruce Gowers. Queen's *Bohemian Rhapsody* was made as a last-minute filler only when the group cancelled a planned appearance on UK music show *Top of the Pops*, and marked a new high level of production values, incorporating early video effects with dramatic lighting.

MTV

Within a few years plans were under way for wall-to-wall promos on TV and in 1981 MTV opened its doors to the relatively small promo industry. Opening on 1 August with Buggles' *Video Killed the Radio Star*, it proved that they at least had a sense of humour. Ratings soared but it quickly became a *bête noire* among old-school rockers, who saw it as ushering in the dominance of image and style over music. But MTV was never intended as a channel for music aficionados. Instead, it aimed at a fast turnover of images. It cut videos when they got boring – never mind the song. It scheduled the videos they knew you wanted to watch rather than the music you wanted to listen to. And in its smartest move it evolved into a kind of visual wallpaper, like muzak: always on somewhere in the background. An advertiser's dream, it grew into a powerful force in music.

Effects of MTV

One of the effects of MTV has been the changes it forced upon filmmakers, and in particular editors. Films had to deliver the goods fast, within seconds, had to be constantly catching the eye, and had to avoid repetition, deviation or hesitation. For filmmakers it was like dancing while someone shoots the sand at your feet, producing a frenetic style that has passed into the lexicon of film school professors everywhere as movie-making for 'the MTV generation', implying a short attention span of near medical proportions.

So which came first, the fast-edited promo or MTV? MTV merely responded to the audience's need for something new, every day. It had to anticipate the viewers' need to fast-forward through the boring bits of videos, so the logical conclusion of this was that directors found you got more air time if you had no moments where you lost the audience. But MTV also gave the promo a commercial buoyancy which allowed directors to try new ideas on a daily basis. Without this quest for originality based on a steady income of cash there would be no promo as we know it today.

The industry now

Today, the music promo has become probably the most fertile place for an emerging director to learn the craft of filmmaking. The TV commercial gave us directors like Ridley Scott and Adrian Lyne and producer David Puttnam in the 1980s, while the promo is giving us directors like Spike Jonze, Michel Gondry, David Fincher and Gore Verbinski.

The reason why the promo is such a good launch pad is its place at the crossroads of new technology, with motion graphics, CGI (computer-generated images) and animation used routinely by the better-funded directors; on a promo, you get to learn a bit of everything. Many videos are made solely on animation software, creating abstract worlds that are picked up by front-line digital festivals like Onedotzero and Resfest.

But for many directors, the obsession with this kind of work has had its day and we are now seeing directors return to their live-action roots. Dave Drummond, director of Edinburgh Festival's music promo strand Mirrorball, keeps a close eye on these developments. 'Animation was a big deal once. But now that technology is accessible to everyone I think you have to do something different to make new stuff. People still see the benefit of traditional filmmaking. Shynola [Blur, Queens of the Stone Age], for instance, started out in animation, made their name in it, but have now started to do live action.' Directors now use animation software as an integrated part of their work in live action.

But there have been big changes as the promo adapts to the new world of file sharing. Illegal music downloading has had a powerful effect on the music industry, leading many labels to cut back on marketing budgets. 2004 saw a 7 per cent decrease in funding for the sector in the UK and many smaller labels are starting to market in new ways. Viral movies are becoming more common – an ultra-short of carefully chosen video images and clips from music sent to phone users, who then pass it on to friends if they like it. These sail a wave of word of mouth, trading on their exclusivity.

Go to: Chapters 10:2 and 10:3 for ideas on how the new environment of downloading is affecting film studios.

Other labels instead concentrate on live video projections at concerts. John Hassey, founder of promo agency Colonel Blimp, has discovered some of the UK's top promo directors. From his angle, things are changing. 'The problem is that labels are having to think about where they can spend their decreasing budgets on a band. They put a lot of it now into tour support because a live gig gives people a whole night out rather than just three minutes on a cable channel.' And with cable audiences now spread over more music channels than just MTV, this problem is multiplied.

So what's it like elsewhere? Japan has experienced a particular growth in the promo, but its promos don't necessarily travel well, at least not to the States. Dave Drummond says:

> 'In Japan, culture is a lot different. Promos in Western culture tend to be more about shock value. In Japan the lifestyle is different – they don't go for shocks. Over here it's mutilation, effects and all that, but in Japan instead they do wacky stuff, really different.'

How music video converges with movies

One of the lasting legacies of the number of directors entering filmmaking from a background in VJ or promos is its effect on movies. Many films now routinely include sections that are essentially music promos, while others rely more subtly on music promo devices, such as dreamlike imagery in movies like *Eternal Sunshine of the Spotless Mind* (Michel Gondry, 2004), *Being John Malkovich* (Spike Jonze, 1999) and *Adaptation* (Spike Jonze, 2002). Elsewhere, movies such as *Moulin Rouge* (Baz Lurhmann, 2001) borrow freely from the music promo repertoire of swooping camera movement, extensive CGI and a breathless, frantic structure.

Ingredients of the music promo

Promos tend to fall into two groups: those that are marketing tools first and foremost, and those that are art films first and marketing tools second. This second group wouldn't get their films made if they were pitched as such to record labels, but certain directors will add kudos to a band if their promo is

Figure 6.17 Music promo group Lynn Fox create organic and subtle images, as in this promo for Bjork's *Unravel.*

Figure 6.18 Lynn Fox's video for Incubus's *Sad Sick Little World* uses a typically stylized and polymedia approach.

unlike the rest of the field. The weirder the promo, the more word of mouth helps it sell the music that inspired it. An example is Chris Cunningham's promo for Aphex Twin, *Come to Daddy*. The images are so striking and unsettling that the music takes a supporting role in the film. It is the sort of film that can be watched in cinemas, rather than MTV.

To cut to what makes a good video, directors and agency executives point to the following as seen in many original and award-winning works:

- *Simplicity*. Some of the best films are the ones with the simplest of ideas, such as Spike Jonze's *California* promo, which is essentially a single 12-second uncut shot slowed down to three minutes, showing a man on fire as he walks casually to catch a bus.
- *Punchy*. Many ideas tend to have twists or punchlines at the end, acting like a twist. It keeps us watching and delivers added interest just as it starts to lose our attention. It also means that cable channels won't cut the video before the end.
- *Style-conscious*. Many videos are highly conscious of the style statements they are making, often referring to other style eras such as the 1950s (Spike Jonze's retro video for Weezer, *Undone*).
- *Low cost*. Many directors never quite lose the ability to think low-budget, even when handed a large budget. The music promo director is used to turning out original effects without using expensive software; the trick is to originate visuals in front of the camera. Michel Gondry's *Eternal Sunshine*, for instance, used extensive visual trickery to show houses falling down, books disappearing and so on. Gondry preferred to shoot these using glass sheets and simple animation rather than resort to CGI.
- *Original*. It is a difficult aim to keep inventing new ways of delivering surprises day after day, but promo directors somehow manage it. Paradoxically, it is often said the absence of big budgets forces the director to be more original, since they have to make a little go a long way.

Ingredients of VJ work

The VJ tends to work spontaneously, creating virtuoso performances of editing in much the same way as the DJ does with sound sampling. For pioneers of VJ work such as The Light Surgeons or Hexstatic, this medium enables the artist to create endless variations, tailored to the environment.

Go to: Chapter 8:2 for more about VJ-ing.

Ingredients of successful work tend to include:

- *Multiple screens*. Two or three screens arranged to surround the audience, leading to an immersive experience.
- *Themed clips*. Specifically shot by the artist and connected by an overall theme or idea. The use of downloaded clips of psychedelic fractals is especially overused in poor examples.
- *Text*. Meanings can be pinpointed through the use of snatches of words or sentences. It enables extra levels of juxtaposition derived from surrealist examples like painter René Magritte's picture of a pipe, with caption 'this is not a pipe'.
- *Repetition*. For the VJ repetition is a structural device. It's a way of ordering the priorities of a piece by selecting certain images and highlighting them as motifs.

- *Manual manipulation.* The development of manufacturer Pioneer's DVD mixer enables VJ-ers to work their video clips in a more hands-on manner, in exactly the same way as DJs use vinyl records. Before this, VJ-ers preferred to manually cut between clips and developed a dextrous style of quickly shifting around a range of clips.
- *Anti-technology.* Interestingly, many VJ-ers reject the high-gloss effects of their counterparts in music promos. It is described as a trend towards 'non-narrative, image-based video, a kind of digital punk aesthetic, low-fi and micro-budget' (Graham Daniels). In the work of digital artist Richard Fenwick, much use has been made of explicitly low-fi effects such as using out-of-date 3D software, and elsewhere artists create levels of juxtaposition by contrasting the non-narrative, twenty-first century nature of the video with effects and software from the stone age of digital video in the early 1980s.

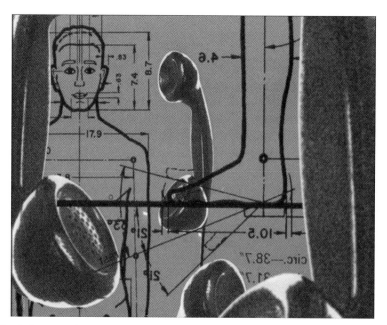

Figure 6.19 The influence of graphic design is evident in many music promos and VJ work, as in this still from *Skitzophonic* by the Mellowtrons.

Interview

'My advice for anyone new to VJ-ing is – Remember: mess has meaning. But there's a fine line between a mix and a mess. Keep it simple, less is more, stay away from wipes, never use special effects if you can help it. Be nice to people on the way up because you'll greet them on the way down.'

Chris Allen, director/VJ artist, The Light Surgeons

Film View
Five music videos you must see:

Come to Daddy/Windowlicker – Aphex Twin. Chris Cunningham's nightmare-inducing promos which helped redefine an industry. Brutal, brazen and clever.

Praise You – Fatboy Slim. Spike Jonze's low-res 'reality' shoot of crazed community dancers taking over a shopping mall. Jonze himself is the uber-jerk lead dancer.

Fell in Love with a Girl – White Stripes. *Eternal Sunshine* director Michel Gondry's typically dreamlike video of animated Lego models is a masterpiece of what he calls 'punk animation'.

California – Wax. Spike Jonze's promo of a listless Los Angeles street failing to notice the burning man running for a bus, it is a lesson in simplicity. Buy Jonze's DVD collection on Palm Pictures series. Available in retailers.

Hayling – FC Kahuna. Lynn Fox's fascinating arthouse promo is ahead of its time, even several years after its debut. An organic feast of weirdness like that glimpsed in 1960s sci-fi movie *Fantastic Voyage*.

Tip: top promo agencies in the USA and UK
Many top directors are represented by just a few agencies. If you want to send your showreel try:

Colonel Blimp: London-based agency headed by the legendary John Hassey, talent-spotter who launched the careers of many of UK's finest promo directors. See some of the best examples to download on their website: www.colonelblimp.com

RSA/Black Dog: Ridley Scott's super-agency has all but cleaned up the promo hemisphere, with Hype Williams, Chris Cunningham and Vernie Yeung in its stable. Offices in New York, Los Angeles and London. www.blackdogfilms.com

Anonymous Content: US-based empire representing many feature directors who also dabble in promos: David Fincher (*Fight Club*), Wong-Kar Wai (*In The Mood for Love*) and Gore Verbinski (*Pirates of the Caribbean*). www.anonymouscontent.com

Independent: London-based office representing many from the Anonymous Content stable plus other high profile UK directors, including Dominic Yeung. www.independ.net

Project 17. Music video

What this project is for: to make a music promo and investigate non-narrative filmmaking
Time: allow two days to plan, two days to shoot and three days to edit

What this project is about

The aim of this project is to put into practice the ideas covered in the previous section and to make a movie that relies wholly on images. A music video offers you ample chances to work whatever you want into the film, linking a wide array of unusual images together under the umbrella of the music track. You can be experimental, creative, and try tricks and ideas you normally can't work into a more straightforward movie.

As with most videos, the aim is to convey the ideas and atmosphere of the piece of music with images that complement it or set off new meanings in it. Avoid the kind of music video that focuses solely on a band performing, as this will restrict your creative opportunities.

Stage 1

Decide what piece of music you will be using. Bear in mind at this stage that if you intend making this part of your showreel, the tape that hopefully gets you accepted in festivals or offered other work, or if you want to show this movie itself, you are going to need copyright clearance from the band or its music publisher. In almost all cases this is going to cost huge sums, so your options are to use this movie as a stepping stone to learning how to make better films, not expecting it to be seen beyond you and your friends, or to use the music of a local or unsigned band who may welcome a free music video in return for waiving any copyright fees.

The kind of music you need to use is that which you already know well, which sparks off images and ideas in your mind whenever you listen to it. If you feel you can relate to the song and get a sense of the atmosphere it conveys, then this will lead to a good range of images to match.

Stage 2

Get a piece of paper and, while listening to the track you will use, write down descriptive words that you feel convey the song. Then write these down a vertical column and start sketching images that match the words, similar to the process used in Project 3 on composition. In that project, you were trying to convey something more tangible: a place or event, while this project asks you to try to put into images something that you imagine in your mind, triggered off by the piece of music.

When you have attached images to each word, define and select these sketches, redoing some of the more obvious, predictable images (to get an idea of the range of music video clichés, watch a few hours of cable music television).

Stage 3

When you have enough images to sustain the three- or four-minute film, you can start to forge the underlying theme in the film. We need some constant thread that runs through each shot to connect the film and stop it looking like a collection of unrelated images. This means looking at the images you have evolved on paper and trying to find connections between them. For instance, you might find that all your images have a certain claustrophobic feel to them, or are dominated by the colour red, or use a similar prop or setting throughout. Get to know your images. When you have decided on the kind of theme running through your images, label one particular image as the central one. Use this one image as the main focus for your film and one that you return to now and then.

Stage 4

At this point you might start to work on a storyboard, working out the order in which these shots will appear, but in this instance it may be more useful to instead move directly on to shooting, leaving open the possibility to add to or expand on shots.

When you are shooting this movie, you will need to be aware of visual elements far more than on other kinds of movie. To a certain extent, a narrative film that uses images so dominantly may look overworked and contrived. A non-narrative movie, however, with only images to make it work, actually requires you to make images more compelling and dominant than any other aspect of the movie. Shooting, then, is going to need a great deal of attention to detail, in each and every shot, in each setting.

Working without storyboards, you need to remain in control of what you shoot by referring to your visualizations constantly. These are your base point, the central ideas that run through the film, and you need to be reminded of them often.

Stage 5

Editing a non-narrative music video is more enjoyable than other kinds of movie. There are many ways in which the film can be developed, even at this stage, rearranging your shots, setting off one against another to see the ideas that arise. It may be useful to take a look at the section on montage (8:3), which goes into more detail about what happens when disparate shots are combined.

Unlike other kinds of movie, place the soundtrack on the timeline *before* you work on the images. This is to enable you to tie in certain images with particular parts of the song and time the whole movie so that it is the right length.

As with shooting, use the visualizations to return you to the central theme of the film, the main images which dominate it. If these have changed significantly while filming, don't worry – check that you were aware of these changes during production and your decision-making in following them, and that they are not having to compete with your previous theme for dominance.

In terms of structure, try using one particular image as the central point in the film and use it as an image we cut to at regular intervals.

To make the project more effective, try to avoid using special effects in the editing stage, including unusual transitions (ways of cutting from one clip to the next).

Evaluation

- How far did your ideas develop during filming? Were they fully formed when you picked up the camera or did you perhaps allow for more development during filming, preferring to keep some options open at this stage?
- In terms of images, look at how they compare to each other. Which ones are the most successful in terms of composition, subject matter, colour, camera angle, lighting?
- Looking at lighting in more detail, what kinds of lighting did you use? Maybe you focused on dramatic, high-contrast lighting or low-key, naturalistic lighting. Are there some lighting effects that you felt worked well in terms of the atmosphere you are trying to convey?
- The structure of this movie is not determined by story, so you were free to put it together in any way you felt best illustrates the music. Look at the arrangement of images in the film: Did you place some images repeatedly throughout the film and was this successful? Were there moments when the film seemed to be going in a completely new direction? If there were, try removing these sections and viewing the film again, as they may have been contradicting the main purpose of the video.
- Finally, leave the movie for a few days or more and watch it without its soundtrack. Does it still evoke the same atmosphere or theme as the song?

I want something more challenging

Option 1

Music promo is a often a sledgehammer in filmmaking terms; it is emphatic, straight to the point and doesn't take prisoners. If the promo is seen in these terms, is it possible to make one which bucks this trend? Could a promo have deeper levels to it, beyond the superficialities of surface image? In Chapter 3:3, we looked at the connotations that films can have, to the wider world, to other cultural references or just to other films. We saw how it is possible to create a film with layers of meaning that operates beyond the levels of action and appearance.

To push the promo project further, try making a film which does the opposite of many promos and ignores convention. Forget the fast cuts, the visual puns, the gimmicks and visual devices. But beware how you get more depth in your film. It will be tempting to throw in meaningful shots everywhere, but paradoxically this will reduce the overall depth of the film by contriving for meaning abruptly. Think about films you have seen where simple shots unencumbered with gimmicks have left a lasting impression. The low-budget American independent tradition has been particularly successful in achieving emotional, deep resonance in simple stories and images. Look at the films of Richard Linklater (*Before*

Sunset, for instance), Todd Solondz (*Happiness*), Alexander Payne (*Sideways*) and Wes Anderson (*Rushmore*). In each of these films, visual poetry is made out of the most prosaic of situations. Is it possible to make such a promo?

Option 2

A further way of pushing this project forward is to incorporate animated or motion graphic elements. Use software like Maya or After Effects (see the book by Curtis Sponsler, *Focal Easy Guide to After Effects*) to create another layer to your film which pushes it to new levels of design.

7 | Post-production tools

Quick start guide: Editing and post-production

How to get to the part you need now

First choose your route:

Quick start guide for documentary makers

First investigate genre editing
Scene setting, pace, continuity

Then see whether non-narrative editing can help in places
Devices in non-narrative editing

Then go into more depth in your sound editing technique
Sound editing principles

And work on titling
Using text and credits

Quick start guide for music promo/VJ

First investigate general non-narrative editing
1 Aims of the non-narrative edit
2 Devices in non-narrative editing

Then investigate montage editing
1 Montage
2 Project 18, 'Polymedia movie', for ideas

And see whether a creative use of text can help
Working with text

1. Condensed guide to editing

As we saw in Chapter 1, editing is the most crucial stage in the film's development, since it is the time when it becomes more than just the sum of its parts, more than a collection of scenes on a theme. The task is daunting: to compress time, to make events filmed days or weeks apart flow seamlessly; to make space contract or expand, or simply to suggest locations or events that are non-existent. It is, simply, deception on a grand scale.

It is impossible to lay down a rigid set of rules that lead to great editing; since the needs of each film are different, such rules would inevitably change for each movie. But there are points that can lead towards a better understanding of what your film needs. The ideas listed below are some of the most common points mentioned by editors, but all will be broken as and when necessary. The purpose of studying editing techniques is to know when you use these and when you break them. Since you probably want to get out there and make movies rather than spend a few years as an editor's assistant, you need to jump the queue of experience and look at how you make a film look good right now.

Editing: this is how it goes

1 Know your footage inside out, viewing it again and again to get to know where your strong points are and what looks (sometimes unexpectedly) good.
2 'Log' your footage tapes. This means making detailed notes, including the description of the shot, the timecode start and end points, its duration and whether the audio is of sufficient quality.
3 Make a rough, paper edit. More on these early stages in Chapter 7:3.
4 Make a first real edit, consisting of all the right shots you want in the film, but without any of the frills such as text, special effects, colour alterations and so on. These separate clips may also be untrimmed, which means they may still be cut down further. Full details of digital editing are given in Chapter 7:2.
5 View this first edit and go away and do something else. Go for a walk, do something physical, think about what you have made and consider all your initial plans, reflect on what you originally wanted and how this cut (or version of the film) relates to your intentions.
6 If you still feel good about it, go ahead and make the next version. This next cut is more defined, is smaller than the last and takes more time to complete. But at least you know that what you are doing is going in the right direction.
7 Leave it a week. In doing this, you are backing off from it emotionally, allowing you to make ruthless cuts if need be, and letting you see the film perhaps as others will see it eventually: objectively.
8 You still like the film. But beware of constant fiddling with the film, adding or taking away pieces as friends and crew see it and make suggestions, or new ideas hit you. The film won't survive as an artefact if you make it endure multiple rebirthing. Try to restrict your editing period to one specific term. After that, note down all new suggestions and ideas and make time for a reappraisal at some date.

2. Starting to work in digital editing

The more you understand about digital editing as a whole, the better you will be at seeing what it can offer you. Software designers do their best to make editing programs as versatile as possible, suiting every possible need but, if you look through the manuals that accompany these products, they are nevertheless aimed squarely at a large middle ground of programme maker. They will not go out of their way to find the most creative uses of their products; it is for you to find what parts of their product suits you and what is superfluous. If everyone uses digital editing software the same way, the potential for the technology to broaden what filmmakers can achieve will be undermined.

It is useful to look at what kinds of technical issues you may have to deal with, what certain bits of jargon mean and, of course, how your needs can best be served. If you are new to digital editing, or editing in general, then this will also explain the kind of route you take in putting a movie together. But we will leave all the artistic ideas about what makes a good edit for another chapter. For now, let's get technical.

Digital editing in six steps

Just about all software for digital editing involves the same basic chain of events. From the most elementary software that cuts and pastes your clips, to those with special effects and added features, the process is the same. Getting to understand this route from camera footage to finished film will give you the confidence to try out other software and will allow you to discover which kind of software is best for your needs.

1 Get hold of your raw footage. The tape will be played on either your camera or a mini-DV player.
2 Choose the bits of footage you want to work with.
3 Get all your clips onto your hard drive.
4 Trim your clips to the right length.
5 Play around with the clips on the timeline or filmstrip.
6 Put the finished film back on to tape.

It's like shopping

To put it in context, you could compare it to a trip to a supermarket. Each stage can be described as part of the wonderful shopping experience that is the modern mall.

● When you get there, you choose what items you want (like stage 2 above)
● Put them in your basket (stage 3)
● Take them to the checkout and put some items back you don't now need (stage 4)
● Go home and cook something edible (stage 5)
● Serve (stage 6).

The metaphor ends there, but experienced editors will have something to add, such as what happens when you change the recipe halfway through cooking (editing) or what happens when you find you don't have enough ingredients (footage).

Getting clips from tape to computer

As you know, there are only two types of information you are going to be working with: digital and analog. You can edit digitally with footage that is filmed in analog, first translating it into digital language – encoding. Digital tape is more straightforward and can be played directly into the computer, using a variety of different connections. The one you choose to work with is dependent on a whole range of factors, which we will look into in detail.

As for the actual device used for playing your footage, if you are working with digital tape you simply use the camera you shot it on to play the clips, although there are mini-DV players available at about the same price as the most basic, domestic camera. Using one of these would be useful only if you need to use your camera while someone else is editing, but it makes more sense to buy a second camera rather than a player.

Capture cards

Apple have stolen a march on most other manufacturers by including FireWire ports – the best way of hooking up a camera – as standard with all units, and now bundle free movie-making and DVD burning software at consumer level. The new consumer-level low-end Macs are a good route for beginners who want a stable system with reliable iMovie editing software.

But with most PCs the options are not sufficient to satisfy the quality and speed needed for filmmaking. This means you may have to invest in a few extras to get your PC connected adequately. A capture card is a small addition to the PC which enables a camcorder to be plugged in and 'captured' regardless of whether it is analog or digital. At its most basic it allows digital video to be connected to the PC or, higher up the cost scale, will encode analog into digital, and beyond that may allow you to return digital films onto analog VHS. The one that will do what you need for straightforward capture of DV to your computer is a card with a FireWire port.

Choosing the right capture card

This means choosing the right one for your particular needs, taking into account the type of film you might make and where and in what form you want to exhibit. Some of the most common options are:

- **Option 1**. Films for showing on the Internet or to be viewed on a PC, possibly also stored on CD or DVD. Choose this option if you intend to make and show your work on the Internet or keep only digital copies, on disc or digital tape. You will need a capture card that has an input port but no means of outputting the film back onto analog tape. These cards are cheaper than output/input cards but still have editing software bundled.
- **Option 2**. Films that can be shown on the Internet but also to possibly make VHS copies to show to potential agents or to enter in competitions. These cards have additional output ports for you to export the finished film back onto analog tape and are slightly more expensive. If you have ambitions for your work this is the better option, because the vast majority of agents, competition jurors and film buyers will watch your work on standard 12 mm VHS tape at home or at the office (but be prepared for requests for digital too). However, if you can only stretch your budget to a digital *output* card, you can make analog copies by connecting your digital camera directly into your VHS player.

Within these two types of card, there are further options regarding the kind of software you need and the way you compress the films down to fit on disc or tape.

Checklist: ask these questions before buying

- *What kind of processor do you need in your PC to run the capture card?* Check whether the speed of your PC is going to suit the card.
- *Has it got a FireWire port included?* There is no better solution to connect your camera to the PC. You don't need USB 2, despite its claims to be as good as FireWire.
- *Has it got a four-pin to six-pin adapter for FireWire?* You may encounter either size of FireWire, so an adapter is essential.
- *What kind of extras are bundled with it?* Many systems will offer you editing and music programs, CD authoring software or DVD authoring, but check whether you are getting reduced versions or trial-only full versions.

● *How much can I afford?* The most basic, entry-level cards are surprisingly inexpensive. Don't forget that the main reason you are buying the card is for the ports, not all the extras, and bundled editing software is rarely the full program. So, if you have to go for one of the cheapest, it will do the job as long as you get the right port.

Which ports?

Ports have their good and not-so-good points. Some of these you may have already in your computer, others you will get as part of a capture card.

FireWire

This versatile and fast link is a brand name devised by its developers, Apple Computers, and is also known as iLink (mostly on Sony machines) or, to give it the proper industry technical name, IEEE 1394. It has grown in popularity to the point where it is now standard on most PCs, but when it was first introduced to the market its power was seen as excessive. In those days it was rare to own a desktop editing system and the digital video revolution was yet to take off. But its attraction was evident: for the first time at consumer level you could reliably capture information at a high rate using a very small and discreet plug. It uses either four- or six-pin ends, Sony preferring the former, Apple the latter, but you may come across either in any system. Adapters are available for connecting one to the other.

FireWire is about four times faster than USB 1.0, transferring information at a breezy 400 MB per second. The net result for the filmmaker is that with a FireWire port, even the cheapest, most basic or free bundled software like Apple's iMovie or Microsoft's Movie Maker will produce better quality movies than more expensive software using USB. If you have invested in a good quality digital camcorder, it would make no sense to then use a port that loses some of that quality in transferring onto the computer. FireWire should be used if you are keen to maintain technical standards in your movie.

USB (Universal Serial Bus)

USB is flourishing in the domestic PC market because it is a cheaper alternative to FireWire and serves the needs of the videomaker doing home movies of weddings, parties or UFOs. It is hard to criticize this port because it has helped broaden the home video market by making it possible for cheap PCs to capture video, therefore encouraging software manufacturers to cater for this market. It is also ideal for small businesses aiming to show short commercial movies on the web, where perhaps picture quality is not an issue. USB is great for capturing video quickly, but only at the expense of full screen capture and smooth frame rate. USB 2.0 is a significant improvement on version 1, but it remains less universal than FireWire.

Version 1.0 transfers information at a relatively slow rate of 800 kB per second to 100 MB per second. This will knock the screen size on your PC monitor down to about two or three inches square if you want smooth quality, with the result that if you later want to stretch the image to fill a full-size television screen or to project the movie, you will be struck by a heart-sinking loss of quality. The standard screen size for the UK (PAL system), for instance, is 720×586 pixels, but USB prefers to work with a screen around 320×240, roughly half the size, and works more smoothly the smaller it gets. You can try to alter this by enlarging the picture while cutting the number of frames per second from the maximum

(25 in the UK, 30 in the USA) by half, but you have to be prepared to put up with the consequent loss in smoothness.

Capturing video onto the computer

Once you are connected using a capture card, you can gather the clips you need to start assembling a movie. Capturing clips does not have to be a precise process; you really don't have to be concerned about how much you select. The aim here is to grab what you think you might use plus a little more, leaving the decision-making about the precise length of a clip until later.

What to capture

There are different approaches to capturing. You may capture according to an edit decision list (EDL), where you will have clearly thought out in advance the shots you want and will have noted where you can find these on the footage tapes. Any larger production is going to benefit from this approach to some extent, simply because of the sheer quantity of material you need to trawl through to get to the useful takes.

Capture loosely

Alternatively, you may prefer to capture in a more intuitive way, gathering the footage you may or may not want to use as you go through the tapes, having first viewed them several times to build up an idea of what sort of film you are building. The advantage of this second method is that while capturing the basic clips you need to edit the film with, you can also gather footage that may add spontaneity to the film. A more likely scenario is to use both approaches, staying to a well-documented path but allowing considerable room for spur-of-the-moment acquisitions; allow room for the film to grow and develop. Do not be too precise about capturing; if a clip looks useful, grab it. You can always bin it later.

How much to capture

When capturing clips, you need to know how much your PC can handle according to the amount of RAM memory and size of hard drive. As a starting point, you should have at least 512 MB RAM available, but double or triple this is going to make editing much easier. If you are working with the absolute minimum of memory, you can maximize space by splitting up a movie into smaller chunks, working on each part separately and storing digitally. If space allows, you may then be able to capture each section individually and piece them together as one movie later, using the space freed up by dumping all the clips you used for each section. But no solution beats getting a more spacious PC.

Tip When you capture video to your computer, it is better to use a separate hard drive. Store everything you normally use the PC for on the main drive and then use a separate one – internal or external – for all video work. Or you could partition your main hard drive into two sections. The advantage of two drives is that problems in either drive will be contained rather than affecting the whole PC.

Systems and hard drives

Whatever computer you have, it is going to become too small for you at some point when the internal size of the PC – what it can handle in terms of data – will start to strain under the weight of your movies.

- Get the fastest processor you can. Athlon processors deal with video better than any other.
- Get the most memory you can, bearing in mind that some programs require at least 128 MB just to get going.
- Add extra hard drive space to that existing on your PC. You are going to need about 40 GB to make short films easily, moving up to 150 GB to make longer movies, allowing you to cope with most situations. But if you can, go for something much larger than this. Work on the basis of 1 GB taking up about a minute of video, allowing the same or more on top of that for footage stored on the hard drive while you edit.
- Use your PC for editing and nothing else, freeing up space used by other programs.

Tips for better capturing

- When capturing, try to break a clip down into small chunks, provided you cut at the end of a take. Avoid capturing one long clip consisting of several takes, as it is easier to work with if you name each separately.
- When you save your clips, name them as descriptively as possible, as this is the title that appears on the timeline and project bin. For instance, rather than calling a shot 'Steps, take 21', call it 'Steps – best take with good audio, 21'.
- If using a mid-range program, you have the option to alter capture settings. Since you will be doing a top quality edit you need to use settings that maximize the equipment you have, capturing audio and video at the optimum rate. This is sometimes referred to as the 'on-line' edit.
- Some programs tell you if they drop any frames while capturing and give you the option to abort if this happens (get used to it, dropped frames is common with some programs), but if this gets to be too frequent, try switching off the 'Abort on Dropped Frames' command, as captured video often drops the very first frame. If you have dropped only one frame, the capture was successful.

Files and saving

As soon as you start to capture, you need to start putting them somewhere that is easily accessible. Create a folder to contain all your clips, rather than within the software folder itself (which is often the default place it suggests you save it). Within this, always save your clips into separate folders with, for instance, titles in one folder, establishing shots in another, audio in another and so on. It is very easy to mislay files given the number you are going to create with each movie, and the ability to wade through files quickly to get to the one you want is paramount.

Importing your clips

The next step is to get the clips up onto the desktop, ready for use. In some basic software, this is called 'Get Clip', but more commonly 'Import'. Look for your clips, which should be arranged in easy-to-find folders. Once you have imported the clips, they will appear as a list with some information about the length and date of creation. You can be selective at this point, choosing only those files you want to use right now. At the end of this stage you are ready to start building the film.

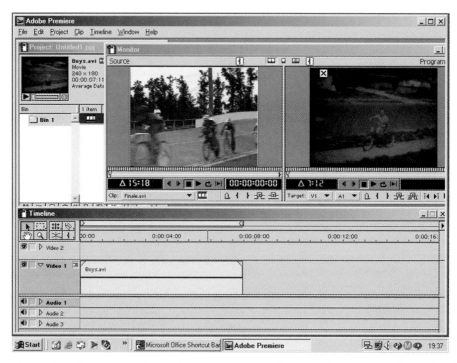

Figure 7.1 In Adobe Premiere, as in most editing programs, three windows are used: a project bin containing clips, a monitor window for trimming and a timeline.

Trimming your clips

This part of the process is where you start making creative decisions. You are deciding which parts of each clip you want to use and whether you need to split them up further into smaller clips. The clips you captured to start with are rough around the edges and need refining before they can be used in the film. Trimming is an exact art. The tools for this are precise to the frame and, provided you can access the original again and again, you can try out several versions of clip if you are unsure of how to construct a sequence.

The obvious question here is why don't you trim them earlier when capturing? Why import a larger file only to cut it down now? The answer is that you need to try to focus all editing decisions into one stage of post-production. Editing is a creative process which requires you to treat the film as a whole; all decisions, such as the nature of the cuts and the order they appear, are creative and need to be undertaken in one process.

> **Tip** Compose a rough cut on the timeline by trimming with the slicing/knife tool. Lay out all your clips for a scene and quickly cut them into shape in the right order. You will have a very quick version of how the film could look, and can then save this and refer to it while you spend longer on the main fine cut.

How much to trim

Choosing how long a clip will be depends on a number of factors and is influenced as much by the previous trim as by the look of all the clips on the timeline. You need to evolve a rhythm and energy to the film when editing, and to do this you should cast your net wide early in the process and focus on the look of the film now. It can upset your momentum if you find you have too few clips and have to go looking for them in the middle of an editing session.

Experiment in trimming

Trimming is similar to part of the old analog editing process and is devised as such to appeal to editors schooled in the old ways. The basic idea is to select 'in' points and 'out' points to denote the start and end of the new cut within the clip. In most software, altering the clip allows you to drag the new revised length onto the timeline but leaves the master copy in the project bin untouched. However, it is worth checking whether your own program alters the original clip, as does Windows Movie Maker. This is more common in free editing software, including those bundled with hardware. Clearly, this is not a popular feature as it takes away one of the great aspects of non-linear: the ability to experiment, for you to see first and make up your mind later, with the option to return to the original if you don't like what you see.

> **Tip** It is often a mistake of first movies to be under-trimmed. Shots tend to be on screen too long. Make your film look more professional by going a little too far with the cutting – try cutting a few frames off each clip and go even further to see how it looks. To see if you are letting clips run too long, give yourself a time limit for each clip of perhaps four seconds (unless dialogue requires longer) and ask yourself to justify each clip that goes beyond this. If you are uncertain, keep a copy of the film without your new trimming to revert back to.

Look at other clips when trimming

One of the basic tenets of editing is that it is all about how one clip looks next to another, not how each looks in isolation. As we saw in some of the projects, clips change dramatically when placed next to others. Editing should become an organic process during which a film gradually emerges, in which decisions about each part of the film are made with reference to the whole. With this in mind, view the last few clips you just trimmed before you trim the next one and, if you can, view the one you think you are going to use immediately after it. In practice, this means looking at the effect of each clip on what has gone before, by playing sections completed so far, but allowing these sections to alter under the effect of later clips.

Using the timeline

The timeline is a central part of the editing process, the place where the film sits and is assembled, and it is common to all software, though it is sometimes referred to as a filmstrip or storyline.

It is usually placed at the foot of the screen, a horizontal track running left to right displaying video and audio, looking like train carriages placed end to end on a rail track. The timeline is one of the most important windows in DV editing and it is worth taking the time to get to know what yours can do. Software varies greatly here, with low-end units offering just one track for you to build a film on, others offering the opportunity to layer text and images on up to 99 tracks.

A–B tracks on the timeline

Another principle seen in software in the mid-range level is the twin A–B track. Yet another aspect that will be a familiar feature to those who have worked with linear editing systems, this operates by allowing a film to be built across two tracks, track 1A and track 1B. This lets you place two clips together but choose how 'A' runs into 'B' (known as the AB roll) using perhaps a cross dissolve, a page tear or a simple wipe. Don't worry if your package does not offer this – great films are the sum of their images and the structure that binds them; if people notice your great AB rolls then the film may have little else going for it.

The method you select from the menu to roll from 'A' to 'B' is called a transition. A clip placed in track A will have a transition placed between it and the next clip, B, where the two overlap.

Play with the timeline

Part of the whole point of non-linear editing is that you can make the film in any order you like, starting in the middle and working outwards, or laying out the basic clips and returning to work on a particular section later, and the timeline becomes the main arena for this. Unlike linear editing, you now have a tool for experimenting, for trying out new ideas about how the film can look. Using the timeline as a creative, intuitive tool enables you to use it to its full potential; it is a place of play and trial and error, and no matter how detailed your plans are for editing, you cannot foresee the exact effect of one clip placed next to another until you see it played on the monitor. Be prepared to change your plans, using the timeline as the place to explore the possibilities presented by each clip.

The implications for this, of course, are that editing can potentially be a never-ending process, with endless variations and versions. Try to be aware of the danger of stirring the pot too much, of refining the life out of the movie. Give yourself a deadline for completing it, perhaps by setting up a first showing for other filmmakers or friends. The objective insights gained by looking at how other people view your film can be invaluable and at least give a solid reason to re-edit if you choose to do so.

Audio

Once the film has been assembled, you can begin to think about audio tracks. The advantage of non-linear editing is that you can see the audio clips and can link sound to vision more easily and more logically than on linear. Some of the lower-end software titles do not allow you to separate sound from vision or add music, but just about all in the middle lower upwards allow this.

The options for gathering sound are:

- importing music from CD or other digital source onto the timeline
- using audio from elsewhere in the film
- using modified sound, created using one of the many sound packages available
- using sound recorded yourself on a mini-disc player or other digital recorder.

If you have gathered the right audio tracks during filming, this process should present few surprises. The best option is to use sound that you have recorded rather than sampled from other sources. Taking sound from other sources stops you from having control over this most important of elements, and in any case, copyright implications should steer you away from it. However, if you don't want to record original sound effects yourself there are some very good programs, some available as free downloads on the Internet, enabling you to generate sounds. Copyright-free CDs are also available, including a wide variety of sound effects. Be aware, though, that these often sound 'canned' or unreal. Natural sounds you have recorded will give your film added realism.

If you are working on a music video (check you have a licence from the copyright owner to use the track), you may find it easier to place the audio track on the timeline first and then add images later. This enables you to match images and sound correctly, with correct timing.

Rendering

Once the film is completed on the timeline, it needs to be assembled as one file. This process is called 'rendering' or building or in some programs is called simply 'make movie'. Rendering takes time and is lengthened if your film has added filters (effects), titles or other layers and transitions, in fact anything other than straight clips.

Mid-range programs will allow you to render as you work through a film, saving you from the trouble of having to re-render the whole film just because you changed a part in the middle. In general, it is better to render in parts as you go, partly for time reasons and definitely if your package is not a real-time editing tool. Rendering is the only way to test the effect of filters, layers or transition; the movie won't play them until they are rendered. However, if you have a fast, powerful workstation then you will expect to render in a time that does not disrupt your evening – in the early days of DV editing, rendering was an overnight job. With up-to-date processor speeds and an average or small memory space of 512 MB to 1 GB, you would expect short films to render during a coffee break, or two coffees if using 64 MB. RAM of 256 or 512 MB is ideal and will release the potential of your software more fully.

Output to tape

Once the film has been assembled in its final completed form, you will need to produce 'hard copies', digitally stored copies so that you can re-edit the film if necessary and VHS ones for viewing, as it is very useful to be able to see a movie's progress after each session. Seeing it projected or on a television screen enables you to get an opinion of the film as a whole and check that it is going in the direction you want, preparing you for the next editing session. It is therefore useful to be able to output the film occasionally as an analog VHS copy. It is also essential to have a hard copy of your film should anything go wrong with the computer during post-production. Output each new version onto something real: tape, CD or DVD.

Output options

1 *Output to analog tape.* Connect your PC to a VCR or camera and follow the instructions on your software to 'export' the movie to tape.
2 *Output to CD.* Typically, a 650 MB CD will hold only a short film. Don't be tempted to compress the movie for storage; master copies should always be at the full frame and full pixel rate. If you really have to use CD and no other method is available but your movie is too big for the CD, store sections of the movie on successive discs. But generally avoid storage on this format.
3 *Output to DVD.* DVD, on the other hand, is a whole different story given its dominance in the marketplace for some time now. Films compressed using MPEG-2, the method used for DVDs, will retain excellent quality and can be reworked repeatedly, while the huge quantities that can be held – feature films plus additional material – make this by far the better storage option. But remember that it is always more desirable to re-edit a movie from an uncompressed original on mini-DV tape rather than disc, even if it is compressed in such an advanced way as DVD.
4 *Output to digital tape.* Once you have wired up your camera to the PC, it is easy enough to be able to reverse the flow of information and get the finished film back onto the camera. Again, FireWire is the quickest and safest method at the moment.
5 *Output to the web.* If you have completed a film and wish to send it to a third party via the web or show it as part of a website, you can output to the web very easily. Most programs, including entry-level ones, have evolved greatly in this respect and allow a film to be saved in compressed form ready for viewing.

Weblink
http://bmrc.berkeley.edu/frame/resources/how_to/premedit/   Useful beginners' guide to editing with Adobe Premiere.

The Crunch

● Digital editing is easy
● Get the right capture card for your needs – don't overspend

- Any edit programme will do – it's what you do with it that matters, not the range of special effects it has
- Use the fastest, most efficient port you can (FireWire)
- Try to get the largest hard drive and RAM within your budget
- Make full use of DV's non-linear approach – edit in any order you like
- Get to know your software and your system
- Play, play, play – experiment and try out anything with your software, whether it is in the manual or not
- To improve your skills, try teaching someone else how to edit – it will reveal any gaps in your knowledge and, in any case, other people ask questions you haven't thought of
- Always store a master copy on DV tape when you have completed editing – keep a copy after you finish editing too in case the unthinkable happens and you lose the movie off the system.

3. Preparing to edit

Although editing has been somewhat liberated by the arrival of the at-home, take-your-time desktop editing system, enabling the filmmaker to make infinite variations of a film, it pays to take some time before editing to consider how to go about it.

Edit log

The edit log is the first step to take. The aim is to identify and mark the clips on each tape that are satisfactory and make life easier by noting where to find them.

The log shown in Figure 7.2 has four vertical columns. In the first vertical column, note the timecode that the clip relates to. In the second column, note the tape on which this appears, if you are using more than one. In the third you may have a shorthand way of referring to each part of each scene, either describing a shot by name or numbering it. The last column gives a description of the shot, including notes on its quality.

Although we look at timecode elsewhere in more detail, there is a point worth noting here that affects your ability to use it in log sheets. Timecode exists as a continuous line of information, labelling each and every frame on your tape. If, however, you interrupt the tape, by pausing filming now and then, you may create a breakage in the timecode information and what you would see when playing it back would not be a continuous timecode but a series, with each new clip starting at zero. This is true of most domestic camcorders, but is easily overcome during shooting by coding the whole tape with timecode before you start filming, simply by recording continuously over the whole tape with the lens cap still on the camera.

Go to: Chapter 7:5 for more detail on how to work with timecode.

Logging software

There are computer programs which are designed for logging tapes and which work along the same lines as described above. The advantage of using a program is that you are then able to compile an edit

0:19:24	miniDV Outside in garden. CU Rachel in foreground, Steve in background	He pushes her
0:20:00	LS. Steve pushing Rachel	
0:20:12	Raising spade from left	
0:20:32	Raising spade from right	
0:20:40	CU dropping spade	Rachel drops the spade
0:20:45	CU dropping spade	Closer than before
0:20:48	CU Steve's feet	
0:20:52	CU Steve's feet	
0:20:57	CU Rachel	Rachel raises her hand to her mouth, gasping
0:21:00	CU Rachel	Walks back
0:21:13	LS Rachel	Runs away from scene, Steve's feet not in shot
0:21:21	ECU Telephone	Very close shot of the handset
0:21:40	CU Keyboard	Hand comes into shot and types
0:21:56	CU Edge of keyboard	Focus throw
0:22:12	CU Keyboard	Letter 'D' in centre of shot
0:22:44	CU Keyboard	Letter 'E' in centre of shot
0:22:51	CU Keyboard	Letter 'E' in centre of shot, shadow pans across keyboard
0:23:07	CU Keyboard	Letter 'A' in centre
0:23:14	CU Keyboard	Letter 'T' in shot
0:23:19	CU Keyboard	Letter 'H' in shot
0:23:25	CU Keyboard	Card bounces up and down
0:23:34	CU Telephone card	Cord swings left to right
0:23:40	ECU Telephone	Shot of 'Redial' button
0:23:48	MCU Lamp	Turns on and off
0:24:12	CU Lamp	
0:24:17	MCU Rachel	In kitchen, Steve paces back and forth in background
0:24:23	MCU Rachel Take 2	Same as before
0:24:42	MCU Rachel Take 3	Same as before
0:24:50	LS Study door	Door opens, Steve walks through
0:24:56	LS Study door (Reverse angle)	Shot from Steve's point of view, he snatches the phone from Rachel
0:25:25	MCU Rachel	She knocks on the study door

Figure 7.2 Example of an edit log.

decision list (EDL) by cutting and pasting each clip you want in the order you want, and if you have been able to label each clip with timecode then you have a fast and easy way of getting hold of those clips.

Edit decision list (EDL)

The EDL is one of the most useful tools for the editor. Although much is made of the need to edit intuitively so that you get to know how one clip affects the next and how your decision-making changes throughout the editing process, it is important to be aware of the way most of the industry works. For today's editors, the EDL is a way of arranging the production as a set of plans for an editor to follow through later. Editing in this case is a technical operation rather than a stage in which possibilities can arise and changes made at any point.

If you are not using one of the many software programs for EDLs, it is equally effective simply to cut and paste the information for real on paper.

The paper edit

The paper edit consists of a series of notes laying out the basic order of clips for a movie. In Figure 7.2, you can see how the paper edit is arranged. Vertical columns show the place where a particular clip is to be found in timecode on the footage tapes and the point at which it ends, followed by a short description of the clip, another column describing audio necessary for that clip or sequence and, finally, the length in seconds of this cut. It follows on from the 'edit log' in that the information you use for the paper edit is taken from the log you have made of each single take you shot on the footage tapes. In the paper edit you have simply extracted the good clips from the edit log and played with the order they occur.

There are many reasons for pausing awhile and working some of the edit out in advance. It is never possible to predict exactly how the film will look after the final cut is in place because you are presented with problems and choices all through this stage, each of which can affect the film in different ways. A more likely reason is that although you may have a good idea of what kind of footage you've got, there is no telling how one clip looks when placed next to another. A 'paper edit' prepares you to make better choices and decisions and gives you a baseline point, a model from which you can deviate or remain with, but which gives you some idea of how close or far you are from the original plans.

Practical uses

In practice – in the real world – the paper edit does not have to be an exact plan as such, but more a way of triggering off ideas about how to edit. If you go into the editing process blind – that is, without any forethought about what kind of movie you are looking to create – you risk making a movie of pieces with no sense of the whole. In a way, the paper edit is like organizing the seating for a table of guests at a party; if you place certain people next to each other you can be sure that more interesting conversations or situations are likely to arise, none of which you can predict yet, but the overall arrangement will make it more possible.

Speeding up editing

If we go into the paper edit in more detail, it becomes possible to save considerable amounts of time by working out the order of shots and the rough timecode points for each clip. You can then start to add up the clips and get some idea of the length of the film and choose whether to cut or alter the overall structure in some way. Trawling through the tapes seems like excessive work at first, but to demonstrate its usefulness, try 'editing' just a few minutes of footage on paper and then try trimming and editing the sequence for real using the paper edit; you may notice the speed with which you work now and the freedom it might give you to concentrate on the way the film is looking as a whole.

Alternative methods

Some editing software programs now include a feature allowing you to import a series of clips, arrange them quickly into an outline of the film and then export the whole plan onto the timeline. This is a useful alternative to the EDL, as it allows you to quickly move and arrange a film as a general plan, in big blocks, before going on to do a fine edit later. Since each clip is labelled beforehand and shows time-code, you don't lose any of the accuracy you might want with the traditional EDL.

The Crunch

- Make an edit log of all your shots
- Use timecode to tell you where the best ones are
- Make an EDL
- Save time editing – do it on paper first
- Plans always change, 100 per cent of the time, when editing for real.

4. Editing with sound

What does good audio do?

Audio is one of the areas of making a film that is often the last to be resolved. Since the nature of film-making is primarily a visual medium, it is often seen that music and sound are there to prop up the images; by the time shooting has finished and you view the footage tapes, it is not easy to consider that there is a further element which can radically alter the effect of the carefully won visuals. Too often, sound is an element that threatens to disrupt the edit-in-progress, but it is the path of least resistance simply to place a soundtrack that adds nothing new to the experience. Digital editing allows much greater creativity and control over audio than ever before, but few filmmakers take full advantage of its tools. The aim of this section is to encourage the use of sound as a central part of a film.

Compensating for low budgets

Sounds fulfil several roles in a film, beyond simply emanating from what is occurring on screen. One of the most useful for the micro-budget filmmaker is the capacity of sound to convince the viewer that more is present than we can see, suggesting a wider world outside of the frame. Cheap sets can be made to seem more realistic, small crowds of extras more populous and action scenes more dynamic, all by using more creative sound. The restrictions of your budget do not necessarily need to be reflected on screen.

Helping continuity

In post-production, sound can be a way of rescuing a scene if unforeseen problems have occurred. A scene can be given a better sense of continuity if a single audio track covers and links shots, acting as an ambient presence throughout. Jarring cuts can be made smoother by covering both with the same sound. Furthermore, a soundtrack can offer stability and continuity so that more abstract visual sequences are sustainable. Whatever the visuals look like when you have finished a rough edit, if you feel that they are not quite as exciting as you had planned, sound can start to turn them into something approaching a full cinematic experience. For the low-budget filmmaker, sound is one way of adding invisible dollars/pounds/euros to the value of a scene.

Editing programs and sound

In many editing software programs audio is not given a high priority, but in mid-range software (not free software like Windows Movie Maker) this improves and the timeline is arranged so that you can work with audio and visual tracks simultaneously. Basic 'cut-and-paste' programs do not always allow the separation of sound from image, although most will allow sound from other sources such as CD. Creative filmmaking is only really possible in one of the more versatile programs. In Adobe Premiere, for example, many audio tracks can be added (up to 99) to bring complexity and depth to the soundtrack. You won't necessarily ever need to use all these, but at least five could be used on a regular basis.

Building a soundtrack

Layers of sound

Building a soundtrack is going to be something that evolves over successive edits. The basic tracks linked to dialogue or essential sound effects will be placed early on in the process, but other layers could consist of a multitude of extras that add, paradoxically, a more natural sound to the film. In the earlier chapter on production sound we saw how sound is dissected and recorded in layers so that it can be manipulated later. That 'later' is now and you will start to see the value of having each part of the soundtrack on separate parts of a tape. Even simple scenes require several layers of sound to replicate the natural feel of real live sound. This illusion is necessary because in real life we are bombarded with many sounds constantly and our brain focuses only on what we think is important: dialogue when talking with friends, the sound of the underground train when waiting at a stop or the sound of a baby's cry to a parent. The way we layer sound mimics the way we order and make sense of the mess we hear. Your main tool is the relative volumes of each of the tracks in the scene.

As an example, we could take apart a sequence in which a figure is entering a room in expectation of finding a crime scene. In this, it is essential that a certain atmosphere is carefully built up, perhaps a feeling of apprehension, fear or anxiety. The actors have done their part, you lit the scene as well as you could and the camera framing is just right. But when played silently, the scene is rendered almost harmless. The way you layer the sounds that relate to each part of the scene will form the basis of how the audience view that scene. So, a list of the kinds of sounds that would be needed would include the main 'diagetic' sounds – the ones that are created from action within the scene as opposed to musical soundtrack or other invented sounds – and the range of sounds that you think generate the kind of atmosphere you are trying to evoke. It is this second part that is the most interesting to play around with.

Add atmosphere

The kind of sounds you could play with could include some extra effects to suggest the exterior atmosphere, outside the room or apartment building. Sounds of rain and wind, of sirens, car horns or other residents arguing in the block could all help create a sense of something wrong. Discordant sounds could be brought to the fore, such as the buzzing of a faulty neon light. In practice, this soundtrack could be composed of several separate sounds, most of which were not present on location when shooting and some of which were created electronically.

Film View

For Hitchcock's *The Birds* (1963), renowned film score composer Bernard Herrmann (*Psycho, Taxi Driver*) was hired to create bird sounds; no music was present in the film. Herrmann used early electronic sound technology – quite unnatural in its effect – to accompany the bird attacks, preferring this to the sounds of real birds screeching. In this case, realism was not going to produce the sounds likely to correspond to our idea of what such an attack would sound like in emotional, subjective terms. And it is that point that tells us most about sound effects in film: that layers of sounds can be used to evoke the *sensation* of what it would be like to experience the action on screen. As a further example, listen to the careful use of silence during the initial beach landings in *Saving Private Ryan* (Steven Spielberg, 1998), which captures the bewildering sense of shock felt by the soldiers.

Prioritizing soundtracks

In every film it is necessary to consider which sounds are made most clear to the audience and which are less distinct. It is something that needs consideration before you start editing, as it needs to be consistent throughout. It can easily be described and arranged on paper, and these notes can be directly translated into what appears on the timeline when editing. When recording sound it is most useful to have recorded each element of the scene separately so that they can be given relative value later in terms of volume.

To see this in action, we could use a scene in which two actors are talking in a bar, with noisy customers and the television permanently switched on in the corner. Later in the scene, another character enters the bar. If one microphone was used in recording the action, the result would be a mess in which everything is heard but nothing understood. The correct way would be to mic up the actors, record presence or ambient sound, record the television and exaggerate the sound of the door opening. There would be a strict order of importance in arranging these sounds later, based on the effect the director wants to create. It is likely that we need to hear the dialogue, so that would be placed as optimum volume. Second billing would be mood music accompanying the scene, also heard over the din of the crowded bar, with ambient sound third. Sudden necessary sounds, such as the door opening, would be brought unnaturally to the front to signal their importance.

Go to: Chapter 5:3 for more details about recording sound on location.

Foreground and background

Throughout this process you are thinking in terms of foreground and background, with shades in between. Prioritizing sounds in this way makes editing far more straightforward, avoiding the chances of sounds pulling in opposite directions to the images, or sending out false messages to the audience. As an example of poor layering order, a scene in which two people are talking at the same bar could be disrupted by the sudden loud sound of an off-screen door being opened. As viewers, our response is to presume that this is significant and start to look for who has entered the room, but placed at a less noticeable volume it would be more natural to the setting.

Make it natural – artificially

This last point is crucial: that sounds must conform to what *seems* natural (in other words, what conforms to what we feel the sounds of the bar should be), not what *is* natural (in other words, sounds recorded by a mic placed randomly in an actual bar). Natural sounds appear artificial, but artificial sounds appear natural. On the other hand, the filmmakers' group Dogme would argue that it is only our dependence on how we expect sound to be heard in films that makes us feel one way is better than another.

Film View
Dogme is a movement of directors which started in Copenhagen in 1995, with the aim of freeing filmmakers from what they saw as increasing artificiality in films. Adherents refuse to use any unnatural elements in their films, such as additional lighting or even period costume. In audio terms, Dogme filmmakers use no ambient tracks, foley or other effects, relying solely on what was present in one track in the actual location at the time of shooting; sound and image are not separated. Initially, watching a Dogme film can be a jarring experience, but after adjusting to their methods, the viewer's involvement in the film is not at all diminished. Try *Dogville* (Lars von Trier, 2003) or *Festen* (Thomas Vinterberg, 1998). Official site: http://www.dogme95.dk/

Getting to know audio – key terms

ADR

This stands for automatic dialogue replacement and is something you will hopefully avoid, but if audio for a scene is below standard you may need to re-record dialogue later and replace the existing track. This is more common when you are limited in the equipment you can use and cannot always record to the desired quality. For example, an actor performing lines near busy traffic needs a particular microphone that picks up only the voice, not the background sound. If it is a choice on set between shooting it with poor sound and overdubbing later or not to shoot at all, it is worthwhile doing the former. Make sure, however, that you have the agreement of your actors to return for post-production work if necessary.

The process involves speaking the problem lines again in a recording studio while watching the accompanying footage. The actor tries to synchronize the words to match. Most actors don't mind doing this, but some filmmakers remark that when you do this the emphasis is always on getting it in sync and not about getting the best performance, with the film suffering as a result.

Film View

At the start of his career, Stanley Kubrick shot a whole movie, *Killer's Kiss* (1955), without sound and then dubbed the entire soundtrack, including speaking parts and effects, later. The movie is also startling for its high-contrast black and white photography and unnerving dream sequences. The making of this movie inspired Matthew Chapman to make *Stranger's Kiss* in 1983 as a fictionalized account of the production.

Non-diagetic sound

This is a widely used device in sound and is present in most movies in some way. It refers to sounds not emanating from what could be called the world within the film. For instance, words spoken by characters within a scene (on or off screen) and sounds from objects in the scene – known as diagetic sound – would all be present in the real world, should this scene take place for real. Non-diagetic sounds, however, could include the voice of a narrator, music or additional sound effects. Ever since the striking uses of subjective sounds in early films, the filmmaker has been able to heighten the dramatic content of a scene with non-diagetic sound.

Film View

Alfred Hitchcock made his first sound movie in 1929, *Blackmail*, and with it provided innovations in his use of subjective sounds to heighten the drama of self-defence, murder and blackmail.

Hyper-real sound

This idea refers to the deliberate exaggeration of certain sounds to make a scene seem more realistic. In real life it would be hard to distinguish one sound from another in most situations, but in a film it is crucial to the story that some sounds are closer than they ought to be. An example is where a scene may need a figure walking along a street at night. In reality, the sound of footsteps would mingle into the other sounds of cars, people and so on. But in a film, that sound would be recorded separately or more likely be reproduced later by a foley artist, someone who specializes in recreating sounds for overdubbing in post-production. It is usually sounds that are important to the information conveyed by a scene that are treated in this way: car doors slamming, keys being turned in doors, phone numbers being dialled and so on.

Sound motif

Sound motif is yet another way in which the aural element of a film can reduce the load on the visual in telling a story. As with visual motif, this is used by the director to convey ideas that help the plot, giving it extra depth. In sound, its uses are often to associate a certain place or character with a sound and in so doing suggest some meaning to attach to it. As a filmmaker, you need all the tools you can get to convey your intended meanings. Ideas about characters or places are hard to put across to the audience, and this is one of those instances when the size of your budget is irrelevant. Sound motif can be a more subtle, almost subconscious way of telling the audience something and does not intrude in the on-screen action. Such sounds can be abstract and quite unreal, but can take their cue from a description of what is being depicted in the script.

Film View

In *Blade Runner* (1982), the sound of a cat wailing accompanies the arrival of Roy Batty, pursuing Harrison Ford's hero, lending an air of menace and cunning. In a film with a complex plot or with several characters to keep track of, the use of such signature sounds helps to maintain clarity.

Music

A music soundtrack undoubtedly helps create mood and yet this is an area where the filmmaker can find some pressing problems. For some directors, such as Martin Scorsese, music not only supports a scene but dictates some elements of it. Scorsese often filmed while playing a recording to the whole set of a piece of music he intended to use. If used well, as in *Goodfellas* (1990) or *Bringing Out the Dead* (2000), it is hard to imagine a particular scene without its musical accompaniment, but for some film-makers, music is a way of lending a film a purpose or style absent from the visuals, as a kind of shortcut.

Permission

If you intend to use a musical soundtrack you need to look long and hard at the kind of sums needed to gain permission to use a track, as well as the legal hurdles to be jumped over. To use a track by an artist you need first to get written permission from the owner of the rights to that track, usually the publisher of the music and the company that releases it. You will probably not get free use of tracks unless you know personally the artist concerned and provided they have some clout with their record company. If you do intend to use licensed music, you need to get an entertainment lawyer on your side, to deal with potential problems such as how much the artist receives or whether a track can be used in promotional trailers.

Sampling tracks

Similar issues need to be addressed when a track is sampled. In legal terms, it is fine to use music that is briefly sampled through no fault of the director, such as the sound of a radio as a character walks past it. But elsewhere, if you use a substantial part of a track without permission you may be pursued by a publisher and it is likely that you will need to pay a substantial sum. But there is no need for this situation to arise; you can use relatively inexpensive software to create unique soundtracks using samples of sounds you have collected yourself from videotape.

Use local musicians

Alternatives exist for adding music to your movie. If you contact an unknown (read: unsigned and not covered by copyright) local band or musician, it may be possible to involve them in your project in the same way you involve other members of a crew, either for deferred payment or as an investment-in-kind, for later reward from the film's profits. Given the exposure this would allow for an artist, it is a deal that works both ways.

Do it yourself

If you don't want to follow that route, it is possible to use music created without copyright, without having to create it yourself. Some software programs designed for use with video have a selection of music that can be used 'off the shelf' – in other words, music that is written to use within films, suggesting certain moods. Music is categorized by mood or situation (for example, car chase, suspense, dream sequence and so on) and you can change the tempo up or down according to your requirements. Critics of this approach suggest that such music is essentially elevator muzak and indeed you do need to think carefully about whether you want to let prefabricated soundtracks near your film.

DIY 2

Of course, there is no reason why you can't have a go yourself. Make your own sounds using a piano, guitar, tin can. David Lynch took this route when he made *Eraserhead* (1976), which has a richly dramatic score consisting of circus-style organs, vaudeville melodies, and industrial thumps and bangs. It is much better than this description, however.

Special audio effects

Many edit software programs allow you to modify a sound, or work with plug-ins which allow this. You can, for instance, give a sound an echo, reverse it, warp it or change the pitch. As with visual effects such as strobe and negative, these should be approached with care, and with the maxim 'if it ain't broke, don't fix it'. Sounds should not necessarily need digital alterations if the original recording was correctly produced and if you are using sound to make up for a shortfall in the quality of your shooting then this is best approached with layered sounds rather than by special audio effects.

Capturing audio

Audio clips are captured and used in the same way as standard video/audio clips and appear as different icons in the project window. You can use this stage to adjust the gain of the audio clips on the soundtrack. So, if a certain clip was too quiet when recorded, you can increase the gain so it becomes louder. But bear in mind that increasing gain too far will emphasize background noise or interference. The audio setting of a clip is 100 per cent for no gain, and anything above this increases the power of the audio signal. Some programs have a suggested gain feature that brings out the track to optimum level without distorting, but in general, try to avoid increasing gain above 200 per cent.

The Crunch

- A $100 film but a $10 million soundtrack
- Record sounds separately and layer them for maximum control
- Create illusions through off-screen sounds

- Beware of unlicensed music
- Sounds can be like extra actors – use them to add expression and meaning to a scene
- Prioritize all the sounds in a scene
- Become a technical master of sound in your editing software.

5. Understanding timecode

Timecode is one of the more complex areas of video and any explanation of it does veer into technical language. Although it is one of those tools in DV filming that you can live without, once you understand what it is you see the benefits for your production and the way it speeds up your work rate. 'Stripe', or timecode, your tapes before you shoot and your computer will really appreciate it; it makes it easier for the PC to locate each clip on your footage. Here goes.

What is timecode?

Timecode is a way of numbering each and every frame of a videotape. Videotape has a certain number of frames in each second. Timecode exists as a separate track – invisible to the viewer when you show the movie – recorded on the tape. It is an eight-digit code consisting of frames, seconds, minutes and hours. An example could be 03:16:45:12, which shows that the particular frame attached to this code is three hours, 16 minutes, 45 seconds and 12 frames into the tape. Those last three words give you a clue as to the purpose of timecode. It is a navigational tool, allowing you to find the exact point of every take and every shot in your tape.

> **Weblink**
> http://www.apple.com/downloads/macosx/video/timecodecalculator.html   Free downloadable timecode calculator.

Different countries, different systems

Unfortunately, to make it all more complicated, each part of the world uses slightly different amounts for their television programmes. In Europe and the United Kingdom, a frame rate of 25 fps (frames per second) is standard and is known as PAL, whereas in the USA a rate of 30 fps is used, referred to as NTSC. This has no discernible effect on the programmes that are made, but it is true that in terms of quality a higher frame rate is desirable.

Go to: Chapter 2:2 for a complete list of international television standards.

Timecode in the USA and other NTSC territories

Timecode in the USA and other countries using NTSC is 29.97 fps. It is fine to round this up to the next whole number of 30 fps, but it may be useful to go through the implications of this if you intend to make productions larger than an hour in length.

The frame rate of 30 fps is actually devised for black and white television and for technical reasons a slightly shorter frame rate was introduced for colour. If you edit assuming a rate of 30 fps then you will end up with a 3.6 second error every 60 minutes. The solution to this is something called 'drop-frame timecode', which removes 108 frames – from the timecode *not* your film – per hour. This requires your counter to drop out two frames per minute, but since this would lead us to drop too many – 120 – we need to *not* drop frames every 10th minute. This is not something you have to think about – your time-code counter does it all for you and when you watch the timecode counter you will see at the end of every minute it will jump suddenly over the dropped frames.

It doesn't affect your movie

Don't worry at all about how this affects your movie – no actual frames are dropped, only their num-bering. Nothing changes about the way it looks and there will be no sudden jump cuts as the timecode jumps forward – it is simply a device to keep the numbers looking good. In most short productions, such as news footage or short business videos, drop-frame timecode is not necessary, but it is import-ant to opt for this rate when you first open your editing program if you intend to sell programmes or movies to television or cable broadcasters using this frame rate and especially if working on produc-tions over 60 minutes.

Timecode in PAL

In territories using the PAL system, timecode is recorded at a rate of 25 fps. As with NTSC, if you are working with a specific client or market in mind whom you know is working on a different system, alter the settings of your software before editing and those of the camcorder before recording. In addition to the 25 fps PAL, there is also PAL 60, which aims to be a more compatible with NTSC territories.

Ways of recording timecode

Timecode is recorded directly onto the tape so that it can be read on any unit, anywhere. There are, however, different ways of recording it, outlined below.

Audio track timecode

In this method, timecode is recorded onto the audio track of the analog videotape using sound impulses, in much the same way as a modem converts digital signal into sound to send down the wire. This is called longitudinal timecode and although it has improved over recent years, it still has two problems: it can only reliably be read when the tape is moving and it can suffer from loss of signal when it is copied or played repeatedly.

Timecode as part of the video signal

This is known as vertical-interval timecode (VITC) and is generally the best method to opt for. This method involves recording the timecode signal using the video heads rather than the audio, leaving all audio tracks available for you to use.

Uses of timecode

This section started with the statement that using timecode could save you time in editing. Much of the technical information above is good to know, but you are not often going to be called upon to use it. The value of having timecode on your tape is that you will need to spend less time shuttling around your tape to find the right take when you come to capture your clips.

Get around your footage tape fast

It is true that getting to know your footage by constant reviewing is a way of speeding up the editing process, but mistakes occur if you rely on notes such as 'good take of Marvin singing, third take after the car scene'. That may be sufficient for home movie family films, but anywhere up the scale from there and you desperately need a more exact and mathematical way of finding that good take. So, on your edit log sheet, you might describe the scene as 'Marvin singing good take: 01:49:12:17'. Now when you want to find that take there will be no mistakes. The edit log sheet is hardly worth the paper it is written on if you are unable to find the precise location of clips whenever you like and, similarly, the edit decision list (EDL) is only really a viable option if you use timecode throughout filming. With this degree of forethought, editing can become something you are more in control of and less frustrated by.

Continuous timecode in filming

It is crucial that you keep timecode as one continuous line, uninterrupted by filming breaks on the tape. If, for instance, you pause and then continue filming, you may have created a break in the code and the new recording will start at zero timecode. The problem with this is that when you start to capture your clips ready for editing, the capture software starts to get very confused, as it soon realizes that there may be several clips each labelled, for instance, 00:00:20:43.

Stripe your tapes

The easiest way to ensure that you have timecode present is to place it on when you start filming. As we saw in the section on shooting, place the lens cap back on the camera and press record. When the camera has finished recording over the whole tape it will have placed continuous timecode from start to end. When you later go and shoot over this, the shots fit into the timecode that has been burned on. This process is called 'striping' the tape.

A further method, and the one to use if your footage was not shot on a pre-timecoded tape, is to make a copy of the tape containing your footage with new timecode burned on. You can do this by capturing large chunks of continuous footage and outputting it back onto digital tape, captured now with timecode. Copying in this way presents no problems with loss of quality, unlike analog.

The Crunch

- Timecode is good for your films
- Get to know how timecode works in your camera

- Get to know how timecode works in editing
- Put timecode on all your tapes before you shoot on them.

6. Working with text

As we have seen, part of the task awaiting the low-budget, independent filmmaker is the necessity to use ingenuity and imagination to utilize what the medium can offer, before having to start spending money. When the main elements of the film have done all they can – camera composition, lighting, shooting, script, images – the use of text in a film can be a further way of supporting the ideas you are trying to put across. This applies as much to the traditional use of text in the opening credits as to their use throughout the film, setting off other meanings or adding a layer of visual density that the images alone could not supply. In this section we will be looking at the way creative use of credits and titles can bring a more professional look to your film and make its meaning more apparent.

On the whole, this is territory most often occupied by the more unusual, non-narrative films, including music videos, commercials and video art. As the projects on non-narrative film showed, there are many lessons for the narrative filmmaker that can be picked up from investigating non-narrative forms. So, stick with this section, even if you can't see a place for text in the films you intend to make; its benefits can be felt in many forms of filmmaking.

Better credits

Every film needs them, and they are most often the first indication we see of the style and mood of a film, but still some films look as if the opening titles are taken off the shelf, selected from a menu of pre-set examples and excluded from the kind of thought and attention that goes into the rest of the movie.

Credits grow out of the movie

When the film has been completed and you are in the process of designing the right look for the opening titles, complete storyboards and visualizations just as you did when devising the look of the whole film. Take your cue from the images and colour schemes seen in the film. If you have been working on the film closely, covering nearly all tasks yourself, it is sometimes difficult to assess what makes the film look and feel the way it does. After a while you can't see what makes your film distinctive, so caught up are you with the glitches or negative aspects of it. Where other people see style, you might see the problems you encountered while shooting or how the scene was assembled.

To get around this, base the designs for your credits on the same notes you made at the start of the production, when you were deciding what constitutes the core of the film, what makes it tick. If we take as an example David Fincher's film *Seven* (1995), the extraordinary and distinctive credit sequence seems out of keeping with the rest of the film. The words flicker and move, are scratched and creased, and are reminiscent words on a shaky Super 8 movie, filmed by looking at etched graffiti on a toilet wall. Given that the film itself is high on production values, this seems out of sync, style-wise. But both credits and film are working towards the same ends and relate right back to the same theme, of a distorted and disturbed world, at its centre a figure sending out crude messages with violence. Looked at like this, the credits do not just fit into the film, but offer a way of understanding the whole theme behind it. Like Fincher, you should be able to use every part of the film to advance your cause.

Stages in designing credits

1 Take the central theme in the film and describe it. Work out how you have manifested this theme on film. What devices did you use, such as colours, shapes, mood?
2 Take the image that you think defines your film. Look through the whole movie and try to see which single part sums up the aims of the film. Think of this as you would for choosing the defining image used for advertising the film.
3 It helps if you have a sense of graphic design or can hire the services of a designer, but try looking for the design characteristics of the credits: font, size, allusions to other films, colour and so on. If you are not sure, try looking through style or design magazines to work out what you do and don't like. If you are doing the designs yourself and have little experience, it is usually better to under-design – in other words, keep it low-key and simple.

Captions

Captions are sometimes used in a film to indicate the start of a new chapter. If your movie has a need for clarifying the time or location of a scene, a caption can help the audience to maintain their involvement. In action films it is common to see them used to build tension towards a specific point, counting down to a meteor impact, an invasion launch and so on. In all cases, captions used to assist theme or plot should be kept low-key, with modest typefaces.

Other films use them to add further layers of meaning to the film, breaking it up into sections marked by theme rather than plot progress. For example, *Hannah and Her Sisters* (Woody Allen, 1986) separates the action by the use of seemingly oblique captions which later make sense. In one part, titled 'Not even the rain has such small hands', Michael Caine ensures he runs into Barbara Hershey, who he is infatuated with, in a bookshop. He insists on buying her a book of poems by ee cummings, from whose work the caption is taken.

Film View
Great credit sequences: anything by Saul Bass – *North by Northwest, Vertigo.* Much imitated (badly) in *Catch Me If You Can* (Steven Spielberg, 2002).

The Crunch

- Credits grow out of the film
- Credits are often the first part of the film that the audience see – make them good
- If in doubt, go for clarity in terms of font, design and size.

Software	Level	Pros	Cons	Cost	Contact
Final Cut Pro	Ideal for all levels, including features	The industry standard, FCP has become synonymous with DV editing. There is very little else that comes close to FCP for low-budget filmmakers. The new version supports any including HD. You can convert interlace to progressive, convert between broadcast NTSC and PAL, and to DVD in one step. Real-time effects help speed up editing time. Try Final Cut Pro Express if you can't afford the full program.	Not available for Windows users.	Around £730	www.apple.com/ finalcutstudio/ finalcutpro/
Adobe Premiere	Ideal for all levels of filmmaker	Pro is a vast improvement on 6.5, with better audio and use of transitions, getting rid of the AB roll line. Very easy for beginners to pick up. Integrates well with other Adobe products After Effects and Photoshop. Web output and compression settings are easy to use and can be adapted for individual films.	Video capture has tended to be problematic, with frames often dropped, but this has improved with 6.5. It is costly, but the new Pro version warrants the price for the first time.	Around £740	www.adobe.com/ products/premiere/ main.html
Vegas Video	Ideal for all levels	A greatly underestimated editing program, it has huge reliability and a big fan base. In tests in PC consumer magazines it slightly outperforms Premiere.		Around £500	mediasoftware. sonypictures.com/ products/ vegasfamily.asp

		Excellent for first-time editors, easy to use.		
IMovie	Ideal for all levels but better for beginners	Very good web and DVD encoding tools. New versions also cater for HDV capture of 720 × 1080i. Audio options are probably the best of any software, with 5.1 surround sound and extensive mixing facilities.	Less friendly when it comes to using audio. You need to own a Mac and have 512 MB RAM available or 1 GB for HDV.	Free (only available for Mac)	www.apple.com/ ilife/imovie/
		Now used on several feature releases, iMovie has built up a reputation in film schools and among low-budget filmmakers as the most reliable software in its range. Macs have always dominated filmmaking and it is no surprise that both Final Cut and iMovie are considered the best places to start and develop your career.			
		Never ones to miss a trick, Apple have now made iMovie compatible with HDV. Excellent output options to web, tape or DVD.			
Windows Movie Maker	Ideal for beginners	Windows answer to iMovie, WMM 2 is an improvement on v1 but still not designed for the serious filmmaker.	Few adjustments in effects.	Free	www.microsoft.com/
			Transitions are limited by poor design.		

Figure 7.3 Editing software guide. This guide focuses on the main market leaders in video editing. Beyond semi-professional or student grade software, there are hardware systems consisting of an entire unit of monitors, hard drive and so on. But for the low-budget filmmaker, software remains the most accessible option.

8 | Post-production aesthetics

1. Editing aesthetics: editing for genre

In the style of editing we are going to take a look at here, it will seem like there are more rules, more restrictions and less room for manoeuvre than in any other kind of editing. But stay with it. It is also the kind of editing that requires more subtle skills and because of its challenges leaves you a better filmmaker than before. In what we can call 'genre editing', we are going to leave no trace at all of our movements. Every trick, device and sleight of hand must quickly be hidden so that the audience have no indication at all of the craft you are practising.

What is genre editing?

This kind of editing is more often called 'continuity editing', and refers to the kind where its sole aim is to get the story (we don't see this style in non-narrative or abstract movies) moving along and get the audience completely immersed in the plot and characters. Hollywood movies have carefully developed this style over the years as the surest way to suspend disbelief in an escape-seeking audience. It draws no attention at all to the fact that you are just watching a movie. It highlights nothing about the

Figure 8.1 In this still from *The Dark Hunter* (2002) by Jonnie Oddball, the close angle requires a faster pace of editing.

mechanics of movie-making. Most of all, it provides the most seamless way for the world which the movie created in its first act to stay real to the viewer. As you can tell by now, it places the viewer before the director in terms of importance; directors' need to make a personal mark and reveal their hand as author is not as important as the viewers' need to get involved and to identify with the world they see on the screen. Genre editing makes you feel like it's really happening.

Realism

Like much in the craft of filmmaking, realism and naturalness are achieved through completely unreal and unnatural means. In shooting, a natural effect of sunlight streaming in through a window is only achieved through huge extra lamps. Similarly, in editing the realistic effect of someone getting in a car and driving to a destination is achieved through a very unrealistic squashing of time and space through cunning editing. Going even further, filmmakers who decide they want a very real look to their movie and dispense with editing rules and tricks quickly find that their movie looks anything but realistic. So, the more trickery and devices you employ, the more the viewer can forget they are even watching a film and engage in a truly real experience.

The aims of genre editing

Continuity

In most genre films the aim is to make sure that no one notices the mechanics of editing. It should be like the silent scene-changer on a stage, whose presence you don't notice until something goes wrong. In continuity editing the aim is to create a perfect visage of realism, maintained through careful use of illusion. In this kind of editing the greater the realism you require, the more the editing has to be exact and conform to certain rules. Realism, in this case, means the way to draw the audience wholly into a story, enabling them to suspend their disbelief that a 2-D screen can become a 3-D world, and that periods of years or centuries can be compressed into hours. What we could call documentary-style realism is also realistic, but its rawness reminds us that we are watching an artificial rendering of reality.

Go to: Chapter 6:2 for more ideas about narrative continuity.

At the core of continuity editing are a range of factors, including:

- consistency of what the camera sees – props, costumes and objects remaining constant
- accurate portrayal of space – using the edit to back up the camera's definition of a space
- consistent direction of movement – a character running through a location moves from left to right or vice versa
- consistent sound, style and colour throughout
- consistency of events – simultaneous events are edited in parallel, while edit devices such as a fade into and out of black before a cut can show past events.

Setting a scene

Editing is primarily concerned with time rather than space, but is central to enabling the viewer to understand a space. When we enter a new place, the editing must enable us to perceive it entirely. The wide shot is the shortcut to getting this, but the editing must then reveal key elements of the place. The dimensions are crucial, and the important characteristics such as door, furniture, windows help us to comprehend the relative distances between these objects. Longer cuts are usually needed at this stage.

Creating and controlling time

Temporal space, or time, is the domain of the editor. No other part of the filmmaking process can define when an event takes place in the frame of the story, nor show what else happened at the same time. The shots and images themselves are mute when it comes to showing anything other than what is in the frame. Almost any attempt at showing the passage of time – in ageing, or the seasons, or just within an afternoon – depends on showing at least two shots side by side. Almost all interactions between people depend on more than one shot, either by switching between shots of two people to show that they are talking to one another, or by showing the relative movements of each person.

Passage of time in particular is a primary consideration in genre editing. The whole idea of telling a story is based on the premise that it is not told in real time, so in children's books Red Riding Hood is shown at only certain dramatic points of her unfortunate trip. We don't have to see the entire journey to Granny's house, nor the entire detail of how the wolf gained entry to the house. Finally, while the wolf is making his excuses to little Red, we also see the woodcutter bearing down on the house, suggesting simultaneity. This way of telling a story is as old as fiction itself. The ideas of truncating events ('later that day') for dramatic effect and of cutting between two events ('meanwhile, at the same time elsewhere in the woods') are the basis of editing for genre.

Setting pace

The events of a narrative need to be fed at a carefully controlled rate to the viewer. A story related without the use of pace would be like reading a police report of the specific times when this or that event happened. The idea of pace is to increase the sense of meaning of each part of the story – for instance, by heightening tension or delaying an event to create suspense. It is a fundamental part of the storytelling process and can radically alter a story by the way it is used. For example, by speeding up events or compressing them in a shorter time frame, a part of the story can be made to seem less significant.

Go to: Chapter 4:4 on story and structure to see how to embed pace into the planning of your movie.

Clarity of vision and sound

This is a more functional part of the editing process, rather than a purely aesthetic one. Editing suggests ideas, helps themes develop and leads the audience towards a reading of the film, but beneath any of this it must do its tasks with clarity and certainty. This doesn't mean that editing has to be overly pedantic or fastidious – as we saw in Chapter 6:1, 'Better looking films', shots that are unplanned or added on the spur of the moment can add an extra dimension to a film to make it less formal and rigid.

But a film must have a clear idea of what it is trying to say. Film has more in common with writing than other art forms in that there is no option other than to make a statement – there is either this cut or that cut, this length or that length of cut, this choice of fade. On the other hand, in painting, ambiguity is a part of the process; paint drips, smudges and other by-products of the art are accidents. In editing there are no such ambiguous moments; everything is a statement and there are no mute parts of editing where you can place a few shots and coast along until the next important part of the movie. The aim must be to have a clear idea of what a sequence is 'saying' and to make sure that every step of the editing for that part works towards your idea.

Devices used in the genre edit

Rhythm

As we saw in Chapters 4:4 and 4:5, on stories, finding a rhythm for your film gives you an overall flavour, mood and pace, and enables you to modulate this rhythm according to the needs of the plot. Rhythm is one of the most important devices in editing. Without it, a film lacks any ability to evolve dramatically.

Arrive at the rhythm of your film in advance, looking at whether the film is to be fast paced and action oriented or slower and more contemplative. When compiling a scene, arrange the shots in order and start assembling them, noticing the relative duration of each clip. Assuming that you are trying to cut for continuity, notice peaks in the action or dialogue. Keep most of the shots surrounding these points at a similar length, but change when you come to these peaks.

Rhythm in the timeline

Use a timeline chart to work out the relative lengths of clips and try to establish some consistency in duration. Label the peaks and devise a different approach for those parts. In some ways, the rhythm of these detailed scenes (what we could call micro-rhythm) should mirror that of the film as a whole (macro-rhythm). In Kubrick's *The Shining*, individual scenes are edited with the same menacing, drawn-out consistency throughout. It takes a long, slow-moving pace towards the climactic action, like Frankenstein's monster, but this very consistency makes it relentlessly tense. It is easy to crank up the action a gear when necessary, by shortening the length of cuts and increasing the frequency of cutaways.

Juxtaposition

One of the most potent tools in editing is the use of juxtaposition – the placing of one shot next to another to alter the meaning of both. As we will see in Chapter 8:3, 'Montage editing', this is an effect with many uses, delivering ideas and feelings not attainable through other editing techniques. Try to find better instances of using juxtaposition in your movie by approaching your footage in a less sequential way. Look for shots that collide with others rather than simply reinforce them; try to find shots that add extra layers of meaning to your images by juxtaposition with contrasting shots. One way to do this is to show widely contrasting emotions in characters, suggesting a different side to their motives. For instance, in *Don't Look Now* (Nic Roeg, 1973), we see two sisters offering psychic advice to a distraught Donald Sutherland and Julie Christie. They undertake the process solemnly and with tact. After the couple's departure we cut to a brief shot of the two sisters in hysterical laughter. The effect is unsettling as it undermines our previous view of the sisters.

Purposes of editing

In genre editing, one of the central places to advance the plot is the action sequence, which acts as a condensed version of many of the devices we look at in understanding editing. These sequences push the plot forward, create new subplots, cram in subtext and heighten emotion.

As Ken Dancyger points out in his accomplished book on editing, *The Technique of Film and Video Editing* (Focal Press), the main concerns of this kind of sequence are:

- Identification
- Excitation
- Conflict
- Intensification.

Identifying with characters

The primary aim of a sequence must be to involve the audience and enable them to identify with a character, usually the protagonist. The aim of the camera is to get the audience close to the character, offering an intimacy where we become the character and start to emulate their feelings. At moments of high emotion the camera often takes on point of view or close-ups to enable us to see as they see.

Thrills and spills

Following on closely from identification is the process of exciting the audience. This is often related to a point of view as we get to know how our protagonist is coping with extreme conditions. But at this stage the point of view itself becomes too detached and the camera needs to become more subjective, using shots that are no longer descriptive but evocative – pans, swooping movements, hand-held shots and fast tracking shots. The aim of the editor here is to let these shots run away with the audience and accelerate the feeling of identification. Not only are we in the scene with the protagonist, but we experience a sensational reaction to what is happening. Montage is a major device in evoking this, but with very short shots of often less than one second.

Conflict is necessary

Conflict in storytelling terms is the bread and butter of the plot. Nothing advances without conflict – no character can change, no situations evolve, no aims accomplished without obstacles. For the editor, the device is to cut frequently between two situations, showing their contrasting aims, which should conflict with each to a high degree. For instance, the chase is a typical example of two conflicting aims: one person wants to catch while the other wants to escape. In *Collateral* (Michael Mann, 2004) we see the hapless taxi driver Jamie Foxx trying to contact the next victim of assassin Tom Cruise.

From where he stands he can see both victim and pursuer in the same building, but is helpless to prevent the confrontation.

Hyping it up

Finally, the use of intensification is crucial at the climax to a scene. Shorter shots and an increase in pace produce a sense that events are leading toward a conclusion. Editing becomes sharper, using shorter shots and devices such as parallel montage to show events converging. So, at the climax to the scene in *Collateral* described above, we get to see a use of hand-held camera to give us further identification, subjective camera angles to push us further into Foxx's viewpoint and sense of frustration, frequent cross-cutting as we see Cruise and close in on the victim, and finally a dramatic conclusion as Cruise fails in his task, but putting further danger in the way of the protagonists.

Tools

Say it economically

In narrative film, one of the purposes of a scene is to convey information. Your job is to show how a scene progresses in terms of the motivations of characters, events that have happened or any other detail needed to understand the plot. Your primary tools are the angle and movement of the camera, but how long do you allow to make sure that the audience have taken on board what is going on? The length of a cut is impossible to prescribe and the answer must contain the proviso that you may not want to hand the plot to the audience on a plate. Sophisticated audiences want to be made to work a little to uncover the goodies you are offering; films that demand something of you are often the more satisfying experience. As a starting point, however, close-ups will take up less screen time than long shots, for the reason that less information is contained in the former, more in the latter. The relative lengths of these will vary according to the pace and rhythm of your film, but you can decide in advance that a certain number of seconds becomes a benchmark.

To begin, you could start with the idea that for medium shots in an action sequence ask yourself to justify the length of a shot lasting beyond three or four seconds, while dialogue will determine the length of cuts in other scenes, but even here you can break edits up into several shots, from varying viewpoints. However a scene is conveyed, whether it is oblique or straightforward, try to make the edit only as long as it needs to be to convey the necessary information, and this is equally true when that 'information' is more ambiguous or abstract. Cut away as soon as you can.

Show clearly what is happening

Unlike reading a book, the viewer will only get one take to ascertain what is happening in a scene. Although your aim is to edit economically, you also have to convey clearly what you want the audience to see. How much you want them to see is up to you: do you imply what is happening in a scene or describe unambiguously? As we will see later, montage is one way of opting out of this argument and making each shot quite plain and defined, but juxtaposing it with others, suggesting more layers of meaning than otherwise would be conveyed.

Use the close-up

As a starting point for describing action clearly, the close-up is the most useful tool. It draws the attention of the audience towards one aspect of an action and therefore tells them that this or that part of the scene is the most important to see. If you are in doubt about whether a part of a scene is prominent enough, use a close-up. Balance this with frequent medium and longer shots, so that the audience can get their bearings as to where the action is and who is involved.

Each clip progresses the action

Equally important is the progression of the action. If a crucial part of the action is missed out or not given enough prominence, then a scene can be rendered meaningless. Take as an example a scene involving a chase through empty train carriages, with no dialogue. The aim of this scene is to show who is being chased, who is doing the chasing and what obstacles are going to get in their way. If we lose track of the information at any stage we lose interest in the film. The main instructive shots in this case are those that show the relative distances of the escapee and the pursuer to each other and those showing how, for instance, the escapee jams a compartment door shut, opens a main door and climbs up to the roof. We need to see how the pursuer releases the door and finds the escape route. In fast action sequences, it will be crucial to make the delivery of information as punchy as possible. Therefore, in these shots, the close-up is going to be the most economical way to shoot, enabling us to see the essential part of the frame without having to scour the screen for it.

Don't use a shot just because it looks good

When you have invested time and money it is tempting, and inevitable, to become emotionally attached to it. You may start to enjoy the footage as individual bits, as great-looking scenes. You may also look at how well certain scenes go with pieces of music you have earmarked for the film. As any artist or writer will testify, being seduced by the work you are in the middle of constructing is a certain way to lose track of it.

Without doubt some scenes turn out to be better than expected and start to assume a more prominent role in a film, but this does not necessarily mean they take up more screen time. A scene on a beach with two characters is going to look even better when, unexpectedly for you, a great sunset appears from behind the clouds partly obscured by a flock of birds. All this does is to make that particular moment more memorable; it does not follow that you have to extend the duration of that cut. This should also apply to scenes that proved unexpectedly difficult to shoot, or cost more than you had planned.

Make a director's cut if you can't decide what to edit out

If you have great shots but you know deep down that you really can't include the full glory of them, then go ahead and make a 'director's cut', knowing that this is an experiment. Reserve the cut-down version for exhibiting but retain what you have in the extended version. Noting which shots you consider to be better than others is crucial self-knowledge and will help you next time around.

> **Did you know?**
> A director's cut is a version of a movie that differs from an originally released version.
> One of the first examples was *Blade Runner*. Ridley Scott was under pressure prior
> to the film's release in 1982 to place a voice-over on the film to make the plot more
> transparent, and to include an ending which resolved the plot in an upbeat way. He
> did so, but in 1991, having established a strong position in Hollywood, released a new
> version without these elements.

Check how your ideas change during editing

Further to this, you may start to notice that the parts of a film that you really like are not ones you had first thought when preparing the film. If you have made an action film but find that you actually want to spend more time on the slower, more reflective sequences in between the action, then you have gained an important piece of information about what makes you different as a filmmaker. In truth, however, if you have a change of heart and try to turn a film into something quite different *during* editing you are likely to get into difficulties. You are still likely to learn a lot from the process of completing a movie, even though it no longer perfectly reflects your ideas. So make your movie as you first intended, but keep track of what you liked about those reluctantly discarded shots.

Cut on movement

This means ending a cut while the subject or camera is still moving. It encourages a fluid transition to the next shot, sustaining continuity and flow, and is going to help maintain rhythm. In many of the points described here, the aim is to hide the mechanism of editing, to place the plot or theme to the fore in the viewer's attention and not draw attention to how the film is constructed. Often called 'continuity editing', this is the dominant mode in cinema. Part of the aim of covering your tracks as editor is to make the potentially jarring cut from one image to another as smooth as possible, and cutting on movement is one way to achieve this.

Don't plan too rigidly

Cutting together the shots for your movie has to involve, frequently, a certain amount of listening and watching. However well you have planned the film, there will be changes and fluctuations as it passes through the hands of the people you are working with during shooting. Your own ideas may have altered and what was once the main theme in the film is now a sub-theme, or subplots may start to take more prominence. It is not uncommon for a director to continue changing a part of the script even as the previous one is being recorded. Viewing the daily takes give you a more objective view about how you are interpreting your material; it could remain very much as it appears in your plans or it could start to deviate. Be aware of these shifts in emphasis and don't reject them out of hand.

The need to remain with your plans and to see them through to fruition, no matter how tempting it is to deviate, is an important lesson, but it is true that the film does not finish evolving at the planning stage. A film in its early planning stage is often a blurred, overall plan, without detail. The main themes, main events and outcomes are evident. But what we might miss at this stage are the ideas lurking in the background which might come to the fore during production. It is possible, of course, to prepare a film so thoroughly that every conceivable angle has been considered, but this degree of planning can sap the life out of a film at an early stage, and many filmmakers would argue that it is, in fact, desirable to make available some aspects of the film to be resolved during production and editing.

Allow, then, for alterations to occur when deciding how to edit. To put it in perspective, this will probably be more the shifting of priorities within the film rather than bringing in completely new concepts.

Edit in sympathy with the film

A key concept in editing is to be appropriate: that every aspect of a film must lead back to the aims set out by the director. Editing filters what goes into the film, so it is the most important opportunity you have to forge each aspect into a coherent whole. If you have, for example, a short, fast-paced action film, you would expect to edit using faster cuts. If parts of this network of filmic elements are out of sync with others then the film may fail, although, of course, there are times when out of sync is what you want, so even this is under the rule of appropriateness. Ensuring this is maintained throughout the film is achieved partly through having and retaining a strong vision of what its core ideas are.

This fault was more common when the filmmaker was less in control of the final stages and needed to pass on editing to a third party, perhaps unconnected to the project until that point.

Film View

The problem of losing control of your work to someone else can occur at all levels of the industry, a famous example being the editing of the classic *The Magnificent Ambersons* (1942). Director Orson Welles was obliged to hand the master print to the frustrated studio, RKO, and a probable masterpiece was ruthlessly cut to excise parts of the narrative, removing much of Welles's vision, and tacking on a false, sentimental ending.

The exceptions to this rule are the occasional necessary diversions (more often in feature films), such as subplots. But even here, the relative infrequency with which sub-elements appear will confirm the dominance of the main direction of the film.

What makes a good editor?

As an artist you need to be a great technician in order to be in control of your film. Achieving this is down to practice; the more hours you spend coming up against problems and overcoming them, the more you will be able to handle every task. To become a good editor takes practice. To become a great one means becoming aware of the pull between two opposing forces when you are editing: the forces of reason and the forces of instinct. It sounds dramatic, but good editing exists exactly between these two sides and you have to steer a course between these two rocks – if you stick to reason too much you risk making a film that is too rigid and soulless, while moving too much towards instinct may make a film too mannered. In practice it means knowing your tools inside out, knowing about structure and knowing when to break the rules.

The Crunch

- Editing is good – you are in control once again
- But the wide range of options are tempting – be decisive and sure-footed, rejecting ideas that seem to divert you from what you set out to do
- Avoid editing too stylistically – editing is subservient to your aims
- Use rhythm to order your editing and take your cue from the overall rhythmic structure of the film
- Become a technical master of your equipment or software – it stops you having to depend on someone who doesn't understand your film
- Don't let your attachment to certain takes lead you to change your plans
- Improvisation is OK
- You won't always know what you are doing – sometimes it is enough to say that a particular arrangement of shots 'just feels right'
- Be aware that the arrangement of themes and ideas in the film may have shifted during filming – edit according to what you have.

2. Editing aesthetics: non-narrative

Working on a narrative movie demands different approaches from a music promo, VJ performance or other non-narrative video. Many of the ideas looked at in Chapter 8:1 are going to be of limited value when working with material where there is no attempt at continuity, where stories are absent and where the demands of the market are wholly different.

In this kind of editing an extra dimension comes into play, where signs and meaning can be conveyed through the style of editing itself rather than simply through what is shown on screen. The very mechanics of editing become as important as the images.

What genre editing can't do

There comes a point in genre or continuity editing when you run out of tools and devices and need to resort to other means. The rules and conventions of the edit start to feel restrictive and prevent certain ideas from coming into play.

When does this happen? One instance is when the ideas mentioned near the start of this chapter of identification and intensification become stronger than the plot. At these points the plot takes second place to the desire to involve the audience. The emotion in the sequence becomes heightened only if we share the protagonist's emotions. At this point we may see a diversion away from the plot entirely, where we encounter a montage of shots with sounds or music, designed to produce an effect of visceral sensation.

Film View

In *Midnight Cowboy* (John Schlesinger, 1969), a night out for the two protagonists, Dustin Hoffman and Jon Voight, leads to a party that quickly becomes like a nightmare for Hoffman as drink and drugs take their toll. The film then switches entirely out of the continuity editing used up to that point and uses other tricks to let us enter his deteriorating inner world, such as ghosting one image on another, echoing sounds, flashbacks to other moments, quick successions of shots, and random images. See Chapter 8:3 for details on how montage works.

In individual scenes, then, there is a need to occasionally break out of continuity editing. But what about on a larger scale, when the entire movie needs help from outside these conventions? In some films, you may want ideas to enter into the film that are not present solely in the story. You may want to use different kinds of structure to push the audience towards other meanings in the film. For instance, *Memento* (Christopher Nolan, 2000) raises questions about who we are, to what extent we can trust our memories and what this means for the way we deal with the world. The plot unfolds in reverse order as the protagonist, Leonard (Guy Pearce), goes further back towards the memories he cannot reach given his short-term amnesia. By placing the effect first and the cause second (for instance, Leonard finds a warning note to himself but cannot recall why; we then go to the day before to see what provoked this warning), Nolan lets us experience Leonard's amnesia.

What is non-narrative editing?

In music promos editing has evolved to keep pace with changes in music, as dance-based music and other urban styles have influenced promo directors towards a more surreal or even abstract approach, having no lyrics to work with as starting points. Editing in these films is about revealing the editing process by scratching and layering shots together to echo the manipulation of DJs with vinyl.

Tip   For examples of innovative non-narrative work, look at music promos by Shynola, Pleix, Chris Cunningham and Lynn Fox. These and other directors have experimented with varying degrees of abstraction away from narrative film. Shynola, in particular, operates more on the level of moving paintings.

Another influence has been the pressure from cable music channels – or more accurately from audiences via the channels – for more eye-catching videos. The result has been to 'micro-edit', where smaller parcels of information are contained in each shot. In a feature film there are signs all over the frame as to the story or theme, including colours, camera framing, composition and so on. But in this kind of movie, shots can be on screen for less than a second and inevitably contain less than is crucial. But this does not necessarily mean we are coping with less information in these films. Instead, it uses montage techniques (see Chapter 8:3) to almost literally pile the shots on top of one another, in what Eisenstein called 'vertical montage'.

But what makes this kind of video work interesting is that it plays with different audience expectations. The same person can see a feature film and then a music promo and read them in very different ways. The feature film has a certain structure (see Chapter 4:4), which asks us to order events and to expect a certain pattern to these. But in non-narrative work the desire to order what we see is less. We don't need to figure out who is who or where we are. We take in the images without prejudice and let them move around our perception until a shape of sorts emerges.

Weblink
http://www.ne-o.co.uk/   International group of filmmakers, makers of commercials and promos.

Figure 8.2 In this still from Bauhaus's *Corps Incorporated*, text and image are layered to create a dense visual mix.

Aims of the non-narrative edit

Sensation

At the upper end of the scale for aims of this kind of editing is the need for sensation. Music video, particularly in the West (Japan has very different approaches), has thrived on shock tactics and revulsion. Often subliminally used, these have the effect of grabbing attention, but also sometimes of incorporating political points with snatches of provocative images. In the club atmosphere, VJ performances use video screens on three walls to envelop the audience in the film and induce strong perceptual reactions. Big screens of colours, lights, text and images fill the vision and ensure total sensory inclusion. It is intense and visceral.

Go to: Chapter 6:4 for ideas on how VJ movies work.

Abandonment of reality

In these films there is no attempt to remain within reality or sometimes anything resembling it. Editing is a powerful tool in removing our sense of what is happening and when. If continuity is a way of sustaining a new reality for the viewer, convincing them that 50 years have passed in one minute or that hundreds of miles have been travelled, then it seems right that non-narrative filmmakers use the same techniques to distort reality. So clips are broken up with other clips, text obscures what we see, and images clash and contradict other images.

Non-narrative simply inverts genre editing to subvert reality.

Space for the viewer to inhabit

Although there is an abundance of imagery and information being thrown at the viewer, non-narrative films are not quite what they seem. A description of the kinds of editing seen would suggest that they

Figure 8.3 Non-narrative work, such as this piece by polymedia group Raya, demands a different approach to editing.

are the equivalent of the swinging pocket-watch, hypnotizing the audience. But instead these films tend to use what we could call 'structural space'. This means that the films offer a space for the viewer to enter the structure of the film. The surface of the film is not flawless as in features, where the suspension of disbelief is all; in VJ-ing there are glitches where video images stop, synchronize, break apart and then start up again. Another way of achieving this space is through repetition, where images recur and are echoed from screen to screen so that the viewer starts to see them as rhythmic devices and takes part in predicting them. In these films you identify not so much with characters, but with rhythm and images.

How to do it: devices in non-narrative editing
Strong rhythm

In music promo and VJ-ing, rhythm is often the driving force due to the use of music. Promos tend to be restricted by the rhythm of the song in question, but VJ-ing tends to use music in the same way as a band uses a drum beat: it uses the music as a way of building up layers of images, again through repetition. The music keeps rhythm but images can be used against rhythm or with it. It is a foil for the development of the images as they cut in and out and then finally reach a cumulative climax.

In *Wild Man of New York* by The Light Surgeons, for instance, footage of a homeless man in the streets of New York is interspersed with cuts of consumerism, TV culture and urban environments. We start with the man himself, and these other images enter slowly, at first for just a few frames but then dominating the sequence until the man has disappeared. Near the end of the piece, the images diversify and we are returned to the man again. His importance in the film is underlined by his recurrence and we start to relate all the other images to him, creating ideas from juxtaposition. It's classic montage but uses structures borrowed from dance music culture.

Did you know?
The Light Surgeons are a UK-based group, run by Chris Allen, which pioneered the use of light and video shows in club settings in the 1980s and 1990s. Their low-tech shows originally used Super 8 film and found their ideal home in the late 1980s rave culture. Since then, they have established a reputation at the forefront of experiments in video and sound, moving their work increasingly towards the art gallery in large-scale installations.

Editing is the story

This idea seems like a riddle perhaps, but this may be because we see editing as a tool for the final stages of a film rather than as an end in itself. Much of VJ-ing is about using editing as the first and last tool. This means that the way images appear is as important as the actual images themselves. As in much VJ work, the better analogies are with music to really understand how it works. In some music the melody is not important and not especially memorable; instead, it is the way different sounds are arranged that is the important element.

How non-narrative structure works in music

As an example of how music can reflect similar approaches to video editing, in DJ Shadow's *Changeling* (from *Endtroducing*, 2002, Universal) sounds are sampled which recur and then disrupt each other. A highly disruptive aural landscape is developed by placing sounds out of sync and having others glitch and repeat as if scratched. The melody here is not the memorable part – the meaning lies in the disruption, fragmentation and clashing of sounds. DJ Shadow wins us over by ultimately making the sounds seem unified at the same time as being fragmented. So where's the meaning in all this? Is it that city life is just like the arrangement of these sounds: fragmented, with sudden shifts in gear, but all adding up to a kind of unity?

www.djshadow.com/landing.html

In editing, then, try to favour adding rather than taking away clips, building up rather than reducing the effect. And the way that you arrange the shots has a sort of meaning all its own, so you don't necessarily need images to carry much meaning. Take a look at dance music and also look for similar patterns in the music of American composer Steve Reich (who incidentally is seen as the grandfather of sound sampling through his experiments with tape in the early 1960s).

Weblink
http:/www.stevereich.com/   Official home page for the avant-garde composer.

Imitation of the dream

Another common element of this kind of work is the way the editing borrows from dreams. This doesn't mean that they are all surrealist, although many music promo directors do favour the dreamlike or nightmarish above other themes. It means that they borrow from the structure of dreams, where continuity is not necessary because the flavour of dreams is based on sudden change and alarming juxtapositions. There is no chronology that we recognize and events seem to occur out of nowhere; cause and effect either disappears or is reversed. This kind of structure favours the music video and VJ more than any other, for two reasons: first, it allows the film to rely just on images and jump straight to the next symbolic shot; second, because it results in a film that constantly grabs the attention, which is exactly what the market needs for MTV and similar channels. To understand dream structure, look at Luis Buñuel's *Un Chien Andalou*, which gets this kind of structure just right.

Did you know?

Surrealism is a running theme in many films over the last hundred years. Artists who devised the movement in the 1920s and 1930s, such as Salvador Dali and René Magritte, believed that dreams and nightmares would enable us to find out the truth about our real desires and fears. Filmmakers dramatize surreal imagery as a way of unfolding the inner lives of characters, often through specific dream sequences but sometimes through visions that develop themes in the film. Martin Scorsese uses a vision in *Bringing Out the Dead* to show the guilt felt by the central character, while Hitchcock's dream sequence in *Spellbound* was hugely influential on a generation of filmmakers.

Symbolism

Symbolism is rife in the non-narrative genres. Symbolism is the less definite sign, more open to interpretation and more stimulating to see. Universal symbols such as fire, darkness, speed, the colour red, the sea and more urban ones such as empty streets, rough sleepers and police sirens are typical examples used in these films. To the non-narrative filmmaker they are like actors and characters – ready to be brought on stage when needed.

Go to: Chapter 3:3, 'Film language and how to speak it', to see how symbols are used throughout film.

Disorientation

The live mix by a VJ is nothing less than virtuoso editing, responding to the film as much as generating it. Disorientation is a by-product of this kind of so-called 'accelerated film'. The scale of the screens and the enveloping nature of the experience make it unlikely that any other sensory information can get through against the wall of sounds and images. This degree of sensory manipulation is profound and means that the slightest disruption of images and sound is enough to disorientate the audience. And as we have seen, it is precisely this kind of discontinuity that the non-narrative filmmaker prefers. For editing in music promos and VJ work, the effect will be disorientating if you follow the ideas above – particularly of editing with rhythm where this can be suddenly disrupted. The free use of sampled images from other movies also means that the unexpected is a constant factor, disrupting not only the structure of the video but also the nature of the images. Anything can happen and that makes for a nervous experience.

Weblinks

http://www.eclecticmethod.net/   Accomplished VJ-ers who edit with gathered film.
http://www.raya.org.uk/   Promo and ploymedia artists.
http://www.ladypat.com/main.htm   VJ artist Pat, with visuals for Scissor Sisters, Lee Scratch Perry and Boy George.

Figure 8.4 Editing with images such as these demands a different approach to conventional editing, as in this still from Daniel Levi's promo for Massive Attack, *Butterfly Caught.*

Figure 8.5 Hardware such as Pioneer's DVJ-X1 enables direct scratching of DVDs to create VJ shows, emulating the way DJs use vinyl.

Project 18. Polymedia movie

What this project is for: to investigate filmmaking for cell phones or hand-held devices
Time: allow a few days to plan, a week to shoot and a week to edit

What this project is about

The aim of this film is to create a moving image product that goes outside your expectations of video. We need to try new ways of using video, to respond to new ways of watching video.

Go to: Chapter 10:2, 'State of the art: expansion and convergence', to find out more about polymedia movies.

Stage 1

Choose from the following ideas:

● A sequence of viral movies to accompany a political message (designed to be seen on phones and hand-held devices)
● A sequence of virals to market a new band or record company.

In both ideas, the aim is to create short films of less than 30 seconds each which compress well – see Chapter 5:5 on shooting for the web and compression for how to do this. In the 2004 US presidential campaign, volunteers went from house to house showing voters short films on palm-tops to swing their opinions, with different films available for the volunteer to choose from according to the voter's race or age.

Music company virals are becoming commonplace as costs of promos force labels to reconsider how to target more directly to consumers. Your viral is being sent to someone who likes another group from the same label and has given their cell phone number for marketing purposes.

Start by planning a series of short storyboards that have strong, bold images.

Stage 2

Shoot uncluttered and clear shots that will translate well to cell phones. Work with hard lighting to achieve strong shapes and shadows. Avoid fast movement with the camera. The virals should relate to each other clearly so that they each seem to belong to a single campaign. To achieve this, use consistent lighting, camera angles and colour in each. Create a visible style which connects each one. For the political viral, make it explicit what you are stating by adding text.

Go to: Chapter 5:2, 'Lighting', for help on getting the right effect.

Tip: common mistakes in polymedia movies
- Too many shots
- Nothing to keep attention focused – try using instead a motif or symbol that recurs
- Weirdness for the sake of it – the film has to travel through many different kinds of viewer, so play for the middle ground of your target audience
- Reliance on sound – many phones have poor sound quality.

Stage 3

Editing may be a short process given the length of the films. Use montage techniques and avoid long, lingering shots. Virals tend to work well when made in an enigmatic way, leaving the viewer curious and eager to find out more. For political shorts, be succinct, punchy and get to the point immediately.

Evaluation

Show your friends the movies you have made and find out how well they convey what you intended. An equally important question is the results of compression. Try putting the movie through heavy compression at around 5–10 frames per second and view on a camera LCD monitor. Freeware is available for compression for cell phones.

I want something more challenging

This is a pretty tough assignment because of the restrictions imposed, but if you want to push yourself further try making a movie where you work with a real-life client, perhaps for a company that wants virals for a marketing campaign. Contact design agencies – not companies direct – and find out whether any are planning this sort of addition to their clients' campaigns.

---

3. Montage editing

Montage is one of the most significant devices used by filmmakers in editing. Many editors see montage as a definition of editing, while others see it as just another device to bring in when other more rational ones don't work.

At the centre of this debate is the view that there are two essential approaches to editing, at least in a theoretical sense. It seems too simplistic perhaps, but does stand up to analysis of editing styles. It could be summed up as being between:

- Those who think editing is about taking away shots to make a sequence

vs

- Those who think editing is about adding shots to make a sequence.

The predominantly Hollywood-style editing is concerned with the first method. Shots are placed to advance the story and anything additional to this is extraneous. Action depends on short cuts with information that the audience can digest quickly. These shots are delivered in 'single file' as it were; they are linear in the sense that they each tell a part of the chain of information we need to understand the story.

But there is another school of editing which says that you need to add more shots. It is derived from the approach to editing devised by Sergei Eisenstein, who many would say practically invented the language of editing in early films such as *Battleship Potemkin*. He talked about 'vertical editing' and suggested a parallel with orchestral scoring, where instruments are layered on top of one another. This kind of editing is concerned with adding shots, to bombard the senses in what Eisenstein called a polyphonic sequence to get 'a synchronization of the senses' (*The Film Sense*, Faber & Faber, 1943).

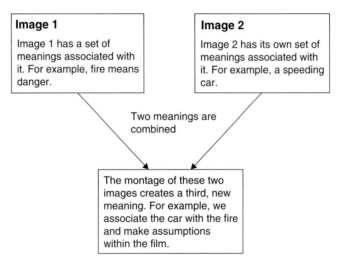

Figure 8.6 How montage creates new meaning out of combining seemingly unrelated shots.

This section is about how to edit in this way and what it can mean for your films.

In keeping with the spirit of montage, the rest of this section will look at a range of ideas in a different way, putting forward ideas without order. Feel free to mix them around, add them up later and make your own versions of this chapter.

In essence, montage centres on the idea that shots do not have to match in order to be placed side by side, but can show seemingly unrelated images with the aim of heightening the emotional or dramatic impact of a sequence. The idea is simple: shot 1 is placed next to shot 2 and gives birth to a third representation, this time in the mind of the viewer. In this way, montage achieves the multiple layers of meaning it wants because there is a net result of more 'meanings' than there are individual shots. It quickly becomes bewildering.

For example, shot 1 is a car journey at night and shot 2 a burning house in daylight. Both have separate and quite individual meanings and have potentially lots of symbolism. We may consider as separate the journey in shot 1 or the event in shot 2, but edited together they trigger all sorts of ideas. Together they create a synthesis that is now greater than the effect of either shot independently:

> *Imagine a scene*:
> Burning house + more shots of house = burning house
> Car + more shots of car = car
>
> *But if you try*:
> Burning house + car + burning house + car + man looking scared = Did he do it? Why is he escaping, if he is escaping? Is he the occupant of the house, reliving the memory? Is he alive? Is he dead?

Montage has become more sophisticated since its beginnings in Eisenstein's movies. In its infancy, montage was criticized for being too literal, inserting shots that did not add to the meaning of a scene but merely underlined what we already knew, such as a cutaway to a shot of a lightning strike when a character falls in love.

Later montage began to fulfil its potential – namely, to create a third meaning out of two shots. It is this ability to conjure up new meanings by simply juxtaposing one image with another that has revealed an enormous untapped reservoir of poetic subtlety in film.

- Working with montage is somewhat easier with non-linear editing systems, which by their nature encourage the user to try out shots against other shots and view the possibilities. Digital editing *wants* to become montage editing.
- *Montage is a kind of anti-editing*, in that it is concerned with building up a sequence, amplifying meaning and effect through multiple cuts and images, whereas more conventional editing, in its classical sense, is concerned with discarding, with *deselecting* images.
- It has a geographical bias in that its greatest exponents are found in European film, while Hollywood has tended to view it as a disruptive influence, upsetting the steady flow of shots in classical 'continuity editing'.
- Montage is not a device as such to add some complexity when a film seems like its becoming too obvious. Instead, as Scorsese's film professor and mentor Haig Manoogian put it, montage 'is the source for a film's power; it *is* editing' (*The Filmmaker's Art*, Basic Books, 1966, p. 215).
- As with any other tool in post-production, montage editing is driven by the content of the film itself.
- With montage, more is better. *Montage is a kind of anti-editing*.
- Formula for Hollywood editing: a–b–c–d–e–f.
- More is better, anti-editing.
- **The**sis + anti**the**sis = syn**the**sis. In this, the letters '**the**' are signs of the ever-present theme in each shot.
- Formula for montage editing: a–d–c–b–e/a–b–e–a/d–a/f–a/a. Note the rhythm as 'a' recurs.
- Meaning of shot 1 plus meaning of shot 2 equals *new meaning*.

Figure 8.7 In this sequence by New Zealand filmmaker Charlotte Clark, a series of images are held together in a fast-moving montage.

- But *randomness is the enemy of montage*.
- Juxtaposition must seek out *similarities* of theme in opposing images for it to work. It is about creating a *unification of theme* so that the unseen meaning in shots 1 and 2 becomes the meaning of both, even though the two images may have little in common at first sight.
- To make sure you have a unifying theme to your juxtaposition, take each shot from the *same source*.

- **The**sis + anti**the**sis = syn**the**sis. In this, the letters '**the**' are signs of the underlying theme in each shot.
- *Accelerated montage* creates what is invisible: in Hitchcock's *Psycho* there are no shots of the knife striking the victim in the shower scene. Shot combinations and speed convince us we have seen it.
- **The**sis + anti**the**sis = syn**the**sis. In this, the letters '**the**' are signs of the central **the**me in each shot.
- A montage sequence can convey ideas, emotions or a series of events more subtly than through purely verbal means, and the director is then free to add a particular twist to the scene, depending on the kind of shots included.

Film View

In Sofia Coppola's *The Virgin Suicides* (2000), the director needs to demonstrate the strange, other-worldly closeness of the sisters. The complexity of emotions could be conveyed through conversations between them, but there is a limit to what words can convey. Coppola's answer is a montage of dreamy, swirling images of the girls dancing against a setting sun. It is unsettling because they are happy yet they plan to die.

- Use montage in an almost improvised way, selecting and using clips intuitively.
- Add more than you discard.
- **The**sis (the shot) + anti**the**sis (another shot which juxtaposes it) = syn**the**sis (a fusion of both as the **the**me present in both is revealed and elevated by repetition).
- '*Parallel montage*' allows the director to show simultaneous events or stories by cutting from one to another and suggesting shared meanings.
- Film theorist Christian Metz suggested eight different types and described the interactions and uses of each.
- In 'accelerated montage', a sequence is built of a succession of fast clips showing a bewildering array of images, trying to effect a particular *response* in the viewer.
- '*Involuted montage*' allows a story to be told without regard to chronology, letting the filmmaker reveal parts of the plot and draw the viewer into a more complex reading of it than a simple a-to-b-to-c of events.
- **The**sis + anti**the**sis = .

The Crunch

- Montage looks weird but try it – it is unpredictable and adds something extra
- Montage takes many forms – try out each method and see what it can offer you
- Look for montage in movies you watch – it's everywhere
- Why should you tell a story straight? Give the audience something else to think about other than the story
- You don't have to be in control – improvise when you compose a montage sequence.

Project 19. Movie spell

What this project is for: to try montage editing techniques
Time: allow about one week for planning, shooting and editing

What this project is about

The aim of this movie is to investigate the full effects of montage editing. This movie is not descriptive and is not trying to make any statements or tell us any messages. Instead, it is aimed at producing an almost physical, sensational effect on the viewer. It takes its inspiration from the movie *The Ring*, and in particular the piece of video tape which forms the centre of the story. In this movie, a video is said to be so potent that it condemns anyone who sees it to death. But can you work magic with a piece of video? If so, can it be like a spell, capable of making someone fall in love, give away all their money or change their life? This movie is going to aim for the jugular in the audience and perhaps produce some startling effects. We will need all the tools picked up so far in montage editing, lighting, sound, structure and composition to produce the desired effect.

Stage 1

Describe the 'spell' that you would like to perform. Then describe in simple descriptive words the effect that this may have on a person. For instance, love may be described in words like warm, rapturous, nervous, anticipatory. Fear could be described as cold, empty, fast, compelling, piercing and so on.

When you have described the feeling you want to induce, make a list of these words on a page and draw images that you think link to them. These will be entirely open to interpretation, but bear in mind that they need to be fairly universal to reach the audience. Then devise a separate list of words which also link to the main idea but are opposing evocations of it. For instance, in love, there are also feelings that are less predictable: hopelessness, change, sudden doubt. These add another dimension to the feeling and will provide us with juxtaposition to add to the spell.

Stage 2

From these images you have a basic series of visualizations. With each image, try to conjure up an intense aspect to it. Always opt for the most dramatic and intimate aspect of a particular word. Go over the top.

Go to: Chapters 4:7 and 4:8 to see how to work with these visuals to create a shooting script.

Outline a plan of where to get these shots and then draw more sketches to define how they could look.

Stage 3

When shooting, keep looking out for images that could fit your movie. Try to avoid perfection, and avoid following the chapter on good composition too closely. The images we need for this movie will benefit from a bit more spontaneity, so try compositions that are deliberately not quite 'correct' in terms of good framing. Consider how much more interesting home-movie footage of UFOs can be; even though they are fakes, they grab the attention by being faint, blurred and uncertain. M. Night Shyamalan used this technique in the movie footage sequences of aliens in his movie *Signs* to use the device that imperfection equals truth.

Stage 4

Cutting for this movie will be better if you follow the ideas in non-narrative editing, Chapter 8:2. Also check out Chapter 8:3, 'Montage editing'.

Evaluation

For this movie, its success is judged by the effect it has on viewers. Show the movie to friends and see how they react. Note where the moments are that affect them most strongly and see whether other sections could be re-edited to emulate them.

Look for whether there are any lessons here in editing for narrative movies. Can you see ways of editing action scenes like this? Could moments of intense feeling be conveyed in montage sequences like this? The most important question here, though, relates to the whole purpose of filmmaking: can you strongly manipulate the audience's feelings and induce strong reactions?

I want something more challenging

Try relying less on quick editing to get the effects you want. A more difficult version of this film would be one that uses images less frenetically, with longer cuts. Is it possible to hold attention strongly through images that are captivating rather than piling up images that are individually less interesting?

9 | Careers and distribution

Part 1: Where am I going?

1. What's a career?

To many people, the idea of a career is something that you have for life – you move onwards and upwards towards greater financial and employment security. In the film industry, however, this doesn't fit. A career in films means a series of jobs, each of them starting and ending with periods of no job in between a mix of employment and self-employment. But it is possible to aim for a situation where you successfully earn a living in films, linking together various skills you have and forming a coherent plan. With this plan you can make the best of your individual talents and where they can be used – all of which will help allow you to make your own films too.

If we use the term career loosely, the closest analogy is probably rock climbing. Forging a career in film is similar in that you know roughly where you want to go – up – and you know the skills to get you there. But each step can be gruelling and challenging because you have to make your own mark and find your own footholds for yourself. So, although the overall route may be clear, the small steps you make along this path may not be easy.

In essence, then, the film industry makes no effort to help prospective entrants into it, despite the seemingly ubiquitous nature of the moving image and the huge industry infrastructure in some territories where jobs are more common. In most places it is up to the individual to adopt an attitude of self-reliance, focus and persistence.

On the other hand, of course, all this talk of making it to the top gives the impression that it is an 'all or nothing' industry where you either become a star or you sink. The key to being successful in this industry is in realizing that there are many other levels to it, that opportunities exist right across the industry at every point, from no-budget right up to large features. If you are willing to multiply the possible aims you have – rather than relying on just one, such as making features – then the chances of your succeeding increase.

In practice: case studies

To get more realistic about what kinds of routes we are talking about here, let's home in on some practitioners who are managing to do what they enjoy and work towards a better future position. All are at the start of their careers, developing skills but also trying to figure out exactly what it is they can offer and where their strengths lie. Names and companies have been changed.

Case 1

Josie is currently preparing a script for a short she has been working towards for six months. She has steadily raised funding for it from public arts agencies and from friends and family, and has been working in part-time jobs since leaving film school two years ago to save money for her projects. Recently, though, she has been working as an editor on several shorts, after a director of a film she edited for no fee recommended her to a friend. Sometimes she gets paid, sometimes not – 'it depends on the movie and whether it will advance my skills in editing, and whether I like the script'. She also has income from a sideline in web design, having found this easy at college. Lately, this has become a big part of her income and is taking up more time. But Josie finds that she is managing to stay independent, make short movies, though not as many as she would like, and is optimistic about the future.

Next?

'I'm going to carry on with these various strands of my life. It's tiring but in different ways I am doing what I love to do. If I can get a short into Clermont-Ferrand next year it'll be a big step forward.'

Case 2

Alex was making shorts while at university but found that he was much more in demand among friends for his skills with the camera. He has just started to get paid for jobs and is thinking of going full-time into camera operating and then making shorts at weekends. He will have more money if he does but is worried about 'selling out' or giving up too much time. But being a DoP (Director of Photography) is better than his current job in a real-estate office, which he got because of his IT skills. A year of freelance DoP work and his résumé looks great, and Alex has had one or two returned calls from directors recruiting for larger projects. Against what he expected, his enforced absence from making films as he works on others' projects has led him to start writing scripts, and spending so much time on sets means he knows just about every mistake directors tend to make.

Next?

'Save and invest in my own films. I don't make many now but when I do I'm quick, professional and everyone knows I know what I'm talking about. I've got some good contacts through DoP work and think I may be able to get a short sold to TV soon. I am also setting myself up as self-employed now that I am making a regular but small amount from the DoP-ing.'

Case 3

Lola has been making documentaries for some time and at the moment her one-person company, Insight, is loss-making in itself, but she supports it through her work as a video trainer. She organizes networking and screenings events for filmmakers, and has found more and more people want to do her basic documentary training courses. The training is so successful that Lola wonders now and then why she doesn't just concentrate on this and stop making her documentaries. But Insight has started bringing other filmmakers on board to share the load and has become more productive. Their last movie, which Lola directed after travelling widely, was bought as a shorter version by a US cable channel and they were able to spend the income on issuing a DVD of the full cut. Her latest movie, an investigation into the World Bank, has been funded by asking for small donations from non-governmental groups in the developing world.

Next?

'Raise funds for a more ambitious documentary. I'm also pitching for a three-minute slot on a TV channel soon because someone had sent the programmer our DVD. I'm getting there slowly – I just don't know where "there" is yet. But I'll know it when I arrive.'

Figure 9.1 Director Richard Graham's short, *Kafkaesque*, was made in between day jobs but went on to win awards at screenings.

What connects these people?

If we look for common threads in each of these cases we can see the kinds of skills and struggles that many filmmakers go through – the conflict between making money and being an artist, the search to find out what particular skills they have, and the need to keep plugging away at opportunities constantly.

Multi-skilled

Each filmmaker is remarkably multi-skilled, able to hop between film skills and less glamorous ones within the working day. They juggle with several tasks at once, running small companies, doing editing or DoP work, developing ideas for projects. In any given week, the 'to do' list is rarely focused on just one task. Instead, there are several strands to their working lives demanding attention, sometimes interacting – as when contacts made in a job can help with getting your films seen.

Conflict

In each case also there is a sense of conflict between personal aims and freelance work. Many people just entering the industry experience a slight sense of disillusionment as the scale of the odds stacked against them becomes clear. But this is often accompanied by a corresponding sense of empowerment as knowledge increases about the industry. Freelance work becomes the way to acquire knowledge that can help personal projects rather than an obstacle to them. In this way, any work at all in the film industry is beneficial in some way, not least because of making contacts. So, paid work can directly help personal movie projects.

Knowing your strengths

Another crucial element which contributes to the success of these cases is that they know their strengths and play to them. They may harbour pet projects that don't seem possible just yet, but they also realize, especially Alex, that their natural talents may lead them to other routes. Alex is clear that he wants to carry on making short films, but knows that if people like his camerawork then he will plough that furrow too. In other ways, too, the other cases use sideline skills such as IT, training or funding to remain independent.

Work in other areas

Each person here also possesses more than one skill area. That doesn't mean they were born lucky, but more that realism has taught them that a few safety nets are needed, financially. They learned pretty soon that they needed to use all they had to earn income and that using skills that people needed – IT, teaching and so on – paid more than manual work like waiting. So each has purposely developed and worked on skills they might otherwise have neglected. Josie, for instance, may make more money from web design for some time, but it will provide for her real aspirations and give her time to realize them.

Self-employment

Each of the filmmakers above is self-employed to some extent; they make some or all of their total income from jobs they find for themselves. In Alex's case, he is practically self-employed right now, getting good jobs as a camera operator or DoP, and is able to consider this as a possibly stable source of income. After several months of this kind of work he may call himself a one-person business and formally adopt the role as one that he has confidence he can accomplish. It is common, then, to have a dual status as partly employed, partly self-employed and this may continue for some time, neither job fulfilling your income needs just yet.

It is also common to have two tax statuses – as employed and self-employed. This does get confusing when you have to declare your annual accounts and find yourself sorting through employment where tax has been deducted at source (as long as the job was not 'cash in hand' or not declared by the employer) and that where you need to settle the tax yourself.

Taxation

It might hurt to pay cheques to the tax service, but it does pay in the long run to become legitimate early on in your business life. As soon as you start earning for two or three jobs in a row and it looks like this may continue, go through the steps of becoming a one-person business. Keep records of what you spend and what you earn and, if possible, keep a separate bank account where you place a top slice of each job you get paid for. The good sell is that tax people are more likely to be nice to you if you are upfront and honest – for instance, by spreading payments to them from artistic earnings over a tax year instead of all in one cheque. Another good reason is that it is quite unlikely that you will pay any tax in the first two years or so because your 'start-up' costs are so large. Just about every spare cheque you get goes into the business in the form of a new Mac, an updated camera, new lenses, cables and so on. Each of these legitimate business expenses can be offset against tax, so you need to keep receipts of each item, even the very small stuff.

The bad sell is that if you get rumbled later in your career that you have not yet declared tax on significant sums, you will get the full force of the bureaucrats coming down on you. You are no longer small fry – the start-up solo business – but a terminal tax dodger. And in any case, an industry where you seek publicity is not the kind to be in if you want to hide your tracks from the tax people.

A final good reason for keeping good accounts and going legitimate is that there is a good feeling if you opt for this professional status. You actually feel more like a genuine filmmaker – you have the business card, the accounts, logo and so on. When times are tough, these kinds of affirmative signs are the ones to keep you afloat and feeling positive.

Checklist

- Contact your tax service – talk to them about getting help with setting up accounts
- Find out what items are legitimate tax-deductible expenses – these stop you paying so much tax
- Keep all receipts and file them
- Be legal about what you earn.

Taxable profits?

The operative word here is 'taxable'. This means that not all your profits are available for the tax people to get their hands on. So how does this work? Suppose you earn $1000 in a year. You may have spent $800 on equipment and other expenses over that year, so this means that there is only $200 for the tax people to take a slice from. If tax was 25 per cent, then you only pay $50 in taxation. Obviously, figures go up and down according to where you live and most corporate tax is complicated enough to employ lawyers full-time. For emerging filmmakers this is the bottom line, but it is dependent on keeping strong accounts and having records of whatever you spend.

2. Careers: essential knowledge

One look at the story outlines in a recent film festival tells you that filmmakers have their eyes firmly looking outwards at the world. The idea of intense inner expression divorced from reality is not an option for most, as films are seen as essentially a tool for communication. They are a way of telling what happens in the places the filmmakers find themselves – whether this is in the social sphere (how we get on with each other), in the political sphere (what we do to each other), or in the moral or spiritual sphere (what we should do and be with each other). Filmmakers have a lot to say and they want to say it.

In most cases, filmmakers tend to be more attuned to the prevailing zeitgeist than other people, but this has traditionally been the role of the artist for centuries. Art often holds up a mirror which reflects the times, even if this is not at all intentional. Film in particular, perhaps because of this need to communicate above all else, tends to hold a clearer mirror than most art forms, reflecting closely what people think about, what they are scared by and what they aspire towards.

In this section we will see what kinds of areas successful filmmakers are interested in, which inspire films and motivate them to work.

What's going on in the world?

Successful filmmakers tend to have a close relationship with the world around them. They do this by being at once detached observers and fully engaged performers in the human drama, stubbornly questioning and investigating how people live together in society. The zeitgeist is the current which they tap into.

Figure 9.2 Andrea Arnold won an Academy Award in 2005 for this hard-hitting short film, *Wasp*.

Zeitgeist

We could define zeitgeist as being the prevailing winds that affect the social, political, personal and spiritual aspects of our lives. It is more than the sum of its parts, however; it is more like an overriding vibe, feeling or atmosphere that is the result of each of these aspects, but is multiplied because of the forms of communication we have. Certainly, a couple of centuries ago it would have been harder to talk about a shared zeitgeist when news from New York took months to arrive in Berlin, if at all. But in the highly talkative world we live in, we now experience rapidly spreading feelings, confined mostly to the industrialized nations but affecting us all.

Zeitgeists tend to change slowly, but occasional events that resonate globally can effect a sudden earthquake in our shared feelings. The 9/11 attacks, for instance, dramatically changed the world in each of the areas that make up the zeitgeist overnight. The destruction of the Berlin Wall, the Cuban Missile Crisis and the Russian Revolution could all be said to have had a similar effect. Other events act as a sudden signal to show us something we had not noticed was changing, such as the birth of the first cloned animal in 1996 (representing a new age in science) or the first TV presidential candidate debate in 1976 (representing the dominance of the media in democracy).

The connection between all the major events that happen in the world is that they affect our hopes and dreams, limiting or fuelling them, and – most importantly for the filmmaker – give us ingredients for our nightmares. What we are scared of has long been the holy grail for filmmakers, from Kubrick's *Dr Strangelove* (nuclear annihilation), through to *The Matrix* (computers getting smarter than us). A film that would once have passed unnoticed can become a cultural must-see – purely as a result of its tapping into our fears. It makes good therapy. Directors who have one finger on the pulse of society notice where the times are heading and imagine the worst and best outcomes. In their films they express (temporary) universal truths about us all.

How you get the knowledge

So how do you get this inside knowledge? It comes about in two ways: one formal, the other informal. Making time for newspapers and journals allows you to soak up the daily mood. You start to notice the slow news (the trends) behind the fast news (the events) and they trigger ideas in your mind for projects. There is no need to force this process of absorption and creating – it is usually the case that after a while the zeitgeist seeps into your work. This results in some subtle investigations of what's going on – such as *25th Hour*, Spike Lee's post 9/11 eulogy to lost time and redemption. It ends up being less ham-fisted than movies that deal with big events directly, such as David O. Russell's *Three Kings*, which looked at the 1991 Iraq war.

Aside from straight news, there are also many signs in everyday life that point towards the zeitgeist. Some are in the streets, some on TV, many in people's dreams – in the form of advertising images, fads or prejudices. Whatever and wherever they are, to the filmmaker they are content, and more importantly they are content that has an immediate audience.

To do

- Watch the TV news – it is the barometer of fear, as Michael Moore points out in *Bowling for Columbine*. Local news will be more populist and therefore more attuned to what we fear or aspire to.
- Don't restrict yourself to national news or sites. Read news from the countries in which events happen by looking on the Internet.
- Sign up for real news networks – emerging sites which promote alternative methods of finding out about the world.
- But don't avoid the mainstream press – read the news weeklies (*Newsweek*, *The Economist*, *Time*) for the status quo viewpoint. This will become the Greenwich Mean Time of your ideas about the world, so you can work out how divergent from this centre – to the left or right – everything else is.

What's going on in culture?

This is kind of zooming in on a particular part of the zeitgeist, but affects not just the content of films but what form they take.

An awareness of the route that culture is taking can affect every aspect of your films – at its best ensuring that they highlight, and are at the forefront of, cultural changes. Film directors such as Baz Luhrmann or David Cronenberg make movies that seem at once a product of their time and a leap forward within it. Luhrmann's *Moulin Rouge* used CGI, a frantic editing style and a cultural melting pot of music to accurately reflect much of contemporary video and music – but at the same time looked like nothing seen before.

Each cultural epoch has its own character. If the 1990s were dominated by the ideas of post-modernism and irony (all those references to genres and movies from previous ages and other cultures), then today's epoch is marked by a change away from this. Post-modernism was useful for the kind of world we lived in then – borders that used to separate different cultures were dissolving and so artists took parts of cultures they liked and fused them with others.

But times change. We have moved into another cultural epoch, which is characterized more by a converging of styles and crossover of technology. For example, video games borrow from cinema, which borrows from comic books, which are influenced by graffiti, which is influenced by consumer branding – and so on. Slicing across these convergent moments are technologies that encourage artistic products to overlap: the cell phone, computer-generated images and the iPod, for instance.

Go to: Chapter 10:2 for more on the place moving images have in our culture.

Absorbing (sub)culture

But why should anyone need to know what goes on in culture and subculture? The answer lies, ironically, in the need for originality. Most filmmakers desire their own personal stamp – a style that is recognizably theirs. This could be expressed in terms of the stories they make and the way they make them – their visual appearance. It could be argued that the filmmakers whose style is most unique are the ones who have absorbed the most from the world around them. They know how to locate themselves within cultural life and can identify where they are different to all the other movies around them. Their own ideas are thrown into relief as they experience those of others, and then see the value in their own work.

Beyond this, a wider range of cultural influences produces a wider range of variables – rather like being able to produce better perfume when you can mix from a thousand very divergent possible sources rather than just ten. As an example, the acclaimed cinematographer Chris Doyle, who photographed *Rabbit-Proof Fence*, *In the Mood For Love* and *2046*, has arrived at a style that is uniquely his own. Widely travelled on the seas after working on ships, Doyle originates from Australia, found his camera style in south Asia and then found his artistic home, as it were, in the Far East, speaking Mandarin and becoming a sought-after DoP. The resultant style is a mix of something from all his influences, and the strength this uniqueness has given him has led him to question everything about cinematography.

The ability to absorb culture and subculture is one that helps to mould your own personal style. How do you achieve it? No single source will keep you in touch, but a mixture of printed, Internet and media sources should, between them, reflect the ephemeral passing trends as much as the resonant cultural moments.

To do

- Read arts pages in journals and newspapers – try online versions of *The Guardian* and *New York Times*. Also try *Time* magazine for what the mainstream thinks – if *Time* has highlighted a trend you know it's the moment you should move onto something new.
- Read blogs and news sites that express opinions, not just facts. It is as useful to know what people think is happening as what actually is happening.
- Argue with friends and other filmmakers. Hone your opinions about everything you see.

What's going on in the industry?

The film industry is notoriously hard to pin down as it shifts and evolves on an almost weekly basis. One week independents are hooking up with the major studios, then the following week one of those studios gets swallowed by a Japanese conglomerate. Lower down the chain, a tax loophole is closed, certain territories become flavour of the month as shooting locations – Mexico, then Canada, then Eastern Europe. Meanwhile, festivals go from independent to mainstream and then back again changing identities, while markets fall out of favour and new ones crop up. Only the most ardent industry-watcher could keep up with the changes.

Tracking change

For the emerging low-budget filmmaker, whether wanting to work in the multimedia underground or direct a feature, it is much easier to track the changes going on in their own sector. With the web this is easier, since the range of sources and news is huge. Bulletin boards, blogs and news sites spread word of what is shifting before the ground shakes – alerting you to changes in every aspect of the industry. By contrast, film magazines are at least two months out of date by publication and are now sensibly taking a loftier position as notaries of the overall direction the industry is going in.

In terms of your overall career, a knowledge of what is going on in the film industry is the first step to getting involved in it. You can then identify opportunities that could help you in terms of festivals that may take your movie, websites that could advertise it or fund-holders that could help on your next project.

To do

- Sign up for every email newsletter you can – public arts, film support boards, finance commissions and newspapers (*Variety*, *The Hollywood Reporter*).
- Network with other filmmakers to find out about opportunities.
- Read *Screen International* and other industry papers.
- Read blogs for emerging news.
- Attend briefings and workshops about film industry issues (check with local film groups, public arts agencies and film schools).

3. Essential qualities

Filmmaking is a multifaceted art form. It utilizes elements from other art forms, such as lighting, story-telling, music and sound, and asks directors to have at least a working knowledge of each area. On another level, the industry itself is composed of different elements – different territories, different economic models and, with technological advances, different ways of watching films.

It seems logical, then, that the smallest but most necessary cog in all this – the filmmaker – needs also to be composed of varying skills and qualities. And as the industry changes, so to do the skills film-makers need.

In this section we will take a look at the kinds of qualities that successful low-budget directors tend to have. At the heart of this discussion, however, there is a big vacuum of something which we can't talk about but which propels each skill forward: talent. Talent is the unquantifiable part of the equation. But some people in education question whether talent exists at all or whether it is simply a mix of five parts inner compulsion to two parts ambition/desire to three parts practical skill. Skills in filmmaking tend to focus on technical aspects more than any other and it could be argued that without this you won't get anywhere. But skills also means the personal qualities you develop, the modes of working, the attitude you adopt and the way you interact with other people.

This list has been drawn up after many interviews with filmmakers working in the difficult environment of the low-budget sector, but who somehow seem to thrive and experience some success in these arid conditions. What are the qualities which have seen them succeed?

Flexibility

This ingredient is going to reappear in various guises throughout this list. Flexibility is the oil that greases all the other personal skill areas. In this context it means being able to think fast, switch plans quickly, adapt to new situations and accept change readily.

At the forefront of this skill is a sense of being focused on what is important – in your movie or in your wider career. This means that you need not be fixed or rigid in many aspects of your work because you have 'ring-fenced' the most essential, core aspect. You have determined what is not negotiable – perhaps a certain theme or idea that the film revolves around – and so you then have a sense of proportion about everything else. It's a kind of 'Blue Suede Shoes' moment, when almost everything can be stepped on – or changed – except the most precious central idea to the movie. An actor may have to be replaced, a location suddenly changed, a scene reshot or even mid-production rewrites of the script – in fact, anything except the key idea that drives your movie. While making *The Shining* in 1980, Kubrick famously rewrote almost every day, eventually having to colour code different versions to clarify which was which. In this case, as in yours, the aim was to boil down the script to its most essential parts, filtering out what he saw as the periphery in the original King book.

Mantra:

'Everything is up for grabs except this scene here.'

Persistence

One common misconception about the low-budget sector – including shorts, music videos, multimedia work and so on – is that only the good stuff rises upwards into more mainstream sectors. It may seem obvious to think that because your film did not get into a festival it was because it was not good enough or that if you did not get funding from a recent public arts scheme it was because you had a lousy script. To get a more realistic view, we need to see that on the opposing side to the director is an essentially entertainment-based industry who see the films they want to and not necessarily the ones that are best.

Caught in the middle are the organizers and programmers of festivals, TV schedules and screenings, and the holders of funding budgets, who tread a fine line between the two sides. Their decisions about whether to accept your movie for this or that event are based on what is good for the event as much as what is good in critical terms. So if in a festival there are programmed lots of politically related shorts, then a few comedies or polymedia works should redress audience balance. Likewise, if a large number of documentaries are being booked, more fictional work might be needed. As one festival organizer said, 'What do people like to watch? They want to laugh – and see something that pushes the envelope a little.'

A filmmaker who sends off a tape may be disappointed by repeated rejections, but if you cast a wide net and keep sending tapes to events then you are likely to find an audience for your movie. Even if ten festivals wanted your movie, less than that number may be able to programme it within a balanced schedule.

Persistence is as essential at this micro-level of day-to-day work as it is on a broader scale of your overall plan. Allow yourself multiple chances and repeated shots at your targets. If rejection comes your way repeatedly, don't interpret this as a sign of anything to do with the quality of the movie – however tempting. Probably the only people who should be able to convince you that what you have made is not right will be those who have supported you at other times – the filmmakers you share ideas and screenings with.

Mantra:

'The harder I practise, the luckier I get.'

Gary Player, golfer

Good organization

Artistic people are chaotic – allegedly. It goes with the image of the creative genius to be unable to sort out the minutiae of life – the bits of paper and the deadlines – because the demands of great thoughts get in the way. Ironically, given its almost innate distrust of maverick genius, it is Hollywood that has done most to foster this view of the artist in movies such as *Lust for Life* (Vincente Minnelli, 1956), *The Agony and the Ecstasy* (Carol Reed, 1965), *Shine* (Scott Hicks, 1996) and *Amadeus* (Milos Forman, 1984).

For filmmakers the real picture couldn't be more different. Filmmakers tend to possess more organizational power than most artists, requiring a whole raft of conditions before they can begin work, as opposed to the needs of writers or painters. Few art forms are as dependent on technology and on collaboration with other people as this. As a result, after making only a couple of shorts, most filmmakers tend to possess the kinds of organizational skills that could evacuate a town, stage a coup or set up a presidential inauguration (a filmmaker would probably be the first to figure out that it is easier to do the first and then the second during the third).

In practice, being organized means foresight, thinking in advance about what you want to happen. The level of your organizational skills determines how flexible and adaptable you can be should your plans not go as you would like. Intense planning can, in fact, enable greater freedom and spontaneity. The producer of *Before Sunset* (Richard Linklater, 2004), Anne Walker-McBay, remarked that given the size of any production, even a moderate budget movie, they needed a strong plan in order to allow themselves the freedom to improvise. In other words, with the safety net of every eventuality covered and every possible need foreseen, the director was able to try out new ideas on set and go with ideas from the collaborating actors.

Good organization means covering all bases, looking at possibilities rather than just what should happen. If flexibility is being able to respond to sudden change, organization is about having several plans up your sleeve to help you know how to respond. It's about having a plan for every part of the production, which everyone knows about, but which is backed up with a plan B and even a plan C.

Mantra:

'If you think you are overdoing the preparation, you've probably got it right.'

Work discipline

This hardly needs emphasizing because any filmmaker – or artist – who feels deeply about a project is going to do just about whatever it takes to complete it. Obstacles and hiccups, diversions and hold-ups only serve to increase their determination. It is a common trait of many successful filmmakers at low-budget level that work is not seen as something separate from their lives. Work spills over into nights, weekends and holidays, and to many there are no off-duty moments. But crucially the filmmakers themselves don't mind. Work isn't just a day job, it is a necessity. On a semi-serious note, the frequency with which the term 'my baby' is used when filmmakers talk about a project suggests a parallel to parenthood, where care of the infant is not questioned even when the days and nights are long.

From another point of view, it is useful to look at what is happening when you feel that you are not working hard. If you know that you are not putting in the necessary hours but just can't figure out why, it may be worth considering whether this is the right project at all (the parallel with parenting ends here, incidentally). Don't make any sudden decisions, but there may be benefit from putting a project to the side for a while, leaving you to concentrate on developing others, and return to it later. Often, though, you just need to drop it. It happens to the best directors too. Terrence Malick famously ditched his biopic of Che Guevara in 2004 to work on his own version of the Pocahontas story, leaving his lawyers to pick up the pieces, although no specific contract or legal small print had been broken.

Mantra:

'Pain is just another opinion.'

From A Man Called Horse *(Elliot Silverstein, 1970)*

Self-awareness

Self-awareness could be defined as having a realistic knowledge of who you are, in terms of what you are good at, where your strengths and weaknesses lie, and how you tend to work. In a sense, if your career plan is like a path, then this skill is like the global positioning system that helps you along the way.

To get a good picture of what your strengths and weaknesses are, make a list that brings together technical, artistic and other aspects to your work. Include ideas such as lacking confidence with editing or the characters you devise in your films. There will be some ideas that some call strengths and others weaknesses, such as being obstinate or stubborn.

Following on from this exercise, also take a look at the obstacles and opportunities – what might be termed respectively the 'shut doors' and the 'open doors' – of the last year or so and ask how you have responded to these. Do you leap into opportunities? Do you stall at the first hurdle? How you dealt with problems and chances is valuable knowledge.

Mantra:

'Know yourself.'

From the temple of the oracle of Apollo

Teamwork and people skills

In today's multi-skilled workplace our expectations about how we should behave to each other have changed a lot. Even a shop assistant is now given voice coaching on how to answer the phone and we expect high levels of interpersonal skills from just about everyone we meet. This new protocol, however, is not the whole story when it comes to how we work with each other; being able to lead a team or collaborate means going beyond this.

The low-budget sector is a highly networked one, where personal contact and relationships are the main ways of establishing deals and taking opportunities. Skins are certainly tough but in this sector, where the main currency is shared respect and mutual assistance, your credit will quickly become low if you don't reciprocate. These skills include: listening; not judging without proof (ignore gossip); involving and valuing people; aiming for consensus (but knowing how to make firm decisions without alienating people); returning favours and calls; taking criticism; and keeping people you work with 'in the loop', or aware of what's going on. No one can fulfil all of these aims all the time, but if you just add 'being able to say sorry' to the list you should have all bases covered.

Equally important is knowing when to unleash the filmmaker's most devastating tool – the ego. Every artist has an ego, but when you only have paint palettes or typewriters around you it doesn't matter too much about keeping it at bay. Successful filmmakers at every level of the industry tend to be successful collaborators (Mike Leigh, the Coen brothers, Steven Soderbergh, Richard Linklater, for example) and yet they are driven by their creative desires as much as those directors whose tantrums are their hallmark (for instance, Ridley Scott or David O. Russell), and probably get more Christmas cards from former colleagues. In the low-budget sector, we have seen how it is the norm to have people working for free on your set and so it makes it even more necessary to rein in the ego slightly. A useful strategy is to allow the development stage of a movie as the arena for the ego, where you can play and experiment with what you personally want to do. By the production stage you can rein it in a little, as your ideas meet reality. The editing stage can be a time once more to let the creative demands of your ego run freely again.

Mantra:

'Slowly, slowly catchee monkey' [or tread softly and you get what you want].

Professionalism

One of the most striking aspects of the low-budget film community is the degree to which filmmakers refuse to act like the poorer cousin of the mainstream industry. Their main weapon in this is their professionalism – a manner of doing business that is thorough, realistic and efficient. It is the maintaining of high standards and high aims in day-to-day work and in all dealings with the people you work with.

Filmmakers adopt ways of working which are consistent with any level of the industry, while the aims they have belie the budgets they work within. Every day there are film productions going on with funding budgets of less than a family's weekly food bill. And yet a visit to these sets would show a production of anything but low expectations. There are quality cameras, rigorous plans, rehearsed actors, and all in a safety-aware set. In short, despite every financial obstacle, filmmakers find a way to live up to their high expectations.

Mantra:

'Start as you mean to go on.'

4. Three stages of a career

For many filmmakers there are stages through which they travel as they become more confident and financially secure. Although this is a simplistic model, it is worth pinning down the stages that you are likely to go through in achieving your aims of being entirely self-sufficient working in some aspect of the film industry. It is a whole lot more gradual than it appears here, but there are certainly incremental steps that occur as you move on. If you label these as they are described below, then you may feel some satisfaction as you see your working life change and you visibly move to another level.

Stage 1: Expansion and investigation

How do you know you have started? When are you actually a filmmaker? It is certainly not like a job where you turn up one day and soon are employee of the month. Many filmmakers have been making moving images in some form since their early teens, while others were writers or actors and then directors. Artistically, you have probably been a filmmaker since your first VHS movie at high school, but in terms of a career, we could tag the date as when you began making plans to become self-employed, to live as a filmmaker.

The first year in this new unpaid job will be the one where your reserves of optimism and positivity are in demand. Sometimes it may be hard to motivate yourself, but it will not actually be the most exhausting – that comes later. This stage consists of a wide-ranging move to make contacts and establish relationships with other people in your position. You investigate every opportunity and collect phone numbers and email addresses. This is a time of trying out every possible way to get films made and get them seen. No avenue is too small for you to try, no competition too local or too small.

Trying anything

You may have no preconceived ideas yet of who you are or what you are good at, preferring to try and fail or succeed to find out where your strengths lie. You volunteer for small productions for friends, try editing, dubbing, recording your own music, try out filmmaking styles and discard them the next day. Failure becomes as much a part of life as success and you learn to enjoy the thrill of not knowing whether you can do something.

You may be working on lots of projects simultaneously and you know that several won't make it beyond the ideas stage. Your projects range from the sort of film you always wanted to make to the ones you would not imagine ever making, but you might find that it's the latter that stimulates you more, boosting your confidence as you complete them.

As well as making contacts, chasing dead ends with opportunities that don't materialize, making films you like and those you don't, you may be considering ways to earn money from all this activity. Is it possible to cut down the day job and do more filmmaking? Is there some skill related to filmmaking that can take over the day job? As your confidence grows and you encounter more people who earn an income from some aspect of the film industry, you start to see the possibilities for devising your own route. With your frantic networking and chasing opportunities, you have been slowly laying down the roots of your career in the film industry, but it is yet to be seen what form the outcome will take. The only obstacle will occur if you try to limit your horizons and focus too much on one kind of opportunity. To stretch the analogy further, roots tend to be far broader and wider than whatever they support. So, try to experience everything and assume that unless you have tried it, there is the possibility that you can succeed in it – whether this is writing, camera work, editing, producing, designing or managing a production.

Stage 2: Focusing and defining

After the first, chaotic year, the next stage is more reflective. This doesn't mean you slow down or become less ambitious. It means that you decide which projects are worth your attention and which are not. You start to adopt a more sceptical, stealthy approach as you try to steer your career for the first time, rather than just hitching a ride with it as in the first stage.

In terms of work, this stage can become the most exhausting, as the stakes are raised in every job you do – whether in productions for other people or for yourself. Everything seems more precious now – the kind of work you do, how you do it and what you do with it. But at the same time you start to get pulled in two directions as the need to earn a steady income doesn't go away and yet the days seem shorter. How do you

Figure 9.3 Polymedia group Raya travel the world performing their VJ sets, pictured here in Taipei in 2004.

fit it all in? Most of the time you don't. In fact, it becomes a hallmark of this stage that overload seems to be your main characteristic of your daily work. But you start to notice more the occasional hits among lots more misses – becoming far more optimistic in the face of rejection and obstacles. The difference at this stage is that last year's jobs were easy come easy go, but this year it all matters so much more, so you are at once protective and fiercely defending of your projects.

Evaluating Stage 1

In this stage the key is to tease out the successful elements from Stage 1 and embed them in this stage. Try, without any preconceived ideas about who you are, to figure out what people liked and what you did well in the first stage. Through quiet, reflective evaluation you can trawl through the good and bad moments of the first stage and try to find out the people who helped you, the movies you made that people liked, the parts of those movies that people really liked (the camera work, the editing, the stories), the technical stuff you found easy. In doing all this you are looking for threads that you can tie together. For instance, look for similar elements in your work, similar comments people have made or more than one good reception at a particular screening or network gathering.

> **Interview**
> 'Doing this job is very tiring, and frustrating, and even when you are 110 per cent dedicated to it like myself, it will not necessarily happen quickly. But when I do get to do a video, that's when it all seems worth it – the satisfaction of creating something original is unbelievable. I am immensely proud of my work, and the only downside is not being able to do more. But hopefully that will all change, because after all this hard work, sweat, blood and tears, there is no way I am giving up. You have to persevere after all – if everything happened so easily, there would be no excitement in it.'
>
> *Lee Barmsey, music video director, London*

Any two instances or more of any positive aspect in the first stage should be noted as a strength. These you can forge on with in this second stage. You may also want to discard certain successful elements because you want more challenges and feel you have investigated something as far as you can. This is positive too, since they can be noted as successes and possibly returned to in later years.

Financially, this period may see some return – though modest. You may sell a short movie, but this is rare. The purpose of the short, after all, is as a calling card leading to other steps forward. But you may find that freelance work for other people's productions is now paid rather than deferred (i.e. unpaid). You may also find that a wider use of the skills gleaned from filmmaking, including associated ones such as web design or training, start to replace the income from manual day jobs such as waiting. As we have seen in the case studies, there may be times when you get concerned that these peripheral skills might take over your creative life. This itself will be good practice, however, for learning how to steer your career rather than being led by it.

This period, then, is one of transition, one of looking backwards and forwards – backwards as you take account of successes and forwards as you focus on where to spend your energies.

Stage 3: Sustainability

This final stage in the development plan is where you establish ways of working that are sustainable, in an environment that supports you financially but also nourishes you artistically. Certainly, there will be many times when you feel anything but nourished, but this stage is not about the day to day, it is about setting up a long-term plan that carries you forwards.

The aim is to have enough financial return from the wider skills you have from filmmaking and enough time to make your creative projects. If you can focus on these aims then it is likely that you will feel successful. But if you start to measure success in terms of rising stardom and bigger cash reward, it is just as likely that you will feel a failure.

Getting a method

The filmmakers who reach this level of sustainability tend to possess many of the qualities described earlier in this chapter, including flexibility, good self-organization, professionalism and a strong sense of identity. Let's clarify how this impacts on your movies. It doesn't mean that you become closed to new artistic challenges nor that your films are any less original than at earlier stages of your career. Artistically, you are still the live wire you were, and in fact you now have greater courage because trying new ideas is harder when you have had some success in old ones. It is instead your working methods that become fixed in a sustaining pattern.

Where next?

This third level is not the final stage, it is more like the end of the beginning and the start of the pattern that can help you to flourish. From here you may move onto more specific routes – types of movies or themes, for instance – that have their own stages involved. But each of these routes will have their own cycle of development, which resembles the overall one described above of: (1) exploration, (2) focusing and (3) sustainability.

5. The career map

The aim of this map is to relate the common experiences of many successful low-budget filmmakers as they have progressed from first steps to a sustainable career. What is most apparent from the many interviews that have built up this picture is that there is no single route guaranteed to bring success; most filmmakers have followed opportunities and taken chances, and in doing so have ended up in a strong position. But the overall picture is that there are smaller routes you can enter that tend to lead towards the same end, like tributaries of a river.

The reason this information is laid out as a chart is precisely because there is no single route, just lots of mini-paths that lead to the same point. It is more appropriate, then, to describe these in a form that shows how they parallel each other, cross over other paths, converge in places and branch off into other smaller diversions.

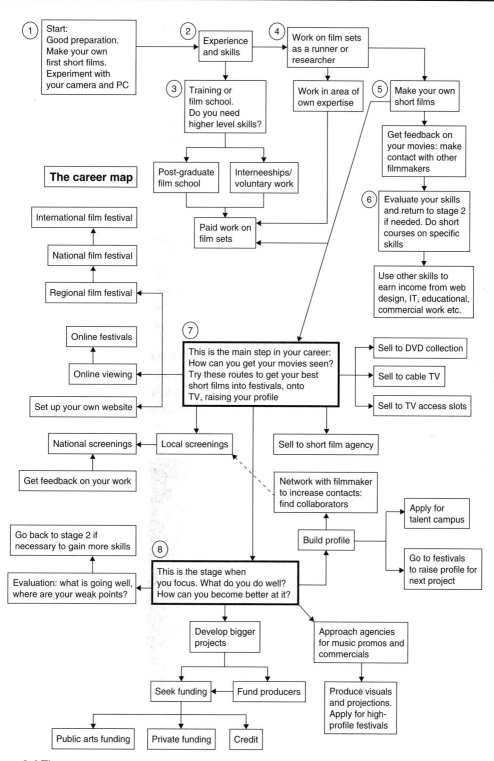

Figure 9.4 The career map.

The advantage of seeing this kind of map is that it allows you to identify certain points as being valuable, that what looks like a dead end is in fact a useful stage. The idea of making a sustainable career in films may seem daunting and unreal when you are at the outset, but seeing it 'from above', as it were, enables you to glimpse how to move from place to place, steadily pacing forward. It is indeed a jungle out there and it is easier to get through when viewed from above.

Below is a description of the stages outlined in the map.

Preparation

What it is

This is concerned with laying the groundwork for future moves. At this stage you are making your first short movies, investigating what your tools can do, picking up the basic skills in shooting and editing. You will aim to make lots of mistakes here, developing the first ideas of what sort of films you like and what you want to make.

What to do

- Make movies quickly and often.
- Go through the checklist of what you need to be and know (see Chapters 9:2 and 9:3).
- Examine what sort of movies you like to make.

Get experience and skills

What it is

This stage is all about equipping yourself with skills and experience, to give you the facilities to become more independent. You are experimenting with many kinds of films, trying styles and discarding them, and trying to figure out what form your particular voice will take: will it be documentary, multimedia work, drama or other forms? You are now ready to start Stage 1 of the three stages outlined in Chapter 9:4.

What to do

- Work on other people's projects and learn what you can in situ.
- Make shorts from the projects in this book.
- Sign up for courses in specific skill areas. Don't look for long-term academy-style courses just yet. Aim for short courses that last a few days in camera skills, editing, scripting and so on.

Film school

What it is

Not all filmmakers go to film school and there is a perennial debate in the filmmaking community as to the merits of long courses. The majority who have completed courses describe its benefits, but there are equal numbers who did not do film courses and who still go on to make films that people want to see. Some courses repeat a tired, out-of-date curriculum, and do not prepare students for the contemporary film industry. But the vast majority do have something to offer the aspiring filmmaker.

Figure 9.5 Central St Martin's College, London, has produced some of the most innovative music promo directors in recent years.

What to do

- Think about whether film school is right for you now. Are you trying to put off having to deal with the film industry proper? Or are you clearly in need of more development before you branch out alone?
- Check whether the film course is the right one. Visit institutions and see what kinds of work the students do, how often they see their professors, how well equipped the campus is. Find out about industry links and whether students get interneeships or placements in companies. Most of all, check the costs – hidden as well as upfront.
- Consider a postgraduate or master's course if you already have a degree. Many film schools do not insist on a film degree to get onto a master's film course. It is common to study English, for instance, as an undergraduate and then practical film at a higher level.

Interview

'I studied at art school for a year, then went to film school for three years and for some people that's great, but I think for others just studying movies and listening to director's commentaries on DVD, reading books and making little films on video can be as good. I think you can learn a lot from books like Robert Rodriguez's *Rebel Without A Crew*, but I also think that if you're writing dialogue it's crucial to understand something about structure and you should read at least one book like *Screenplay* by Syd Field. Then once you've learned the basics you're in a good position to throw that stuff away.'

Colin Spector, filmmaker, UK

Crew member: runner/researcher

What it is

At this point you are in the thick of Stage 1 in the three-step plan in Chapter 9:4. You may already have experience of low-budget productions and now you want to gain experience at a higher level. You start to move on from films made by friends and peers into applying for positions in larger, funded productions further afield. The pressure will be greater and you won't get paid at first, but soon the paid positions will trickle in.

This may be a stage that has great potential. In the map this area branches off into a route of its own, enabling you to work in parallel with boxes 5 and 6 in Figure 9.4, where you are actively making your own films. Increasingly, you may then get jobs on films that are more within your own area of expertise, the result of skills you have built up over the last period of study in boxes 2 and 3. You may also find that you build up contacts widely through your work on these productions, and are more able to recruit reliable crew for your own projects.

What to do

- Subscribe to filmmaker bulletin boards and news sites.
- Prepare a c.v. or résumé.
- Make a showreel of your work and have copies ready to send to productions.
- Apply for many jobs, expecting most to be unsuccessful.

Making your own films

What it is

This area is the reason why all the other routes are being pursued so hotly. You are seeking contacts, money, skills and opportunities so that your own films can have a better and longer life. This area forms the backbone of the map from now on. You now have the tools to make films that you actually want people to see.

At this point you are entering the second stage of the three-step plan in Chapter 9:4. You are starting to be more careful about what jobs you take – including those on other people's productions in box 4 of Figure 9.4.

What to do

- Keep revisiting Stage 2 to refresh and update your skills. Attend short courses and one-off events. Find out what is going on in the industry more closely and identify the opportunities that are right for you.

Figure 9.6 Filmmakers at the Berlin Talent Campus attend a series of workshops in Berlin parallel to the film festival, giving a boost to the careers of the participants.

Figure 9.7 Berlin Talent Campus 2004.

- Although you have been making films throughout this whole map, it is only the ones you make now that are going to get exposure.
- Enhance your knowledge of the industry, so that you are more aware of opportunities. Also keep your ear to the ground with broader social and political events to give your films greater depth. See Chapter 9:2 for more on this area.

Get feedback constantly

What it is

This is an integral part of your career plan and is going to become a constant companion route through every stage you enter from now on. Your films now deserve a greater exposure and in the next box you will be finding ways to do that. But right now you need to find out what your films are like before everyone else tells you. This involves getting a network of people whose views you trust to help you evaluate your work. All this feeds into your work as you move through the creative cycle of filmmaking to evaluating, taking on board new skills or ideas and then back to filmmaking again. Your peers and colleagues are crucial to the process of evaluation.

This process is not, however, like running focus groups, where cross-sections of an audience can influence a film before it is completed. Instead you are seeking constructive views on what you have done, like holding up a mirror to your work. Being at the centre of the creative process offers the worst possible vantage point for viewing it objectively.

What to do

- Build links with other filmmakers, via screenings, local film groups and productions.
- Offer feedback to your colleagues, suggesting constructive proposals rather than generalizations – expect your peers to do the same with you.
- Don't be shy about your work – spread the word about your new screening and hire a cinema or arts centre to show it.
- Evaluate carefully what people say about your films. If responses are negative, albeit nicely worded, look at every aspect of the film. Weigh up whether you agree with their ideas. If you reject advice, that's fine too – the process of evaluating has simply reinforced what you thought so you are stronger in your opinions now.

Get your film seen

What it is

This box represents a process that may occupy you for some time, as you investigate outlets for your movies. In terms of the three-stage plan in Chapter 9:4, you are somewhere near the end of Stage 2 right now, having moved on from the frantic period of investigation and expansion into the more focused period where you concentrate on making better films and getting the right opportunities. In Chapter 9:8, which looks at the full range of options for getting your work seen, you can take a longer look at each possible route and figure out which one looks right for your movie.

Some individual routes in this area branch off to more specialized areas – for instance, in online viewing sites. In these cases, let your film move as far forward as it can, even if it was not quite the route you had in mind originally. Let the film find its audience. For instance, if your film has a slightly futuristic tone you may find sci-fi cable channels want to show it, which could lead to sci-fi festival showings, even if you had not envisaged being a part of this genre.

Interview

'To make a film you need passion and perseverance. You need the passion to get out there and get the film made in the first place, and then the perseverance to get it out into the world. You may find that this is the longer of the two processes (depending on how much time you have been developing the idea and finding the money). Once you have finished your film, you need to devote a year to getting it into festivals, as festivals usually regard a new film as one that has been completed in the previous 12 months or two years. Start with big festivals and work down. Someone somewhere will screen your film, but as I say, you have to keep going. It took me a year to get my first feature, *Mystery Play*, accepted by a festival.'

Sean Martin, filmmaker, London

What to do

- Use the chapter on getting your film seen.
- Prioritize which outlets you go for. If you want to sell through DVD or get a limited theatrical release (for features), don't put the film out into the public arena on the web or on TV.
- For multimedia work (VJ-ing, for instance) try clubs and party organizers first.
- For music video directors, apply to smaller labels more willing to take a chance on you. Also contact agencies who represent promo directors. See Chapter 9:8 for more details.
- Decide whether you want sales or exposure (shorts are more like calling cards rather than money-spinners).

More ambitious projects

What it is

At this stage you have had some success with showing your films at local and national screenings. You may even have had your work selected for compilation DVDs by music video or short film organizations (Onedotzero or Resfest). You have had your share of rejections and have found which outlets are more open to your particular work. Your list of contacts is large and you have many opportunities to find out what other directors make and what they think of you. Your confidence is high and you know exactly where your strengths lie. At the same time you are now restless for the next challenge and start to seek out more ambitious projects.

You may also be working on projects which support you financially, as a crew member in other productions or using your skills in other ways: you may be involved in training or education in film or video, or making commercial films for corporate clients or advertising firms. You are now entering the more sustainable period of your career, as you have the support to let you make your films, feedback from peers, a knowledge of the industry, and have a strong sense of your own identity. Now is just the time to challenge it all in new and more daring projects.

What to do

- Check your showreel, résumé and promotional tools (DVD, website and so on).
- Investigate more specialized and higher level sources of funding from public and private sources.
- Look for creative ways of getting support – for instance, in borrowing cameras and equipment.
- Develop a sustainable cycle of working where you overlap post-production on your last project as you plan and prepare the next.
- Into this cycle you can now incorporate a new element of promotion, where you maintain your links with the more successful routes you identified in the last box. So if a certain festival liked your work, keep up to date with their next submission deadline.
- Visit more film festivals and start to seek out how your larger projects could be funded and displayed.

6. Career troubleshooting

In this section we are going to look at the most common problems filmmakers find when they feel that their career is not going forwards. Like those irritating troubleshooting guides in software manuals, the exact question you want may not be here, but the general issues covered below may apply to most questions. The ones selected are often the most frequently heard by film professors and help bulletins.

Problem: My career has stalled

Many filmmakers find themselves far from where they actually want to be for protracted periods. It seems like some wind has blown them off course and they start to question what they are achieving. Each project becomes a chore and frustration and disillusionment set in.

Solution

Slow down for a while. Although it may seem as if you have stopped moving in any direction, it is often at times like this that people tend to thrash around in desperation trying to hitch onto any passing object that will take them forwards.

- Take a long look at the path you are on and figure out how far you are from where you wanted to be. Have you in fact arrived somewhere else, but don't recognize it yet? For example, you may have yet to make a short film you like, but have successfully written scripts for other filmmakers.
- Look at the three stages outlined in Chapter 9:4 regarding career development. Have you opted out of Stage 1 early, with the result that you are trying to focus and narrow your sights before you have actually investigated more possible avenues?
- Try hyping up your milestones more often. Take a look at what you have achieved and mark them in some way. For instance, you may have completed short films but let them slip into a life on the

shelf without showing them around. Arrange a screening of your work for other filmmakers and friends and make a big deal out of it.

- Take a more long-term view. You are in the middle of a blip, a temporary downturn which will pass. Take this period as a chance to reflect on and evaluate what you have achieved so far. Use the time positively and you will start to see it as a necessary period in a creative life.

Problem: I don't like anything I make

It is healthy to have a certain level of inbuilt self-criticism regarding your work. You should subject it to a rigorous set of criteria that you alone have devised. In this way your movies will gradually evolve. But for many filmmakers this goes too far and starts to interfere with the creative process rather than nurture it. For some, the thought of watching their own movie brings on something near to depression as they see only the negative aspects of it. The signs of this self-criticism become more apparent when the movie needs its maker to push it out into the world and find an audience, but instead gets disowned and then shelved. Part of this problem stems from the long production life most films take. From ideas through to shooting to editing and promotion can take one or two years.

Solution

- Give yourself a break. You are probably making the mistake of applying your current standards to past projects. Accept as a given that you are partially going to dislike any film you make after a certain time has elapsed. The important idea to remember when viewing past work is to try to tap into what stage you were at when you made it. OK, you might make it more subtly now, or edit differently, or use better lighting, but try to value what you did then and see any film you make after it as being a descendant rather than an orphan.
- If you find yourself being too critical of your work, make a list of what is negative about it but try to balance it with a list of equal length of the positive aspects of it. If necessary, give the film to friends or show it at screenings. Other filmmakers tend often to be complimentary at local screenings because they know what it means to you.

Problem: I keep abandoning movies halfway through

Filmmaking can be fast and furious at times, slow and relentless at others. Keeping enthusiasm constant in the dry season of hold-ups and obstacles is not easy. Many filmmakers find that it is easier to start another project rather than persevere with the one that is causing all the problems. It is common, then, to find more projects in 'development hell' than in completion, though this is no more true than in the mainstream film industry. But this can be dispiriting and leads to frustration and inertia. You lose out on the most rewarding moment when the film finds an audience, even if it is just in a local screening.

Solution

- Have a look at where you enjoy working most: is it in the development stage before you commit to anything? If this is you then perhaps you enjoy generating ideas and working on scripts rather than shooting. Is it time to refocus the work you do and start to get work as a scriptwriter?

- Do you find it invigorating when you are flying by the seat of your pants – working late and hard – but come crashing down to earth the next day and have little enthusiasm to finish the job? All art forms attract their share of creative binge-workers, who fast in a creative desert for long periods and then change into workaholics overnight. Their energies are used up quickly and they approach burn-out with relief. If this is you, try to spot the pattern emerging and place obstacles in its way. For instance, arrange meetings weeks in advance so that you are committing yourself to an aspect of the project. Try using a wall-planner to pinpoint the places when you tend to crash down and plot a course where you slow your work rate down immediately prior to it.
- Are you over-planning? Perhaps you are taking the life out of later stages in your production by planning excessively, so that there appear to be no chances or opportunities arising. Try to spend your energies developing the content of the film rather than the exact way you intend to show it. Leave deliberate open areas in the production where you have not planned certain scenes but rely on collaboration instead. Allow whole areas of the film to change dramatically or even to be taken out, even when you are in the middle of filming.
- Are you clear about the central theme in the movie? Many unfinished films tend to have experienced a pulling apart of the main ideas in it at some point, usually during shooting. This means you have divergent ideas forming about what you are trying to say and can't settle on one particular theme to dominate. If you feel you don't know what your film is about any more, try talking it over with trusted crew or friends (don't announce it openly as you may freak people out). Show them what you planned and let them reflect back to you what your initial aims were.

Problem: I haven't got all the skills I need

Filmmaking can be seen as a highly skill-centred art form. The different levels of making a movie include as diverse a range of skills as any job, requiring drawing, budget management, writing, team-work, camera work, editing, as well as others to do with marketing. It is also true that there is a big industry out there that offers shortcuts to getting these skills, in the form of short courses and work-shops. Lots of people want you to part with thousands of dollars so they can make you into a director. Anyone looking at the filmmaking magazines would quickly become less than confident about their skills when they see so many courses on offer.

But try looking at this from another angle. Just about every filmmaker interviewed for this book offered the same piece of advice for emerging filmmakers, which was to make films regardless of what you know or don't know. 'Just do it' was the common phrase. Each of these people are skilled but none believed that it was these skills that helped them get where they are, believing it was more to do with personal qualities such as persistence and hard work.

Solution

- You don't need to know everything about filmmaking. Read a few books, make a few films and you will quickly know what you need.
- When you are ready for the next level of skills, you will know it. Wait until you become frustrated by your lack of knowledge. Wait until it is necessary for you to know about compression ratios or sampling rates.

- Put more work into your imagination and ideas than into your technical skills.
- Know the basics about making films and ask other people for more help.
- Know your strengths – maybe you will never be good at a certain aspect of filmmaking and need to work with other people. They probably need your help because you have something they want too.

Problem: I can't get jobs

As an industry, filmmaking is notoriously overstaffed. It is dispiriting to consider just how many people want to become filmmakers and how many want to get into films at any level. For someone wanting to break into the industry it can be difficult to get jobs in film, even at the lowest of levels – for instance, on productions as runners. Many productions are aware of the number of people who want to be interns or take paid jobs and interview widely for these posts. Applications are high. So what can be done to improve your chances?

Solution

- Although the potential workforce for filmmaking is huge, no one has your particular point of view, so it is good to value, before anything else, the unique vision you have. You bring to bear all your experiences, work, hopes and strengths, and are unlike any other filmmaker.
- Try to value what you have that makes you different. Look at what other people see as your strengths and ply these, applying for jobs that address what you know you are good at, not necessarily what you think you want to do.
- Apply for many jobs. Expect a success rate of perhaps only 1:30.
- Be organized, persistent and professional. But back off straight away if you sense you are being too persistent. Take a break and come back for the next job.
- Look at your promotional package – the résumé, business card, covering letter – and ask yourself and friends to be brutally honest about whether any element looks wrong.
- Above all, keep yourself buoyant by putting your energies into more than one area. So if you are applying for jobs, also try to have your own project at the same time.
- Keep your own circle of networking going – many jobs are already filled by contacts before they are advertised.

Part 2: How do I get there?

7. Where to get your movies seen

In this section we will look at the range of outlets where you can get your movies seen by an audience. In the section on distribution (Chapter 9:8) we identify which are the main routes to selling films and how to access some of these.

Distribution routes: where you can show your movie

- Terrestrial national broadcast television
- Terrestrial local broadcast television
- Cable television
- Satellite television
- Internet
- Cell phones and small content providers
- DVD.

No single potential market alone is likely to bring any significant return for your movie, but a combination of several of these will be the best possible way of getting what you can for your film. But there is a hierarchy regarding which you need to approach first. Some outlets won't buy your movie if it has been shown elsewhere, so you need to pick your first distribution point carefully. For instance, if you sell it to a cable channel, a DVD sale would be flawed since it is already in the public domain.

Terrestrial television: local and national

While feature films are more suited to theatrical release, the short film succeeds more often on the small screen. Broadcasters are showing more short movies than they ever have, the number of accessible slots growing steadily in many countries. In the USA, there are several venues which may show your movie, but for the most part these are in local stations. At the top of the league in terms of prestige and audience numbers is PBS, in the United States. They run a slot for documentaries (*POV*) and another for both fiction and documentary (*Independent Lens*). PBS provide fees for films they show and the exposure you would receive is a great confidence boost.

Did you know?
PBS (Public Broadcasting Service) is a private, non-profit corporation operating 349 non-commercial television stations across the United States. To Americans, PBS offers a respite from relentless ratings-led entertainment shows on commercial stations and instead focuses on educational, arts and community programming. Available to 99 per cent of American homes with televisions, PBS serves nearly 100 million people each week.

Local PBS stations offer other slots for shorts, including:

- *Reel New York* on WNET 13 New York. See http://www.thirteen.org/reelnewyork7/
- *Image Union* on WTTW Chicago. See http://www.wttw.com/
- *POV* on KPBS San Diego. See http://www.pbs.org/pov/

Acquisition fees for these local stations are low compared to what you could receive with larger broadcasters, although they are often up to $100 per minute.

In Britain, Channel Four's *The Shooting Gallery* acquires films directly from the filmmaker and may also offer considerable back-up in completion costs. Submission to this and other slots is straightforward but highly competitive and can be accessed through their websites. If you encounter a slot that asks for payment before viewing your film, think again. Most slots are free, or even pay you a small fee on transmission.

Possible success: 6/10
Possible return: 8/10

Weblink
http://www.channel4.com/film/ Dedicated film page for Channel Four and its cable sister channel, Film Four.

Cable television and satellite

In cable television, there are more specialist programmes offering the chance to show your work, but to a far smaller audience. For documentaries, HBO/Cinemax run the *Undercover* and *Reel Life* series, which pay the filmmaker far above the usual rate and 'place you alongside a very eclectic and interesting group of documentaries' (Greg Pak, filmmaker). The prestigious film festival Sundance is also involved in broadcasting and its channel, The Sundance Channel, buys short films from unknown directors. Acquisition fees are up to $2000, but although prestige is high, actual audience share is low. A similarly discerning and prestigious cable channel, The Independent Film Channel, is also a good agency to submit to.

Weblinks
http://www.hbo.com/docs/americaundercover/ Documentary strand on US network.
www.sundancechannel.com Features and shorts news.
www.ifctv.com Strong support for short films alongside established names.

Before submitting a film to a broadcaster, make a few decisions first about the kind of 'return' you want. You need to decide which has priority: prestige, audience numbers or pay. If it is audience numbers you are after, national television is the route, while prestige and good acquisition rates are sometimes to be found in the same area. A good rule to follow whichever route you intend to follow is to start with the biggest, most well-known, highest-paying stations and then work down. Many of the larger slots prefer it if your film has not first been seen by local audiences, though this will not automatically preclude you from selection.

Possible success: 8/10
Possible return: 5/10

Educational

A further market, though considerably smaller than those looked at so far, is educational sales. This may include university courses and community groups, who may be particularly disposed toward your film through subject matter. You could attend screenings as part of a discussion or lecture. A film dealing with racism, for example, could bring DVD sales on campuses and communities where this is an issue. Another dealing with industrial relations could arouse interest from union groups. However, this market is not easy to engage with as its buyers will probably not be a part of the usual buying/selling community at film festivals, although a distributor may have appropriate contacts.

Possible success: 1/10
Possible return: 2/10

Internet distribution

The number of sites offering to show your movies has increased in line with the comparative ease with which video can be downloaded on the web. This route can offer some very strong audience figures, outstripping that which can be achieved in a theatrical release, and some sites have developed enough of a profile to lend considerable kudos to the offer of a showing.

Broadcast sites vary widely, from those at the top of the scale offering payment and the chance to place your résumé and contact details to those offering no fee, some of whom are online only intermittently. In the short time that webfilm has been a possibility, a handful of sites have come to dominate the field, but this is not to say that smaller sites have nothing to offer.

Jess Search, co-founder of Shooting People, a widely used site for filmmakers in Britain and New York, believes broadcasting on such sites is becoming more important to filmmakers:

> 'It will only increase in importance as a distribution medium as quality improves and it does remain an easier way to refer people to your work than sending out tapes. Ifilm and Atom have a certain kudos – a bit like being accepted for London/Edinburgh/Berlin Film Festivals – and it certainly helps to say your film is on their site rather than just your own site, just as it helps to be shown at a festival rather than your own screening in encouraging busy industry people to take the time to look. There are still huge limitations to web viewing to be sure (the things that work best have been shot for web), not too much movement, music sequences (music videos work well) and more heavily lit than usual – but the only way is up, especially as broadband becomes more popular.'

Weblink
www.shootingpeople.org   London based but now operating a successful New York mailing.

Low return on deals
The larger sites have struck deals with television broadcasters, passing on shorts originally shown on the web, and have supported filmmakers by offering a percentage of advertising revenue according to how many downloads a film generates. The financial return of these deals tends to be very low, but the reviews that viewers post, and the use of such sites as part of a larger promotion plan, makes it a worthwhile option.

Festival links

Some sites are also linking up with festivals to show short films and in return lend sites the credibility that tight festival selection offers. The US festival South by Southwest in 2000 selected ten short films to show on Atom for three months. Although there was no payment to filmmakers in this instance, it has set a precedent that others follow.

Possible success: 9/10
Possible return: 3/10

Weblink
http://2005.sxsw.com/   Also hosting a range of other arts festivals in Texas.

Cell phone movies

Content providers at this level are relatively new and have yet to establish agreed methods or ways of dealing with filmmakers. We could break this area down into two dominant areas: music videos and advertising. These form the bulk of content delivered in this format, but take several different forms. Music videos are often provided through agencies, which house directors who they know can attract contracts for new promos. RSA Blackdog, based in London, or Anonymous Content, based in Los Angeles, between them cover the most prestigious promo directors, including Dougal Wilson, Gore Verbinski and Dominic Leung. Contracts for products often arrive via these agents. If you can get an agency to represent you, then your music promo work should reach a wider audience than before. In some cases, however, a more direct route has been established. In 2003 a major record company awarded the contract for a new promo to a student at film school rather than an established filmmaker, citing the fact that costs would be lower but the film itself would be highly original.

Weblinks
http://www.rsafilms.com/   Ridley Scott Associates home page for several companies, including Black Dog.
www.anonymouscontent.com   Highly regarded media agency.

As for advertising, design houses will assign a contract to a filmmaker after initial pitching of ideas from invited directors. But further down the scale, smaller companies or political movements may commission work from less established filmmakers. Advertising can take the form of a straight ad downloaded to a phone, or in the form of virals, short films of less than 30 seconds to a minute that the recipient receives and then sends on to a friend. These are the ultimate proof of the success of word of mouth and have seen a shift in the kinds of films made for this arena.

Another format gaining popularity for more up-market companies is themed short films, where filmmakers are asked to make a short on a theme connected to a current campaign. The resulting shorts tend to be original and innovative, and most of all rely on soft sell techniques, where the viewer simply associates the product brand with the positive experience of watching the movie.

Possible success: 4/10
Possible return: 7/10

DVD

As we have seen, the potential for this route is huge. It used to be the case that theatrical was the first port of call for anyone seeking to get their film shown, but ancillary markets in DVDs are becoming more dominant. Furthermore, they are becoming a market in their own right rather than simply a tag at the end of a theatrical run. To demonstrate this, there are certain kinds of film that do better on DVD, certain stars who attract more rentals and sales. It is clear that this market has its own taste and is separate to mainstream theatrical tastes. When in 2003 the point was reached when sales of DVDs outstripped ticket sales in theatres, a corner had been turned where cinemas no longer had the lead in distribution. It could be the case that from now on the most successful route for getting all kinds of films seen – features, music videos, multimedia work – is the DVD. The only possible contender to this lead could occur if or when the main studios decide to enter the legal film downloading market, allowing movies to be bought along the lines of Apple's successful iTunes online store.

1. **Self-produced DVD**
   Potential success: 5/10
   Potential return: 1/10

2. **Distributor-produced DVD**
   Potential success: 8/10
   Potential return: 6/10

Tip: how to get ahead in music promo directing in seven steps

It's different for music promo makers. Getting into music promos is not easy and as a career it is not for the faint-hearted. The daily need for eye-catching originality on an ever-reducing budget takes its toll, but also makes a director capable of creating innovation under pressure and on budget – an attractive proposition for feature film companies.

1 Make movies. Make them original, punchy, preferably with a twist at the end (stops MTV cutting it). Work with local bands for free.
2 Try to get jobs with up and coming bands. Contact record labels of emerging bands – be pushy to get a job. Send the showreel and pitch an idea – work for free if you need to at first.
3 When you have a good showreel, send it to the major agencies for some comments.

4 Some record labels at the top end are contracting out videos to complete unknowns, including students, in the hope of reducing costs. Be cheeky – ask Sony and the like to let you make a promo for peanuts.

5 At the same time, make a name for yourself by getting your films seen by the big digital festivals like Onedotzero and Resfest. Send them to Mirrorball (Edinburgh Festival's promo strand) and local and national screenings.

6 Meanwhile, teach yourself the full range of gear, including low-fi effects programmes like Maya and After Effects and stalwart animation software of yesteryear like Auto-CAD. The low-fi look is well liked by some digital festivals.

7 You need a separate career to run next to promos. Visuals for live performances are preferred by some record labels to promos as they target fans directly. Get into VJ-ing and video projections by offering to work in local clubs for free. When you are confident, try pitching for work with big labels – mention your reliability, low costs and stunning visuals.

8. Guide to distribution

What is distribution?

One of the most challenging tasks is to push your film out into the wider world, and it comes when perhaps all your energies are drained by the process of getting the film made in the first place. Distribution – the process of finding someone somewhere to show your movie – is nevertheless a time when you must be prepared to make decisions that affect whether the film has any life beyond your immediate friends and family. The kinds of questions we need to look at in this chapter include: Where can you get your movie seen? What kinds of deals are common? What you can expect to get as a first-time filmmaker and how do deals for short films differ from features, whether for theatrical, DVD, television, phone or the Internet?

Distribution is going to take many forms. Despite the obvious kudos of seeing your film in a cinema, theatrical receipts account for only a small part of the overall gross a film could return.

Distribution today

Over the last few years the industry as a whole has been transformed from a primarily theatrical one to one based much more on home entertainment. The profits of the majority of feature films are derived as much from DVD sales and rental as from cinema tickets. But if you go down a few levels to the low- and medium-budget sectors, the influence of DVD is now huge. Films now bypass the established sales and distribution system because high quality versions – DVD – can be issued cheaply and manufactured as needed. Even very small productions can release films onto the market and expect some return. For others, the return from DVD far outstrips tickets.

Film View
The Football Factory (2003), a small-scale British movie focusing on violence in soccer, found that what was a break-even return in cinemas became a runaway success in DVD rental, where strong word of mouth spread, and the film raised over five times its ticket gross.

Distribution has changed in other ways too, the result of new formats for watching movies. This expansion in outlets for viewing means that the traditional distribution system has to rethink what it does.

Go to: Chapter 10:2 to find out about new formats.

Changing the system

So what may change? For many filmmakers, the system where companies decide which films get a release and which stay on the shelf has been an unacceptable stranglehold on the industry for too long. For every movie released, at least a dozen more get refused, with the winners tending towards Hollywood franchises and sure-fire hits. Indigenous movies rarely get a look in in some countries. This set-up has been a kind of glass ceiling for independent filmmakers, preventing new ideas from surfacing. With a multiplicity of outlets, however, it seems likely that this monopoly is being pierced, if not yet demolished.

In practice, this means that as an emerging director it is more likely today that you will get your film into profit, with a sale straight to DVD, where the real profits are starting to lie. For shorts, music videos and experimental work, the doors are open as never before, with what some people term a content shortage to fill the new viewing outlets.

Getting a distributor

If you decide that the brief outline above is more than you wish to handle, you may want to find someone who will take the strain, for a fee. Many law firms and PR agencies will take on films, helping you find the right exposure for your movie. This would include trying to get the film seen at screenings and festivals, but there is also a network of reps within the film industry who may take on your movie, either at the pre-production finance stage or in marketing of the finished product.

Weblinks
http://www.launchingfilms.com/   Home page for the UK Film Distributors Association.
http://www.artificial-eye.com/   Notable distributor of arthouse and Asian films.
http://www.optimumreleasing.com/   Ardent supporter of low-budget and independent film.
http://www.lib.berkeley.edu/MRC/Distributors.html   Comprehensive address book of US distributors for home entertainment.

What is a distributor?

A distributor is a person or company who will try to sell your film to markets you could not have previously reached. They will have extensive knowledge of each market, from theatrical to home rental, and will, more importantly, know how to pitch your film to achieve the highest levels of exposure at each event or screening. They will take a sizeable cut of your receipts and they will have many other movies they are trying to sell, but if you want to make any money at all from your movie, the service they are going to provide is extremely valuable in terms of getting you seen by the industry.

Actually getting a distributor to act for you is an uphill struggle. They receive dozens of unsolicited tapes each day and as many scripts and unfinished movies. If you win a slot in a festival and get some profile from this, distributors may seek out a deal with you. The main festivals are visited by many international buyers and sellers, each trying to make deals with each other, based on what critics, film juries and audiences claim to be the best of the crop. For a short film, you have opportunities to sell the movie itself with a sales agent or use it to strike an informal deal with funding partners about future projects. Features may find deals with ancillary markets in DVD.

Did you know?
Ancillary markets refers to other ways of selling a film apart from theatres. In practice this tends to mean DVD.

Film View
If your film is noticed, most of the buyers you encounter will offer a distribution deal involving either an advance or no advance. Piotr Skopiak, whose directorial debut *Small Time Obsession* was sold at the Edinburgh Film Festival, was happy to have sold his movie even though he received nothing upfront. 'My distributor did not pay for my film. He raised the money we needed to finish and release the film. The reason he did it is because he now has a cut of overseas sales. Without that he would not have taken the film at all.'

Foreign distribution

Foreign sales may account for a substantial part of your overall revenue and should be explored fully. It is, however, unlikely that a small independent film will find a theatrical or DVD sale in territories other than its own. Many of the stronger territories to challenge the Hollywood hegemony, such as South Korea, China, Japan and Latin America, have healthy film markets where new talent can emerge on DVD or in small theatres. If you are considering trying to sell a feature to other territories, be realistic about how likely it is that a profit will be made. Higher up the film industry, though, non-US sales now account for far more than they used to, so it is clear that audiences are more receptive to global products than they were, but at the same time quite capable of producing their own too.

Shorts for sale

Short movies operate under a wholly separate set of conditions, with separate markets and festivals to cater for them. The short film has experienced a renaissance in recent years, quite simply because there are more outlets for them now. Before online viewing, DVD collections and cell phone distribution, shorts had no real home to speak of and yet remained the best school for producing new directors. For a while advertising filled the gap, producing directors such as Ridley Scott, but today the short film has renewed purpose. Sales of short films are more common and there are more sales agents who specialize in this area. However, expect little or no return on your short film.

Roseann S. Cherenson, Executive Vice President of Distribution at Phaedra Cinema, sees the short film as:

> '… a calling card towards getting a feature film or television career. I have to say that while there is the possibility that you could make some money domestically or internationally from your short, the vast majority do not make any money, just get the filmmaker good festival exposure and hopefully prizes (maybe even Oscars) that help boost a filmmaker's chance of getting full-length gigs.'

Figure 9.8 Oscar winner Andrea Arnold took her short films – including this film, *Dog* – to many festivals, winning several awards.

Self-distribution

The tough option

Marketing movies is a complex, unstable field. The marketplace changes rapidly according to the most recent successes and is subject to geographical and economical variations. It is therefore undoubtedly difficult to attempt to market your film yourself unless you have knowledge of what each market offers, of what constitutes a good sales price, of foreign sales, of percentages, and you have the contacts to make this happen. This route means you will be involved in the business side of filmmaking more than ever before and that takes away valuable filmmaking time from your next project.

Domestic theatres

With domestic theatres, you will be negotiating directly to place your film for a limited run, but this is unlikely to yield results. Theatres specializing in independent movies are going to be more open to this possibility, but usually will want you to have some exposure at a film festival first.

Handling advertising

You will be responsible for advertising. This means compiling a press pack and other promotion material used by theatres. Don't spend unwisely on advertising, because it is likely that you will receive less than 30–35 per cent of gross box-office takings from a theatre. In real terms, this means that if a 200-seat theatre sells a quarter of its tickets (it is an unknown film, don't forget) at $10 apiece, with a revenue of $500, you receive something like $150, which is going to cover only basic publicity.

Terms

You will need to negotiate with theatres how much of the box-office gross you will receive, but be aware that a theatre taking 65 per cent of gross receipts of mainstream films is probably going to increase this if they think the risk is greater for an unknown movie. You need to ensure that the deal you have negotiated tells you when your movie will be shown, and for how long. Some independent cinemas show short films for free before a main programme, or have unknown features as part of special slots in a programme and these functions are built into their educational programme. University cinemas, arts centres and local film societies are also likely to be more receptive to flexible rates.

Projection

A theatre's method of projection must match your print. A theatre equipped to show 35 mm film may not have the facilities to show a digital film, nor even a 16 mm film, although some smaller independent chains or campus theatres may be equipped to show S-VHS video. But the move towards digital projection of digital films is inexorable and will lead eventually to more and more theatres accepting this format, though it is more likely to be larger, high revenue cinemas leading the way for some time. Digital projection is going hand in hand with digital broadcasting, and films are being broadcast directly to some theatres. Studios are very keen for theatres to pursue this; with more films being made within the digital domain, the massive costs of producing prints would diminish.

Did you know?

Digital projection is becoming a reality in many cities. Theatres are being equipped with projectors which require a digital copy of a film rather than a celluloid version. Many filmmakers already working in digital – such as George Lucas – and companies such as Pixar see digital projection as the only way to view their films at their best.

Tip   The main film-going markets are, in order, the USA, Europe, the Far East, Latin America, Australia/New Zealand. Within these areas, the countries spending the most on movies, which would be at the top of your marketing list, are: Europe – United Kingdom (25 per cent of European market); Far East – Japan (60 per cent of that market); Latin America – Brazil and Mexico (25 per cent each of that market). Of remaining foreign markets, Australia and New Zealand together take up about 5 per cent.

Weblink
http://www.digitalcinema-europe.com/pages/EUScreens.html   Comprehensive list of all European digital cinema screens.

Figure 9.9 DVD collections of short films are increasingly common.

DVD

This is more likely to be a route you pursue after you have first investigated the possibility of theatrical and television release, but if you look at this area after or before other routes, consider carefully who you deal with. There are many companies now offering to make copies of your movie on DVD and purport to sell these. Don't forget that a company saying they will try to sell your DVD is not the same as a company saying they will go out and actively push your movie, advertising it and making sure it gets seen at the right markets. Given the ease with which DVDs can be produced, in very small numbers, there may not be much investment on the part of the distributor and you may well end up being part of a mail-order list with low sales. DVD burners are now a fraction of what they once cost, so doing it yourself may prove to be no more expensive than via an Internet DVD distributor, with the advantage that you can include additional material such as commentary, interviews and other marketing tools as needed.

Did you know?
DVD stands for Digital Versatile Disc, so called because it can hold a range of media from video to text to images, all of which are accessible freely.

Contracts and distribution deals

In each of the routes described above, you will have to deal with contracts. It depends on the cost of your movie as to whether you hire an entertainment lawyer or decide to rely on advice from other film-makers and your own judgement.

Advance deals

If you get an offer with an advance, the buyer takes their distribution fee from any money your film makes – often around the 35 per cent mark – and then takes off the advance you were paid at the start of the deal. It doesn't stop there; they then start to recoup their expenses, which may be considerable. For most filmmakers taking an advance, that is the last return they see from the movie, so it is important to make the right level of advance to begin with; calculate your figures based on the idea that this is all the money you will ever get for the movie. In calculating the advance, the buyer is not plucking figures out of the air, but thinking coolly and with much experience about the revenue the film is likely to generate. They take into account all costs and then think about making some profit for themselves. If this seems like a tough deal, bear in mind that the exposure you receive is going to be more helpful in the long term. Tarantino's *Reservoir Dogs* (1991) made more of a splash culturally than it did in terms of actual box-office receipts, and the rest is history. If you do receive an advance, make sure that you stay in communication with the buyer to make sure that you receive your 'overages' when or if your movie starts to make profit beyond the expenses outlined above.

Non-advance deals

The other kind of deal, with no advance, means you don't see any returns for some time, at least six months after release. If the film starts to make good returns, you will see more of a share of it than if you had an advance, but only after the distributor has taken a cut and taken expenses. However, you will have negotiated in advance what you both agree is a reasonable amount to spend on advertising and other expenses, referred to as capped expenses.

The cut they take will vary, but as a baseline figure, in North America the figure is 50 per cent for theatrical, roughly 40 per cent for video and television, and 20–40 per cent for foreign sales. Films will almost never recoup what they cost and then have enough to share around to the crew if you rely on domestic theatrical receipts alone, even in countries with a large population. The most likely chance of seeing returns – overages – is from video or DVD sale and television, with the only obstacle to this being whether the film had more spent on paying for theatrical release than was recoverable in the cinemas. Any other possible markets that could generate returns are opened up only after theatrical release has been fully mined. If you are relying on sales other than theatrical to recoup your costs as director/producer, you will have a long wait if the film performs poorly in domestic release, but the spread of these other markets is enough to raise the possibility of some return.

Check your contract

Whatever deal you look into, make sure you understand the whole contract and the kind of terms used. Ask for clarification on any term you are unsure about and insist that standard terms are agreed upon. For example, theatrical release may be agreed but you need to know within what time-scale this would happen, and if the words 'reasonable period' are the answer, insist this is put in terms of months, years, centuries or whatever.

Agree acceptable cost limits

One of the valuable services of the distributor is in advertising and pushing the movie to the right places, such as film festivals. These costs soon add up and you need to agree in advance how much is a reasonable amount to spend on marketing. Take into account the cost of the movie and what you expect a low estimate to be of return from all markets. Then agree a cap on expenses above a certain amount. If you don't cap you may not actually have to pick up the bill for disproportionate expenses, but it does mean you will have to wait far longer before any revenue comes your way. Don't let the unscrupulous distributor use your movie as a free travel pass, recouping more than they should from your sales.

What is your share?

Ask for clarification about what part of the potential revenue is being divided up when your percentage is worked out. You need to know whether you are sharing in the producer's share or whether your share comes from total profits. If we take a case of a producer from New York who was in dispute with a filmmaker reluctant to give much of a slice of the profits, should there be any. Starting at the top of the chain, the theatre takes 65 per cent of gross receipts and gives the rest back to the distributor. The other 35 per cent that the distributor received was the net money and had to be big enough to recover all advertising and print costs. The producer was seeking a deal in which he received 12.5 per cent of gross receipts, leaving that 35 per cent which the distributor received diminished down to 22.5 per cent. This set-up would have been unlikely to attract interest from distributors, but if the producer was asking for 12.5 per cent of the distributor's share, a deal would have been possible. Alternatively, the producer could have sought gross receipts of theatrical release only, which as we have seen accounts for only a small proportion of total revenue; the distributor will be more concerned about video and television rights.

Weblink
http://www.marklitwak.com/   Noted entertainment lawyer based in Los Angeles. Site has useful information and books for sale.

If your film does the unexpected and starts to make money at the box office or in other sales, you will receive statements from the distributor detailing what money is coming in from what source. But if you decide you want to check up on the progress of your film if you feel not enough revenue is coming your way, you should not be asked in your contract to waive your rights to audit these figures and you should not be required to audit before enough time has elapsed for the film to make some profit. If you think that your share of profits is not forthcoming, an audit can be costly but the only effective way of recovering money from the distributor. Your contract should allow you to ask the distributor to cover the costs of an audit if it reveals that they have withheld money owed you, although this is rare and often down to mismanagement rather than malice.

If the distributor forwards you an advance, check whether you are paying interest on this money. If so, check whether interest is being gained by the distributor from money received in advance from theatres. If you can't eliminate interest, try to reduce it.

Arbitration
If you disagree with your distributor and are unable to resolve an issue, you need to have a clause on arbitration built into the contract. Lawyers fees will hurt you far more than they hurt the company, so it is in your interests to have a binding arbitration agreement, avoiding costly court battles.

Weblink
http://www.bfi.org.uk/facts/publications/fmguide/index.html   Free downloadable document to film distribution for filmmakers from the British Film Institute.

Film on the Internet
What the Internet can offer

There is something rewarding about having finished your film – you can show it to your friends, play it over and over again and use it as a calling card to get further into the industry. But until the arrival of video on the web this was about as far as you could hope to push a short film at the start of your career.

On the plus side, the web:

● enables you to show your films to anyone, anywhere
● lets you do this without the need for 'the middlemen', such as distributors

- lets you devise your own marketing campaign for a film
- lets you communicate directly with potential buyers or other people you might want to work with
- lets you watch what everyone else is doing.

All of which looks good until you see the potential down side of this technology:

- the net is unstable – its infrastructure is shaky to say the least
- it takes too long for many users to download a short film
- picture and sound quality are poor.

Video streaming

Video streaming has branched off from the web to become a field with its own growth rate and millions of dollars of research going into finding quicker ways of showing movies. In this section, we need to get to grips with this technology and find the best way of exploiting it for the use of the low-budget film-maker. It won't solve your problems overnight or guarantee a great career – artistic merit is and always will be a deciding factor. But it does give you more control over your work than anyone working 20 years ago might have dreamed.

What is web film?

Webfilm is basically any moving image which is downloaded as a single file or 'streamed' for viewing on a PC. At the start of the twenty-first century it is estimated that there are something like 300 million Internet users and although the net was once the preserve of information, communication and consumer services, the prime use of it for most people – 70 per cent on average – is entertainment. As use of home PCs evolves in this direction, the Internet industry has put more time and money into pushing it further, with better ways of compressing these massive video files over tiny phone lines.

File sizes

One of the issues at the centre of video on the web is infrastructure. Most people don't possess the right sort of connection – broadband – needed to watch films at a reasonable rate. The kind of modem most people have is one that conducts data at a rate of 56 kb per second; put this against the size of a video file lasting only a few minutes, which could be up to 650 Mb, and you start to understand why something had to be done to squash these files down into a more manageable size, and to find a way of starting to show the movie before the whole length of it has downloaded.

What types of films are out there?

The rules and hierarchies of Hollywood have no currency here. In webfilm, it is common to see a site where first-time filmmakers are on the same bill as established, well-known directors. There is no limit to the kind of material seen. Animation is popular, since web-specific software like Flash means that it is downloaded or viewed at a fraction of the time that video takes. Independent film dominates, and students of film courses use it as a way to get seen quickly. Interactive film has evolved, where you can zoom in or out on a scene, or choose the outcome of the film. Experimental artists have never had it so good; work usually destined for a poorly attended gallery now has wider potential. Film has become more of a fun 'hit' to be had at work or at home, and webfilms are perhaps the espresso of the entertainment world: quality compressed into a short space.

Go to: Chapter 9:11 for more ideas on Internet movie sites.

Who shows films?

There are many sites that specifically show webfilms and several high profile sites that are forging close links with the traditional film industry and attracting support from leading names in directing and acting. Most offer the viewer a small screen, roughly two or three inches across, together with information about the film and a chance to comment on it.

The Crunch

- Decide whether you distribute it yourself or involve a distributor
- If you do it yourself, are you sure you can handle the market?
- If it's a feature, try DVD and theatrical first
- If it's a short, try festivals, TV and cable first
- Avoid the Internet as the first option if you want to sell to other routes.

9. Strategies for promotion

These sections on promotion and distribution are aimed at pointing out the possible routes available to get your films seen more widely. Before entering into the world of publicity, press relations and profile raising, we need to take a step back and look at how to devise a coherent approach so that the time and money involved is worth it.

You will only get one chance to promote the film; if you get it wrong, you can't ask people to give you a second chance, with so many filmmakers vying for the same attention from public or buyers. Whether you buy into the whole idea of film as a commodity or not, you may still agree that people won't see your work unless you compete with every other bit of culture trying to catch their eye. If you ran a business, you would expect to have to actively promote your products and would not rely on the maxim, 'if it's good quality, they'll find it'. Any movie that involves an outlay of time or money needs to have behind it some promotion plan.

Get a plan

Promotion must be worked into the overall production plan right from the start, as a part of the overall budget. You will then spend only what is appropriate to the size of the production and won't feel too bad spending it because you have allocated it specifically for this purpose. If you involve investors in funding your film, they will take you far more seriously if you include in your costings some budget for selling the product they are supporting.

Before you move on to a plan, decide first what is it you are hoping to achieve in marketing your movie. We could narrow down the options to the following:

1 *Beginner's route*. I want to get the film seen but I don't expect to make any cash this time around – I'm building a profile.
2 *Intermediate route*. I want to get the film seen and I need to make a small amount of money to recover costs.
3 *Advanced route*. I have not yet made this movie and I want to attract large funding to get it made.

Beginner's route

This is likely to be the aim for those at the start of their careers, possibly making short films for entry into festivals, competition or cable television stations. In this case, the right route is to approach festivals, television short film slots, independent cinemas and websites with the aim of securing some small exposure for the movie, but which you can then build on. Just one showing of your movie at whatever level and in whatever format is enough to launch your campaign of getting recognition for this or the next movie.

Intermediate route

This second route is likely to be followed by those who have made movies with a bigger budget than the average short and are aiming to see some return from their investment. They may have already made a few shorts and have some experience of showing them at festivals or on television. The more profitable routes will involve gaining entry to television slots that pay for the right to show the movie, or others that commission further projects. Retail sales will be crucial, centring on limited DVD release, and these must be spread on as wide a geographical base as possible. Theatrical release is a possibility for feature films but may drain any profits that could result, and would need to be well placed in the right cinema.

You do, however, need to be realistic about the chances of making any return on your movie; getting it seen does not mean making money and even getting a distribution deal doesn't necessarily mean that the future is bright. For most producers, the advance is all the money they will ever receive due to the distributor first taking out all costs from the producer's portion, leaving very little left over as 'profit'. For this reason, get the highest possible advance on offer.

Advanced route

This last route is more likely to attract those people who have more experience of filmmaking and have now decided to move towards more elaborate, fully funded feature-length films. They may have made a small section of the movie and hoped to get finance for completion costs. If this is your position, you may need to find a producer's rep, with the aim of securing a financing deal with a distribution company. A round of hard selling is going to centre on how well your film – or more likely a script or small section of it that you could afford to shoot – can perform at festival screenings or special screenings for selected agents. In many cases, there is the expectation that you have first invested heavily in the film yourself, demonstrating your commitment by having raised some finance and gained the confidence of investors. Festivals may put you in the right place to find a rep willing to push your movie and conscious of the right route for you, nationally and internationally. Don't expect to be able to handle the detail of foreign DVD sales or other unfamiliar markets without some outside help. Getting on the books of the main festival film markets is a big step forward. For instance, independent-friendly festivals like Rotterdam help a selected number of filmmakers to meet with investors. While fewer actual deals are made at Rotterdam than at many other festivals, investors like the intimacy of the set-up, with everyone accessible throughout the event, and the relaxed feel to the event. Many later deals are finalized elsewhere but instigated in Rotterdam. Berlin promotes a selected number of filmmakers through more substantial sales packages and supports a Talent Campus simultaneous to the festival, which also promotes a small number of filmmakers each year.

Weblink

http://www.berlinale-talentcampus.de/   News on Berlin's filmmaker residential workshop.

In all these options, it should be recognized in advance that there is a long-term goal (to make more movies and eventually enter profitability) and there is a short-term goal (to get a profile, with any exposure at all). If you make any profit at this early stage, consider it just the icing on the cake.

Interview

'The best way to get publicity is to never take no for an answer! In this industry, you have to push and push and push. If you believe you can get your film screened at the local cinema, then do it. If they say no, then ask again, ask at a different cinema. The media is about who you know rather than what you know, so make friends with people in high places; just being friendly can reap dividends when you need something from them.'

Kevin Lapper, filmmaker, ReelRaine Films

Marketing strategy

Research screenings

You need first to get views on what sort of movie you have made, since you are the last person entitled to be objective about its strengths and weaknesses. Maybe psychologists should coin a term to describe viewing one's artistic efforts in an exaggerated positive or negative light, where a filmmaker can no longer see the film, only the time and money invested in it (how about chronic artistic dysmorphia?).

Weblink
http://www.filmeducation.org/filmlib/JDredd.pdf   Educational paper on the selling of the movie *Judge Dredd*.

Screenings

Arrange screenings of the film with friends and other filmmakers, on a small level at first. Try to recruit a range of viewers with different expectations, but don't make life difficult for yourself; choose people for your pre-screening with care, preferably people who see independent movies often. Ask them to write their positive and negative comments about your film on a postcard, or hold a discussion if you have a thick skin. You need to know what kind of audience is going to respond best to the movie; what issues are raised in it and how they are conveyed; and whether any part of the movie is unclear, including parts of the plot.

Interview
'At the screenings there's always a buzz because the work to be shown is kept secret until the night itself, and also just the fact that the industry rubs shoulders so closely with the public makes it really good fun for everyone – the directors meet the fans, the fans meet the directors. Probably my favourite bit is in the bar afterwards where you see everybody talking about which video was their favourite or which one they weren't so crazy about.'

Jordan McGarry, organizer, Antenna film screenings, London

Weblink
http://www.antennapromo.co.uk/   Monthly screening of music promos in London.

Listen to other filmmakers

Although the practice of using focus groups by Hollywood is frowned upon in the independent sector, it must be remembered that our aims could not be more different. In Hollywood, it is possible that the film's conclusion may be altered if focus reports suggest so, or that certain characters be excised, all with the aim of avoiding alienating any section of the viewing public.

But in our own case, we are looking at defining the film, assessing how it is viewed, and may not consider cutting unpopular parts. However, if you have investors on board, think carefully about this sort of screening as the investor may insist on changes as a result of unfavourable pre-screenings. For wider audiences, try a screening at a film school, university film clubs or local filmmaker groups. Attend in person so you know at what point people started to walk out or how much applause there was.

Form a company

Project a more professional air by forming a company, perhaps with other filmmakers. Forming a production company can force you to become much more organized about your marketing and encourages your tax department to see you in a more favourable light, offsetting costs against tax if and when your movie takes off. The company could be a long-term venture to support all your movies, or could be formed for one project only. Go the whole way: get a company logo and headed paper. It won't legitimize your work as great film but does legitimize you as a filmmaker.

Set up a website

This is as crucial as your calling card and as useful as an office full of assistants. A huge amount of information can be displayed and accessed by those you want to impress.

Make a press pack

Prepare material you can mail to the media to garner publicity for the movie. Use it also at festivals, in meetings with possible deal-makers and financial backers. Include a DVD or VHS copy of the film, JPEG stills at 300 dpi or more, business cards, publicity and press cuttings, information on crew, cast, director, scriptwriter, an outline of the film and some information about the making of the film, including trivia (the worst and best moments, for instance).

Tell the acquisitions execs about your movie

This is the first stage to getting a deal. Although getting a deal is not easy, getting an acquisitions executive to look at your film is not too hard. They are always looking to buy films, for theatres, home rental and television, in domestic and foreign markets. Various factors give you a head start, such as having a known actor or having had a good response in a festival. Since most films have neither, the job of attracting the attention of the acquisitions executive is difficult.

Use the following ways to achieve this:

- *Tell everyone.* If there is a dedicated filmmaking press or there are trade publications in your country, alert them to the existence of your project, usually in the last few weeks before shooting begins. In the USA, for example, this would include *The Hollywood Reporter* and *Daily Variety*. In the UK, use www.shootingpeople.org, which is accessed by thousands of people daily.
- *Film Finders.* Place a notice with Film Finders, a resource for buyers and sellers to get information about movies in production in the independent sector. This is a publication run by a successful former acquisitions executive, Sydney Levine, and is available online (www.ifilmfinders.com/). It has established a strong reputation as a meeting point for filmmakers and buyers, and helps to create a profile for the movie before completion. The service is free – just download a questionnaire and return. Set up links to your site from well-visited sites connected to the film industry, including online trade press such as *The Hollywood Reporter*, which welcomes such links as they direct visitors to their own sites in return.

Submit your film to an online buyers/sellers site

These sites offer the chance to show your film to distributors directly and are primarily for completed movies. They usually ask for a fee, but this does not guarantee that the film gets viewed any further than an initial submission stage. Before passing a film onto selection committees, the initial selectors will need to be convinced that your film is legal. Prior exhibition will greatly harm your chances of being considered.

Did you know?
A film that is referred to as 'legal' has a clear chain of ownership and no aspect of the film is part-owned by anyone else. Music licences are also looked at to check that you have clearance to use music.

If your film makes it beyond these first stages, panels of filmmakers or industry people then view these movies and grade them according to suitability for the market, technical quality, story and so on. You may then be invited to submit your film for viewing by distributors or other buyers. However, most insist that the movie is at least 75 minutes long and is finished. Some sites are more directly geared towards selling and have some prior reputation in the distribution business, while others offer a wider service, with news, reviews and industry statistics. These sites act as galleries, selecting the best unsigned, legal, independent films and directing them at distributors. For the buyer, they offer a filtering service, making the process of seeking new talent more focused.

If your film is only partly financed, in other words, you don't yet know where the funding for the rest of the movie is going to come from, you can still place notices in Film Finders and the trade press. Acquisitions executives and sales agents may negotiate to finance a movie that is only partly made in return for an equity stake in the movie, but usually you must expect to have something that entices them, such as a known actor or previous festival success.

Figure 9.10 Festivals such as Raindance, held each year in the UK, provide a chance to network and create interest for new films. Shane Meadows and Paddy Considine are pictured here at the 2004 event.

Get a producer's rep

These people work hard at putting together finance deals for independent movies, but also act as agents to finalize distribution deals after completion. They are highly experienced individuals who will devise a strategy for marketing the film, so that it reaches the right festivals, is screened to the right people and is positioned correctly so all marketing possibilities are realized to the full. Producer's reps take between 5 and 10 per cent of revenue.

Create a buzz

There is no hard and fast way of doing this, but it remains the most effective way to attract the attention of the acquisitions executive. A 'buzz' means that industry people are talking about your film and suggests that there is some mystique surrounding it, an air of excitement and expectation. You will find a 'buzz' at festivals, at its centre a film that has in some way created attention because of who is attached to it or what others say about it through advance screenings – that single most effective of marketing tools: word of mouth. Since everyone tries to create a buzz surrounding their film at markets and festivals it is a scarce commodity, but a producer's rep will greatly help, with the most well-known creating interest about a project simply through being involved with it.

Free publicity

Finally, mine every possible route through which you could raise the profile of your movie. Does it, for instance, have a particular minority-interest angle that may attract certain publications or news agencies?

Shorts are different

The options are different for a short film or a feature. Distributors do indeed buy shorts for theatrical release, but they are more difficult to sell. On the other hand, television and cable slots for new film-makers almost always prefer to screen short films. Theatrical release is rarely the right route for a short film unless it is picked up for exhibition alongside well-known movies. In many ways, however, the availability of outlets for shorts has dramatically increased in recent years as a result of the Internet and a rise in public broadcasting slots for new filmmakers.

Web film

Although webfilm sites are visited by acquisitions executives – the people who buy films for distributors – it is very rare for any to be offered deals as a result. Getting a film entered into the wider market of theatre exhibition, television and home video or DVD sales involves a more circuitous route. In this option, there is no limit to the amount of time and effort you can expend on getting the right people to see your film. You have to be prepared to believe in your project without question, moving on relentlessly after each rejection. At every step of the way there are stories of filmmakers who have persisted when all avenues seemed closed. Not getting a deal at all is not the end of the story; some filmmakers go on to sell a film direct to theatres, or market DVDs direct to the consumer.

The Crunch

- Decide what you want first – be realistic and aim to get a small amount of exposure first time, then get more next time and so on
- Develop your filmmaking slowly and surely without aiming too high just yet
- Get opinions on your movie from filmmakers
- Attend film festivals
- Submit applications to film market sales sections
- Choose your ultimate aim for the movie, then select the right route
- Prepare all the information you need in advance as if you expect a deal to be made
- Don't be caught out: interest from an acquisitions executive is more common than you may think – they call even if they are only slightly interested and will keep calling to ask for information until they have everything they need
- Work out in advance the route you see the film moving along and check whether you rule out other options in the process – for instance, broadcasting on the web may preclude a television deal
- Set up a website
- Enjoy it – you've earned it because you made a great film.

Project 20. Showreel: who am I?

What this project is for: to help get jobs, and to try editing for ultra-short movies
Time: allow around one day to shoot and four hours to edit

What this project is about

Your showreel is one of the most important aspects of your promotion kit, along with your business card and cell phone. It consists of a series of clips from your films, or whole films if they are under a few minutes in length. The aim of this project is to complete a central piece of your showreel – a film to sell yourself. This is a film that shows someone who you are, what you do and how you think. It offers a fast way into projecting your personal style on a showreel. In applying for jobs on film productions this is a way to stand out from the crowd.

Stage 1

You have 60 seconds to show who you are. Be aware that your shooting and editing skills are under scrutiny, but perhaps more importantly so is your creativity – pack the film full of interesting ideas, sudden changes, quirks, anything that is different and is your personality.

Avoid putting yourself in the frame too much – in fact, many of these have only a few seconds of the film-maker, the rest being images that represent how you would like to be perceived. For example, you could take the idea of showing five items you could not live without (iPod, Gucci shoes, high-spec headphones an so on), or list your top three most memorable experiences, perhaps with quick dramatizations, or three personal heroes and why you respect them. Anything irreverent and left field will catch attention.

Stage 2

When editing this movie, use short, concise cuts. Go straight for the very best, funniest, most intriguing parts. You need to grab attention from the very first, so throw all your best shots here.

It is crucial to put a permanent contact details line at the foot of the frame, with name, number and email address.

Evaluation

The real test of this film is in the reception it gets when you first use it. This film is not for use when sending your shorts to festivals or competitions for selection. It is instead aimed at those jobs where you need to make a splash to get noticed, and where you are dealing with media-aware people, who may respond well to such an approach. Many universities also ask for this sort of film before they consider you for selection for film courses.

Look at the finished result and work out how you think attention levels will fall in those who watch it. Show it to friends and (encouraging them to be brutally honest) ask them to signal to you when they get bored. You need to know whether this happens after 10 seconds, 20 or 40. If you get to 40 you can count it a success.

I want something more challenging

This idea can form the basis for a more serious movie where you explore your identity. Create a film that takes a more measured look at who you are, delving into the past, showing hopes and fears, and adopting an open, revealing attitude. Take a look at Jonathan Caouette's movie *Tarnation*, which uses archive footage and reconstructions to create a story of the filmmaker's life.

10. Film festivals

Pushing a film around the festival circuit is described by some filmmakers as one of the most important moves they made in marketing the film. Greg Pak, a filmmaker based in New York, found it essential, as he described in this diary entry:

> 'I met many great people at the [South by Southwest] festival, several of whom have made distribution offers for my movie. I'm keeping my mouth shut till I nail things down but it looks like I'm pretty close to achieving my distribution goals for the film. The experience has confirmed for me the importance of going to festivals and meeting people face to face. I might have gotten these offers had I not been at the festival, but there is nothing like meeting people in the flesh for establishing real trust.'

Entry into some festivals is considered to be a huge boost to a career. The best known rarely act as simple showcases for great and upcoming movies, but are the points at which buyers (distributors) and sellers (reps and agents) meet, with filmmakers hoping to be in the crossfire. In the independent sector, the festival is a chance to test public reaction in screenings. Critics may attend and review films not yet signed to a distributor, increasing or decreasing the chances of its sale.

For feature films this route is crucial, but for shorts also the festival is a great chance to market your film and obtain a deal in markets other than theatrical. Some festivals specialize in shorts, while others offer special short films among the feature-film screenings.

Weblink
http://2005.sxsw.com/   South by Southwest festivals.

Film festivals as markets

The main festivals are also markets, helping the acquisitions executive spot unsigned films that could be picked up. This is the place where you and your sales agent can start to cash in on the buzz that you have worked hard to create through screenings at smaller festivals. There are five major markets, spaced throughout the year:

● European Film Market in Berlin in February
● American Film Market (AFM) in Santa Monica, now in November
● Marche International du Film in Cannes, France in May
● London Film Festival in October.

Weblinks
www.berlinale.de/   European Film Market web pages.
http://www.ifta-online.org/afm/   American Film Market details.
http://www.cannesmarket.com/   Cannes Festival market site.
http://www.lff.org.uk/   Details on the London Film Festival.

Finished product vs short clip

If you are trying to sell a movie to potential distributors, it helps if you have a finished product; surprisingly, up to 80 per cent of films submitted to Sundance are incomplete.

Did you know?
Sundance is the most prestigious festival for the North American independent sector. Its filmmaker workshops, in which unknown directors make and shoot a sequence for viewing by well-known directors, have been the springboard for many careers, including that of Quentin Tarantino.

Figure 9.11 Independent festivals such as Raindance attract high-profile directors such as Ken Loach, seen here at the 2004 event.

However, incomplete projects are bought in special forums at most of the main film markets. For example, the Independent Feature Film Market each autumn in New York attracts buyers who are able to see special screenings of partially completed work. Incomplete movies are inevitably less attractive because the producer usually asks for completion funds, but distributors are well versed in deciding whether to buy based on just a small section of a film; even in full screenings, potential buyers make up their minds from just short sections of a movie and may leave midway through in order to attend other screenings.

Interview
'I went to the Edinburgh Film Festival and put the film into what was then the NBX section, a section within the market part of the festival that lists all the UK films made the previous year and allows all those films to be booked out and viewed in a video room. Buyers and distributors then look through the booklet they are given and they can choose to watch any film at their own leisure without pressure.'

Piotr Skopiak, director, Small Time Obsession, *UK*

Weblink
http://www.ifp.org/   Site for the Independent Filmmaker Project, which hosts the Independent Film Market. An excellent site for a wide range of filmmaker information.

Figure 9.12 Festivals such as Emergeandsee offer filmmakers the chance to screen films and find contacts.

How to submit to festivals

Many larger festivals deal with huge quantities of submissions. Sundance, Montreal, Berlin and London, for instance, are all intensely competitive but are worth entering on the basis that you have nothing to lose aiming at the top and working your way down to smaller festivals. There is certainly no lack of festivals; just about every capital city has its own, with up to 40 each month in the United States alone. Many larger festivals do not need to advertise for submissions and yet still receive thousands of submissions each year.

> **Interview**
> 'We asked for submissions on VHS in the first instance, and then made our selections as to what would be shown after our preliminary viewing sessions. For us, it made no difference whether publicists, agents or filmmakers themselves approached us – the film itself was more important than who sent it.'
>
> *Lydia Wysocki, former festival curator, UK*

Specialist festivals

Further down the scale, at regional or state level, applicants are more likely to be successful. Some festivals focus on certain types of work or specific formats. For example, the Chicago International Film Festival shows the full spectrum of film in October, while more challenging work appears in the

Chicago Underground Film Festival the previous August. Other festivals specialize in much more particular works, such as the H. P. Lovecraft Film Festival, which shows only adaptations of the novelist's work. Others still offer an outlet for those filmmakers rejected by the rest, such as the Reject Film Festival. Make sure you check out the kind of festivals that best suit your film and the level at which it sits within the industry as a whole. A film centring on gay issues should also be entered in gay and lesbian film festivals, such as the annual London or San Francisco international events. Other festivals specialize in ethnic groups, such as Latin American or Asian or religious groups.

Weblinks
www.chicagofilmfestival.org   Details on the Chicago Film Festival.
http://www.britfilms.com/britishfilms/   Comprehensive global list of festivals with email addresses and submission guidelines.

Short film festivals

The number of short film festivals has increased over the last few years. The Shorts International Film Festival in USA and the Clermont-Ferrand in France are two of the most highly regarded, with distribution deals made in a competitive environment. Most general film festivals also have special screenings and awards for shorts.

Interview
'Keep to under 12 minutes. Keep to as short a story as possible; many people make the mistake of making what is essentially a 10-minute short and dragging it out to 20 minutes. A cohesive short story with a beginning, a middle and an end. Precise and clean edit. And of course, original ideas, innovative style and creativity.'

John Wojowski, curator, Kino Short Film Festival, Manchester, UK,
on what helps get a film selected

Weblinks
http://www.clermont-filmfest.com/   Home page of the world's foremost short film festival, Clermont-Ferrand.
www.filmfestivals.com   Searchable database of film festivals.

Getting information

Getting hold of listings will vary from country to country, but details are available on filmmaker noticeboards. In the USA, the Association of Independent Video and Filmmakers has listings in its magazine, *The Independent*, though the West Coast is better served by the Film Arts Foundation magazine, *Release Print*.

Fees

Most festivals demand a fee for looking at your movie, but this varies between those asking for enough to keep the festival running and those operating more on a profit basis. Submit your film at least three months before the festival, using their application form – never send unsolicited tapes. Some festivals operate an office throughout the year, while others open for business in the quarter prior to the festival. When you submit your movie on VHS tape, make sure you have available a copy more suitable for screening, such as DVD, and which you are able to lose for up to three months. In response to the move in the industry towards digital technology, many festivals, particularly the larger ones, will have digital projection facilities.

Making the most of a festival

If you are accepted, devise a thorough marketing plan and consider hiring a publicist or sales agent. A publicist may cost you dearly but may be a worthwhile investment if you are accepted at a high profile festival, where there will be press attention and you are against wide competition from other film-makers. A sales agent, on the other hand, is likely to have a more lasting commitment to the movie and will be more specifically geared toward the film industry, knowing how and when to cash in on festival success and translate this into sales.

Interview
'I sent my film to 20 or 30 festivals, just sticking a VHS in the post. The big break was when it got accepted for the library section in the Clermont-Ferrand Short Film Festival [in France]. A sales agent from Hypnotic in New York saw it and liked it. He emailed me saying he could sell it and license it, taking 30–50 per cent. It sounds like a bad deal but they know it is not about the money, that the director is getting exposure. It got me into festivals, TV stations around the world and on Atom.com. Sales agents are good because I just don't have the time or the money to push the film like they can. Festivals are good; you never know where it will lead you. I was at the Santa Monica International Short Film Festival and left the postcard for my movie *Crush* lying around. A Hollywood manager saw a postcard advertising the film – not the film itself – and thought it looked interesting. He called me to a meeting in Hollywood and passed my name to Dimension Films, who invited me to pitch for an upcoming project. It was a long way from where I started.'

Matt Sheldon, filmmaker

Prizes

Festival prizes are given to encourage and reward talent, rather than provide the sort of money needed to make further movies, and are a great boost to promoting a film. Buyers will be more inclined to take a look at your film if a festival draws attention to it.

Online festivals

There are a growing number of festivals operating solely online, broadcasting films in specific periods, attracting mainly short films.

Interview

'Technically, lighting and camera movement are currently important for compression reasons. However, I believe in the importance of what's being said by the filmmaker. First, make sure that the film is only as long as it needs to be; that means convey the meaning of the film as quickly as possible. Keep the subject matter and locations simple; less is more when making a digital film. Be clever. In a short film, you don't have time to be really profound. Just convey a simple idea simply. Be original. There are tons of films out there and making them is difficult. If you're going to spend the time and money, then make sure it's a tale worth telling.'

J. C. Calciano former festival organizer, USA

Online festivals are diverse, with some specializing in films that just happen to be shown online, while others show films that have been made specifically with the web in mind, including Flash animations. Don't confuse these with digital film festivals, however, which showcase films made on this format but in a conventional theatre setting, such as the Onedotzero Digital Cinema Festival or the Resfest Digital Film Festival. Clearly, the opportunities for buyers to make contact with you are greater in a more conventional environment as opposed to a virtual one, which cannot cater for filmmakers to meet and network. Yet these online festivals are popular with filmmakers because of the potentially global catchment area of their viewing public and the lower entrance costs. These festivals should not be seen as focusing purely on a film's mode of production; most are run by filmmakers sympathetic to the independent ideal and more interested in the content of a movie than its format.

Weblinks

http://www.torontoonlinefilmfestival.com/   Online strand to the famous Canadian festival.
www.sundanceonlinefilmfestival.org   Online festival running from January to June each year.
www.onedotzero.com   Events and festival news from leading digital festival.
www.resfest.com   News from innovative film festival.

Interview

'In Resfest, we look for new innovators, those who push the envelope of what one can do graphically or how one can tell/show a story. Comedies and those films that tug the emotions are more successful, but again, those filmmakers showing us something new or showing how to look at something in a new way, that's success in my opinion.'

Sid Goto, curator, Resfest online festival

The Crunch

- Film festivals help get your film noticed
- Go to film markets – hang out and take in the atmosphere
- Put together a press or distributor's pack for market screenings
- Look for specialist festivals
- Investigate online festivals
- Festivals are about more than just watching and selling films – go there to meet other filmmakers and exchange ideas.

11. Using Internet broadcast sites

Submitting films to a site

Getting a film accepted on a high profile web movie site has acquired some prestige, with sites such as ifilm.com or Atom/Shockwave establishing reputations as places to see the best short films. They cater for every (legal) kind of movie, including dramas, comedies, music videos, experimental films – even *Star Wars* homages. Some lend weight to their sites with extensive back catalogues of work by established filmmakers such as Bernardo Bertolucci and Spike Jonze.

Submitting films for these sites is straightforward. The most popular sites ask you to complete a registration form and pay before submission. Each site offers different incentives to attract filmmakers and have different terms; check on the specific requirements of a site before submitting.

Film specifications

- Most films tend to be less than 20 minutes in length. Shorter ones are more popular with viewers due to quicker download times.
- Films should be reasonably fresh, made within the last two years at least.
- Films should have all clearances and rights available. Make sure you have cleared the rights for any music in the movie before submitting. Some sites, such as AtomShockwave, distribute successfully to airlines, television and hand-held devices, and they will insist that no rights are going to be infringed elsewhere.

- Some sites screen only narrative work, while others include sections on experimental film, spoof and animation (iFilm).
- Tapes are mailed to the site operator on DV tape or Beta SP. However, don't send films that have been compressed already at home. The provider wants to be able to compress it themselves to their own specifications (and probably with better software).

Did you know?

Betacam SP is the highest grade analog video format, producing quality that far exceeds consumer-level VHS. Sony have also introduced a Betacam SX system, a digital version that records broadcast quality video.

All screen formats are accepted, including PAL, NTSC and SECAM.

Tip   Find out which broadcast standard you need to send by checking www.ee.surrey. ac.uk/Contrib/WorldTV.

Interview

'I made a short film which has been screened on the Internet – *This Ain't Your Business* – a very low budget, tongue-in-cheek gangster film. I didn't sell the film [to the site] but I do think it is an advantage to have a film on the Internet. First, it is something to put on your résumé. You've made the film and in a sense you've distributed it. You can also direct people to watch your film without having to send tapes. Second, there are so few outlets for short films, it would be crazy not to take advantage of what is offered.'

Carlo Ortu, filmmaker

Weblinks

http://atomfilms.shockwave.com/af/home/   Mainstream online film-showing site.
www.ifilm.com   Once quite discerning but has become more mainstream; heavily reliant on *Star Wars* homages, trailers and action.
www.sputnik7.com   Music promos, anime and music in a stylish and reliable site.

Rights

The better sites will offer individualized deals based on the market potential for your movie. You don't lose any rights simply by submitting a movie, though check that you don't have to give any undertaking to this extent in online registration forms. The larger sites look to acquire worldwide rights and will actively seek to exploit markets for mutual benefit, though you need to check what percentage the distributor takes in each market, weighing up the benefits of signing over rights to an online distributor and losing the chance of selling through more traditional distribution methods.

Interview
'Use the Internet when trying to get your short film shown. There are a number of sites that showcase short films. Be careful, though, as many have an annual fee and some demand all world rights to the film. You may get some payment for the film, but by losing your world rights you are giving up a lot. Go for sites that let you keep the rights to your film.'

David Norman, filmmaker

Paying to show your movie

Some sites ask for a fee to show your work, though for some of the larger sites with more industry experience and contacts in the wider distribution field, you are effectively getting a sales agent as well as a screening; they will actively push your film towards wider sales internationally. If you want this sort of site, look for ones that have evolved out of existing distribution and marketing companies (for example, Atom Film). Depending on the quality of the format used to screen your movie, costs can vary between $50 and $300 for a specific run of 3–12 months. Getting the film online may take several weeks, though some sites will offer 'express options' (read: more expensive) to get it screened more quickly.

Bear in mind that not all sites ask for payment to show your movies. The sites that offer more, such as a dedicated home page for your movies, do so because filmmakers are willing to pay for these services. Sites such as Atom view films and select only those they feel have marketing potential – which is different from, though not always opposed to, artistic quality, so don't be discouraged if your film gets rejected.

Weblinks
www.dfilm.com   Stylish film and festival site.
www.heavy.com   Music-based and underground movies.
www.newvenue.com   Web-specific movies showcased.
www.undergroundfilm.com   Mostly American short films, independent and original.

The Crunch

- Showing on the web can help you – the feedback you get helps you move on
- Keep movies short
- Beware losing your rights to the movie

- Not all sites ask for a fee
- Aim at the best sites first
- Capitalize on your successes – tell everyone you know to watch your film on a site and post a message on a filmmakers' bulletin board to say 'watch my movie'.

12. Your rights: protecting your movie on the web

Just as you sign over the right to show a film with a particular distributor in theatres, so the Internet also works by giving all or some of the rights over your movie to a particular site. In the rush to sell a movie, you may be tempted to accept any deal, ignoring some of the finer points in a contract. You need to consider some areas very carefully.

Distribution agreement

If you are offered a showing on a website, you will receive a 'distribution agreement'. Check whether the site is offering to actually broadcast your movie, as opposed to selling video copies of it via the Internet, or doing both. This sounds like an obvious point, but if you later strike a deal with a foreign buyer to sell video copies of your movie in a certain country, the fact that the consumer can buy your cassette already from another country over the Internet may affect your deal.

If you have already allowed your movie to be broadcast on television, or in theatrical release, regardless of how limited this may have been, you must be open about this when agreeing your contract. Similarly, a television company will need to know whether your movie has first been broadcast on the Internet. Withholding this information could lead to problems later, if the TV company perceives that you have violated their exclusive rights to show the film.

Royalties

Royalties have yet to be standardized on the Internet. Choose a site that offers you a cut of the advertising revenue generated by people viewing your movie. Check whether you are receiving equal share with other films, although some sites include confidentiality clauses restricting filmmakers from revealing what their cut is. If a film is your Internet debut, and you have no profile in the wider industry, you have no real bargaining power and will probably have to take what you are offered. Bear in mind also that disparity of rates is inevitable, since some filmmakers regularly generate many more downloads than others.

Did you know?
Royalties refer to the total that artists receive for their work after it has been sold by a third party. In this case, the third party is the website trying to find viewers for your movie.

Rights

In signing a contract, you are granting rights to that website, exclusive or otherwise, and you need to ensure that you have the authority to do this. If your movie has music which needs permission to be included, or literary rights which must be acquired, have you first obtained the necessary permission? Some sites, offering broadcast or video and DVD sale, don't let you past the home page without first asking whether you have music or screenplay rights to your movie. Music is usually the biggest hurdle, as some makers of short films are unaware of the need to obtain permission for even a few seconds of music, or perceive that an unknown musician with few sales won't be aware that their music is being used on a movie.

Written agreements

If you do sell a film for viewing in any setting, you must make sure that you have full acceptance from your actors and anyone else who appears in the film. To get your film shown in a prestigious venue or television slot and then have to withdraw because you don't have clearance would be heartbreaking. To free your production from these potential problems, ask everyone who appears in the film to sign a written agreement that they accept your right to exhibit this film in a 'public showing'. You need this for any kind of movie, including documentary. Written agreement may have special relevance where young, up-and-coming actors subsequently become famous overnight, and in documentaries tackling outlandish and extreme subject matter. Certainly, broadcast television would expect to have complete clearance from everyone who took part before transmitting your film.

If you are in a position to offer rights, look at how those rights are arranged. Some entertainment lawyers suggest seeking a reversion clause in which rights are returned to you after a set period, perhaps six months or a year. Rights could be retained by the site only if a certain amount of revenue is generated during that period.

Use the Internet for marketing, not financial return

In general marketing terms, remember that since a film shown on the Internet can be accessed theoretically from any territory in the world, just about all your future marketing deals will be affected once you have shown the film on the web. Since it is unlikely that you are going to see any reasonable return by selling to the Internet, it may be more prudent to seek deals first with markets offering higher rates, such as television and video. In addition, copyright laws vary enormously from country to country, and if you are at all protective about your movie and the possibility of its being copied and sold, think twice about Internet broadcast. The Internet should not be seen as a way of recouping costs or making a profit on your movie, rather it is an effective marketing tool, enabling people to see what you do, remember your name and check out the next movie you make. Although it certainly lacks any financial gain for the filmmaker, it somewhat makes up for this by offering the widest possible return of opinion. Many people find the comments and suggestions made by viewers enlightening and encouraging.

So, to recap, decide in advance what your aims are in seeking Internet broadcast. Since financial gain is unlikely to be high, viewing figures are the main attraction, and that means going first to sites with high profiles.

The Crunch

● Always read the small print before you sign your film over to a site
● Don't expect financial return – it's about exposure
● Make sure you have permission and ownership of all parts of your film – music included
● Check what the copyright law is in the country where the website is hosted.

10 Mapping the industry

1. State of the art: mapping the film industry

We've spent some time looking at the main issues affecting the new world of moving images. Next, we need to look at who pays the bills, the industry itself. What kind of health is the film industry in and what are the trends that stand to affect filmmakers?

An overview

A possible analogy for the film industry is that of an iceberg. Only a very small amount of the total is actually visible and yet it is that small part that is most visible and draws our attention. Mainstream feature films are still the backbone of the industry and there are no signs that audiences are about to desert their second favourite pastime (after gaming). In fact, the need for newer twists on tired genres and for more flexible means of watching movies is the result of larger appetites on the part of audiences rather than disillusionment. Hollywood's response, as we have seen, has been to draw in international cultures to inject new life into its staple genre diet, and it is tentatively seeing the possibilities for interactivity in DVD.

Within this surface mass of the movie world, there are a range of smaller industries with different economic models – where expectations for profits are smaller but have corresponding budgets. In these models there are established audiences that coexist with the mainstream fare, often within the same company. So, a large studio can support left-field directors like David O. Russell (*I Heart Huckabees*, 2004) or Michel Gondry (*Eternal Sunshine of the Spotless Mind*, 2004) because a Harry Potter or other lucrative franchise covers losses. Furthermore, such movies – which are independent in spirit if not in pocket from the major studios – often return greater profits than many blockbusters in terms of the ratio of money spent on actual production (the negative cost) to money earned. Further afield, markets in territories such as Asia and Latin America are surprisingly buoyant, despite economic struggles, and are resilient to the flood of bigger budget films from Hollywood.

If we go slightly below the waterline of our iceberg, we see the hundreds of movies which don't make it into theatres – or don't surface. The iron grip of the distributor prevents them from getting to the upper levels of visibility and profitability. The distributor has, for a long time, been seen as preventing new directors from breaking through. They are arguably culturally conservative and determined to preserve the profitable status quo.

Amma Asante, BAFTA-winning director of *Way of Life* (2004), found distribution a serious obstacle:

> 'The most limiting thing is distribution. A film is not a film until it gets an audience. It can be the best film in the world but until people see it, it is not a film. We make great films in the UK. They are meant for the big screen but so often they just end up on the TV in the corner of the sitting room and that's a really sad thing.'

Did you know?
A distributor is a company that specializes in selling a movie within a particular country, or 'territory'. They act as go-between with film studios on one side and theatres on the other, getting a sizeable cut of box-office takings. They decide whether a film gets seen by audiences by assessing whether it will be a box-office success. If they don't think it is a big movie, they don't release it widely.

The issue of feature-film finance in countries such as Britain, Australia and Spain has always been seen as important. But the distribution problem – how to actually get untried, untested movies into theatres – remains intractable, which is why many people see the possibility of legal downloading of films offering a way forward.

Pushing further down below the waterline we see the even larger numbers of filmmakers making features that do not expect distribution on the scale seen above, and instead opt for DIY releases. Revolt Films' *Asylum Night* is an example of a movie made with little funding but which was able to find its own distribution route. Rather than waste time pushing at closed doors, these filmmakers bypass theatrical release by aiming for the more easily targeted home viewer, through specialist cable channels (in this case The Horror Channel, UK) and a self-financed DVD. Knowing their audience and where to find it has proved to be a highly efficient way of target marketing.

Moving further down we start to encounter a part of the industry which has arguably the fewest resources and yet has the most intense pool of talent. The short-film directors making movies with maximum originality, innovation and professionalism but with minimum budgets are the main motivating factor in this floating berg. Their circulating momentum pushes new talent upwards, encourages first-timers from down below, and spreads opportunity and support throughout.

Parallel to this part of the iceberg are the directors who sustain and energize the music promo and advertising fields. Lucrative and with high stakes, these areas attract ambitious directors who may also wish to enter feature-film production later, as do the short-film directors next door. The high turnover of their work often gives them the edge when it comes to moving further up the industry, giving them room for development and experimentation while getting paid.

If we take a quick side-view of these layers of the industry for a moment, we can see the way funding affects production.

Public funding is a fact of life for many countries, but less so in the USA, given its more established industry infrastructure. If we looked at an Australian version of our iceberg, for instance, we would see a generous core of state funding that affects many levels of production, from scripts, to shorts, to features. But the Australian Film Finance Commission is criticized for not helping innovative or unique voices of directors, preferring the conservative middle ground, a charge rebuffed by its commissioners.

The UK sector, meanwhile, has several sources of public funding, including large initiatives such as the Film Council, to Lottery franchisees, down to local arts support for scripts and training. But a pertinent criticism is that these operate out of sync to one another, offering no coherent pathway for filmmakers to move through. Pots of funding exist for parts of production, but not for other areas. Filmmakers find themselves looking for bridging capital to reach the next pot of cash ahead. But these higher levels of funding have been criticized for poor project judgement; the Lottery excursion at the turn of the millennium, where several companies were offered cash effectively to operate as mini studios, has been deemed less than successful.

Tip   Skillset in the UK is a government-backed agency offering training and support to filmmakers. Check out their website for details of how they can help UK-based filmmakers: www.skillset.org

---

Other territories such as India have industries where production costs have yet to reach the exorbitant levels of European/Hollywood movies and are correspondingly profitable. Unlikely pockets of vibrant production exist in some other countries where conditions are least favourable, such as Argentina and Mexico, while emerging economies such as China loom large in the distance as they develop film industry structures with festivals, a DVD market and a distribution system.

Moving back to the view of our iceberg, again plunging down further, the expanse of the lower strata becomes clear. The no-budget filmmakers, making films at the start of their careers, populate this level in their thousands. From here emerge the talented directors and technicians, cinematographers, scriptwriters and producers who will be drawn up into the middle of the iceberg, and eventually try to push into the upper reaches. In this environment, budgets are small and funding smaller, or whatever is left over after food and bills are taken out.

Go to: Chapter 9:4 – the no-budget level corresponds to Stage 1 in the three-step career outlined therein.

Each of the levels in the iceberg are dependent to a great extent on the success of the topmost layer. In practice, this means the chain of people who make it their job to visit the lower layers of the industry to scout for talent – buying scripts, awarding prizes, providing funding, bringing investors and producers together. They act as a natural filter to how many filmmakers rise through the levels to the top, basing their decisions on the health of the industry and allowing through only what the industry can support.

2. State of the art: expansion and convergence

After working hard on your own films for so long now, this section is going to let you take the soft seat and watch as we go through the landscape that is the contemporary film industry. On this journey we are going to see what has shifted over the last few years, plot where we may be headed and spot the possible threats on the horizon.

At the end of each subsection there are points which need to be chewed over some more in the form of questions. Knowing what will happen in the future is all about knowing what questions to ask.

From a professional point of view, too, it is paramount that your understanding of the industry is not restricted to a knowledge of who sells movies, where and how you get them screened, how you promote them and what your rights are. What is needed is a joined up approach where your understanding of the industry as a whole is informed by a bird's eye view. From up there you can see what is happening to the industry as a whole, and from this can plot your own route through it.

In Chapter 9:5 on mapping your career we looked at what your route could be to get from beginner to self-sustaining worker in the industry. In this section we will look at what sort of environment this route or path is going through. To achieve this, we will look at the key issues that are affecting filmmakers today at different levels of the moving image world.

Viewing

The audience has always been a crucial part of the equation whenever filmmakers talk about their work. Every film needs to find its audience and this body is seen now as a crucial part of completing the jigsaw of what a film means – the audience colour the experiences within the film with their own ideas, prejudices, knowledge, fears and aspirations.

So far so good, but today the difference is that the audience is no longer just a passive receptacle for the entertainment offered it. Many filmmakers have always struggled with how to devise ways to wake up and engage an audience, but often this has been in the arthouse sector, where audiences don't mind the cat and mouse game they play with the director as they piece together what the film means.

Did you know?

'Arthouse' is a term which refers to a type of movie. It comes from the fact that these films were often seen in arthouses, or arts centres, rather than in mainstream theatres. Arthouse films tend to be very different to the Hollywood model and concentrate on theme and meaning rather than story and plot, and are pitched at a more niche and usually adult audience. However, a film that is a mainstream movie in its home country can often be seen as arthouse in another, such as New Zealand's *Whale Rider*.

Viewing alone

But now, quite literally, the audience has gone home. They are no longer sharing the viewing experience together. They don't even watch the same movies at home as they did when networks aired the big film and we all watched simultaneously; the hundreds of channels now accessible, including pay-view, mean that watching a film is now a solitary experience. The movie in the theatre has diminished while other platforms to watch have grown – the personal DVD player, the phone movie, web films on the PC. As if to define our viewing habits further, films now use a horizontal spread of formats to reach the audience, creating a fictional world that is only experienced in its entirety if you watch the movie in the theatre, then go home and watch the animated story background on the web, then download story updates onto your cell phone. Further deleted scenes are added in the DVD and perhaps a director's cut is issued. Today, then, the viewing experience is exhausting – it no longer gets delivered to our door; we have to go and search for some of it.

The DVD is a particularly fertile area for the new interactivity of films. It is now possible that a film can be regarded as a work in progress on its theatrical release and then revisited by the director for different audiences for the DVD.

Film View

Oliver Stone, when he was about to release *Alexander* in 2004, was asked whether there would be a director's cut later. 'This *is* the director's cut,' came the reply. Only two months later Stone revised this idea in the light of poor press reviews of the film, saying that the DVD would be very different and he would 'add more' to the film.

This is not inherently a negative development and could perhaps be seen as producing a relationship between maker and consumer which is more of a dialogue. The 2001 film *Donnie Darko* fared badly in the box office on its release, was a word-of-mouth hit (we used to call these 'cult films') and then re-released in 2004 with more material, becoming a best seller.

Bite-size content

We also want to be able to watch our moving images in various environments – the result of having hand-held or portable devices for viewing on. The effect on viewing habits is on the content of the films themselves. Content has become more bite-sized, in recognizable 'scene selection' chunks, ready to be played repeatedly like a favourite CD of songs. Movies in this noisy environment – watched on the train, in class, at the breakfast table – need to shout louder. They need to travel well to any format, from two-inch screens to 30-foot screens.

One more complicating factor here is the need for films to travel well in geographical terms. For Hollywood films, the foreign market now accounts for a significant amount of income, and no big-budget film can make strong profits in the domestic market alone.

It's not only feature films that have changed; the content we watch has become very different. On cell phones we now view bite-sized content such as film trailers, ads, virals (shorts you send on to a friend) and music promos. These fill a need for media products that are easily digested and can be viewed without the commitment needed to enter into a two-hour feature film.

Converging forms

But it also affects what we are accustomed to seeing: non-narrative, music video-style images that look more like graphic design than movies. At this point we can introduce a key concept in this chapter: convergence. This means a process where different art forms and styles meet and overlap. It is not so much a fashionable watchword as a real way of working for media makers. So, for instance, videos look like graphic spreads in magazines or films resemble computer games – and one of the reasons why we like convergence, as consumers, is that it means familiarity. Many media products (print, video, web) resemble each other in style, design and purpose.

Finally, the whole act of watching has become a different kind of experience and that calls for different kinds of movies. Once upon a time – before home entertainment – watching a film was an immersive activity, set in a dark, sensory-deprived environment where the film was the only stimulus. You could describe this as a 'hot' way of viewing – in other words, it was intense and intimate. But viewing on the platforms we now have is a much cooler experience – our senses are being fought over by a hundred other stimuli. We tend to watch with only one eye and with one ear.

Work it out

- How is the same film affected by being viewed on different platforms – cell phone, PC, theatre?
- Directors now need to vie for our attention in several different ways at once using the web, short films, extra DVDs, all to support the main feature movie (as in *The Matrix*). Is this just another marketing wheeze?
- Does more interactivity on DVDs mean that the director hands over the final cut to the viewer?

Content overdrive

Content is the stuff the movie is about. It used to be simple – this or that happened in chronological order and then the credits came up. The story, style and theme – that was the content.

But today content is tied strongly to the form it takes to reach you. So, a viral movie is ultra-short, enigmatic, gimmicky and has 'share-it qualities' to encourage you to send it on to a friend. Whatever the point of the viral – to raise the profile of a new recording artist or broadcast a new political campaign – it will have to contain a certain kind of content because that is what people expect.

Did you know?
A 'viral movie' is a short film of usually under a minute or two. It is so called because it is sent from person to person via email or phone. If you see a viral movie and like it, you would send it on to a friend; they like it and so the chain goes on. In practice, virals tend to be related to music promos and often sell a product – for example, raising awareness about a new band.

Now that there are so many new ways of viewing there is a need for more and more content. This platform explosion is good for small, independent makers because it has led to increased jobs available. But pricing structures are less rigid in this arena, so corporations are taking advantage to define this

Figure 10.1 The computer-generated animated short *Bungalow* by Giffentoast.

field on their terms – usually by aiming to produce products for less money. One of the reasons companies have embraced this new form is, ironically, due to downloading and file sharing. The net loss in financial terms to the industry has been significant – most of it felt by music labels and film studios – and the result is the need to target content more efficiently at the 'right' audience. For example, music labels have started to target the live performance as the place to market a recording artist as opposed to the music promo, aware that you can target more effectively when you have a captive audience of a certain age group all in one place. This means that some have started to reduce money spent on music promos in favour of video projection at a live concert and then targeted virals to those who sign up for updates by phone.

Did you know?
New forms of movie have led to the term 'nanotainment', a suitably enigmatic description for such short bursts of video. The 'nano' part of the term refers as much to the short length of the videos as to their shelf-life.

But this new form of content is not actually that new. In the early days of cinema there were short reels of spectacle – a speeding train coming at the audience, a bullfight, a daring circus trick – which audiences experienced rather than simply watched; audiences ducked when the train zoomed towards them.

Film View
The early playful films of George Melies are examples of mini-spectacles where musicians appear out of thin air or a coronation is replayed in Melies's small studio. Many of the routine camera tricks we take for granted today originated in Melies's studio, such as layering multiple images of the same actor together to give the effect of clones.

Narrative was not what it became later; thrill and spectacle were more prevalent. Today, perhaps, we are rediscovering this idea and opting for quick-fix imagery. But maybe it is not so much a product of the short-attention-span society but a return to cinema's roots.

With all this new content emerging, how does it look? The result has been to cut out reflection and pauses, since time is at a premium – both in terms of how much air time costs and how long our attention spans are. These are the sorts of films that don't stop for a breath. Camera language has been rewritten in favour of a constantly engaging, unpredictable style. Editing too has emerged as more jagged, jumping quickly from shot to shot. Movement of the camera has been reduced due to the blurring that occurs when the movie is compressed – in its place the jump cut has taken over. Close-ups are more common and long, detailed shots rare. On a more general note, the space – literally, in a room or on a location – that films create has been foreshortened, as the dominance of the close-up and the need to avoid distance detail has brought the field of vision much closer to the viewer.

Film View

Phone Booth (2002) is an example of filmmaking as short continuous bursts of action. It takes the audience on a bare-knuckle ride in the first few minutes as we trace the route of a phone call from handset to satellite to cables to phone box, a trick which has previously appeared in *Three Colours: Red* (1994). The whole movie tells its narrative in terms of easy-to-digest images, where the camera goes straight to the action and literally focuses only on what we need to see.

Moving on to feature films, there has been an effect, due more to the influence of many directors emerging from the music promo business. Spike Jonze and Michel Gondry both developed their unique styles in award-winning music promos. More recently, a new generation of directors has grown out of this field, including David Slade (*Hard Candy*, 2005); David LaChapelle (*Rise*, 2004), Tim Story (*Fantastic Four*, 2005), Steve Carr (*Rebound*, 2005), Jonathan Glazer (*Birth*, 2004), Joseph Kahn (*Torque*, 2005) and Mark Romanek (*One Hour Photo*, 2002). These directors bring a style honed on fast editing, strong imagery and quick delivery of narrative. They have the skills to truncate stories and to develop character and plot in small glimpses. In many cases, they are aware of the weight of information that each image, each frame, needs to carry and so they aim for economy of shots with tight delivery of story elements. Whatever its artistic merits it is certainly what the target audience wants and is familiar with.

Work it out

- How does the scale of the image on the new formats affect how you make a movie?
- Is 'nanotainment' really as innovative as it looks? Or is it simply top-slicing the good bits off cinema without putting in the depth of meaning? Will movies resemble trailers?
- Is nanotainment returning movies to popular, street-level roots?
- How will the Hollywood studios adapt?
- How will working in promos affect directors?

The rise of video games

A quiet coup took place just after the turn of the century when the total size of the Hollywood film industry was overtaken in the entertainment-scape by the video game industry. In this velvet revolution the insurgents don't want to depose the long-standing king of the screen – the movies in the theatres – but they do want to pull a few more strings than they were.

Cinema, on the other hand, has had different plans and has seen in this upstart video game industry possibilities for marketing. It has not been averse to flattery through imitation as movies start to resemble game scenarios and even imitate camera shots, in an effort to bring the gaming generation into theatres. Audiences are overlapping in that gamers tend to be cinema-goers and treat their media fixes as extensions of each other. So they want films to have strong plots with parcels of action in varied situations, with obstacles mounted like Pac-Men against the protagonist. Similarly, they want their games to be more and more realistic, with camera angles that borrow from established movie camera language, and with texture mapping that creates more illusion than before – obscuring the fact that it is just a screen of coloured-in polygons.

Films have not, as was suspected a while ago, become like video games themselves, and any attempt at pure interactivity where you can determine the story outcome is seen as gauche. And films which have self-consciously tried to use video game 'style' as a production look have been unsuccessful, such as Cronenberg's *eXistenZ*.

Instead, the most impact gaming has had on movies is on the industry itself, but this may in time prove to be a strong effect on the movies themselves. Now that game companies are returning profits equal to those of small film studios, it is possible that these companies will establish themselves in the wider entertainment industry, reversing the flow chart where game follows movie. But this may not be simply a case of filming the narrative of a successful game – like *Lara Croft* or *Resident Evil* – but the simultaneous development of stories and characters in both gaming and movie worlds.

Perhaps the most clear example of this is LucasArts. As a studio it resembles no other; it has its feet firmly planted in media of every type, masterminding game, movie, CD, DVD and merchandising in one stroke. The latter trilogy of *Star Wars* films has arguably been subject to a business sense that perceives a multimedia audience. These films lend themselves so directly to taking a form in video games that it is hard not to think that script meetings may have been attended by game developers. Certainly, the range of fight and flight scenarios that make up a successful game are all evident in each of these later films, with action staged with a variety of craft, weapons and obstacles in settings such as the jungle, desert, frozen wastes, industrial complex and so on. Could it be that LucasArts is the model for the new breed of studio which makes story franchises that are suitable for delivery in both passive (movie) and interactive (game) modes?

Work it out

- Is there a chicken and egg question here relating to the camera framing seen in games: did games borrow from cinema convention or did they invent their own framing style? Or is it that films now borrow from game framing (as in *The Matrix* fight scenes).
- If a game company controls which films get made, how will this affect directors?
- And will CGI (computer-generated images) become the preferred production method for such films where motion capture can be used both for the movie and the game?

Territory shift

The gravitational centre of the film industry has shifted over the last century, starting off in Berlin and Copenhagen, then Los Angeles. But its latest home has been restless too and has led critics and industry-watchers to question whether Hollywood can claim to be the start and end of the movie world. The reason for this doubt is the number of franchises and blockbusters that have been handed to directors coming from the emerging industries in Latin America, Asia and Australasia, and by the movement of production to other parts of the globe. Has Hollywood found itself with few directors for the new world of movies today? Has it had to rely on world cinema to sustain its talent base?

Two factors suggest that Hollywood is having to adapt to these new territories. First, there are vibrant industries with developing infrastructures in countries such as China, South Korea and many countries in South America. New directors challenge their domestic audiences with home-grown products and tempt them away from their Hollywood viewing habits. Second, audiences in the strong Western markets in Europe have broken with tradition and embraced the foreign subtitled film in box-office hits such as *Crouching Tiger, Hidden Dragon, Amélie, Hero* and *The Ring*.

Figure 10.2 *Futureshock* by polymedia group, Neo, displays the shift from territories that has moved many filmmakers to shoot in the Far East.

Studios have seen the benefit in bringing directors who speak the language of the foreign audience to Hollywood. They refresh tired franchises and genres by bringing a new cinematic language to audiences, reaching domestic markets with their freshness and foreign markets at the same time. John Woo's contribution to the *Mission Impossible* series brought a fresher Hong Kong toughness to the action genre, while Alfonso Cuaron's third Harry Potter (*The Prisoner of Azkhaban*, 2004) balanced the inevitable effects-driven action with a greater sense of place. Meanwhile, Romanian Gore Verbinski took on Disney's *Pirates of the Caribbean*, Chris Nolan took on *Batman* (*Batman Begins*, 2005) and Jean-Pierre Jeunet the *Alien* series (*Alien Resurrection*, 1997). The effect of this importing of talent into what some have termed the 'talent vacuum' in Hollywood has in the most part brought significant box-office returns, though the Harry Potter series has made successively less money as it has progressed, regardless of director, and the *Alien* movie by Jeunet was the least successful of the series.

These new industrial centres have exported more than just directors. As the identity of Hollywood genres has undergone something of a crisis, mutations have occurred regularly as we have seen in the western (a brief re-emergence in the late 1990s) and horror genres (resurrecting 1970s movies or combining franchises such as *Freddy vs Jason*). But it is the influence of movies from new territories that has really revitalized genres. The Japanese horror film has been synonymous with originality for some time, with English-language remakes planned for most major hits. The Hong Kong action movie has become the standard for all action scenes as far as young audiences are concerned and Eastern cod-spiritualism has become the mainstay of films such as *The Matrix* trilogy.

To add some perspective to all this, the family-oriented, culturally conservative movie retains its loyal fan base and will carry on doing so. But arguably, the artistic centre of the film industry is quietly migrating to the Far East to reflect the need for booming ticket receipts in these new markets. Financially, too, shifts have occurred, with electronics giant Sony acquiring Universal and having stakes in other major studios.

Work it out

- The independent movement in the USA has been the keeper of the flame in opposing Hollywood with original and new cinematic voices. Will this sector be squeezed by similar innovative directors from other territories?
- Do Japanese/Hong Kong films simply ape Hollywood in terms of action, spectacle and entertainment, or do they offer a seriously new approach?

The polymedia artist

We talk about the DV revolution as an ongoing series of incursions into the mainstream film industry, where new technology has led to filmmakers being able to bypass many of the obstacles that used to prevent them making movies. It has democratized filmmaking to a large extent. But at the forefront of this revolution since the mid-1990s has been a new breed of filmmaker who find themselves diametrically opposed to the filmmaking tradition as it stands. They have developed a complete stratum of the moving image industry for themselves and have turned it into one of the most profitable areas for a filmmaker to work within.

On the sidelines, this kind of filmmaker has been cutting a vertical slice through the other strata of the film industry, making inroads into animation, advertising, television and even feature films. DV is now moving through filmmaking at a fast pace, making some filmmakers question how long celluloid can coexist with its upstart technology. If film has had an assassin in the shadows waiting to enact a *coup de grâce*, it is the polymedia artist/filmmaker. In his book *The End of Celluloid*, Matt Hanson, director of the highly influential Onedotzero festival of digital polymedia video, asked:

> 'How do you rebel against … three-act structures and happy endings you can predict from the opening scene. The safe commercial formulas are breaking down as genres become overfamiliar and tired.'

Hollywood, he predicts, will naturally decay as audiences demand video products – you can't call them movies as such – that reflect new watching habits. The theatre will no longer be the venue of new moving images; that will give way to the party, a place of random collisions of video images and music in an atmosphere where video is experienced rather than watched. The VJ artist, mixing live from pre-arranged clips, reacts to the 'audience' to produce one-off video events. Video is used for synaesthetic ends, inducing sensation rather than delivering information.

So what does the polymedia artist do? The term itself derives from multimedia, but is seen as a more accurate description for the simultaneity of media in the work, as opposed to a serial use of it. It suggests a contraction of media together to form a new kind of medium, rather than a use of separate media.

The polymedia artist tends to be a part of one of the many groups or companies that operate across the fields of filmmaking, VJ-ing, art, architecture, web design and graphic design. The groups are often highly profitable, their bread and butter work the visuals at party venues. They produce films perhaps described as the *haute couture* of the video world – without obvious function, but having a large stylistic trickle-down effect on other parts of the industry. They organize workshops, produce music promos, develop art installations and devise films that are more like theses on ideas such as urban isolation or corporate greed.

These groups experiment with every aspect of the moving image product, challenging it so severely that there would appear to be no common ground at all between the polymedia artist and the film director. Blast Theory, a successful UK-based group, worked on a collaboration with Nottingham University's Virtual Reality lab to produce an event in Rotterdam in 2003 which combined video with design gaming and animation. Players were recruited to track with GPS systems a group of 'runners' – players who needed to be caught within a simple narrative. On video screens they could view their own

Figure 10.3 In *Can You See Me Now?*, Blast Theory created an interactive game where players were tracked by satellite. The audience becomes both viewers and directors, helping to steer the course of the film/game.

participation in the narrative of the chase and be director, actor and viewer at the same time. Online participation added another level to the event.

The most visible product of the polymedia artist is as a VJ, producing visuals for parties and events. Eclectic Method use gathered footage from movies to create collages that are syncopated with music, displayed at closing night parties at the Sundance Film Festival in 2004 and 2005. The Light Surgeons emerged from art school experiments with Super 8 to light shows and then progressed into live video mixing with the arrival of DV in the 1990s. Large projections surround the audience and engage more senses than just sight and sound, making for a more visceral experience that translates poorly to DVD.

In terms of distribution routes, this field is well catered for, with high profile festivals Onedotzero and Resfest offering a rolling schedule of localized and online programming. Spin-offs from these festivals have proved lucrative, including the best-selling Onedotzero DVD collection and Resfest's magazine. The DVD, in particular, was an unexpected development. Bringing together the best examples of this kind of work, they were unlikely hits, with one newspaper (*The Guardian*, UK) describing them as 'the equivalent of having a mixtape made up by your coolest friend'. They tapped into a home market already making hits out of Addictive TV's *Mixmaster* series of DVDs – an audience schooled on the 1990s home DJ and rave culture, who immediately felt at ease with a visual form that scratched and sampled freely in the same way music did.

Did you know?
Resfest and Onedotzero are agencies dedicated to supporting and promoting new and innovative digital video work. Both operate festivals and related products, including DVDs. Resfest also runs a successful magazine, *Res*. Resfest is based in the USA, while Onedotzero is based in the UK, with outlets in Japan.

So how does all this affect the wider film industry? As the makers themselves develop their own culture, it seems less necessary to knock down the mainstream film culture. It is becoming more separate from the film industry, but has a one-way route into it that is the envy of other filmmakers. Many animators and artists move onto more high profile jobs in the mainstream industry, such as Tim Hope, maker of experimental animations, who went on to work at Disney.

In an increasingly safe position, polymedia doesn't need to evangelize for new recruits. It has a completely parallel system of production and distribution, and is comfortable in its position outside the film world. It does have a lasting legacy though. It is slowly but determinedly changing the moving image landscape – not by changing the film industry, but by changing the audience.

Work it out

- Is polymedia merely technology-led? Is it just about playing around with new software and gadgets?
- Do these artists pose any threat to filmmaking or are they doomed to forever be the street protester outside the studio gates?
- Is subject matter (themes and ideas) limited because everything has to be dealt with in small bites?

Figure 10.4 Dougal Wilson is one of the top music promo makers, winning awards for his witty and ground-breaking work. This still is from a promo for The Streets.

Threats to the industry

The colossal size of the film industry masks the fact that threats exist which have created leaks in its structure. Anyone entering the industry needs to know where these leaks are, which are haemorrhaging cash at an alarming rate. To studios and filmmakers, film piracy is the biggest of these leaks, made up of illegal downloading and counterfeit DVD sales. Efforts to reduce illegal copying of DVDs have proved fruitless because of the ease with which it can be accomplished, despite encryption software. Moves towards HD DVD are based to a large extent on tighter security measures in this new technology.

The issue of downloading is more pressing because of the widespread use of the web, whereas pirated DVDs need to be produced and shipped to consumers. Quality is improving and file-sharers take pride in producing accurate copies with extra credits containing their own pseudonyms. Still largely recorded by camcorder illegally in theatres, studios are increasingly worried about copies straight from DVD, using screeners – tapes sent to critics or members of industry associations. This led to some companies refusing to issue screener DVDs of certain films prone to piracy, altogether against the wishes of voters on important awards like the Oscars or BAFTAs.

Did you know?
The value of the market in illegal downloading – hinting at the loss incurred by film production – is estimated to rise to over $1 billion by 2008, and has grown extremely quickly, with a 1768 per cent increase in pirated DVDs between 2002 and 2004.

Lost revenue is at the crux of this issue, but it is not just those at the top who stand to lose out. John Hassey, leading agent for some of the world's top music promo directors, has seen available funding from music labels shrink due to music downloading:

> 'The effect of downloads is very bad. When I was a kid there was talk about how home tap-ing was killing music, but that was nothing. For some people it is difficult now. There was about 7 per cent less money now [2004] than last year on videos. The problem is that labels are having to think about where they can spend their decreasing budgets on a band.'

In Hollywood, the most vociferous body against piracy is the MPAA, representing the interests of the major studios. But it could appear that this anger is more a voice of frustration that the mechanism is not in place to exploit downloading as a retail area. Home video was seen as a similar threat in the 1980s. It eventually led to a shift in viewing habits and has emerged as the saviour of the industry, as revenue from these ancillary markets now accounts for more than total box-office receipts. A workable and legitimate method of downloading films – perhaps even during theatrical release dates – is arguably the only solution to this threat to the film industry.

What next?

Futurology and film don't make a good mix. Predictions tend to be exercises in compromise, filled with caveats. And there seems to be little point in talking about how the industry could change next year when it is in a state of perpetual change. But any filmmaker entering the industry needs to have some sense of what's on the horizon. If we can't figure out all the answers just yet, perhaps the next best route is to work out which are the right questions to ask. This is a way of raising issues and offering multiple scenarios for reflection, so that you know where to look when you hear about changes going on.

Questions for the future of the moving image industry

- With *CGI and motion capture*, will the actor/star system in movies decline? An actor's movements can be mapped and encoded, with movies realistically animated later.
- Will *multiple formats* of viewing mean that we need to have new ways of telling stories?
- Will *viewer choice* become more prevalent? Could DVDs offer sad or happy endings, arthouse or mainstream versions, pre- and post-18 cuts?
- *Is the cinema doomed* as the place for new movies? Will it become like *haute couture* at the Paris catwalk – seen by few but widely influential?
- What will happen to *cultural differences* with the new global market for movies (same-day release times, cultural references from around the world to capture each market)?
- Will film studios have to become *universal deliverers of media content* rather than film production companies? Will they seek story or character franchises to sell though DVD, downloads, games, themed parties and web movies?
- How will *shared software and online rented hard drive space* on a central server affect no-budget filmmakers? They will have greater resources to store, edit and promote their films independently.

- Is there a model in Apple's successful *iTunes online music* store for shorts and music videos and other polymedia products?
- Will plasma screens and *High Definition* affect the way we shoot? Does greater picture realism and detail change content?

3. Trends affecting film

Earlier in this book (Chapter 9:5) we looked at how the changing landscape of the film industry affects individual filmmakers. In this section we can take this a stage further by zooming out to look at the entire environment we call the film world, where it is located in wider culture and technology, and how filmmakers can track their way through it. In this way, the map we will enter is as useful as a career guide as it is in identifying the changes in the industry.

Since film is a visual medium it follows perhaps that we resort to images when trying to convey the more complex ideas. The most useful effect of an image in this case is in being able to highlight the simultaneous effect of many of the ideas discussed here; convergence, plurality and multiplicity are the watchwords that run throughout this new environment, so it is appropriate that we take an approach which shows everything to us at once.

How to read the diagram (Figure 10.5)

Figure 10.5 takes as its focus the image of a filmmaker walking towards the horizon that is the future. S/he is going from one landscape into another. The clear path that used to exist is starting to peter out and the filmmaker is faced with a landscape with many paths, crossed by opportunities.

In symbolic terms, the landscape is the entire cultural breadth of the industry, the path through which filmmakers used to tread. The fact that the path no longer points one way suggests that filmmakers have options about where to head towards and are not restricted from changing routes and crossing into other areas of the landscape.

Key

- The lakes and ponds are – for the moment – discrete areas of the moving image industry. Some are larger than others, while some are currently dry beds awaiting attention. The main point of interest here is how each of the pools is developing furrows to connect one with another, trenches dug by new developments in technology. Note how this 'convergence' will overfill some areas and threaten to swallow up others.
- Feeding lots of these lakes or ponds is the major lake of narrative cinema. Vessels floating on it represent the numerous ways we have of navigating this lake – the film festivals, critics and industry-watchers. Note how the audience are in the lake. They jump in and raise its level accordingly, allowing it to take up more land to accommodate them.

Figure 10.5 Trends affecting filmmakers. Drawing courtesy of Mark Wilson.

- You can see how this major lake is now being fed by new tributaries of small but significant streams of water from very different landscapes. This may represent global cinema replenishing the pool with new talent.
- The gated and walled Hollywood citadel is surrounded by lakes, including one that threatens to flood its lands. It has ring-fenced itself with its success, but also needs sustenance from the bigger pools if it is to survive.
- Moving to the path, it starts at a point in time roughly a decade ago at the foot of the page. At this point notice how the filmmaker is having to travel by large truck, carrying expensive and bulky equipment. By the time we reach the person on foot at the end of the path, we notice how it is possible to travel more lightly, with fewer costs and better equipment.
- Notice how many members of the audience are deserting the main lake to find fresher waters. The more they tread the ground between ponds, the more they make furrows between them. Waters then flow into other ponds.
- Craters here and there pose threats (highlighted in Chapter 10:2) to the lakes and ponds.
- The waters themselves – the pools of creativity that make up the industry – are growing in size. The video games pool, fed strongly by music video, animation and narrative cinema, is rising quickly.
- On higher ground is the pool of documentary filmmaking. Unlikely to be affected by rising tides, it exists in a loftier position, able to survey the rest of the landscape but offering few chances for replenishment. A separate pond related to the documentary has sprung up nearby, which has found massive sustenance through siphoning water from the narrative pond, and the animation and music video ponds.

Go to: Chapter 6:3 for more ideas on new documentary forms.

- The distance is cloudy and uncertain, but the filmmaker is unconcerned with this as the here and now is more attractive. The imminent changes to the landscape as ponds rise and merge and others disappear present challenges and opportunities to her or him. Their newly nimble status means they can move quickly between areas, covering ground fast and drawing from various pools at once.
- The clouds above show rain falling into various pools. These clouds are carriers of water, which favour some parts of the landscape above others. They move like the zeitgeist, focusing our attention on certain areas more than others. Unpredictable as yet, they move heavily over some ponds while others on the fringes of the landscape await their turn for rain, when the climate changes and audiences discover its freshness.

Glossary of film and video terms

4:1:1   A way of measuring the ratio between brightness signal and colour signals. This ratio is the smallest and is roughly 50 per cent of the value of 4:2:2 in terms of horizontal colour resolution (vertical colour resolution remains the same). Panasonic's DVC Pro uses this ratio.

4:2:0   This sampling ratio is very similar to 4:1:1, except that it is the vertical colour resolution values which are reduced by 50 per cent, while the horizontal remains the same.

4:2:2   This is a higher quality resolution used by many high-end cameras, including Digital Betacam and Sony's DVC Pro 50. Resolution is about twice the value of 4:1:1 or 4:2:0.

4:4:4:4   This sampling rate is as high as 4:2:2 but has an additional Key signal.

A

Accessory shoe   A standard way of mounting a light or microphone on camcorders.

A/D conversion   This is another way of saying analog-to-digital conversion. Data coming from an analog device such as a VHS camera or a VCR will need to be translated into digital information before editing software can read them. It looks at the curved electrical waves present in analog information and reduces them to jagged shapes able to be described in numbers.

AE Preset   The pre-programmed settings in a camcorder designed to deal with unusual lighting or subject movement conditions.

AES/EBU   These abbreviations refer to the Audio Engineering Society and the European Broadcasting Union, and relate to standards that have been agreed for transmission of audio data.

Aliasing   Aliasing refers to the degrading of video pictures by high-frequency video information. This results in jagged edges or lines, and strobing effects on sharp horizontal lines and rotating objects such as wheels.

Alpha channel   Alpha channel is used for placing transparent elements over your picture, such as text. When you type in a line of credits, for example, they will need to be seen with the text opaque and the background transparent. This transparency is the alpha channel function.

Alternative cinema   A loose term ascribed to any group of films defined by common characteristics, which is in opposition to the dominant, narrative, mainstream film.

Ambient sound   Also referred to as 'presence', this is the natural background sound of a set or location. It needs to be maintained throughout a scene to ensure continuity. Also known as 'buzz track'.

Analog   This is the method of storing information that was dominant until digital arrived. It involves the recording of information using variable waves, as opposed to digital, which operates only in terms of yes or no, one or zero. Analog data is transferred by the recorder copying the electrical information, but it will lose some of this information each time it copies, leading to an increasing loss of quality in each subsequent copy.

Angle   The point of view of the camera.

Animatic   A simple animated sequence made from a storyboard, mostly used for television commercials.

Anti-aliasing   This is a way of getting smoother pictures in video and graphics. It works by blurring the edges slightly on curved or tilted objects.

Aperture   The round hole, the iris, at the front of the lens through which light enters the camera. It is measured in f-stops, with a smaller f-stop number referring to a larger opening, which allows more light to pass through. Each stop admits 100 per cent more light than the last. F-stops also affect depth of field, smaller iris holes allowing more objects to remain in focus.

Art cinema   A term loosely applied to any film which rejects the dominant mode of filmmaking and is characterized by a high degree of personal expression. For example, Ingmar Bergman, Peter Greenaway.

Artefact   This refers to interference that occurs on video images due to technical limitations or due to excessive data compression.

ASC   American Institute of Cinematographers.

Aspect ratio   This is the relative lengths of the horizontal and vertical sides of the video image. Television tends to use a ratio of 4:3, with 16:9 becoming more prevalent.

Audio mixer   A device or software program for mixing sounds from various sources, such as microphone, CD, tape.

Auteur   A term ascribed to a particular kind of director whose control over their films is such that they can be said to be the 'author', despite the large number of people involved in the movie. Auteurs develop a body of work through repeating, or developing, certain key concerns in their films.

Auxiliary input   Also known as line input or external input. A port which allows a VCR to receive images from an external device such as a camcorder. In the UK few camcorders have DV inputs because of fears from industry regulators regarding piracy, should the user be able to digitize VHS images.

B

Back light   Any light that comes from behind the subject, lighting up the background and reverse of the subject.

Bandwidth   This describes the rate at which certain amounts of data can be transmitted over a given period of time, usually a second. Modems are graded by how many bits of information they can accept per second, while the level of connection to the telephone network also affects the data rate.

Batch digitizing   Batch digitizing is the process of recording data consisting of video clips onto the hard drive, from a DV tape or other format. Only when it has been digitized onto the hard drive can it be edited. When a movie is being cut on digital equipment, a great amount of footage may require a high compression rate, resulting in less data taking up space on the hard disk. However, as the movie gets cut together, space is left over from the redundant footage and the remaining clips used in the film can be redigitized at a lower compression rate, resulting in a much higher quality image.

Battery   A rechargeable power cell used for camcorders. The most common is a Nicad or nickel–cadmium combination, although lithium-ion types are seen as more reliable and capable of holding more power.

Betacam   Until digital, this was the highest analog video format available. Recent years have seen the development of Betacam SX, a digital version using MPEG-2 high compression rates.

Bidirectional mic   A microphone which picks up sound on two sides of the mic.

Bit   A binary digit, the most basic unit in digital technology, not to be confused with a byte.

Boom   A microphone attached to an extension arm which is held above or below the action, out of view of the camera.

Breakout box   An attachment to a computer commonly bought as part of a capture card set-up, which allows the user to plug in and digitize analog signals.

Bricolage   The combination of different styles and genres of cinema, it reflects the use of post-modernism in film.

Broadcast quality   This is a standard which all television licensees are required to adhere to, maintaining the highest possible picture resolution. Betacam SP is often regarded as the benchmark and those DV systems which match it are seen as broadcast quality. In technical terms, a compression rate of 1:2 (which is as low as possible) or a data rate of 50 Mbits per second are correct.

Browser   A piece of software which allows the user to view Internet contents.

Byte   One byte is equal to 8 bits of digital information.

C

Call sheet   A daily list of who is needed for that day's shooting, what parts of the script will be covered and where this will be.

Capture   The means of digitizing analog material or recording digital material onto a computer. Specific software is available to accomplish this, but it is also a part of editing software.

Capture card   Also known as a digitizer, this is a board that connects to the computer and enables video digital signals to be read. Some also allow analog to be read by first converting it into a digital signal, hence the name digitizer.

Car clamp   A type of camcorder brace designed to keep a camera fixed to the side of a car.

Cardioid mic   A type of microphone which has a range spreading in a heart shape on both sides of the mic.

Charge-Coupled Device (CCD)   A chip situated near the camera lens which converts images into digital information.

Chrominance   This is the colour part of the video signal referring to hue and saturation, the other being the luminance, or brightness, of the signal.

Clip   A single sequence of video footage.

Close-up (CU)   A shot of a subject which usually shows the head from the neck up.

Codec   Compressor/decompressor. A piece of technology which enables the compression of video. In order to be able to view (to decompress) the compressed movie, the viewer must have a copy of the same codec as the sender.

Colour temperature   A term describing the colour value of certain light sources. Light sources which are blue/white, such as winter sunlight, have a high colour temperature, while candlelight, which emits an orange cast on the subject, is very low.

Compression   Since so many data are generated by video files, methods have been developed for reducing the sizes of these files and making editing more feasible for smaller systems. There are many methods of compression, differing in what parts of the video signal they economize on and what information is excluded. Compression often results in a loss of visible picture quality, but in some cases, notably MPEG-2, quality is visibly equal to the original uncompressed version.

Contact mic   A microphone which is attached to a surface, for recording musical instruments.

Continuity   The means of maintaining the smooth flow of events within narrative film.

Continuity editing   A method of editing, dominant in Hollywood cinema, which determines that the style of editing must be as invisible as possible and that the viewer can become immersed in the plot and characters.

Contrast   The degree to which the brightness (luminance) of the video image contains light and shadow. A high-contrast picture has few middle tones and mostly bright light and deep shadow.

Crane   A piece of camera equipment which can move in any direction. Video cranes now also have the facility to be remotely operated, obtaining greater varieties of shot.

Cross-cutting   A way of editing a simple dialogue sequence in which the two actors are shot symmetrically, cutting between the two.

Cut   The transition from one scene to another in editing.

Cutaway   A shot away from the main action.

D

D1, D2, D3, D5, D6, D7, D9   Video formats for recording, developed by different companies to provide varying levels of sound and vision resolution. D1 is the most expensive form of recording, used in high-end work. Sony's D2 has all but been discontinued as the rival to this format, Panasonic's D3, has gained ground. D5 is the favourite for post-production work because it works without data reduction. D6 allows for 12 audio channels, developed by Philips, while D7 is the standard for Panasonic's DVC Pro. D9 was developed by JVC and marketed as Digital S.

DAT   Digital Audio Tape offers three hours of digital sound on a tape half the size of an analog audio cassette tape. DAT is the only consumer recording standard that does not compress audio data, meaning that the whole signal is held on the tape. DAT is easy to use on location; indexing of the tape and rewinding are extremely fast (50 seconds for a 120-minute tape), so you can quickly access any place on the DAT tape.

Data rate   The amount of data that can be transmitted in a set period of time.

Dead acoustic   Describes an environment where there is little or no echo, resulting in a sound recording with poor atmosphere.

Depth of field   The area within which objects are in focus. It varies according to the aperture (size of the iris).

Diagetic   This refers to the parts of a shot that directly relate to the narrative. Diagetic sound, for example, would refer to sounds emanating from the scene itself and not added later in post-production.

Digital   In video terms, a system of recording which records images in binary language, representing a mathematical model of the original signal. They do not degrade when copied, but are prone to other problems from the system that plays or stores the digital information.

Digital 8   A format for recording digital signals on Hi-8 tapes instead of the smaller DV tapes.

Digital S   See D9.

Digitize   The method of translating analog information into digital information.

Distribution   A term referring to the marketing of a movie between the production studio or filmmaker and theatres and broadcasters.

Documentary   A form of film which uses real events, either recorded or retold, as part of a thesis or narrative.

Dolby Digital   A multi-channel sound format in which five channels are stored as well as the additional woofer effect channel. Dolby is a trademark of Dolby Laboratories and is used in DVD and cinema projection.

Dolly   A camera support on wheels that can be moved in any direction.

DoP   Director of Photography, a person responsible for overseeing how the camera is used on a movie and how the set is lit. To the DoP, lighting is as crucial as camera angle.

Drop-frame timecode   A form of timecode which caters for the odd frame rate of 29.9 fps in NTSC television standard. It works by removing 108 frames – from the timecode *not* the film – per hour, but does *not* drop a frame every 10th minute. The result is accurate timecode in a whole number.

Dropped frames   A common problem of many editing software capture facilities. When capturing, a clip may lose several frames and this can lead to problems if the amount of these frames is sufficient to lead to jumps within the edit. Designated capture software, rather than editing software, is less likely to drop frames.

DV   A format for recording sound and vision on 6.35-mm-wide tape. It compresses data at a rate of 5:1, sampling the image at 4:2:0 for PAL and 4:1:1 for NTSC. It functions at a rate of 25 megabits per second.

DVCAM   A format for recording sound and vision, developed by Sony. The difference with DV is that it runs on wider tape track (15 mm) and the tape speed is higher, resulting in shorter playing times for cassettes.

DVC Pro   A format for recording video and sound developed by Panasonic. It is similar in quality to DV, but uses wider tape (18 mm) and has a slightly higher chrominance level.

DVC Pro 50   A tape format similar to DVC Pro, but using a higher sampling rate of 4:2:2 and double (50) the megabits per second to that of DV.

DVD   Digital Verstaile Disc. A method of storing large amounts of video material on small, CD-sized discs (12 cm diameter).

Dynamic range   The difference between the quietest and the loudest usable sounds.

E

Edit Decision List (EDL)   The EDL is a list of shots that are to compose a final cut for a movie, listed in the form of the timecode at the start and end of the appropriate clips on the footage tape.

ENG   Electronic News Gathering. This refers mainly to the use of light, mobile equipment for news reports in situ.

Establishing shot   A shot, usually at the start of a scene, which informs the audience of the basic elements of the scene: who is present, what period in history, what time of day and so on.

Exposure   The amount of light that enters a camcorder lens, hitting the CCD chip.

Extreme close-up (ECU)   A camera angle which, when on a face, focuses only on the eyes or mouth.

F

Fill light   After a key light has set the main focus of light on a subject, a fill light softens the effect.

Filter   In non-linear video editing, a filter refers to a special visual effect, such as cropping, stretching or recolouring an image.

FireWire   See IEEE 1394.

Fluid effect   A more expensive type of tripod where movement is eased through lubricant oil.

Focal length   A measurement of the magnification of a lens indicated in millimetres. A zoom lens allows the camera to film closer or further from the subject, without moving either, because it has a variable focal length.

Focus   A point at which the rays of light from a subject converge after passing through a lens, resulting in maximum sharpness of vision.

Frame   The smallest unit of video footage. In each second of video there are, in the PAL standard, 25 frames per second (fps). NTSC uses 29.9 fps.

Framing   The process of arranging the elements of a scene within the camera viewfinder.

Fuzzy logic   A complex series of settings in a camcorder designed to ensure that, when changing exposure, white balance or focus, a change in one leads to a slight change in the others.

G

Gaffer   A crew member responsible for the placing and rigging of lighting equipment.

Generation loss   In video reproductions, this refers to any loss of picture or sound quality resulting from the copying of information. In DV editing, it is rare to encounter losses, but successive compression and decompression of a clip will result in losses occurring.

Genre   A way of categorizing movies in which a group of films share characteristics such as story, style, setting and so on. Genre is becoming increasingly fragmented, with movies fusing different genres together.

Gigabyte   One gigabyte equals 1024 megabytes.

Grip   Crew member responsible for handling props, scenery and equipment.

H

Hard disk   A magnetic storage component of a computer for recording large quantities of data. A hard disk is measured not just by the amount of data it can store, but by the speed at which it revolves, enhancing performance.

HD   High Definition. A video format which is a vast improvement in picture quality over other DV formats. It records at 720 × 1080 pixels, interlaced. It requires large amounts of storage when recording.

Hi-8   An analog 8 mm video format geared towards the consumer market.

HMI lamps   Very powerful lamps which replaced arc lamps on sets.

Hollywood cinema   A term ascribed to a collection of conventions of filmmaking, including continuity editing, character identification and certain moral codes, which gained its peak in the Hollywood of the 1920s.

Hot spot   The point at the centre of a beam of light which has greater intensity.

Hypercardioid mic   A type of microphone that has an extremely narrow pick-up, but which works well in picking up sounds at long distances.

I

IEEE 1394 (FireWire, iLink)   A standard method of transmitting data, connecting a peripheral (camera or VCR) to a computer. It is far superior to any other cable used in video and transmits at a rate of 400 Mb per second, four times faster than the main consumer connection, USB.

Independent film   Strictly speaking, an independent film is one that has not been financed by a major production studio, but with independent production houses being bought up by larger companies, it has also come to denote a certain approach to filmmaking based on challenging movie convention, either in terms of subject matter or style.

Insert   A cut that is inserted into the action as a cutaway. It also refers to a method of analog editing in which clips can be inserted into a programme without disturbing the control track.

Interlace   A term used in video referring to the way picture information is split up. A first field contains all the uneven lines of the picture, while the second field contains all the even lines, so in the PAL standard, 50 fields are transmitted, leading to 25 frames – the human eye cannot distinguish between the two sets of fields, reading them as one image.

Iris   The opening at the front of the lens which allows light to enter the camera.

ITU   International Telecommunications Union, a body which oversees technical standards in broadcasting.

J

JPEG   A method of compressing data for still images, standardized by the Joint Photographic Experts Group.

Jump cut   A tool used by some directors to introduce disturbance into a scene, produced by cutting between two shots of the same subject but from slightly different angles, within the 30-degree rule.

K

Key frame   A way of determining how a clip is altered, by the use of filters, transitions or fades. A key frame is marked at the start, middle and end of the clip, with appropriate settings given for each part.

Key light   A main dominant lamp that focuses on the subject.

L

Lavalier mic   A type of microphone that is clipped to the actor or attached to a section of a set, with limited pick-up range, but discreet and flexible.

Layers   A term referring to the layers of video that are composited together to form a final cut, including superimposed images or text.

LCD   Liquid Crystal Display. A small monitor attached to consumer camcorders which enables better quality viewing of an image.

Levels   Commonly used in association with sound, this refers to the relative volume of different audio tracks. In compression, the term is used to describe the quality steps in MPEG.

Linear editing   A term referring to analog editing systems in which two or more VCRs are connected and clips are recorded from one to another in the correct sequence.

Logging   A term referring to the searching and noting of takes on a tape of footage. If timecode is used, this will determine more easily where tracks are located.

Longitudinal timecode (LTC)   A way of recording timecode in which the signal holding the code is recorded onto a soundtrack or separate longitudinal track.

Long shot   A wide image showing a panorama or landscape.

Luminance   The brightness element of an S-video signal.

Lux   A measure of light. It is equivalent to one lumen per square metre, or the same as 0.0929 foot candle. A well-exposed picture needs something around 10 000 lux.

M

Match shot   A way of setting up two shots so that the camera cuts between them with no loss of continuity. Movements of the subject, lighting and camera angle are all arranged so that the matched shots blend seamlessly with each other.

Medium shot   A shot that shows the subject from the waist up.

Modem   A device for decoding data sent across the Internet via telephone cables. The speed of the modem determines the amount of data that can be received per second, measured in bits. Most consumer modems operate at a speed of 56 kb per second.

Monitor   A television screen attached to a camera while shooting so that a clearer view of the shot can be seen. It is useful for ensuring that colour, contrast and light values are kept at the same level throughout shooting. In digital editing, it is used to refer to the window in which clips are cut down to a more exact size before placing on the timeline.

Monopod   A one-legged camera support.

Montage   An approach to editing in which seemingly unlikely shots are placed together. Two shots can be made to create or suggest a third meaning. There are many variations of montage editing, including parallel montage, in which simultaneous events are told in parallel, and involuted montage, in which a narrative is told without regard for chronology.

MPEG   A standard for compressing video data. The difference between MPEG and other forms of compression is that MPEG is more sophisticated, analysing data from groups of frames and making decisions about what data can be excluded. MPEG-1 and MPEG-4 work with relatively low amounts of data and are suited to telecommunications. MPEG-2 is one of the most widely used versions, used in consumer DVD compression, and results in high quality images.

Multimedia   A much misunderstood term used to refer to any interactive medium. Strictly speaking, it refers to the combining of more than one means of communication in one medium.

N

Nanotainment   A term referring to new forms of video product that are very short, often less than 30 seconds. But it also refers to video that asks for a short attention span, delivered in continual short bursts of interest.

New Hollywood   A term referring to the development of a new kind of Hollywood movie in the 1970s, including such directors as Scorsese and Coppola.

Noise   A term referring to the variations in picture signal that produce unwelcome disturbances in quality. It refers most often to vision, despite its connotations with sound.

Non-linear editing   Also known as digital editing, this term is the more accurate one, since it refers to the ability of the editor to access and rearrange any part of the movie, without having to re-edit the rest of it, as was the case with linear, analog editing.

NTSC   National Television Standards Committee, a body which set standards for television transmission adopted in many territories, including the USA.

O

Off-line editing   When editing a movie, this refers to the process in which clips are edited on lower cost systems first and then passed on to an on-line editor for final cutting on more expensive systems. Since digital editing allows for high quality at very little cost, this practice is becoming obsolete.

Omnidirectional mic   A type of microphone which picks up sound from all around the mic.

On-line editing   This refers to the practice of compiling a final edit of a movie as a second-stage cut, derived from the earlier, off-line edit.

P

PAL   Phase Alternating Line, a broadcasting standard used in the UK, Australia and other territories, which is based on a lower frame rate than NTSC, at 24 fps. But PAL also uses a greater number of lines on the screen, at 625, leading to a slightly higher resolution.

PALplus   A new system derived from PAL, but which uses a slightly different aspect ratio, 16:9, and which produces a higher quality of picture through pre-filtering of the video signal.

Pan   A horizontal movement of the camera at a fixed position to show several aspects of a setting, or following a subject in movement.

Parabolic mic   Not a mic as such, but a dish-like attachment to a mic that greatly enhances the pinpoint range of the mic, used with cardioid mics.

Pixel   A picture element or picture point, the smallest dot on the television screen. Video pictures are measured in pixels with PAL at 720 × 576 pixels.

Plan sequence   A French term referring to a single, uncut shot involving several camera movements to make a whole scene.

Plug-in   An extension to software which serves to extend the capacity of the software in some way. For example, many editing programs promote plug-ins capable of enhancing the range of special effects available in the program.

Point of view shot (POV)   A shot which aims to show the viewpoint of a subject, typically with a hand-held camera.

Polymedia A term referring to moving images that incorporate more than one medium – for example, video, text, sound lighting, environment. It is gaining currency as a replacement for 'multimedia'.

Post-modern A term referring to a cultural development in the late twentieth century which still affects cinema. It is characterized by the borrowing and fusing of different elements from global and historical culture to forge provocative and interesting new combinations.

Post-production The stage in filmmaking in which shots are edited, soundtrack is added and any further effects or modifications are made.

Post-structuralism The movement away from the academic confines of the structuralist approach to analysing movies, gathering pace in the 1990s. It sought to move attention in film studies away from the movie itself and look at the spectator and the context within which the film is viewed.

Pre-production In filmmaking, the stage in which the film is planned in terms of the script, visuals, budget, schedule and other demands, prior to the start of shooting (production).

Production In filmmaking, the shooting stage of the process, in which all clips and sounds are gathered.

Progressive download In video streaming, this refers to a method of sending video data on the Internet that enables a movie to start playing before the whole file has downloaded. Picture quality is greater than with real-time downloading, though there is a slight wait to start playing the film, the length of which depends on the speed of your connection. A calculation is made as to how long it will take for the whole movie to download and the film starts playing only when there is enough video to sustain uninterrupted playback.

PZM A pressure zone microphone, a small sensitive mic often fixed on the camcorder.

Q

QuickTime A trademark of Apple Computers, this is one of the most popular video formats, enabling high quality video data to be used on all types of computer.

R

RAM Random Access Memory, the temporary data section of a computer that the processor is currently using at any given point, erased when it is switched off, when the data must be saved and transferred elsewhere.

Real-time downloading A term used on the Internet to refer to video that is sent to the viewer without waiting for it to download. Picture quality is sacrificed for speed and it is mostly used for news clips and interviews, where resolution is less of an issue.

Real-time editing   A version of editing programs that offers reduced rendering ability, enabling the user to see effects and transitions on clips as soon as they are placed on the timeline, without having to wait for the program to render, or build, the files into a complete film.

Redhead   A type of lamp that has become a generic term for a strong, usually 800 W, tungsten halogen lamp made by the Ianiro company. It is versatile and can be used as much for main, key light as for other softer lights, using barn doors and reflectors to bounce the light.

Rendering   The process by which editing software builds video files and effects as one complete sequence. When editing, it is not possible to watch the film as it develops because each clip, and any effects placed on them, do not exist as one complete file and must first be rendered to see the movie. Certain programs offer real-time editing, but these are often limited in their reduction of rendering.

Resolution   The clarity of the video picture, often another word for sharpness. In technical terms, resolution is measured in lines on the screen, pixels or megahertz. Although the screen may accept a certain level of resolution, each stage of production, including the kind of camera used, through to post-production, including the standard of editing equipment, can affect final picture resolution.

Rushes   Rushes are your footage, usually called this because you are looking at them soon after shooting in order to check how the film is progressing.

S

Sampling ratio   The amount of data displayed in terms of brightness and colour, or luminance and chrominance. Luminance is often sampled at a much higher rate than colours, often double the amount. Quantities such as 4:2:2, for example, refer to luminance and colour sampling, and vary according to the camera.

SCART   Syndicat de Constructeurs d'Appareils Radio Recepteur et Televisuers. A common European standard 21-pin connector, carrying audio and video signals. Known for being unreliable and prone to breakages.

SECAM   Sequential Couleur Avec Memoire, a television broadcasting standard developed in France and used in many Eastern European nations. It is most similar to, and compatible with, PAL.

Server   A piece of central equipment which acts as a conduit for a user to access the Internet.

Shotgun mic   A type of microphone which has a narrow range and is pointed at the subject.

SMPTE/EBU timecode   The current standard timecode used in professional video. It consists of four pairs of digits – hours : minutes : seconds : frame. The last pair differs depending on what broadcasting standard is being used (maximum of 24 out of 25 frames for PAL or 29 out of 29.9 for NTSC).

Structuralism A movement in academic circles in the 1970s which sought to understand the structures by which a film is made, but ignoring the variables inherent in the spectator's viewing of it. It was later superseded by post-structuralism.

Studio system A term referring to the dominance of major studios in Hollywood in the classic period of Hollywood production from the 1920s until the 1950s, when a lawsuit broke the majors' stranglehold on film production and opened the doors to independent production.

Supercardioid mic A type of microphone with a limited width of range, but which can pick up sounds up to four metres away.

T

Timecode See SMPTE timecode.

Timeline A window in digital editing programs on which the film is built clip by clip. Layers of images or text are placed on separate tracks on the timeline and the final arrangement is rendered to produce a movie.

Tracking shot A movement of the camera alongside a moving subject.

Transition A visual effect in editing programs, in which one clip merges into the next – for example, by a dissolve, a wipe across the screen or other effect.

Trimming The process of reducing the size of clips in editing programs, to the exact length required.

Tripod A three-legged camera support.

U

Unidirectional mic A versatile type of microphone which picks up sound in front of the mic.

USB Universal Serial Bus. A type of cable that allows the camcorder to be plugged into a PC. But it is not effective in transferring DV as it cannot carry sufficient data, being around four times slower than FireWire. USB 2.0 is an improvement but has yet to catch on in the video market.

V

VHS Video Home System, the most common consumer analog format, developed by JVC, using 12.7 mm tape. VHS is not suitable for professional use because of its poor resolution.

Viewfinder A part of the camera through which the image being recorded can be seen.

VJ   Video jockey, referring to the use of video tracks mixed live often in a club or party setting, developed from DJ audio mixing.

W

White balance   A feature of consumer camcorders which assesses the correct balance of light to ensure accurate colour representation.

Wide-angle lens   A lens with a short focal distance but which can focus on a wide range of objects in a frame.

Wild sound   Also referred to as non-synchronous sound, this encompasses all sounds not recorded on location or set, and not related to the action, but which add realism or effect.

X

XLR   In audio technology, the XLR-3 is a cable connection able to transmit high quality audio signals.

Y

Y/C   A video signal connection in which luminance (Y) and chrominance (C) are transmitted separately, leading to higher picture quality, better than that achieved with composite signals. This connection is often referred to as S-Video.

Z

Zoom lens   A lens with a variable focus, enabling the camera to focus on subjects in the distance.

Bibliography

Careers in Film and Video – Ricki Ostrov and Alison King. Kogan Page, 1992.

The Cinema Book – eds Cook and Bernick. BFI Publishing, 1999.

Dealmaking in the Film and Television Industry – Mark Litwak. Silman-James Press, 1994.

Developing Story Ideas – Michael Rabiger. Focal Press, 1998.

Digital Video A–Z. Fast Electronic, FAST, 1999.

Dogme 95 – Richard Kelly. Faber & Faber, 2000.

Don't Look Now – Mark Sanderson. BFI Publishing, 1996.

The End of Celluloid – Matt Hanson. Rotovision, 2004.

Film Art: An Introduction – Bordwell and Thompson. McGraw-Hill, 1993.

The Filmmaker's Art – Haig P. Manoogian. Basic Books, New York, 1966.

Film Production, The Complete Uncensored Guide – Greg Merritt. Lone Eagle, 1998.

Film Studies – eds John Hill and Pamela Church Gibson. OUP, 2000.

Film and Video Budgets – Michael Wiese Productions, 2001.

Focal Easy Guide to After Effects – Curtis Sponsler. Focal Press, 2005.

Genre, Star and Auteur, Introduction to Film Studies – Patrick Phillips. Routledge, 2003.

The Hidden Order of Art – Anton Ehrenzweig. Weidenfeld and Nicholson, 2000.

Hitchcock on Hitchcock – ed. Sidney Gottleib. Faber & Faber, 1995.

How to Read a Film, 3rd edition – James Monaco. OUP, 2000.

Independent Feature Film Production – Gregory Goodell. St Martin's Griffin, New York, 1998.

An Introduction to Film Studies – ed. Jill Neames. Routledge, 1996.

Key Concepts in Film and Cinema Studies – Susan Hayward. Routledge, 1996.

A Man with a Camera – Nestor Almendros. Faber & Faber, 1982.

A Personal Journey with Martin Scorsese Through American Movies – Martin Scorsese and Michael Henry Wilson. Faber & Faber, 1997.

Postmodernist Culture – Steven Connor. Blackwell, 1989.

Premiere Quick Start Guide – Antony Bolante. Peachpit Press, 1999.

Spike, Mike, Slackers and Dykes – John Pierson. Faber & Faber, 1995.

The Technique of Film and Video Editing – Ken Dancyger. Focal Press, 2002.

Techniques of the Selling Writer – Dwight Swain. University of Oklahoma Press, 1981.

Time Out Film Guide – Penguin, 2004.

The Videomaker Handbook – ed. Jim Stinson. Focal Press, 1996.

Video Production Handbook, 3rd edition – Gerald Millerson. Focal Press, 2001.

Index